Managing Multicultural Lives

Managing Multicultural Lives

Asian American Professionals and the Challenge

of Multiple Identities

Pawan Dhingra

Stanford University Press
Stanford, California 2007

Stanford University Press
Stanford, California

Printed in the United States of America on acid-free, archival-quality paper

Library of Congress Cataloging-in-Publication Data

Dhingra, Pawan.
Managing multicultural lives : Asian American professionals and the
challenge of multiple identities / Pawan Dhingra.
    p. cm.
    Includes bibliographical references and index.
    ISBN-13: 978-0-8047-5577-1 (cloth : alk. paper)
    ISBN-13: 978-0-8047-5578-8 (pbk. : alk. paper)
    1. Hybridity (Social sciences)—United States. 2. Group identity—United States. 3. East
Indian Americans—Ethnic identity. 4. Korean Americans—Ethnic identity. I. Title.
    HM1272.D45 2007
    305.800973—dc22   2006023580

Typeset by Newgen in 10/14 Minion

To my parents, for making all that
came before and afterwards possible

Contents

Acknowledgments

As is obvious to anyone who has written a book, it is not a solo endeavor, regardless of how many names appear (or do not appear) on the cover. Without the assistance of probably countless people, I would not have been able to complete this. My most sincere appreciation goes out to all of those who participated in this study. You gave some of your time and shared part of your life with me. Each conversation was enjoyable and worthwhile. Those conversations provide the backbone to this study and are used to provide whatever insights are to be gained in the experiences of immigrant minority communities. I learned so much from talking with you. I have not tried to speak for you but to take from those conversations and present the book's arguments.

This project started as a dissertation, what seems like a generation ago. My dissertation committee held me to a high standard, gave me strong feedback, and made the process even enjoyable. My appreciation goes to Victor Nee, Elaine Wethington, and most of all to my dissertation chair, Penny Edgell. You have opened intellectual doors, and you continue to be a support. I also want to note the friends from graduate school who meant so much to me then and still today, and without which I might not have finished: Andy Buck, Moon-Ho Jung, Bikku Kuruvilla, Will Morris, and Brent Simpson. In addition, my professors as an undergraduate both in my major and outside of it gave me the tools and inspiration to pursue academics.

Having left graduate school and entered life as a faculty member, I have continued to benefit from generous colleagues. At Bucknell University colleagues both in and out of the sociology/anthropology department inspired me to focus intently on this book project while teaching. Similarly, my colleagues and friends in the sociology department, the Comparative American Studies program, and elsewhere at Oberlin College have encouraged the completion of this project while making both work and life here pleasurable. My heartfelt

thanks go to all of you. My students also have been a source of feedback. I especially want to note my seminar class of fall 2004 for their energetic discussions
and critical remarks on relevant literature.

I also have enjoyed being part of a broader intellectual community, one that
includes scholars whose own work has motivated me. I have met some of you
and become close colleagues with a smaller number. Some have commented on
either this book or related work of mine and/or have offered advice along the
way, for which I am extremely grateful. These include Carl Bankston III, Yen Le
Espiritu, Elaine Howard Ecklund, Amy Foerster, Viktor Gecas, Emily Ignacio,
Russell Jeung, Grace Kao, Nazli Kibria, Sara S. Lee, Sunaina Maira, Pyong
Gap Min, Viranjani Munasinghe, Dina Okamoto, Vijay Prashad, Sharmila
Rudrappa, Purvi Shah, Jiannbin Shiao, Linda Võ, and Min Zhou. I also thank
Gary Okihiro for giving me an intellectual and physical space at the Center for
the Study of Race and Ethnicity at Columbia University as I finished the disser-
tation, and for his guidance both inside and outside of the classroom.

Others near both the end and the origins of the book project deserve recognition. Peter Kivisto and Christena Nippert-Eng reviewed the manuscript
for Stanford University Press. You both went above and beyond the call of
duty with your constructive criticism, time, and enthusiasm. Simply put, you
took a text and helped turn it into a book. Thank you both. In a similar vein I
am greatly appreciative of Kate Wahl at Stanford University Press. You were
encouraging from our first conversation about the book, and you guided me
through the publishing process with a quick hand and delicate touch. Kirsten
Oster at the press also gave valuable time and assistance.

Well before I got the manuscript into book form, I was pilot testing interview questions. I thank Vijay Parekh and Mala Mahendroo for sitting with me
for that. Other friends supported this project with your time and simple cheer-
fulness. Rather than name you all (and extend this for another few pages),
please know that I am sincerely grateful.

My family—nuclear and extended—has been a key, if not *the* key, source of
support throughout this project. Your doors were always open to me. Moreover, your love and enthusiasm were limitless. And my deepest thanks go to
my wife, Charu Gupta. I could not have asked for a better partner. There is no
way I could have finished this without you. You gave comments on drafts, put
up with late hours, and always encouraged me. And most recently you have
given us our first child, Talvin. Expecting his arrival helped me finish this
project, and he inspires me to continue our work for social equality.

Identity is not as transparent or unproblematic as we think. Perhaps instead of thinking of identity as an already accomplished fact, which the new cultural practices then represent, we should think, instead, of identity as a 'production' which is never complete, always in process, and always constituted within, not outside, representation. This view problematizes the very authority and authenticity to which the term 'cultural identity' lays claim.

—Stuart Hall, "Cultural Identity and Diaspora"

1 Introduction

Opening Up the Margins in the Mainstream

HOW DOES AN INDIVIDUAL MAKE SENSE of and handle his or her multiple, sometimes conflicting identities? When I asked how he hoped to maintain his self-defined Indian culture, Samit, a twenty-four-year-old second-generation Indian American, replied:

> The biggest way is marrying an Indian. Getting involved in the community and temple and attending its cultural events. Language is a big deal. . . . There are things you can talk about with Indians that you can't talk about with others. . . . I think growing up here it's very hard; a lot of culture and attributes of being Indian are lost. Sometimes I think I'm no different than Joe Smith who lives next door.

Later in the interview he also fondly recalled a ras garba festival held at his parents' home, which involves dancing in concentric circles while clapping sticks and hands—part of a traditional religious event for Gujarati Indians:

> We used to have garba at our house growing up. My [White] American friends came over and they loved it. We had a blast. It was fun teaching them how to do it and doing it with them.

These two quotes suggest the multifaceted nature of an answer to how people maintain multiple commitments. Samit feels highly Americanized yet still attached to an ethnic culture that distinguishes him from the majority, as seen in the first quote. At times he is able to bridge those parts, such as with a ras garba festival that translates well to other Americans, as seen in the second quote.

Similarly, when I asked James, a twenty-seven-year-old second-generation Korean American, what effect the model minority stereotype of Asian

Americans as diligent had on him at work as a financial advisor, he smiled and said:

> That's why I wear glasses. I wear glasses because I think [that] people think "Asian American, glasses, studies hard, works hard." I wear contacts on the weekend when I am with my friends. Maybe I play the race card a little bit. Sure, why not, if people think, especially in financial advising, [that] I am good with numbers.

He works in the primary labor market, is fluent in standard English, and has the dress, accent, and other commonplace signifiers of middle-class Americans his age. Yet, contrary to popular assumptions, he does not leave his minority status at the door when he enters the workplace. Instead, he makes an effort to appear racialized. By consciously acting as a "model minority," he hopes to climb the job ladder. Like Samit, he looks for ways to bring together the various elements of himself.

These anecdotes draw attention to how people deal with contrasting identities, whether as an ethnic minority who grew up in middle-class America, a mother with a full-time career (Blair-Loy 2003), a gay man living in suburbia (Brekhus 2003), and so on. This study analyzes second-generation Korean American and Indian American professionals living in Dallas, Texas—a geographic region under-explored for Asian Americans—to investigate how they both differentiate and integrate their ethnic, racial, and American identities in daily life. I frame these professionals as the margins in (instead of versus) the mainstream in order to move away from the presumption that minorities always separate, both cognitively and in practice, their ethnic and racial identities from the majority. The term "margins in the mainstream" refers to people who are connected to yet separated from a social space, in this case the mainstream. As a result, they have multiple sets of commitments. Allowing for both tensions and associations between group identities not only captures the experiences of ethnic minorities, but also draws attention more broadly to the agency we all have in dealing with contradictory interests. Moreover, this perspective offers new insights into assessing identity development and performance, immigrant adaptation, and racialization. The study is based on in-depth interviews with almost ninety individuals as well as participant observations (see chapter 2 for research design). Informants' voices dominate in the text. I emphasize how the experiences of Korean Americans and Indian Americans overlap, while noting their particularities.

So much of the discourse on ethnicity, including fiction, autobiographical essays, and academic research, refers to American culture as modern and as prioritizing the individual relative to a traditional and constraining immigrant heritage. This discursive dichotomy conceals the cultural conservatisms found in America, including the constraints placed on women and the rise of overt religiosity. The West is extolled at the expense of "Oriental" countries, which are criticized as pre-enlightened (Said 1978). Yet Asian Americans themselves often interpret their experiences within this framework, and denying its power would misrepresent their subjectivities and practices. "Asian" and "American" values presumably contrast with one another. The former is read as an emphasis on family, elders, and social conservatism, and the latter as a prioritization on personal autonomy and individualism (Ahn 1999; Jo 2002; Kibria 2002; Maira 2002; Min and Kim 1999).[1] I accept that people understand their lives within this dichotomy, but in this study I demonstrate how they also move beyond it in their expressions of their identities (Zhou and Lee 2004), signaling the constructed nature of this dualism while recognizing its felt effects.

MAKING SENSE OF ETHNIC AND RACIAL IDENTITIES

Samit and James make sense of their backgrounds in ways that both differentiate them from and allow for association with Whites. This latter possibility breaks with the standard framing of ethnic communities—that immigrant groups' identities only create a severance from the majority. Previous research suggests that rather than maintaining divergent identities, the second generation privileges one over others. Groups presumably either assimilate into a segment of American society while keeping a weakened symbolic ethnicity, or they remain embedded in an ethnic community (that may or may not encourage success in mainstream institutions) (Alba and Nee 2003; Child 1943; Gans 1979; Waters 1990, 1998).[2] Child (1943) posited three resolutions to the second generation's internal conflict between ethnic and American interests: to assimilate and break ties with one's ethnic community, to assert one's ethnic culture and fortify relationships within one's local setting, or to be "apathetic" and feel lost between cultures.[3] Each of these scenarios hypothesizes choosing primarily one community as the healthiest means of adaptation. If one is extremely committed to a role identity, then that identity might always be active, merging with the person to form a core part of the self (Heiss 1992). For instance, Blair-Loy (2003) finds that many career women, particularly those of earlier generations, opted not to have children because of a commitment to their professions, which seemed at odds with being a mother (see also Stryker and Macke 1978). From a different perspective, postcolonial scholars argue that the nation incorporates diversity often by essentializing immigrants as the "Other" rather than by treating them as equal competitors for resources, which still affirms the either/or binary of identities (San Juan 2002).

Other researchers accentuate groups' sustained ties to multiple identities, rather than a primary one—identities that lack any connection, as if they were in distinct worlds (Uba 1994).[4] One acts "Asian" at some times and "American" at other times, with no interaction between the roles. Even theorists who allow for ethnic lifestyles to change and emerge from one's local environment emphasize the distance that such identities create from other groups, rather than a possible alignment of group commitments (Roosens 1989; Yancey, Ericksen, and Juliani 1976).

As fitting a margins *in* the mainstream perspective, I consider how individuals develop an ethnic identity in order to be not only distant from but also at times accepted by other Americans, with whom they also identify, as in the case of Samit. Informants noted significant tensions between their self-defined ethnic and American lifestyles, as fitting the standard dichotomous framing discussed earlier. As explained in chapter 3, they also believed that a commitment to an ethnic community would give them group pride and allow them to associate with Whites despite tensions. First-generation immigrant parents prescribed a selective assimilation, hoping that honoring cultural differences in private and selectively presenting them in public would facilitate mobility despite one's minority status. The second generation tried to adhere to parental expectations in developing ethnic identities, although in often overlooked ways and with varying results. Actors hoped to integrate by developing salient ethnic identities, rather than preferring a "post-ethnic" America in which group differences are voluntary and secondary (Hollinger 1995).[5] Still, even when parts of informants' background were accepted by others, they were not automatically embraced. When Samit invited his friends to take part in a ras garba, it became simply a dance in which they learned how to clack sticks and move their feet, rather than to be part of the religious significance behind it.[6] The majority culture's selective tolerance of ethnic differences impacts how Korean and Indian Americans form ethnic identities and ultimately adapt.

Informants interpreted their racial minority status in a similar way, as both distinguishing them from and allowing for links to Whites. Asian Americans are racialized as foreigners (Ancheta 1998). This means that they encounter a general discrimination as non-Whites and a more specific and pronounced racial treatment as inherently Asian and un-American. How they make sense of race relative to other minorities and the majority remains in question. These second-generation professionals' class status does not erase the effects of race but instead alters them in a way that suits the needs of the state and capitalism (Omi and Winant 1994; Small 1999). For instance, middle-class-specific stereotypes include the model minority, who is passive and lacking social skills but who contributes to the economy, and the "yellow peril," whose hyperfeminine sexuality (for both women and men) and accomplishments construct one as a foreigner who threatens the nation's purity, safety, and prosperity during times of economic decline and war (Fong 1998). Asian Americans' ethnic background (including religion or food preferences) also becomes racialized, that is, evaluated not based on its merits but on members' racial status. Emphasis within this perspective falls on deconstructing essentialist depictions of Asians and Asian Americans, such as that of the "Easterner" not only as different from the enlightened "Westerner," but as his or her inferior opposite (Okihiro 1994; Said 1978). Other research examines individual and institutional discrimination within the social structure, along with actors' resistance to it (Collins-Lowry 1997; Feagin and Sikes 1994; Massey and Denton 1993; Pattillo-McCoy 1999). Such standard framing of minorities and immigrants is necessary in order to draw attention to injustices and group agency. In all the chapters, but especially chapters 3 and 4, I explain participants' general critique of discrimination from their perspective as supposed non-White foreigners, discrimination that includes instances of cultural intolerance, property damage, and physical threats.

Still, this critique of racism is not the total sum of Korean and Indian Americans' identities as racialized communities within the mainstream. As explained in chapter 4, contrary to common assumptions regarding U.S.-born minorities, actors did not embrace a pan-ethnic or person-of-color identity or develop a reactive ethnicity of themselves as "real minorities."[7] Indian Americans in particular had weak pan-ethnic and even South Asian ties. This is despite the fact that both ethnic groups live in supposedly one of the more racist states of the country.[8] These college-educated professionals did not claim to be beyond the effects of racism but instead made sense of the racialized image of potential invaders in ways that connected them to the majority, in particular to other immigrants, and kept them distinct from other minorities. In this way Asian Americans, rather than identifying themselves as either marginal or mainstream, can critique Whites for racism while still maintaining camaraderie with them.[9] This in turn has implications for other minorities and class groups. Overall, informants made sense of both their ethnicity and race in ways designed to encourage their integration into mainstream society *as* ethnic minorities, not despite that status. I pay particular attention to the question of whether their efforts likely lead to an equal status with Whites or perpetuate stratifications.

PERFORMING IDENTITIES IN CULTURAL SPACES

Understanding the ethnic and racial identity formations of the second generation explains only half of how individuals handle their status as margins in the mainstream. I now turn to how they deal with their commitments to their dissimilar ethnic, racial, and American identities in daily life. How do Asian Americans decide which identity to act on and in which manner as they encounter racial, class, gender, religious, and other hierarchies, and as they cross distinct contexts? For instance, do women and men go out of their way to act "American" at work, or do they allow themselves to express an ethnic identity? Do they accept parents' expectations of how to act in the home sphere, and if so, how easy is it to fulfill those expectations? Do they support an ethnic community but engage in leisure activities, such as drinking, in order to appear "American"? Although much has been written on multiculturalism from the perspectives of philosophy, history, politics, and cultural studies, how individuals embody multicultural lives remains underexplored. To understand how groups perform their identities, we must appreciate two factors: the influence of a cultural space on people's behaviors, and how that influence in turn impacts their commitment to multiple, at times contrasting, interests.

People do not present any identity they wish or in any way that they please. Everyday actions occur within cultural spaces, which I refer to as domains, and must be contextualized. Little attention has been paid to the effects of domains, including one's office, home, leisure activities, and civic associations, on identity choices (Brekhus 2003). Recent research on culture and cognition argues that the culture of a place itself, apart from the particular actors within it, shapes how people think of themselves and process information (Cerulo 2002; DiMaggio 1997; Zerubavel 1993). Individuals make sense of the same stimuli differently based on the setting, even when the same persons are present across them (Lave 1988; Resnick 1991). More research is necessary on the effects of context on individuals' self-expressions (Hall and Okazaki 2002). As Douglas (1986) argues, institutions "think" for us, telling us how to make sense of items and events within them. Regardless of one's personal inclinations, a cultural schema impacts which self-conceptions and skills we consider most appropriate in that context. How people decide how to act depends, then, not only on others in the interaction, but also on the cultural code, or implicit cultural rules, of each domain (Swidler 2001).[10] Though there are subtle differences between the terms code, schema, frame, and script, I use them to refer to people's mental image of a setting's expected mode of behavior (Fiske and Taylor 1984).

Interviewees put in concerted efforts to conform to the cultural frame of a setting (Goffman 1974). For example, Sangeeta, a twenty-three-year-old Indian American woman, said she engaged in "silly" practices in the home that she felt obligated to do given its cultural code, which is to create an atmosphere reminiscent of one's own upbringing, as explained in chapter 6:

> In my little apartment I have a little area, and I do my thing in the morning and . . . at night I do my prayers. And I feel bad if I don't, like I am neglecting something, and it is all mental. It's kind of silly. I don't know what I am doing, but I still need to do it to fulfill my own desire. A lot of it is based on how I was raised; it is pretty much a family tradition. It is a family tradition not related to God, but to the house.

Even though she lived on her own, she felt the "need to fulfill" a desire attached to the notion of her "house." Understanding the effects of space explains why people engaged in emotional reactions and practices that did not feel natural. Informants similarly made an effort to fit the codes of civil society, the leisure sphere, and the workplace. In chapters 5–7, I elaborate on each location's cultural frame, and on how participants went out of their way to observe them.

The cultural schemas also shaped how individuals dealt with commitments to multiple identities, such as whether to express one's "American" lifestyle at home or marginal interests in the public sphere. The dominant perspective on identity management allows individuals to maintain contrasting roles, which are compartmentalized in separate spheres. As individuals we can incorporate numerous symbols and competing value sets (DiMaggio 1997; Swidler 2001; Hurh and Kim 1984).[11] Current literature actually celebrates the biculturalism of both the first and second generation as the healthiest way to adapt (Buriel 1993; Portes and Rumbaut 2001). For instance, Portes and Rumbaut (2001) argue that maintaining strong connections to one's private community offers support as young people go through school (see also Gibson 1988; Zhou and Bankston 1997). The notion that groups choose a different identity as they cross distinct realms is supported by both theoretical work in social psychology (Alexander and Wiley 1992; Stryker 1992; Tajfel and Turner 1986)[12] and cultural sociology.[13] Empirical work on ethnic identities (Maira 2002; Saenz and Aguirre 1991), pan-ethnicity (Cornell 1988), and the experience of minorities in the workplace (Anderson 1999a; Bell 1990) indicates the same.[14] According to these studies, ethnic minorities supposedly act "American" or "pan-ethnic" in mainstream, public spheres and "ethnic" or "racial" in marginal, private ones. Individuals' agency is seen in their ability to switch between identities as context dictates, which can be emotionally challenging (Danico 2004). People bring together various identities when those identities are defined as comparable (Brekhus 2003; Nippert-Eng 1996).

Contrary to this widespread assumption, though, we do not always compartmentalize contradictory identities in discrete spaces or times (Danna-Lynch 2004). In chapters 5–7 I explain the tensions that interviewees encountered within various locations between their identities and then stress how they dealt with those tensions. It is too simplistic to say that people feel or perform only one identity at a time. I look for how actors displayed multiple roles rather than always switch between them.[15] As already noted, James conveys a racial identity in his workplace. It is true that interviewees commonly went out of their way to perform one identity at a time as expected within a domain, such as Sangeeta's attempt to act traditionally religious at home. But rather than *only* segregate identities in discrete spheres, actors also pursued multiple, competing interests within each space, even at times through what I refer to as a "lived hybridity." That is, they engaged in practices and decision-making processes that brought together elements of their ethnic, racial, and American lifestyles, at times simultaneously, to form a distinctive way of being.[16] The current academic use of cultural hybridity concentrates on cultural products, such as music or films, or on liminal spaces and events (Zhou and Lee 2004). These are separate from people's everyday experiences, which supposedly remain within static categories segregated in distinct spheres. Such presumed segregation in turn makes hybrid products and spaces so emotionally resonant (Maira 2002).[17] I apply the lens of hybridity to daily life. Even Sangeeta expressed "American" interests in the home in deciding whether to work outside the home when she has children. She resolved this dilemma by finding a way to maintain a self-defined gendered, ethnic lifestyle and simultaneously identify as an American feminist despite its felt contradictions, discussed in chapter 6. Although Samit carried out an ethnic and religious festival in the home sphere, he did so in a way that made non-Indians feel welcome. Participants struggled to express their multiple interests as they moved through the domains of work, home, leisure, and civil society.

How interviewees handled their various roles depended, in turn, on the cultural scripts of a space. James illustrates a lived hybridity by acting on a racialized image of "Asian" in a way that concurrently promoted an employee identity in the white-collar workplace. He used the prop of a pair of eyeglasses to demonstrate that he is a *model* minority (Goffman 1959), enabling him to suit the cultural and financial goals of his workplace, as discussed in chapter 5. Rarely did actors consider violating domain codes by, for instance, wearing ethnic attire in the corporate workplace, which would appear too foreign and disrupt employee unity. Actors stayed within other domain codes as they brought together diverse sets of interests. In civil society the expectation is that organizations connect people who otherwise would not interact (Alexander and Smith 1993). Informants enjoyed bonding with co-ethnics in their organizations, but they went about their activities in a manner that still conformed to the schema of civil society. This shaped, for instance, the kinds of conversations members had relative to those in which they engaged in the leisure sphere, which had a different set of cultural expectations, as elaborated in chapter 7. In the home sphere informants found ways to express their Americanized interests when making key decisions, such as whether to move away from parents, whom to marry, whether (for women) to stay at home when children were born, and other issues. They accomplished this in ways that supported the home-domain schema of a semitraditional ethnic lifestyle, as explained in chapter 6. In these ways they could affirm an ethnic solidarity across multiple spheres and still appear as proper workers, moral families, and full cultural citizens, instead of as dangerous or inept outsiders.

So we see that by adopting a margins-in-the-mainstream perspective, second-generation immigrants have multiple identities that they define as both in tension and as in dialogue, not just the former. Similarly, they act on their multiple lifestyles by at times embracing one over another but at other times bringing them together even when they feel as if they contradict.

ASSESSING ADAPTATION, UNCOVERING STRATIFICATION

The fact that second-generation Asian Americans can make sense of and enact their identities in a combined, not only segregated, manner offers additional means of assessing immigrant adaptation and considering stratification, elaborated upon in chapter 8. Dominant adaptation theories, such as assimilation (Alba and Nee 2003; Gordon 1964), segmented assimilation (Portes and Zhou 1993), reactive ethnicity (Bean and Stevens 2003; Portes and Rumbaut 2001), and pan-ethnicity (Cornell 1988; Espiritu 1992) allow for individuals to have multiple roles but assume that people separate both what their identities mean and where they are performed. Individuals supposedly define their life-styles in competition with one another, and so a preference for one category means an aversion toward another. For instance, prioritizing a pan-ethnic or ethnic identity rather than an American one suggests a resistance or even hos-tility toward Whites. Conversely, acting "American" presumably signals a lack of interest in an ethnic or pan-ethnic identity, even if done more as a racial strategy to not seem foreign. But, as seen for Samit and James, this inherent re-sistance is not always the case. We first must understand how actors interpret their identity categories in ways that both contrast one another and allow for dialogue. Their interpretations, explained in chapters 3 and 4, indicate whom they feel close to and distant from, and so how they begin to adapt.

Following this reconsideration of identity meanings, it is important to in-vestigate the assumption, seen in chapters 5–7, that people segregate where they perform their identities. As mentioned earlier, ethnic minorities suppos-edly adopt a mainstream role in public and a marginal one in private. Accord-ing to prevailing theories, the more one does so, one furthers one's integra-tion because one acts like everyone else in public institutions and is treated accordingly. Conversely, the more one experiences one's ethnicity and/or race at work, in leisure spaces, or in civil society, the stronger the pluralism. But if we allow groups to express multiple identities within a single sphere in daily life, we start to question this assumption, and so theories of adaptation change too. James, for instance, fits in at work as an ethnic employee and is likely rewarded by his employers for acting "Asian" to the extent that he brings in more profits. Similarly, civil society and the leisure sphere may endorse mul-ticultural themes, in which ethnicity and race are selectively welcomed.[18] To what extent "mainstream" spaces even exist, in which ethnicity and race have little relevance, remains in doubt (Waldinger 2003).

Actors may not only express unexpected identities in ways that clearly suit the domain code but also in ways that are not anticipated and are even con-troversial, but without disrupting the domain schema. It is difficult to nego-tiate implicit rules of conduct, yet this becomes possible when one is highly motivated (DiMaggio 1997; Heiss 1992). For instance, one may speak a foreign language at a workplace despite its clear preference for English. He or she could violate the code by using the language unabashedly and so draw explicit ethnic boundaries from others, or could actually fit within the schema if this was done strategically so as not to disturb workplace expectations.[19] Similarly, one may date outside one's ethnic group, which challenges the guidelines of the home but could, with effort, be reconciled with the home domain code and not promote simply assimilation. The extent to which one conveys a marginal identity in the public sphere or a mainstream identity in private, then, does not clearly signify one's adaptation. The question of how groups integrate has been reduced in the literature to a list of measures, such as language fluencies, intermarriage rates, organizational memberships, and so on. I am not interested in assimilation versus pluralism per se, but in what Asian Americans' identity practices mean for the assessment of adaptation.

As explained in chapter 8, based on this study's findings we see that adaptation does not depend only on *how much* Asian Americans care about their ethnic minority background or *how much* they participate in mainstream versus marginal spaces, but also on *how* they define and express identities in various spaces. We must understand what the domains of workplace, home, popular leisure activities, and civil society actually mean and how informants fit within or challenge those norms as they express their multiple identities.[20] Fitting into the domain code increases actors' integration. This book addresses the fact that increased attention must be paid to how individuals go about their multicultural lives, not just whether they do. Assimilation and multiculturalism outcomes that supposedly contradict one another are reconciled with this new formulation of adaptation.[21]

Korean and Indian American professionals' identity management also affects their stratification. Rather than stopping with the question of whether they are integrating, we must also ask, integrating into what? This book concentrates on the stratification the second generation and other minorities face. How informants define their ethnic and racial differences may promote group pride and resist certain stereotypes, but it may still exacerbate their minority status in the long term and so contribute to their own and others' inequality. How they deal with domain schemas also affects groups' hierarchies. Because Asian Americans are racialized as foreigners, they must actively appear as desirable workers, families, and public citizens by adhering to the domain codes. The state indicates "proper" expressions of difference through the logics inside local settings, such as the workplace or home. Domain scripts are not simply rational responses taken to create highly functional institutions. Instead, capitalist structures and the state reproduce themselves and their racial (as well as other social) hierarchies through support of the codes that reward and punish certain expressions of difference (Lowe 1996). Abiding by domain frames may result in a continuation of hierarchies, even when actors boldly infuse unwelcome identities into a domain in order to make themselves more comfortable. It is important to continue to open up studies of stratification to account for how marginalized groups' agency in resisting oppressions can have unexpected ramifications. Without analyzing group identities relative to the domain frames, we will not be able to explain behavior, nor to assess group relations and stratification.

The setting of Dallas adds another dimension to this study. Over one-third of north Texas is either foreign born or the direct descendant of someone who is foreign born.[22] Dallas is the ninth-largest city in the country in 2005, and does not fit its stereotype as a place of only big oil, big cattle, and big hair.[23] At the same time, the state of Texas, including Dallas, has a politically and socially conservative majority that may enhance racial tensions. The city also lacks a history of Asian American pan-ethnicity. How Indian Americans and Korean Americans build communities there is an intriguing question. The demographics and history of Dallas, along with those of Asian Americans, will be discussed in chapter 2.

This book addresses a set of questions about how Asian American professionals make sense of and control their various identities. These individuals are well integrated in the cultural, social, and economic mainstream. How do informants define their multiple positionalities given their involvement in both immigrant communities and White-dominated neighborhoods, schools, workplaces, and so on? Also, how do they balance their ethnic, racial, and mainstream American interests as they move between distinct settings? And what are the implications, both intentional and unintentional, on the second generation's adaptation and stratification? As a case study, this book cannot give definitive answers to these questions. Instead, it offers points of consideration that further research can pick up, contest, and elaborate.

DEFINING ETHNIC AND RACIAL IDENTITIES

The term identity has become so fashionable that it is impossible to find a consistent definition of it. It has been applied to individuals, organizations, and nations. This book focuses primarily on individuals' identity development and enactment. People develop personal interpretations of social identities (Snow and Anderson 1987). Social identities refer to the locally defined meaning of a group, which is influenced by popular images, discourse, community leaders and members, and others within local, national, and transnational contexts. A person's ethnic identity as a Korean American, for instance, is his or her own personal interpretation of the ethnic social identity. The meaning of identity can vary based on whether one was raised in Los Angeles or in rural Texas, or on whether one grew up in the nineteenth or the twenty-first century. Regardless of the exact meaning of one's identity, invoking it prioritizes one's cognitive and emotional commitments to that community over other group memberships (Tajfel and Turner 1986). We embody multiple identities in which we have different degrees of interest and commitment. The more people we know who are associated with one identity, and the more important to us that community is, the more salient the identity is (Stryker 1992). Having a group identity typically involves an affective commitment to it and participation in its activities (Phinney 1996). To the extent that people express their identities, they create group boundaries from others.

Both race and ethnicity are constructed forms of group membership whose meanings and boundaries vary based on social, political, and economic forces and on individuals' own assertions in response to those forces (Spickard and Burroughs 2000). An ethnic identity refers to one's sense of self as a member of an ethnic group, that is, a group that considers itself having and is believed by others to have a shared culture, geographic origin, history, and possibly interests. The more embedded one is within an ethnic community, the stronger one's ethnicity. A racial identity refers to one's sense of self as a member of a racial group, that is, a group of people distinguished from others based on supposedly common physical characteristics and stereotyped culture (Cornell and Hartmann 1998). Racial groups typically are assigned different degrees of power and moral worth, often by the state, which has an interest in maintaining such divisions (Omi and Winant 1994). Without an environment that promotes pan-ethnic affiliations, such an identity will be weaker.

Ethnicity and race overlap for Asian Americans because of their racialization as foreigners. Characteristics relevant to one's ethnicity, such as having been born in Korea, can be interpreted as a "racial" difference and cause one to be stereotyped as a foreigner who should go back to Asia. Asian Americans can therefore be considered to have a "racialized ethnicity" (Ancheta 1998; Kibria 2002; Purkayastha 2005; Tuan 1998)—that is, ethnic traits of one group, such as the stereotype of "chink" or of eating dogs, are assigned to other groups in the race. It also means that ethnic characteristics, such as religion or cultural norms, are evaluated based not on their own merits but on the racial status of the group, in particular as presumed foreigners. A group may be criticized for being Buddhist or Hindu, for instance, in part because the religion is associated with (non-White) Asians. This critique may then be applied to other Asian American groups, even if it is not culturally relevant. As a result, expressions of ethnic identity, such as wearing traditional clothing, can become racial expressions because through such expressions actors may reinforce their status as foreigners rather than as simply Americans with a distinct heritage. Referring to wearing traditional clothing as invoking an ethnic identity alone can be misleading, depending on the context. The identity of Korean American or Indian American can be a racial, not only ethnic, identity if it signifies a contrast from other races, such as Whites or Blacks. I refer to ethnic and racial identities separately when helpful in distinguishing analytically between primarily cultural differences and hierarchies between groups, respectively. But the two often overlap, so that acting on one implicates the other.

I use the concepts of boundary work and identity work to examine how individuals express their desired interests relative to social expectations. Boundary work and identity work refer to the practices and references one makes to affirm a commitment (or aversion) to a socially defined identity (Nippert-Eng 1996; Howard 2000; Snow and Anderson 1987). The concepts draw attention to the practices and cognitive processes that signify people's differences across settings.[24] I look for the actions and references informants consciously or unconsciously make to designate themselves as being like some people and different from others (Lamont 1992). That is, their boundary and identity work affirm one (or more) of their identities (e.g. American, ethnic American, Asian American, Asian, etc.), such as through whether they don glasses or contacts at work, what leisure practices they pursue and in what manner, whether and how they critique racist acts, what events their organizations sponsor, how they refer to their decision to date, how they refer to being a stay-at-home mother, and much more. Without placing migrants into cultural contexts, we cannot understand their choices of boundary and identity work, nor the impact of those choices on their adaptation.

Chapter 2 explains my choice to study second-generation Korean Americans and Indian Americans, and to base my study in Dallas, Texas. Research on immigration generally is sorely lacking in the South (Bankston 2003).[25] The rest of the book divides into two major sections. In the first (chapters 3 and 4) I explain the development of ethnic and racial identities. In the second (chapters 5–7) I explore how individuals actually express their multiple and possibly contrasting identities within the cultural spaces of work, home, leisure, and civil society, along with related issues. The final chapter considers the implications of how these margins in the mainstream managed their multicultural lives for the study of identity, cultural sociology, immigrant adaptation, and racial stratification.[26]

2 Uncovering Asian Americas

Examining Korean Americans and Indian
Americans in Texas

RESEARCH ON ASIAN AMERICA typically concentrates on one group. I analyze second-generation Indian Americans and Korean American adults because they share important similarities and differences. Both are recent populations who have built up their communities predominantly since the 1965 Immigration Act. The first generation of each group arrived with different occupational patterns, but the second generation has succeeded in the education system and labor market to similar degrees, with a high level of educational attainment and gradual residential integration (Cheng and Yang 1996). As a result, both communities break down the margins-versus-mainstream dichotomy central to this study's focus. They also have noticeable differences, such as religion, appearances, pan-ethnic solidarities, heterogeneity of home country, and others (Min and Kim 1999). Although the differences between Korean and Indian Americans receive ample attention in this book, I concentrate on the overlaps. "Asian America" is a social construction and is often depicted as extremely heterogeneous.[1] A look at commonalities speaks to shared themes within their adaptation and race relations that give meaning to a single population. Research on each group rarely addresses the other. This chapter first explains Indian Americans' and Korean Americans' histories of immigration and racialization in the United States. It then describes their current demographics nationally, the setting of Dallas, the social demographics of the area, and the participants in this study.

HISTORICAL AND CONTEMPORARY RACIALIZATION

Asian Americans have been described as wanted more for their labor than for their lives (Espiritu 2003; Prashad 2000). Historically, they have entered the United States mostly for work, but they faced systemic hostilities as they pushed for real acceptance in terms of both employment and their social-cultural lives. Although today's conditions differ politically, culturally, and economically from those at the end of the nineteenth century, similar patterns arguably remain in terms of the role of Asian Americans in the U.S. economy and their treatment from other Americans. Many immigrants generally appreciate the opportunities available in the United States relative to those in their homeland. And when they arrive and work in the United States, they often receive greater returns on their capital. Yet, they remain constructed by the state as both racial minorities and foreigners, apart from other races and immigrants (Ancheta 1998; Omi and Winant 1994). Asian immigration has been and continues to be a product of U.S. needs in global capitalism. It has been designed to fill gaps in occupational sectors ranging from white-collar positions to sweatshops (Ong, Bonacich, and Cheng 1994). By bringing in Asians, the government has also limited its social service spending on the education and training of local minorities and has helped businesses alleviate the costs associated with labor and training.

As Asian Americans become successful, suspicions turn on them, especially during times of economic insecurity and political tensions with Asia, which affirms the image of the United States as a White country, despite changes in the economy (Lowe 1996). They become racialized as the "yellow peril" bent on overtaking American industries and national defense. They are no longer the "model minority" who kept to their place and worked hard to sustain national and local economies (Okihiro 1994). This notion of Asian Americans as the "enemy within" was displayed most vividly with the internment of Japanese Americans during World War II and the Japan-bashing of the 1970s and 1980s (Chan 1991). Another literal example was the mistaken identity of Vincent Chin, a Chinese American killed in Detroit partly because he was assumed to be a Japanese American during a time of strong economic competition by Japan in the auto industry. Violence, distorted media images, and nativist laws reinforce the symbolic and practical boundaries between White Americans and immigrants, whether they live in separate countries or as neighbors (Chang 2000).[2] Gendered and sexual images of Asian American women and men also serve to uphold White male heterosexual dominance by positioning Asian Americans as either the deviant characters that Whites should define themselves in opposition to or as the desired objects that serve as a warning to other Whites of how they should behave (Espiritu 1997; Lee 1999). This structural racism becomes difficult to address through individual, as opposed to collective, efforts alone, even though people in daily life have little other option. Indian and Korean immigrants, while uniquely different from one another, have histories that fit these general experiences. This chapter does not offer an exhaustive history of each group but instead provides a backdrop to the experiences and attitudes of the current first-generation interviewees, discussed in the following chapter. The history of the two groups fits the trend of Asian Americans wanted more for their labor than for their lives.

Indian Americans

The greatest numbers of Indian immigrants to the United States have arrived since 1965. But Indians have been in North America since as early as 1750. Our best records start with those on the West Coast at the turn of the twentieth century. They arrived in western Canada and the northwestern United States at that time to work in lumberyards, farms, and railroads (Sheth 1995). Violent incidents and even anti-Indian riots ensued due to racial prejudice and economic competition. Many Indians moved to California to avoid racial violence, welcomed at first by farmers needing to replace Chinese and Japanese labor. There were about 7,000 Indian immigrants in California by 1914. Along with Japanese and Chinese Americans, these Indian immigrants substantially changed the agricultural landscape of the state, in particular the Imperial Valley area (Leonard 1997). Still, the usefulness of their labor did not translate into an acceptance of their lives. The immigrants, predominantly Sikhs and Muslims from Punjab, were misnamed "Hindoos" and stereotyped as slaves (Takaki 1989). In the rural areas in which they worked, they often were denied entry into White restaurants and hotels and instead found acceptance in segregated parts of the town, along with Chinese and Mexican immigrants (Leonard 1992). Indian immigrants also were targeted by the Asiatic Exclusion League in California, which previously had sought the removal of Japanese and Korean immigrants. As a result of their economic threat, dark skin that resembled that of "niggers," and Asian origin, the league sought restrictions on them as well. The notion of yellow-peril Asians overtaking U.S. culture, politics, and economy became that of the brown peril.

Citizenship and land ownership laws limited the impact of this brown peril. Following the Ozawa case of 1922, in which Asian Americans were denied citizenship because they were not "Caucasian," Bhagat Singh Thind argued to the Supreme Court in 1923, that he deserved citizenship because he was Caucasian. The courts rebuked the argument and concluded that though

Thind was Caucasian, he was not "White" as defined by "common sense" (Lopez 1996). At that moment the United States outwardly defined itself as a racial and racist state, with Asian Americans denied full acceptance, no longer defended by "science" but attacked on the basis of ideology. This ruling, along with the Alien Land Law of 1920, which denied noncitizens the right to own land, meant that Asian Americans lacked economic security and control and were forced to accept a subservient position relative to Whites and to go outside the legal framework to attain land (Leonard 1992). In other words, Asian Americans could work in needed occupations but were not accepted as real Americans.

Not only Asian Americans but also those wishing to migrate into the United States faced discriminatory treatment. As the labor market grew tighter in Asian-concentrated occupations at the turn of the century, many Americans lobbied to have all Asian immigration stopped (Chan 1991). In 1882, Chinese laborers were excluded from immigrating. Other Asians were denied entry into the United States in 1917, when Congress created the "barred zone." Still more were prevented with the Immigration Act of 1924. Almost no women entered at this time, leaving a predominantly male immigrant population. Without co-ethnic women, families were more difficult to start, and immigrants would presumably either return to their homeland or slowly die away. They could not form legal unions with White women owing to antimiscegenation laws aimed at protecting the sexual "decency" of White women and the durability of the "White family" (Lee 1999). Some Punjabi men in California married Mexican women, often sisters of laborers on their farms (Leonard 1992). The family was a metaphor for the nation, and the laws helped define the nation along racial lines. This limited Asian immigrants' status to a minor presence of likely sojourners.

Practically all migration from Asia ceased from 1924 until 1946. In 1946, the Luce/Celler Act, widened in 1952 with the McCarran and Walter Act, allowed a small quota of Asians to immigrate and obtain citizenship (Sheth 1995).[3] The majority of Indian Americans arrived after 1965, following the Immigration Act of 1965, which eradicated the limited quotas against Asians.[4] Although the act was not intended to result in a sizable increase in Asian Americans, many fell into the preference category for highly skilled professionals and relatives of citizens. Indian Americans arrived as doctors, engineers, professors, students, or managers, women and men in equal numbers. Given their proficiency in English and their human capital, they rarely formed segregated residential and commercial districts comparable to those found in Chinatowns or Korea-towns (Helweg and Helweg 1990). In contrast to many other Asian Americans, a sizable minority of Indian Americans have settled outside of urban centers, taking those professional or small business openings least preferred by natives. Still, enclaves of Indian American–owned shops and residences, known as "Little Indias," can be found in or near major cities, including Queens (in New York City), Edison (New Jersey), Chicago, and Los Angeles. Many—not all—of the men and women working in these areas lack the professional degrees and/or English abilities of their sponsoring relatives and represent the chain migration of the professionals who arrived in the 1970s and early 1980s (Khandelwal 2002). One of the more graphic forms of anti-Indian violence were the "dotbusters" in Jersey City, New Jersey, in 1987 (Lessinger 1995). (The "dot" referred to the bindis on Hindu women's foreheads.) A group of mostly White teenagers threatened Indian Americans. Among their other attacks, they beat to death a bank manager named Navroze Mody while chanting "Hindu! Hindu!" and beat a doctor so severely that he was in a coma.

The stratification within the Indian American community is stark. In addition to the "brain drain" during the 1960s and 1970s, a large number of computer programmers and businesspeople more recently have established a reputation in Silicon Valley and elsewhere, including Dallas. At the same time, South Asian Americans increasingly own and/or work in gas stations, convenience stores, and motels. Patels alone, a subset of the population from the state of Gujurat, India, own more than 50 percent of motels in the country (Bhakta 2002). Other South Asian Americans drive taxicabs or work as seasonal farm laborers. The image of Indian Americans as economically affluent hides this diversity as well as community problems such as domestic violence, glass ceilings, anti-immigrant violence and rhetoric, and cultural intolerance. Some of these issues facing the first generation receive attention in the following chapter. The occupational diversity is matched by the religious, regional, and linguistic diversity of the diaspora. Most individuals are Hindu, with a significant number of Jains, Sikhs, Muslims, Christians, and Hare Krishnas. These religious groups have built temples or churches that serve as community spaces as well (Kurien 2002). The largest segment of Indian Americans originates from Gujurat, although areas of the entire country have come to be represented. After 9/11, Indian Americans, in particular Muslims and Sikhs, have encountered increased attacks and general suspicions. I discuss this further, and its impact on the local community, in later chapters.

Korean Americans

Korean Americans share a history with other Asian Americans as immigrating primarily for economic incentives and encountering opportunities as well as resentment and hostility as "foreigners." As with Indian Americans, the largest influx of Korean Americans in the United States has occurred since 1965, with limited numbers relative to other Asian American groups before then. Few Korean Americans immigrated at the beginning of the twentieth century owing to restrictions by the Japanese government, of which Korea became a protectorate in 1905 (Henthorn 1971). This first wave of Korean Americans was made up of male laborers who arrived as contract workers to Hawaii to toil on sugar plantations, displaying Asian Americans' historic role in global capitalism. Their labor was needed because Chinese had been excluded from immigrating, Japanese American laborers had gone on strike protesting their conditions, and European Americans proved too expensive (Hurh 1998). Koreans looked to escape harsh economic conditions in their country, including a famine in 1901 that loosened emigration restrictions (Min 2006b). Although the labor of Korean Americans on the sugar plantations was valuable, they too had great difficulties establishing lives for themselves. The work proved dangerous and lacked adequate compensation, and an extremely imbalanced sex ratio ensured that many would stay bachelors. Some moved to California. Barred by Whites from owning land and restaurants, they formed Koreatowns with their own residential and commercial buildings (Takaki 1989). When they could no longer even own farmland—a result of the Alien Land Law Act of 1913—some Koreans left California entirely.

As Korean immigrants tried to build a community in the United States, they also organized around Korea's attempt to attain national independence from Japan (Lyu 1977). Korean intellectuals gave money to newspapers and patriotic funds, and parents emphasized the need to maintain Korean culture, which was being threatened by Japan. Such transnational organizing is similar to the international Gadar movement by Indian immigrants in the 1920s to overthrow British colonial rule. Gadar members, including those in the United States, tried to bring arms to India, wrote newspaper articles on the need to overthrow the British, and even tried to start a revolt in Singapore (Singh 2002). Korean Americans pushed for independence but, at the same time, also strove to accommodate to U.S. society by stressing their Christian background. They believed that Chinese and Japanese Americans inflamed tensions with Whites by not trying to assimilate sufficiently (Hurh and Kim 1984). (The strategy of advancing national interests while trying to integrate into U.S. society is adopted by current immigrants as well, as discussed in chapter 3.) A small number of men sent for "picture brides" (women in Korea who wed Korean immigrant men based on mailed photos and who subsequently immigrated to the United States) between 1910 and 1924, which resulted in a mixture of some positive and some very negative unions. By 1908 Japan had political control over Korea, and the Gentleman's Agreement between the United States and Japan put a stop to all further Korean migration. With a lack of continued migration, the community did not grow, and in 1924 almost all Asian immigration ended.

The next major wave of Korean Americans occurred in the 1950s, resulting not from economic needs of the United States and the immigrants, but from the war between the countries, in which Asian Americans often find themselves caught in the middle. War brides, war orphans, and students arrived as a result of the Korean War (Hurh and Kim 1984). As the Soviets and the United States fought the cold war on Korean land, they facilitated the split of the country into two. This furthered the exodus and the number of war brides. Upon arrival in the United States, however, many of these women experienced culture shock and depression as they tried to adjust to their new country, often in marriages that proved extremely difficult.

The third wave of Korean immigration has taken place since 1965, and mostly since 1970. The current second generation sampled here for both ethnic groups consists of the children of this wave of immigrants. In fact, the Korean American population increased by almost tenfold after 1970. Many Korean immigrants arrived, as did other Asian Americans during this time, as students or professionals in highly specialized fields. Once they received admission, they could sponsor their families under the preference system of the 1965 act rather than being constrained to living alone.

Korean Americans are predominantly Christian, even though Koreans are not. The Korean American church, probably more than any other ethnic religious institution, serves as a central site for local communities. Such churches proliferate as new ones break off from existing ones. Members not only attend religious services regularly but exchange information of both internal dynamics and external opportunities. People often learn of employment possibilities or access to financial opportunities within the church setting. With educational degrees that were not transferable to the United States and with poor

English skills, many Korean Americans experienced downward mobility after migrating (Hurh 1998). Many in cities entered low-paying service occupations, such as janitors. About a third have started family-run small businesses, often stores that cater to co-ethnics or to native minorities. Koreatowns, where some Korean Americans but also other minorities may live, comprise major business districts in Los Angeles, Oakland, Chicago, Philadelphia, and New York City, not to mention Vancouver and other North American cities. Other business owners serve racially diverse clientele, such as greengrocers in New York City, who work long hours and stock a large selection of merchandise to accommodate customer preferences. Although few of these businessmen had experience running stores in Korea, the businesses helped many realize, albeit slowly, their motivations for migrating to the United States: economic attainment, educational opportunities for their children, and reunification with family members. At the same time, intense competition among co-ethnics often limits profitability, even though many Korean Americans accrue the necessary money for their businesses from co-ethnics (Abelmann and Lie 1995). In addition, they can encounter dangerous work environments within some inner-city neighborhoods. For instance, 20 Korean Americans were murdered by African Americans in Los Angeles County between 1987 and 1991 (Min 1996).

As "middleman minorities" Korean Americans have filled a service gap left by grocery and retail corporations in poor, urban neighborhoods. Like other Asian American immigrants, Korean Americans serve capitalist needs caused by fluctuations in industries within U.S. capitalism. Capitalism rewards companies not for serving the public but for limiting costs and increasing profit, and many corporations have exploited this fact by abandoning poor communities (Abelmann and Lie 1995). Because Korean Americans are caught between White (as well as Korean) suppliers and native minority clientele, they often find themselves the brunt of hostilities by both groups. The 1992 Los Angeles riots and numerous boycotts in New York City, at times violent, have brought to the forefront the tensions between communities and the challenges facing Korean Americans' acceptance as equal members of U.S. society (C. Kim 2001; Min 1996). They are targeted as culturally insensitive and as patronizing toward their inner-city, African American customers while at the same time relying on their business. At other times the business owners are lauded for their entrepreneurship despite their foreign status. Korean Americans illustrate the complicated racial and class dynamics within urban areas today, as well as the continued role of Asian Americans as buffers between White and Black America.

CURRENT POPULATIONS

A major similarity for both groups is the model-minority stereotype, that is, as hardworking immigrants who stay in their place. This image is assigned to our current populations of Indian Americans and Korean Americans. Versions of the stereotype date back even earlier, to the fictional character Charlie Chan, which originated in 1925 (Okihiro 1994). Chan was an overweight, subservient detective in Hawaii who used his mind instead of his weak body to solve problems. He could not threaten local or national security, given his almost effeminate style. He spoke broken English and hoped to please Whites through his obeisance. He fit the desired image of how a minority should behave by staying in his place and earning praise through serving Whites. This model-minority caricature gained more popularity as it became attached to real Asian Americans in the 1960s. The stereotype grew at the time of the civil rights movement as a means of countering the claims by Blacks that discrimination impedes the socioeconomic equality of its minority population (Chan 1991). The supposed success of native- and foreign-born Asian Americans enables the United States to appear as an open, modern society benevolent toward its minorities. The model minority also serves as a warning to Whites that they should not complain about their working conditions, for if they do, a more acquiescent labor force is available.

The model-minority myth is currently being challenged by an influx of working-class Asian Americans. They face heightened danger in their occupations and are more likely to be victims of hate crimes. Discrimination in wages, promotions, and interpersonal relations against Asian American immigrant professionals also continues as they struggle to be rewarded for their labor and gain acceptance for their lives, as discussed in chapter 5 (Fong 1998). The experiences of first- and second-generation Indian and Korean Americans in Dallas support this historical perspective and the current racialized stereotypes, seen in the ensuing chapters.

According to the 2000 U.S. Census, Asian Americans make up more than 4 percent of the U.S. population. Indian Americans and Korean Americans comprise 0.66 percent and 0.44 percent of the country's population, respectively, which makes the former group the third largest Asian American con-

Table 2.1 Family income, U.S.

	Median family income, 1999	Mean family income, 2000
Whites	$50,046	$70,000
Indian Americans	$70,708	$94,000
Korean Americans	$47,624	$71,000

SOURCES: Census 2000 Summary File 4 (SF 4)—Sample Data, U.S.; Sakamoto and Xie 2006, 71.

tingent and the latter group the fifth largest.[5] Foreign-born Asian Americans outnumber native born as of 2000, 69 percent to 31 percent. Korean and Indian Americans had comparable percentages of native born, 22 percent and 25 percent, respectively (Min 2006a). There are still heavy geographic concentrations of both groups, in particular Korean Americans in California, but migration has spread throughout the country, even into rural areas of the South and Midwest, especially for Indian Americans (Bhakta 2002). In fact, 19 percent of Asian Americans lived in the South in 2000, up from 7 percent in 1970 (Min 2006a).

The median family income in 1999 was $70,708 for Indian Americans, $47,624 for Korean Americans, and $50,046 nationally for Whites (see Table 2.1).[6] The mean family income offers a slightly different picture, with both Korean Americans (at $71,000) and Indian Americans (at $94,000) above the average of Whites (of $70,000) (Sakamoto and Xie 2006). In terms of employment, more than half of employed Indian immigrants worked as managers, professionals, or executives in 2000. Korean Americans have the highest percentage of business owners among Asian Americans. Twenty-three percent of Korean Americans owned a business in 2000, down from 25 percent in 1990 but up from 17 percent in 1980 (Min 2006b). Regarding educational attainment, Asian Americans also rank more highly than other racial groups. In 2000, 63 percent of native-born adult Indian Americans and 61 percent of native-born adult Korean Americans had finished college, well above the average of 29 percent for Whites and even the 45 percent for native-born Asian Americans (Sakamoto and Xie 2006) (see Table 2.2). So, although Korean and Indian immigrants have different occupational trajectories, those of each group who were born in the United States have comparably high average education levels. In addition, despite differences among the first generation, the native born of both groups are well represented in professional occupa-

Table 2.2 College attainment, professional and related occupations, and poverty rates, U.S., 2000

	Percentage in U.S. who completed college, age 25–64	Percentage in U.S. with professional occupations	Poverty rates in U.S.
Whites	29	22	9
Indian Americans, native born	63	43	10
Indian Americans, foreign born	66	44	10
Korean Americans, native born	61	42	15
Korean Americans, foreign born	46	23	12

SOURCES: Min 2006c, 82; Sakamoto and Xie 2006, 59 and 73.

tions: 43 percent of Indian Americans and 41 percent of Korean Americans, with very little variation between sexes, relative to 22 percent of native-born White Americans (Kibria 2006; Min 2006b, 2006c). In fact, native-born Korean Americans show no greater tendency for self-employment than do native-born Whites, 8.6 percent and 11.2 percent, respectively (Min 2006b).

Asian Americans' impressive degree of economic and educational success should not overshadow the fact that many Asian Americans live in poverty. The poverty rates for both Indian Americans (10 percent for both foreign and native born) and Korean Americans (12 percent for foreign born and 15 percent for native born) is higher than that of Whites (9 percent) (Sakamoto and Xie 2006).

Whether Asian Americans born in the United States show a disadvantage in returns on their educational attainment as measured by income is under debate, with some arguing that they continue to suffer discrimination in this regard (Cheng and Yang 1996) and others arguing that they no longer do (Sakamoto and Xie 2006). If they no longer do, one explanation besides the decline of discrimination could be the overrepresentation of Asian Americans in science and technology fields, which pay higher wages than other fields that require similar education. A glass ceiling may continue to threaten Asian Americans trying to achieve promotions into the ranks of upper management (Woo 2000). As explained in the following chapters, Asian Americans often are perceived as unequipped to represent a corporation despite their credentials and knowledge of an industry, and so they remain in middle management. I now focus on the general trends as well as the particularities of being Asian American in Dallas.

WHY DALLAS?

This book draws attention to growing Asian American communities in the South. Research on Asian American communities traditionally has concentrated on either Chinese or Japanese Americans on the West Coast, primarily in California. Case studies have focused on a single group and marked its peculiarities to the region. New work has been carried out in New York City and Chicago as post-1965 immigration waves have settled "east of California." The South is an increasingly significant site of Asian American settlement, but there is a dearth of information on this phenomenon. By drawing attention to multiple groups outside of our normal geographic range, we open up the field of Asian American studies to incorporate its social, cultural, and physical diversity. I chose Dallas for two major reasons. First, it was a practical setting because I grew up near there, which made me familiar with the geography. I knew that there was a sizable Asian American population there, despite its lack of attention in the literature. I had not been there for ten years before conducting the research, except for occasional visits to family. So upon starting the fieldwork, I was encountering a city that was a collection of memory snapshots taken over the past decade, rather than walking into a well-known environment. This combination of familiarity with and distance from the city proved highly valuable. Because I had been away for so long, I did not have presumptions of the city or of immigrant communities that could have led me to focus only on only particular geographic areas or types of questions. At the same time, I knew how to navigate the city and could understand residents' references to various highways, landmarks, and surrounding cities.

Second, and more important, Dallas makes an excellent research site because of its size, location, and growing number of Asian American residents. As the ninth largest city in the nation,[7] Dallas has a noticeably smaller Asian American population than the major urban destinations of New York City, Los Angeles, San Francisco, and Chicago, which have received the most attention in this subject. Yet, because these select major cities are so large and have such long histories of Asian immigration, studies on them speak more to the particulars of those areas, rather than to how immigration is taking place throughout the rest of the country. Cities such as Atlanta, Dallas, Denver, Houston, Nashville, New Orleans, Phoenix, St. Louis, and others mostly remain overlooked even though they are home to tens of thousands of Asian Americans. Although Dallas cannot represent any other place besides itself, it opens up insights into the ethnic and racial dynamics in these smaller yet sizable cities.

In particular, the South remains an underresearched site of immigration (Bankston 2003; Ebaugh and Chafetz 2000; Jung 2006; Loewen 1971; Um 1996; Zhou and Bankston 1998). The Association of Asian American Studies recently has recognized this gap. Yet, it has had more panels discussing the lack of research in the South than there has been actual research taking place in the South.[8] Literature on race in the South predominantly concentrates on Blacks and Whites, with a growing interest in Latinos as one moves farther west. This is despite the fact that in 2000, Texas had 562,319 Asian Americans (5.5 percent of the total in the United States), the third-highest percentage in the country, behind only California and New York (Min 2006a) and surpassing even Hawaii. The presumption that the South lacks diversity beyond African Americans and Whites only reproduces itself when insufficient attention is paid to its immigrants. Asian immigrants ranging from gas station attendants to information technology programmers have moved there, in both rural and urban areas. Asian Americans are also making a name in politics in the South. For instance, an Indian American, Piyush "Bobby" Jindal, running as a conservative Republican, almost won the Louisiana governorship in 2003 and now is a U.S. Congressman. In Texas, Martha Wong won a seat on the Houston City Council and then was elected to the Texas House of Representatives in 2002, the first Asian American woman to do either. In 2004, Hubert Vo became the first Vietnamese American to gain office within the Texas Legislature.

The Dallas that Korean Americans and Indian Americans are entering has changed drastically from its history of cattle ranching and oil connections (Kemper 2005). Images of Dallas consist of cowboy hats and boots, the self-titled television show, Southern accents, the Dallas Cowboys football team, the presidential assassination of more than forty years ago, and a pervading notion that everything is "big." The city, founded in 1841, served as an agricultural center of north Texas, with its rich soil, and became a trading post and transportation center for people migrating from east to west.[9] It has been mostly business friendly, run informally and formally by business elites throughout most of the twentieth century (Hazel 1997).[10] When oil prices rose in the 1960s and afterward, the Dallas–Fort Worth economy grew and attracted major corporations, such as 7-11, Alcatel, American Airlines, Blockbuster, CompUSA, Ericsson, ExxonMobil, Greyhound, JCPenney, Mary Kay Cosmetics, Neiman

Marcus, Nortel, Pier 1 Imports, Radio Shack, SBC, Southwest Airlines, Texas Instruments, and others. The city has expanded recently, and areas that were less developed in the 1980s have become gentrified and now offer prime real estate (Prior and Kemper 2005). The downtown area has experienced new growth since the early 1990s, when it was losing residents (Payne 2000). Since then it has turned abandoned buildings into condominiums, and it now has a growing arts district. The image of Dallas as an uneducated, ultraconservative city is belied by its growing cosmopolitan population and feel, in contrast to even much of the U.S. South and Southwest. For instance, Dallas city residents watch less football than the national average and avidly consume the latest fashions.[11]

There had been significant racial diversity in the city even before the arrival of Asian Americans in the late nineteenth century, with often tense relations between Native Americans, African Americans, Mexican Americans, and Whites. The Dallas chapter of the Ku Klux Klan was the largest in the nation in 1920. Immigrants and both racial and religious minorities were victims of violence and intimidation, even as the city depended on their labor. By the year 2000, 35 percent of the north Texas population (including Dallas, Tarrant, Collin, and Denton counties) were either foreign born or the children of foreign-born residents.[12] The area is home to a vast range of immigrant groups from Central and Latin America, Asia, Africa, and Eastern Europe (Adler 2005). A number of first- and second-generation Asian Americans have gained employment in the city since the 1970s because of its growing telecommunications industry, strong business climate, and health care system. In fact, from 1980 to 2000 Dallas had the third-highest increase in the nation in the percentage of immigrants coming in, with the Fort Worth area fourth.[13] Dallas receives more description throughout the book.

Korean Americans and Indian Americans in Dallas

Unfortunately, little is known on the background of Korean and Indian Americans in Texas owing to a lack of systematic research. In north Texas, Korean Americans rank in the top seven immigrant groups in terms of size; Indian Americans rank in the top three, behind Mexican Americans and Vietnamese Americans.[14] Unlike Hawaii and California, Texas saw significant numbers of Korean Americans only after 1965 (Brady 2004). In contrast, the first Asian Americans in Texas were likely Chinese, arriving in the late 1870s to replace African American slave labor on the Houston and Texas Center Railroad. Korean war brides entered following the war and settled near military bases in San Antonio, El Paso, and a few other towns. Upon arrival after 1965, those with English proficiency and technical skills found work in the oil industry. However, as they did throughout the country, Korean Americans opened up small businesses in response to language barriers, occupational discrimination, and labor market recession. Today, in addition to stores in ethnic enclaves and inner-city neighborhoods, Korean Americans own businesses along the Texas-Mexican border, selling to Mexicans Korean items purchased from wholesalers in Korea. Korean Americans make up the highest percentage of small-business owners in the state (Brady 2004).

According to community leaders, many Korean American small-business owners have achieved middle-class status and have reputations as relatively successful entrepreneurs. (All of the interviewees' names are pseudonyms, to honor confidentiality. Traditionally Korean and American names refer to Korean Americans, most of whom had comparable names, and traditionally Indian names refer to Indian Americans. Organization names also have been changed for the same reason but retain their original meaning.) According to Chul Park of the Organization for Korean Americans (OKA), an umbrella organization that serves primarily first-generation Korean Americans, Dallas residents found it easier to open up businesses there than in Los Angeles.[15] "There is more competition there, such as grocery stores or laundry or stores in those field. They find out that this area is relatively easier than big cities." Many Korean-owned stores are situated in African American neighborhoods. In addition, enough stores have opened in a once-dilapidated section of northwest Dallas as to qualify the area (although not officially, according to the city) as a Koreatown, albeit a small one, with store signs in Korean. Peter is a second-generation store owner whose father owned a store as well. I asked him about the district near Harry Hines Boulevard and Royal Lane:

> This place used to be known for prostitution, and it still is now. When my dad opened a business in '84, there was only one other Korean business here. Then it just started to develop. The rent was cheaper but not anymore. Look around—there used to be a lot of vacancies, but not anymore. Overall the rent is cheaper than north Dallas or Plano because a lot of these buildings are older, but that's going to start changing pretty soon.

The district has wholesale shops, restaurants, grocery stores, karaoke bars, and more. Some suburbs north and west of Dallas, where many Korean Americans live, have a smaller nucleus of stores. This Dallas Koreatown is all commercial; it has no residences.

For Korean Americans, the church is the main organization, with report-edly more than 130 Korean churches in the Dallas–Fort Worth area. There are also three daily newspapers, three weekly papers, and a radio broadcast sys-tem. There are also a number of voluntary organizations that serve members of the community. Park of the OKA listed some of them:

> In the community there are a number of organizations: athletics club, women's league, trading commission, chamber of commerce. The organizations occasion-ally have a conflict. We are the coordinators and resolve conflicts. We represent the Korean community. We also help Korean Americans in getting visas, real estate. Service functions. We are representing the Korean community.

Because of the high number of Korean-owned small businesses, there is also a Korean American Small Business Association. There was no political official of Asian descent in Dallas at the time of the fieldwork. Perhaps the most fa-mous Korean American in Texas is Wendy Lee, the wife of former U.S. Sena-tor Phil Gramm. Lee's parents arrived in the United States at the turn of the twentieth century, as did many Korean Americans, to work on sugar planta-tions in Hawaii.

Of the numerous Korean churches in the area, there are four English Min-istries (EMs) that serve young professionals. These are conservative churches geared toward the 1.5 (immigrants who arrived as adolescents with their par-ents) and second generation, with services in English and little outward dis-play of Korean culture (Dhingra 2004). They typically start within a parent Korean church and may break away over time (Chai 1998). I did research in three of them, all Protestant denominations: God's Light, which is the biggest EM in Dallas–Fort Worth and is north of Dallas; World Gathering in Dallas; and the Good Book, also north of Dallas.[16] The other major organization of the second generation was the Korean American Professionals (KAP), a primarily social group for young professionals. The president of KAP in 2000 was Susie. At the time of my follow-up fieldwork in 2002, the organization no longer met regularly. A comparable organization that few Korean Americans attended was a pan-ethnic Asian American young professional association. Most of its members were Chinese American. I discuss these organizations, in particular KAP and the EMs, throughout the book.

Indian Americans also arrived in Texas for the most part after 1965. Like other Indian American men and women who arrived at that time, many in Texas had advanced degrees and entered white-collar professions in medi-cine, engineering, and universities (Brady 2004). The population has increased steadily since then. One Indian American elder estimated that there are four professional occupational groups for the ethnic group: doctors, engineers (including computer scientists), motel and other small-business owners (including convenience store owners), and nurses (Ghosh-Pandy 1998). Indeed in 2000, a quarter of all employees in Texas's high-tech firms were of Indian origin, and Indian Americans make up the highest percentage of international students in Dallas-area universities.[17] Very few have settled in ethnic enclaves; most instead live in urban, suburban, and rural areas. The most significant concentrations are in Houston, Dallas, and Austin. Recently, a more varied occupational representation has emerged. One sees South Asian Americans in such positions as clerks in convenience stores and gas stations, working in ticket booths at airports, as auto mechanics, and in other lower-status occupations. Naresh Shah, past president of the Asian American Small Business Association, noted the change in the Dallas community:

> But in the last fifteen years, the inflow is coming on the blood relations. So now you have every type of people coming in: high school graduates, nongraduates, never went to the college people, some laborers—everyone is coming in. In the Indian community particularly, leaving all the professionals apart, the concentration is of small businesses in retail, motel, dry cleaners, and gas stations.

Many immigrants are here on H1 or family visas.

With their financial resources, Indian Americans have formed Hindu temples, Jain temples, Sikh gurdwaras, mosques, churches, and other religious organizations throughout the state, including Dallas. Among the relevant ones for this study, there are three Hindu temples in Dallas alone. The major temple in the city is an ecumenical one that combines various types of Hindu worship, and is located in a suburb west of the city.[18] Because of its goal to unite the Dallas–Fort Worth Metroplex's various types of Hinduism, I refer to it as the Metroplex temple. Another is the main Swaminarayan temple, representing a particular form of Hinduism popular in Gujarat. There is also a Hare Krishna temple in Dallas (ISKCON). In addition, there are a Jain temple and Sikh gurdwaras in surrounding suburbs. I did fieldwork at the three largest Hindu temples—the Metroplex, ISKCON, and the Swaminarayan temple—as well as at the Jain temple, all places of worship that informants attended. The temples serve as community sites as well, hosting classical music concerts, language classes, lectures, and social services, such as medical assistance or college preparation.

Most Indians in Dallas are from Gujarat and Uttar Pradesh. Still, there are also more than 50 voluntary cultural, professional, and religious organizations of various sub-ethnic groups, including Bengali, Tamils, Gujaratis, Punjabi, Sindhi, Zoroastrians, and others (see Brettell 2005b). The mission of the major umbrella organization, the Indian American Association (IAA), is to help the ethnic group become more integrated into the local area and to honor Indians' ancestry.[19] To that end it has health fairs, information sessions on visas, women's meetings on balancing Indian and American values, and major celebrations of national Indian holidays, such as India's independence day. It receives more attention in chapter 7. Because Dallas has few Indian Americans relative to some other cities, the city facilitates a stronger ethnic rather than sub-ethnic identity for the first generation (Brettell 2005a). Dallas also has an Indian chapter of an international and multiethnic charity agency, comprised of the first generation.

The older generation is more segregated into distinct cultural groups than is the second generation (Ghosh-Pandy 1998). For the second generation, the major organization was the Indian American Network Association (IANA). This, like KAP, served young professionals of the 1.5 and second generation mostly. It is a Dallas branch, started in 1993, of a national organization, unlike KAP which was an independent association. IANA receives more attention throughout the study.

Dallas offers a wealth of cultural opportunities as well. Classical Indian dance lessons are offered. There are movie theaters showing primarily Bollywood productions and numerous Indian grocery stores in strip malls. Restaurants, including a fast food restaurant, serve food from regions throughout India. There is no "Little India" in Dallas comparable to that of Chicago or New York City. Still, the residential concentration in mostly the northern and western suburbs, especially in Richardson, has created a sector of grocery stores, restaurants, and clothing and jewelry stores. Other areas with a high number of Indian Americans are Mesquite east of Dallas, Collin county north of Dallas (which includes the suburb Plano), and Denton county northwest of Dallas (see also Brettell 2005b). In addition a new, for-profit establishment that serves all South Asians with a movie theater, banquet facilities, and restaurant has opened in the suburbs. Local ethnic papers carry mostly advertisements for satellite televisions, grocery stores, real estate brokers, immigration lawyers, restaurants, and so on.

Neither Korean American nor Indian Americans are represented in politics, but their organizations are attracting political attention. Local elected officials attend major ceremonies and meetings of ethnic and pan-ethnic groups.

Table 2.3 Population, Texas and Dallas County

	Texas	Dallas County
Total population	20,851,820	2,218,899
Asian Americans	657,664	100,447
Chinese Americans	112,950	13,208
Indian Americans	142,689	25,830
Korean Americans	54,300	10,115
Vietnamese Americans	143,352	22,612

SOURCE: Census 2000 Summary File 1, 100% Data, Dallas County.

Group leaders have reached out to politicians as well to learn about programs that will impact their members and to signal the needs and resources of their constituents. There are a few pan-ethnic associations, mostly business and political. The most prominent is the Asian American Small Business Association, near Koreatown; it not only serves the needs of business owners but also acts as a representative of Asian Americans more broadly (see chapter 7).[20] The ethnic organizations that Korean and Indian Americans have most access to, then, encourage an ethnic more than a pan-ethnic identity, one focused on cultural, social and economic concerns. In both ethnic groups, men dominate leadership positions.

Time does not stand still in the field after the researcher leaves to write up his findings. The bulk of the fieldwork and interviews for this book took place in the summer, fall, and winter of 1999, with follow-up fieldwork in the summers of 2000 and of 2002. I have made an effort to monitor from a distance the ethnic organizations pertinent to Korean and Indian Americans in Dallas and to keep track of new ones. I make tentative references to activities after the fieldwork ended in order to signal the continued growth of the communities. However, a detailed account of those activities is not possible.

According to the 2000 U.S. Census, Texas has a total of 20,851,820 people and 657,664 Asian Americans, which is practically 3.5 percent, below the national average.[21] Dallas County's social demographics consisted of a total of 2,218,899 people, of whom 100,447 were Asian American (see Table 2.3), about 4.5 percent of the county's population—higher than the national average. Of these, 10,115 were Korean Americans and 25,830 were Indian Americans, making the latter group Dallas County's largest Asian American contingent. Indian Americans comprise 4.3 percent of the area's foreign-born population.[22]

Table 2.4   Household income and poverty rates, Dallas County

	Median household income	Poverty rates
Total population	$43,324	13.4%
Indian Americans	$56,759	8.5%
Korean Americans	$36,522	15.9%

SOURCE: Census 2000 Summary File 4—Sample Data, Dallas County.

Table 2.5   Percentage of men and women married age 15 and above, median age and percentage who speak only English . . . , age 5–17, Dallas County

	Percentage of men married	Percentage of women married	Median age	Percentage who speak only English
Total Population	56	53	31.3	63.8
Indian Americans	63	74	29.6	27.2
Korean Americans	72	64	35.3	11.5

SOURCE: Census 2000 Summary Files 2 and 4—Sample Data, Dallas County.

Local leaders of both groups estimated their population to be much bigger, between 40,000 and 50,000. Korean Americans are the fourth-largest Asian American group in the area, just behind Chinese Americans at 13,208. Vietnamese Americans make up the second-largest group, at 22,612. Vietnamese are more likely than other Asian Americans to live in East Dallas, but they also are spread throughout the region, including the suburbs and the Fort Worth area. Many came from Vietnam directly in the late 1980s. They often work as medical and clerical assistants and own nail and beauty salons as well as convenience stores, frequently in low-income neighborhoods.[23] The community has its own organizations, as do Chinese Americans, Filipino Americans, Taiwanese Americans, and others.[24] None of the informants in this study made more than passing reference to these groups.

In terms of class status, the median household income in Dallas was $43,324, according to the 2000 Census (see Table 2.4).[25] For Asian Americans as a whole, it was slightly higher, at $49,382. Indian American households earned slightly more ($56,759) and Korean Americans less ($36,522) than the county average. The same discrepancy applies to poverty rates. The individual poverty rates are 8.5 percent for Indian Americans in Dallas and 15.9 percent for Korean Americans, while the Dallas average is 13.4 percent.[26] In regard to education, in 2002, 70 percent of Asian American men and 63 percent of Asian

American women in Dallas County had at least some college education.[27] As for social demographics, both groups are near the average age for residents of Dallas County: in 2000 Indian Americans' median age in Dallas was 29.6 and Korean Americans' was 35.3, while the average age in the county overall was 31.3.[28] The 2000 Census also showed a greater percentage of both groups aged 25 and older who were married than for Dallas as a whole (see Table 2.5). The county marriage rates are 56 percent for men and 53 percent for women, while for Indian Americans it was 63 percent for men and 74 percent for women. For Korean Americans the rate is 72 percent for men and 64 percent for women.[29] Finally, and not surprisingly, the groups are less acculturated than others in the county. In terms of language, for example, of those aged 5–17, 27.2 percent and 11.5 percent of Indian Americans and Korean Americans, respectively, speak only English at home. Overall in the county, the rate is 63.8 percent.[30]

The Korean American and Indian American populations are spread out, more residentially structured by class than race. Like other middle- and upper-middle-class newcomers regardless of ethnicity, many live in north and west Dallas and the surrounding suburbs (see Figure 2.1).[31] For the most part they live segregated from other minorities, in particular from African Americans. For example, in the suburb of Richardson just north of Dallas, 12 percent of the residents are Asian, but only 6 percent are Black; 10 percent are Hispanic and 71 percent are White. Lancaster, on the other hand, has 53 percent Black, 1 percent Asian, 12 percent Hispanic, and 34 percent White residents. Those cities with the highest concentration of Blacks (Lancaster, DeSoto, Cedar Hill, and Duncanville—all with a Black population of 25 percent or more), had some of the lowest concentrations of Asians (1 percent, 2 percent, 3 percent, and 3 percent, respectively) and are located just south of Dallas.[32]

Many Asian Americans live near the "telecom corridor" in Richardson, which houses telecommunication and other high-tech companies. The areas north and west of Dallas, home to a number of Asian Americans, are areas of urban sprawl. Various highways serve the north, and either said of them one sees corporate headquarters.[33] The farther north one drives, leaving Dallas and entering its suburbs—such as Plano and Richardson—more highways appear, along with strip malls with chain stores, restaurants, major malls, and billboards for hospitals, beer, apartments, and so on. As one drives through the residential neighborhoods, one finds blocks of newer houses with one- or two-car garages. There are a number of public schools, supermarkets, drugstores, and churches in the area. This description of north Dallas pertains to

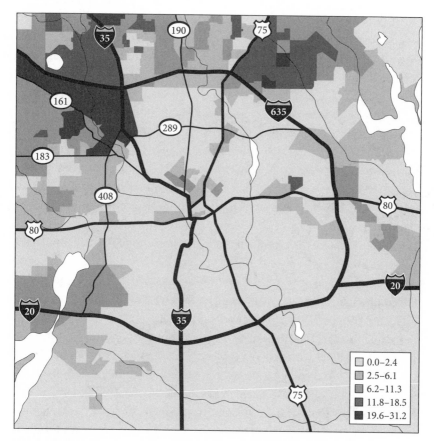

Legend:
- 0.0–2.4
- 2.5–6.1
- 6.2–11.3
- 11.8–18.5
- 19.6–31.2

Figure 2.1 Map of Korean American and Indian American Populations in Dallas.

parts west of Dallas. Parts of Dallas just north of downtown are more metropolitan than the city's edges and suburbs. In the city one finds some of the
most expensive houses, apartment complexes, restaurants, and bars, as well as
art galleries and the city's main art museum, hotels, specialty boutiques, music
clubs, cafés, and a multi-entertainment complex. Participants lived in equal
numbers in central, north, and west Dallas.

Dallas's racially diverse population includes Latinos and African Americans as well. In fact, Texas recently has become "majority minority," meaning that racial minorities constitute the majority of residents in the state.[34]
African Americans have a long history in the city and have a strong political,
economic, and cultural presence. There were 450,557 African Americans in
the county in 2000—20.3 percent of the population, a much higher percent-

age than the national average of 12.3 percent.[35] The former mayor of the city, Ron Kirk, is Black, as are many city council members. Numerous cultural organizations showcase African American talent, including the Dallas Black Dance Theater and the African American Museum. The city has had the usual urban racial problems between African Americans and Whites, such as criticisms of police relations, underrepresentation of minority contractors in city projects, racial segregation, and so on (Payne 2000). Eighty percent of African Americans live in south Dallas.[36] Throughout the city's history, racial segregation has been the norm for African Americans (Hazel 1997; Prior and Kemper 2005). The greatest concentration of poverty is in the southern area of the city. In fact, it has a higher level of racial segregation than other cities, although signs of change have begun to be seen as middle-class African Americans and Latinos move out of the central and southern portions of the city, leaving the poorer behind.[37]

There are Latino pockets in the southwest section of the city, but because of the group's size, members live throughout the area. Latinos make up the largest minority population in Texas and in the Dallas area. In 2000, there were 662,729 Latinos in Dallas County—30 percent of the population, more than double the national average of 12.5 percent.[38] Nor does immigration show signs of letting up.[39] According to Miguel Hernandez of the Hispanic Small Business Association, about 90 percent of Latinos in the area are Mexican Americans who work primarily in low-income employment, such as landscaping and service jobs, as well as in the public sector. They also have their own cultural associations and political organizations, and there were three Latinos on the Dallas city council in 2005. There is even a weekly advice column targeted to Latinos in the *Dallas Morning News*. Despite this large and growing presence, their lives are often framed within the same lens as those of African Americans. Discourse around Latinos resembles that around African Americans: living in high-crime neighborhoods, attending segregated and underfunded public schools, working in low-status service occupations, having cultural celebrations, and voicing political concerns often with the Democratic party. Unique in conversations about Latinos are the issues of illegal immigration and members' close proximity to their homelands. Newspaper articles tailor discussion of community issues based on those dynamics.[40] Unless one becomes involved in local political issues, such as public schools, one would not hear much about the Latino population per se that would challenge its general image as a low-income "minority" struggling for mobility.

In order to get a broader sense of the Asian American community's local image, I interviewed representatives of the African American and Hispanic Small Business Associations. Asian Americans were seen as the successful minority, and these organizational representatives did not comment on the problems that recent migrants and refugees, not to mention members of flourishing groups, face. For instance, Cheryl Davidson contrasted African Americans and Asian Americans, in particular Korean Americans, who have a stronger presence in African American neighborhoods:

> I know we all have the same struggles, but I tend to feel like we've struggled so much longer, and it's just worn down some of our resistance to the negativity that's out there toward all minorities. Which is a good point, I think that Asians, Koreans have more, I don't want to say energy, but they have more of a positive mentality toward going out into the business world and starting a business than we have. We feel like we're defeated before we even start. . . . My opinion is probably, of the three ethnic groups, I would probably say you hear less about Asians as far as maybe crime is concerned. Work habit, as what I've been told, is superior. It's like you're both minorities, but it's kind of like, they may see [Asians] as the lesser of two evils. I think people won't say it, but it's the mindset that people have.

Similarly, Hernandez commented on Asian Americans' image as financially successful:

> I think Asians come from farther than anybody else, and if they are in the lower social class and they are starting their own businesses, they have united families and they work together. That's something that we [Hispanics] don't have. If they're in the upper ends and are well-educated, they're hardly . . . it's hard to find someone that's fallen through the cracks in the Asian community.

Given the smaller size of the groups, Asian Americans have not been, nor do they seem to be, in line to encounter the same degree of hostilities with the majority or with other minorities they have in New York City or Los Angeles. Of course, racial tensions exist and are volatile, which means minor disputes suddenly can become major explosions. Korean American and Indian American leaders hoped to prevent such tragedies in the area by setting up ties with other communities, as discussed in chapter 3.

SAMPLE POPULATION

Because my sample case is of ethnic minorities placed within the mainstream, I made sure that all interviewees were residentially and occupationally integrated. Seventy Korean Americans and Indian Americans made up the main interviewees, thirty-five in each group, with practically equal numbers of women and men in each. They all worked in the Dallas area, and lived in predominantly White communities, both in the city and its suburbs. It was important for this study to sample those who were not solely college students, unlike most of the current research on the second generation, in order to assess their experiences across diverse settings. One interviewee was finishing college but also worked as a teacher at an elementary school. People employed full-time can speak to one of the main issues of this book, which is how individuals express difference across various cultural codes, such as work versus home versus leisure versus voluntary associations. College students often do not experience these categories as distinct, so they cannot shed as much light on how cultural space affects adaptation.

With respect to occupation, informants included financial consultants, computer programmers, telecommunication experts, doctors, lawyers, teachers, engineers, managers, and small-business owners. Both women and men were about as likely to have these professions, except that the three computer programmers, two lawyers, and two engineers were men, and all five teachers were women. There was little variation across ethnic groups, except that the two small-business owners were Korean American (one man, one woman) and most of the doctors were Indian American (both men and women). The participants had been in their workplaces for an average of one to two years. About half grew up in Dallas or the surrounding area, while the other half had moved to the city for employment from somewhere else in the country. Practically all the Korean Americans were Christian. Most of the Indian Americans were Hindu, although with some Jain and one Hare Krishna and one Sikh; most were Gujarati. The informants typically came from two-parent homes. About a quarter of both women and men had married, all to co-ethnics, and one had been separated and another divorced. None were children of racially or ethnically mixed marriages.

Second-generation informants were all college educated and had full-time careers. Korean Americans had an average income of $48,476, and Indian Americans an average of $60,320 (see Table 2.6). The per capita income of all residents of Dallas County in 2000 was $22,603. For Indian Americans, it was $24,880, and for Korean Americans was $16,386.[41] It makes sense that the Census-figure incomes would be much lower than those of respondents, because they refer to the aggregate income of the population divided by the total

Table 2.6 Economic status: informants and Dallas County residents

	Average personal income, informants	Per capita income, Dallas County
Total population		$22,603
Indian Americans	$60,320	$24,880
Korean Americans	$48,476	$16,386

SOURCES: 35 second-generation Indian Americans and 35 second-generation Korean Americans, personal interviews; Census 2000 Summary File 4—Sample Data, Dallas County, both first and later generations.

number of people of that background in the county. Many people do not work or work part-time jobs, which lowers the aggregate income for a community. Furthermore, the second-generation informants are college-educated, full-time professionals. These salaries are all the more impressive given that many were in their first job after college, and a number had worked at their place of employment for less than a couple of years. This demographic profile fits the role of the population in this study as margins within the mainstream and is comparable to national averages for second-generation Korean and Indian Americans.

I had not previously known any of the participants whom I had interviewed. I first made contact with them through posting an e-mail on listserves of the young professional organizations that served each ethnic group and the pan-ethnic group, which gave a brief description of the project and a request for second-generation participants to be interviewed. I also attended meetings of these organizations and the EMs. I solicited people to interview throughout the course of the fieldwork, using a snowball sampling method of asking interviewees for their contacts, then asking those people for their contacts, and so on. I made strong efforts, which proved successful, to reach those who did not take part in ethnic organizations and had few co-ethnic contacts. I often interviewed participants at their homes, at coffee shops, at their workplace, at libraries, and so on. After completing the bulk of the fieldwork in 1999, I returned to Dallas in the summer of 2000 to reinterview some participants and collect more observations. In the summer of 2002 I returned again to increase the sample size from fifty to seventy, with ten more interviewees for each ethnic group, and to pursue topics that had arisen since the previous fieldwork. In particular I was interested in participants' ethnic and racial identities post–September 11, 2001. I also reconnected with some of the original participants.

Interviews lasted between 1.5 and 3.5 hours and took place one-on-one with the author. All interviews were conducted in person and in English. Questions were open-ended and intended to get at respondents' conceptions of and experiences with ethnicity and race during adolescence and adulthood. Emphasis was placed on the ways in which they lived their ethnicity and race day-to-day and when making life-course decisions. (See the appendix for a list of the interview questions.)

In order to ascertain the social and organizational levels of these communities, I also conducted interviews with first- and second-generation community leaders, in addition to the seventy main interviewees.[42] These leaders represent the heads of the major organizations that serve the Korean American and Indian American communities in general, and the informants in particular. They included the presidents of KAP and IANA; the pastors of three EM churches; the leaders of four Indian American temples (three Hindu and one Jain); a representative of a second-generation Asian American professional association; a board member of the Asian American Small Business Association; a prominent member of the IAA; both the president and a presidential candidate of the OKA; the head pastor of an Asian American Christian church; the president of a gay Dallas Asian American organization; and representatives of the African American Small Business Association and the Hispanic Small Business Association. (See the appendix for the interview guide for organizational leaders.) In total, there were eighty-nine interviewees; some were interviewed more than once.

I also conducted observations in most of these organizations. Observations included, but were not limited to, frequent church and temple services, after-service lunches, a singles-night church meeting, a Bible study class, Hindu temple youth group meetings, guest lectures at the Hindu temple, an Indian American Baptist Church service, group-sponsored parties at local clubs, informal dinners and dinner meetings, monthly social networking meetings, outings to bars, a monthly dinner club, a Diwali dinner and food and clothing drive, a seminar on e-commerce, a seminar on the Asian American glass ceiling, a pan-ethnic meeting with television executives, a pan-ethnic small-business networking event, a pan-minority business networking event, a ras garba dance and religious festival, a community retreat for Indian American youth, a volleyball tournament, a health fair, youth group retreats and meetings, children's cultural classes, Korean American Christmas parties, and more.

I am a second-generation Indian American, half Hindu and half Sikh. I was concerned when starting the fieldwork that my background would make it more difficult to get to know Korean Americans than Indian Americans, or that preconceptions of the Indian American community would lead to biased questions and assumptions. Korean American organizations and informants were very welcoming. I grew comfortable with being the only non-Korean in an organization meeting or church service after a few visits and soon felt like a regular. During interviews with both groups, informants of both ethnic groups on occasion would say, "You know what I mean," or "You know what it's like." Sometimes I thought I did, and other times I knew I did not. In either case I tried to get them to articulate exactly what they meant so as not to superimpose my own assumptions onto them. Still, my ethnicity, gender, age, and other factors influenced the interviews in likely subtle and unconscious ways. I do not suggest that because I am Asian American I can offer a truer account of informants' experiences. This is just one perspective. The interview questions stem from a grounding in academic literature, and the coding followed established methods (Strauss 1987). Still, human subjectivities are never removed entirely.

This case study is not meant to represent the Indian American and Korean American populations, not even those just in Dallas. Despite my efforts to the contrary, there may be a higher percentage of people in the second generation with stronger ethnic boundaries in the sample than in the communities, given that those with salient identities are more likely to find such a study personally relevant and to be most accessible via ethnic and pan-ethnic social networks. Also, the second-generation interviewees grew up in lower-middle-class to upper-class households. They did not represent the working class or poor, especially as they grew older and their parents became better established in their work. None noted that they had been in gangs or in jail, although one Korean American man said he almost had joined his friends in a gang. Their success does not mean that they had not experienced the social and psychological obstacles facing many Asian Americans and analyzed in the following chapters. Still, rather than try to represent all of each community, I intentionally carve out a specific piece to understand how being within the mainstream shapes, and is shaped by, one's marginal status. I next turn to how the first generation spoke of their ethnic minority status and hoped youth would make sense of their differences, along with how the second generation developed ethnic identities in turn.

3 Growing Up Takes (Identity) Work
Developing Ethnic Identities

IDENTITY FORMATION IS A PROCESS of negotiating external expectations with personal preferences (Snow and Anderson 1987). In chapter 2 I explained part of the history of Korean Americans and Indian Americans, both nationally and as it pertained to Dallas. Yet how these groups have made sense of their backgrounds remains in question. A group identity is not static but is instead an assertion, even an intervention, to promote one's place within various hierarchies. Social statuses based on race, immigration, class, gender, and sexuality intersect to shape the meanings and salience of these group identities, as do local and community-level factors. The assertion starts with the immigrants themselves, who influence but do not determine the responses of the next generation, who are the main focus of the book. Immigrants' opinions deserve focused attention but rarely receive it when the second generation is studied (Romanucci-Ross 1991).

I find that the first and second generations of both ethnic groups endorsed ethnic identities that distinguished them from others but that still allowed them to feel comfortable with middle-class Whites, as margins *in* the mainstream. Immigrants promoted cultural symbols and values that generally fit within a multicultural America. The first generation hoped that these efforts, along with an endorsement of mainstream institutions in the public sphere, would gain them approval from Whites as hardworking "immigrants" rather than remain stigmatized as non-White foreigners and comparable to other minorities. Such a strategy also would provide a path for youth to develop pride despite a racialization of their backgrounds and to succeed economically. Both the national and the local Dallas environment shaped expressions of their background.

The first generation's definitions of Korean American and Indian American establish the ethnic social identity for youth, that is, the socially accepted meaning of each ethnicity. The second generation internalized these expectations and developed identities as Korean Americans and Indian Americans instead of fully acculturating. How and why informants did so depended on their personal experiences during adolescence.[1] They approached the ethnic social identity in three distinct ways based on their upbringing, so as to form ethnic identities that suited their particular needs and let them feel connected to the mainstream. This chapter first explains immigrants' experiences with racism and how that subsequently affected the development of their ethnic social identity. It then analyzes the three ways in which second-generation Asian Americans developed ethnic identities (with racial identities addressed in chapter 4). Attention is paid to ethnic and gender differences.

THE FIRST GENERATION'S EXPERIENCES

Economic Successes and Threats

The next two sections elaborate on immigrant leaders' encounters with systemic racism, which shaped why and how they articulated an ethnic social identity. In both ethnic groups, the first generation encountered a series of historically grounded discriminatory attitudes and treatment as presumed foreigners, in particular as the model minority and the yellow (and brown) peril, as introduced in the previous chapter. As the model minority, Asian Americans are supposed to remain passive and subservient to Whites. For instance, Shah, head of the Asian American Small Business Association in 1998–1999 and a leading member of the IAA, commented on the mixed image of some Indian American professionals as highly skilled scientists yet docile:[2]

> I felt that the mainstream saw us as very well-educated, economically successful, but they thought, "We can use these people for our own good." Like, Bill Gates has so many Indians working for him, or Asians. Why? And NASA. I was so surprised to hear that 300 top scientists in NASA are Indians. So what they thought [was], "Hey, we can achieve our goals as a company [with] half the costs if we don't hire locals." So that is respect.

Immigrant scientists encounter a combination of respect yet patronization, much like the first model minority, the fictional Charlie Chan. Asian Americans continue to fill the role they did when building the railroads—doing work others lacked either training or interest in for potentially lower wages. Even though the migrants mentioned worked for the governmental space program, they still were known to some degree as non-"locals."[3]

The model-minority stereotype also disguises national and local challenges facing Asian Americans, such as high poverty rates, health problems, and hate crimes (Fong 1998). For instance, Park of the OKA said:

> Well, the sad thing is that two months ago, in another town in the USA, there is some hate-crime and racism. However, I believe that that's one area; that's not main [concern].

Such violence did not constitute a common threat, and he voiced more alarm over the lack of English-language-assistance programs in Dallas that could help Korean Americans attain loans (more than Indian Americans, who are often more proficient in English). Still, with the popularity of the model-minority image, it becomes all the harder for the public to hear about incidents of hate crimes, even more to accept them as true.

Along with the model minority, first-generation immigrants simultaneously had to contend with the label of the economically threatening yellow peril, especially when they appeared to work *too* hard. Seung Chang, who recently ran for president of OKA, spoke with a tentative voice as he explained the contradictory Asian American predicament:

> Asian Americans have shown very successful progress in education, business, and in politics compared with how much time they have been here and compared to the population of other immigrants. Nobody denies that Asian Americans have made very successful progress. Mainstream people have a little bit, [are] kind of scared. "They are trying to get too much. They showed off a lot, but they did not really contribute to this society." We have to change this kind of attitude. We know this. . . . All blame goes to us.

As middleman minorities Korean Americans found themselves in the common dilemma of appearing too inwardly focused and receiving the "blame" of other groups' problems (Bonacich 1973). As mentioned in the previous chapter, Korean American businesses have come to be associated with a particular section of Dallas, which exacerbates this image. Similarly, Wendy, a second-generation interviewee, shared her frustrations over the negative attitudes of residents toward older immigrants. Her parents had run a hotel in a small Texas town. When it came time to sell, their ethnicity and background worked against them. They lost money in the sale—in part because of their poor English skills, in other part because lawyers may have taken advantage of the situation:

Since it was a hotel, [local residents] would go to the restaurant on Sundays, and they had problems with [my parents owning the hotel]. People saying things and not coming in. It is OK if you don't come, but talking about it [is not right]. . . . By selling it [my parents] were set for life, but they lost all their money because the company that bought it from them declared bankruptcy. In a small town like that all the lawyers know each other, and they know the judge, and there is all of this behind-the-curtain kind of talk. My parents didn't speak English back then, but the feeling comes that there is something wrong. I don't think that's gone away. I think [racism] is a little stronger when you look different, because Americans already have the feeling that Asian Americans are taking over their country and stuff.

Nativist can often be interpreted as patriotic. It is our civic duty to "buy American" (seen most vividly following 9/11), which may not include Asian American. In the late nineteenth and early twentieth centuries, the yellow peril united White Americans—a demographic full of disparate European ethnic origins (Chang 2000). Today, not much may have changed in that regard at the local level.

Moral and Safety Fears

The first generation encountered another element of the yellow-peril stereotype: morally suspect cultural backgrounds. To immigrants, such criticism seemed to reflect a double standard. Their labor was useful to the country (even if controlled to an extent). But welcoming them fully threatened the nation's well-being. One excuse for barring Asian Americans at the turn of the nineteenth century from entering the United States was their supposed ethical depravity, an image that still resonates (Chan 1991). For example, Mary became increasingly distressed as she recalled a number of attacks on her parents:

When I was younger, I think my father would get customers being rude to him and telling him to go back to his country. I remember a bunch of kids threw a broken glass bottle at him, and he had to get stitches. I was slapped in the face once and told to go back to my country while working at my friend's parents' store, and I caught someone stealing. . . . Another incident, we lived in Westchester. And there was a hurricane once, and a tree from our property went across on the road and blocked it off. There wasn't anything we could do. Our neighbor across the street was an odd woman. She came to the house and told my father that he better do something about the tree and stuff, and I went and spoke to her. And she started saying all kinds of things about eating your dogs and all of these awful things.

Asians represent foreigners who either need to be civilized by the West or remain separate from it (Okihiro 1994): the savage has left Asia and entered the city and suburbia, and so he must be contained, especially when he threatens Americans' property.

Indian Americans encountered specific types of discrimination based on the racialization of their religion and as perceived terrorists. Hindus supposedly threaten Judeo-Christian tenets with their "pagan" beliefs. At times, this sentiment manifests itself in public defamation. For instance, in October 1999, after targeting Muslims and Jews, the Southern Baptists' International Mission Board leveled their harshest critique against Hindus in their prayer booklet. They wrote that Hindus live with "darkness in their hearts that no lamp can dispel" and are "slaves bound by fear and tradition to false gods."[4] In some cities, including Houston, Southern Baptists even entered temples to proselytize.[5]

Even before 1999 Hindus in Dallas had to deal with tensions from Christian conservatives. Hindu leaders seeking to construct a temple in the mid-1980s relocated out of fear for their safety. Jagat Maraj, past president of the Metroplex Temple, explained in a calm, resigned voice their move from a wealthy suburb north of Dallas, where many Indian Americans lived, to another suburb west of Dallas:

> The temple where it's located right now is not the original purchase. The property was in Plano, in Parker County, which is east of Plano, and it's in an area where the Southern Baptists are predominant. Anyway, there was a lot of opposition when we applied for a permit to build a section, and there were a lot of protests and everything, and so we had to move from there. Fortunately we were able to sell [the property].

> Q: What was the protest based on?
> The protest and petition were based on the fact that being a predominantly Christian community, they didn't want to have another religious organization come in—something that they didn't understand, that they were afraid of. All the normal things that come from people who have got certain hang-ups over different religious groups. . . . We knew that if we pursued it, our temple would always be in a hostile environment. We've got to have security escalated, and one day we'll come and find the place burned down or bombed or something like that. And those types of things were not something appealing to us, so we just moved out.

The fear over physical violence and destruction of property is potentially justified. Hindu temples throughout the United States have been attacked. For

example, in February 2003 in St. Louis, someone threw a firebomb at the door
of a Hindu temple; police recorded the incident as a hate crime.[6] A similar
attack occurred at a temple in Matawan, New Jersey.[7] (Mosques and Sikh gurdwaras have also been targeted since September 11, 2001, and at higher rates.)
In this climate, Hindu Americans have found it difficult to gain acceptance not
only of their labor, but also of their lives.[8]

Prescribing Selective Assimilation

Immigrants encountered a set of prejudices against their background based on
their racialized position: wanted primarily for their labor yet labeled as perpetual foreigners. These experiences, in turn, shaped how immigrants hoped
their communities would adapt. The adaptation process of middle-class immigrants remains poorly analyzed. Those with high human capital may try to
assimilate residentially and occupationally and to integrate socially and culturally, following the path of earlier European migrants (Alba and Nee 2003;
Kitano 1969). Alternatively, they may endorse a selective assimilation and hold
on to much of their ethnic culture and social capital. The intention is to en-
able the success of the second generation (Rumbaut 1997).[9] A privileged class
status can facilitate maintenance of an ethnic culture because individuals take
pride in their group's accomplishments, can afford travel to the homeland,
purchase cultural objects, and so on (De Vos 1991). However, assimilation into
the middle class need not mean the irrelevance of race but can in fact depend
on it, as groups create distance from African Americans in order to gain social
acceptance (Prashad 2000).

Korean Americans and Indian Americans adopted this latter strategy of
selective assimilation to fight their racialization as foreigners. Their response
did not grow out of a naive embrace of the United States as a free and welcoming society, nor out of a bitter resentment toward it with strong opposition to
Whites. They recognized that they were wanted primarily for labor but believed that they had attained a respectable class and racial status as the model
minority. They hoped to inch up in progress by building on their accomplishments, rather than challenging the system directly, by taking advantage of
mainstream Dallas institutions. Doing so would promote a public identity as
immigrants who followed the trajectory of previous Europeans, rather than
as native minorities or the yellow or brown peril. At the same time they built
up an internal community that would accept their lives. Neither ethnic group
endorsed a pan-ethnic or person-of-color identity outside of occasional instrumental alliances.

Joining Mainstream Institutions and Practices

Immigrant leaders recognized the racialized use of their labor, but they believed that the labor market and other institutions were generally fair to immigrants with high human capital rather than necessarily exploitative. They embraced a more socially conservative approach to gaining racial equality: fitting into dominant institutions that advanced mobility and avoiding the stereotypes of the unaccommodating minority. Specifically, the first generation advised youth to integrate through educational and occupational attainment, political participation, involvement with local communities, and one-on-one self-presentations. They also framed their cultural elements analogously to mainstream ones.

Immigrant minorities usually advocate educational attainment for their children as a means for them to adjust to the new country. Parents often emphasize choosing college majors that lead to well-paying careers (Louie 2004). As we stood in the parking lot of the Swaminarayan temple, Ramesh Kuba spoke in a paternal tone of his hopes for those involved in a youth group:

> College education is a necessity. As a core group, they have common thoughts, common goals, and they'll say computers are not my deal, but I may go into medicine or law or information system or whatever it is. But they can talk to people who have a common goal, whatever it is. Out of ten people, if two have not made up their mind, they're more encouraged, so that group is good for itself just because of this.

Advanced educational degrees also break Asian Americans out of the occupational enclaves that weakened their reputation as fully committed Americans. This applies especially to Korean Americans as business owners in ethnic enclaves. Chang said as we sat in his store in Koreatown:

> They have made in this area a Korean American business community. Some say this is very good. But a disadvantage of making this like Chinatown, Koreatown, we make this a closed environment. No group can come [in]. This is a diverse society.

The political system offered another means for communities to accumulate power, in particular for those with economic resources, while demonstrating a commitment to democracy as previous immigrants had done (Glazer and Moynihan 1970). Like Jewish Americans, Indian Americans have gained attention for their financial donations to politicians and their influence on India-U.S. relations.[10] Korean Americans often lacked the proficiency in English to feel comfortable doing the same, according to Park (though a Korean American political action committee exists in Washington, D.C.). He had confidence in the second generation's prospect to "succeed in America":

> We are Korean American. To succeed in America, maintaining your own culture is important but at the same time, do not think of just your own generation but think of the next generation. To do that, there are politics and other key issues in this country that face you—registering to vote, voicing your own opinion. I think that you should get involved with the mainstream more actively; that's the way to the next generation. They can speak fluent English, good with the computer, good background in college. I have a great hope for the next generation.

Participation in politics as an ethnic group did not heighten Asian Americans' image as foreigners, according to Park, but, on the contrary, made Korean Americans more like other groups.[11]

Succeeding within political and economic institutions depended also on the manner, not only the degree, of immigrants' participation. According to community leaders, it is not enough to simply acculturate, as suggested by assimilation theory. Rather, groups must distance themselves from the prevailing image of native minorities in order to raise their position relative to Whites. Shah explained the goal of a pan-ethnic Dallas organization:

> The Asian Small Business Association is to put you to the mainstream, of how to melt faster than others. You cannot neglect that we're Asians, so the Asian Association's job is that hey, "Hello, we're sitting in the corner too. We're not going to shout, we're not going to do anything, but don't neglect us. We don't want to shout, we don't want to fight."

> *Q: African Americans and Hispanics, do they fight more?*
>   Right.

Shah considered the racial status of Asian Americans as between Blacks and Whites:

> If it were not for Hispanics and African Americans, we would have been discriminated [against] just like them. But I feel like that they are cushion for us. [Whites] have seen them for a long time, and they have seen us. So, we are discriminated [against] less, but that means we have to get involved and act just like an American, but in doing so don't forget your roots.

Political participation can be an act of racial identity formation instead of assimilation—to designate themselves as *model* minorities and so hopefully to "melt faster," as European American immigrants have done (Omi and

Winant 1994). With this optimistic view of race relations relative to that of other minorities, community leaders had little reason to encourage a reactive ethnicity in the next generation.

Groups must show links not only to major public institutions but also to local communities in order to gain acceptance as full citizens. For Korean American business owners, this meant connecting to African Americans in Dallas. As we sat in the OKA office, Park expressed a grassroots-based optimism regarding inter-minority race relations:

> About ten years ago, I served as the president for the Korean Small Business Association and at that time, it was during the L.A. riots. Fortunately [during] those periods in Dallas nothing happened.
>
> Q: Why is that?
>   I think communication. I tried to educate the [Korean] business owners in south Dallas area [where most African Americans and many Latinos live], and I tried through seminars and newspaper, and what happened in L.A. and New York. We are the same people. When you have some profit from a certain area, why not help the people of the area, if there are churches, Salvation Army, etc. I like to do that. I used to be an active member with the Black Small Business Association, but I still have good friendship with the people back in those days. Personal record, communication, a lot of seminars—we exchanged scholarships every year. Korean Americans select five excellent Black community students, and the next year, it's the other way around. . . . I especially found out from minorities, through their festival. I get invited time to time to [Blacks'] national holidays or events. I found that they are very much similar in terms of emotion. When we share historical background, [we are] getting more and more close.

Nationally, Korean American businesspeople with stores in urban areas heavily populated by African Americans and Latinos have adopted a more open strategy with neighbors and clients as a sign of goodwill, especially since the 1992 Los Angeles riots (Min 1996).[12] In a related vein, Neelam Jain, a leader of the Jain Temple Center in Dallas, helped start for Indian Americans a Dallas branch of an international volunteer organization.[13] He smiled as he told me of the group's service outside the Indian community:

> We started with community service for communities outside of our own. We are part of a larger community, and we need to be visible in that community to make sure that we don't get perceived to be as selfish and isolated from the mainstream. We have taken so much from this community that we need to give something back. We became the number one club in the district. Our fund-raising was the top.

By giving back locally, leaders were able to present the groups as the very opposites of the yellow or brown peril. Instead, they could be seen as immigrants who contributed to the American mosaic.

In order to fit in on the interpersonal level with Whites, the first generation even prescribed pretending on occasion to be someone one was not.[14] As Ashok Mehta of the Metroplex temple said:

> If I am in India, I am a doctor in Bombay University and I go and practice in Calcutta with all Magnolias, do you think the people will come to me? So I have the discrimination in my own country. Let's take the example of America. If you come from a blue blood from Boston, do you think that you are going to marry a Jew or a Negro or a Hindu? You are trained to marry a blue blood. We have a problem with our face. We have a problem with our food. We have a problem with the things that we wear and even the accent. And, we should not compound that problem. When I visit an American family, I never tell people something that I don't eat. No, whatever is there I just eat. Like drinking. I don't drink, but I always have a glass in my hand so people don't know. They don't know, but when you make it evident, then there is a problem.

Despite multiculturalism, the first generation did not consider all differences welcome, especially because prejudice was somewhat natural. This necessitated a public-versus-private division of self-presentation (Goffman 1963; Saran 1985).

Not all cultural elements could or should be hidden, according to immigrants. Yet even when they shared cultural differences, they strategically communicated them as supportive of dominant values and institutions. They combated being racialized as foreigners by presenting themselves as fellow upstanding immigrants with a background amenable to mainstream mores. Indian American Hindus demonstrated this with references to religion. They defended Hinduism as tied to their class status and to Protestantism, not by counting on the rhetoric of religious pluralism to persuade critics. For example, in response to the Southern Baptists' charges against Hinduism described earlier, Maraj, who served as the Metroplex temple's representative in this matter, endorsed the response by the National Federation of Indian Americans (NFIA). The NFIA issued a statement addressed to national leaders and government organizations, including President Bill Clinton, Attorney General Janet Reno, and the FBI, that challenged such discrimination on the basis of the fact that Hindus and Indian Americans were in general responsible professionals: "We are law abiding, tax-paying, patriotic Americans yet proud (like any other immigrant family in the USA) of the culture and heritage of the land of our origin, India." The president of the Durga Temple in Fairfax, Virginia, also said, "Why should [Southern Baptists] try to change us? We have a value system people crave in this country. We teach respect for others, for marriage vows, for elders."[15] Using similar logic, representatives of the Swaminarayan temple discussed an expansion of the temple with local residents. Kuba summarized the dialogue with an air of satisfaction:

> We invited these neighbors to come and talk with us; they have. We had problems originally. They didn't understand who we are, what we're doing, what we're trying to save in our culture. . . . The basic dialogue was to convince them that we are not a cult, we're all professionals here. . . . I suggested that we hire a professional company to talk with our local council members, to our neighbors. There was no one out there to oppose the deal.

Leaders effectively used the commonly assumed association of economic success and private lifestyle to argue that their religion should be tolerated.

Presenting one's class status is not in itself sufficient for immigrants to gain acceptance as culturally American. Groups must also press a diluted multicultural rhetoric. Hindu Americans framed their religion as practically mirroring Christianity and so deserving of respect. Maraj was a member of an ecumenical organization comprised of major religious groups in Dallas that has an elaborate building in the central area of the city. He defined it as

> an interfaith group here, multicultural, multiethnic, multireligious organization. . . . We try not to use the word "different" too much. We try to focus on similarities. [Our] god is no different than the god of the Muslim or the Jew or the Christian, because it's the same one. We just worship through a different path because of tradition or culture or what have you.

Seen here, religions varied based on culture, not ideology, and so should be respected. He took pride in his work and believed it helped Hindus be accepted, even in rural Texas areas:

> Think about Texas. . . . Over 100-some years, all there was [was] Christianity, and suddenly they have Muslims and Hindus and Buddhists. So there are obvious questions that they asked—things like cows and the dot, because those are the things that they see. They do ask about the many gods. This one time I went to an Episcopalian church in Abeline, Texas, in west Texas, and I was somewhat apprehensive when I went there at first—*this is west Texas. What am I going to tell these people*? I found that there was a genuine interest. . . . As a matter of fact we look for common ground. (Speaker's emphasis)

The presentation of religion (like that of political involvement), not simply its practice, matters in creating goodwill with fellow Americans, especially in parts of Texas. Securing acceptance for one's religion in this manner, however, rests on a highly debatable premise—that Hinduism is almost equivalent to Christianity. Still, these efforts served as a practical and even courageous response in combating a foreign image in their local environment.

Following 9/11, the need for South Asian Americans to appear like other civic and religious groups only intensified. Jain spoke earnestly of his community's efforts as we sat in the conference room of his workplace:

> In this very office we brought together the leaders of the various Indian organizations, including the Muslim organizations. We had a big press conference. Every one of these religious leaders spoke against any idea that we are for what happened there. Even the Muslim clerics came here and spoke. . . . The IAA, they were trying to promote the idea that we are united as a community, and we are rejecting what is being perpetuated by those Islamic people who sent those guys here. We came here to pray for the victims. This was the first time we saw a Muslim cleric in such a setting. They brought people of different beliefs together. As part of the IAA, we raised a lot of money and we sent it to the 9/11 victims. We collected over half a million dollars. . . .

The IAA's action fits its mission to help Indian Americans of all backgrounds integrate into the mainstream. Since 9/11, South Asian American community leaders generally have painted themselves as "good immigrants."[16] Even though the leaders did not worry about misguided retaliation on their buildings, second-generation individuals carried themselves differently after 9/11, as will be discussed in chapter 4.

In making the argument for social and cultural respect, both Indian American and Korean American leaders highlighted their groups' accommodation to mainstream institutions. This distinguished them implicitly from other minorities and allowed them to frame themselves as immigrants who were in line with previous waves of Europeans, rather than as foreigners or as native minorities. In this manner they hoped to gradually improve their racial status while holding onto an ethnic culture.

Prescribing an Ethnic Social Identity

Parents' push for integration was not meant to weaken their children's ethnic commitment in the private sphere. Just the opposite. Portraying themselves as like other Americans hopefully would help immigrants gain tolerance from outsiders for group differences. Yet convincing other groups to respect their unique culture was not the only hurdle. Immigrants had to convince the second generation as well. The first generation worried that a racially maligned cultural background, along with the lure of American popular culture, would lead youth to reject their heritage. First-generation leaders believed that a cohesive ethnic community could encourage pride in one's ancestry and even present advantages over Whites. An ethnicity with semiconservative attributes also would affirm their desirable image as immigrants tied to a respectable homeland rather than as potentially subversive minorities.

Celebrating Differences in the Face of Racism   I first briefly describe ethnic organizations' efforts to build support for members and then the content of the cultural prescriptions. Leaders themselves faced tensions in adjusting to the United States and looked to co-ethnics for acceptance of their lives. For instance, Kuba's immigrant minority status had left him feeling insecure. He explained with a defiant attitude why his community built a temple in Dallas even though they knew that would upset local residents:

> Opposition we'll always have. But our home is India. And, to protect that, we're creating this [temple]. We want our youth to know not to be ashamed. They can take away the color of your hair, the color of your skin. I had a problem when I came here, with the language and keeping up with the Joneses. But you fit in. There is nothing they can do that we can't do better. And we've proved that in many cases, in business, in social activities, the professionalism that we put out for people, you've got to mix in. We can't just say we are we and you all stay away.

Religious associations have historically been a common way for groups to find social and cultural support while learning of opportunities and norms within the local area (Fenton 1988; Williams 1988; see chapter 7). While Kuba wanted space away from Whites, the broader goal was to eventually "mix" with Whites rather than "stay away." How groups addressed members' desire for exclusive spaces while helping them associate with outsiders is discussed in chapter 7.

Similarly, Park explained the importance of positive portrayals of Korean heritage for the second generation:

> They may have an identity crisis at some period, but as long as we are patient about it, and do our job, I don't see any problem. Language and cultural background, we need to hold on [to]. America is successful because of immigration, one of the best in the world. . . . Several times a year we have our own festival:

Koreans' day, year-ending party, art festival, a few holidays, like Korean National Holiday. We get together and show our traditional art. This year at the Korean festival we also had a traditional Korean marriage. When young guys are curious and ask questions like "what's going on," we explain it, and they always talk about it later. Someday they will realize that their parents and grandparents tried to help raise awareness to the culture, and they will realize it after high school.

He recognized the process of identity development in youth, which frequently left them ashamed of their background when young, their interest in it developing only after high school (Cross 1995; Phinney 1990). Organizations hoped to compensate for possible shame, in part so immigrant communities could make America "successful" rather than promote a reactive ethnicity. The IAA held cultural events, such as on Indian classical music and dance, and celebrated the country's independence day, as other immigrant groups do.

Historical teachings joined cultural displays as a means of passing on an ethnic heritage to youth. Mehta described the components of his class at the Metroplex temple:

One is the religion and really the religion; taking it slow, understand the meaning, what is the philosophy behind it. All theory of karma, law of reincarnation. The second part is the great personalities of India. Like by the time that they finish, they should know at least 100 great personalities of India—religious, political, conformist, historical. So they know 100 of them by the time that they leave.

Although a national history that overlooks internal tensions and contradictions clearly misrepresents that country, the goal here was less to create critical thinkers than to increase respect for the student's heritage. In primary school students rarely hear any mention of Asian history, except in Orientalist references to a war with the United States or to "barbaric" practices that, in turn, distinguish the United States for its "enlightened" perspectives.[17]

In these attempts to instill pride in a homeland, only certain definitions of the ethnicity receive attention. Major holidays, wedding ceremonies, and "great personalities" come to represent national histories. Such displays suggest to both community members and outsiders that their ethnic group's culture is nonconfrontational and lacks social movements that question institutional authority (Prashad 2000). In addition, social relationships outside of the nuclear and extended families, such as homosexual partnerships, do not have a voice. Domestic violence and the histories of immigrant women who become brides in the United States yet lack legal status apart from that of their husbands, also are downplayed (Bhattacharjee 1998). The result is a notion of ethnicity that suits groups' efforts to gain respectability within a local environment that lacks much historical presence of Asian Americans.

Teaching a Moral Life and Cultural Heritage to the Second Generation   The first generation hoped to instill in youth pride in their ancestry, which their integration and the racialization of their culture threatened. Their minority position also shaped what constituted the culture. The following cultural prescriptions constituted a moral order, that is, a moral standard of observable conduct that marked one as "proper" or "improper" within the community (Wuthnow 1987). The moral order consisted of such values as putting the family first, obedience to authority, education, religion, and conservative gender and sexual norms, along with appropriate use of cultural symbols. The first generation believed that these factors gave their groups a superior culture to that of most Americans and would facilitate further economic mobility and social respect (Purkayastha 2005).

Interviews and observations indicate these expectations. For instance, Mehta spoke on what distinguished Indian Americans from other groups, including other minorities:

> Education and the cultural values. Cultural values means my son is in tenth grade, but ever since day one, I have been involved in his homework, every day. My wife is the same. We have a family stability. I don't know how long this will last, but African Americans and Hispanics are acting just like Americans. There are lots of divorces, instability in the family, and so many things. So they have gone through all these things, while our kids and us have not gone through it. So that gives us more solid footing to respect other cultures and mingle into it faster.

A commitment to marriage and even education comprises an "ethnic" value for these professionals, despite the generally low level of educational attainment in India. Such values serve the margins in the mainstream well, for they promote a moral life in private that facilitates integration into preferred dominant institutions in public, such as the education system, despite the group's minority status (Portes and Rumbaut 2001).

As the second generation left home and entered religious and other community institutions, they continued to hear references to the values of honoring elders and family and getting an education.[18] For example, I attended the Thanksgiving service at God's Light, which was a joint service of both the first and second generation, attended by at least 600 people of all age groups.[19]

The first-generation pastor led the near-capacity service in Korean, and Pastor Chung of the EM stood by his side, translating into English. The head pastor, in a not-so-subtle reference, asked children to applaud their parents for sacrificing for the children's benefit. He did not mention this as a Korean virtue, but his comments as a first-generation elder, in Korean, to a multigenerational gathering reinforced the value of respecting family and working hard to make parents and elders proud. A similar recommendation to the second generation took place in the Swaminarayan temple. During one session at that temple, the priest sat in a chair facing a group of young people, all of whom were sitting on the floor, and said that they had made their elders proud with their work during a health fair.[20] He also mentioned the need to respect parents even though life may seem tough during adolescence. Many of the youth nodded their heads in agreement.

Practicing customs and religion also reinforced commitment to desired values. As Kuba said, "You keep your cultural values and keep passing them through the generations. Through temples, through all these cultural activities." For Indian American informants, none of whom were Christian, religion represented a fundamental element of their culture (Ebaugh and Chafetz 2000; Fenton 1988).[21] Parents varied in how much they practiced religion in the home or took their children to temple. But no informants reported that their parents did not care about religion. The church is also the most important and popular institution in the Korean American community. Even in Dallas there were reportedly more than 100 such churches (see chapter 2). Many second-generation informants attended church at least on occasion. (Korean and Indian Americans' religious customs are further discussed in chapter 6.)

In addition, both Indian and Korean Americans recognized fairly traditional gender roles as part of their ethnic social identity. Men were presumed to be in charge of the outside world and women were to keep the home spiritually purified and generally take care of that sphere, even when women had full-time careers (Chatterjee 1989; Kim and Kim 1998). Even when gender roles change in the homeland, they often remain static in the diaspora as immigrants try to maintain the cultural norms they grew up with. Religious leaders, even among the second generation, advocated more or less traditional gender roles (Chong 1998; Park 2001). The conservative nature of Texas made this especially pronounced in Dallas.[22] In a sermon Pastor Kwon of the World Gathering EM mentioned in an aside the need for such a gender hierarchy within families, with the husband as the head of the household, though he was expected to respect and listen to his wife.[23] I glanced around the congregation to see if anyone's body language or facial expressions suggested surprise or discontent but observed none. I later asked one attendee what she thought of the remarks, and she agreed with the pastor and thought most women did as well.[24] Not obeying these customs threatened not only their spiritual well-being but also their place within the ethnic and religious community.

The first generation also monitored women's sexuality and children's marital choices, both of which further signified a community's public morality, in contrast to the notion of a seductive and corrupting yellow or brown peril. Women's sexuality is a particular concern of the family and of immigrant culture in general. In the United States a discourse already exists that blames minority women for becoming unwed mothers who then reproduce a "culture of poverty" for their children (Steinberg 1989). Thus, sexual practices have political implications that can affirm or discredit immigrants' desired image of a respectable homeland. The notion of the chaste woman also allows immigrants to indulge in a kind of cultural nostalgia; they imagine their homelands as virtuous places relative to the sinful United States, even as sexual norms and displays change in the homeland (Maira 2002). Mehta urged parents to bring children to the temple so that they could learn righteous behavior, including as it pertains to sexual activity:

> The problem that I am facing, if you don't bring them to the religious classes, they will marry anybody who comes along. They don't know the difference between Muslim or Christian or Jewish. I have no problem [with religious intermarriage]. If their parents want them to marry with freedom, then fine. But parents come and cry. They say, "Oh, what can I do?" Well, you're too late. She's twenty-two, her hormones are telling her that she likes a boy, she needs a man, and the man needs a woman. My telling is not going to do it, your telling is not going to do it. I think it's teaching it.

Marriage became a source of tension between the generations. Religion had different effects on marriage for each group, as discussed in chapter 6. Homosexual relationships were so taboo in the communities that leaders did not even bother to preempt them.

Along with certain historical facts, values, and customs, the ethnic social identity also included cultural symbols, such as language, foods, clothing, and rituals. Within a multicultural America, so many Americans have claimed these symbols of their heritage that Asian Americans did not stand out by accentuating their own in private. This again allowed groups to assert an ethnic lifestyle without creating tensions with others. Elders, according to the second generation, viewed more favorably those who could express themselves and their culture through such symbols, as is discussed in more detail later. Ethnic organizations run by the first generation suggested the same. Because this study examines primarily the second generation, I concentrate on those intergenerational organizations in which they took part, namely religious ones.

While technically open to all types of people, religious institutions stressed keeping symbols such as language, dress, food, and other characteristics (Ebaugh and Chafetz 2000; see chapter 7). At the Swaminarayan temple, for instance, a guru normally spoke to adult members in Gujarati, not English. Lay leaders did the same to convey even general information, not only religious teachings. In a reversal of typical generational norms, the adult men dressed in standard American clothing of slacks and collared shirts, but most male children and teenagers began wearing white kurta pajamas.[25] I asked one second-generation participant why this was the case, and he replied that a visiting swami had suggested that the youth do so to instill in themselves pride in their culture, and the ethnic attire had caught on.[26] In this setting, the older generation's hopes that adolescents would find support for their parents' preferred lifestyle, at least symbolically, seem to be materializing. Through an emphasis on language, rituals (often religious), clothing, food, and values, the temples prescribed a more traditional ethnic identity than did the Korean American EMs (Min 2003). However, because second-generation Indian Americans participated in religious organizations less than did Korean Americans, in practice, Indian Americans did not have more traditional identities, seen in the second half this chapter.

The EMs did encourage some cultural symbols. In joint services with the first-generation congregation, Korean was the primary language. The second generation sometimes spoke Korean with immigrants in the hallways of the church. Predominantly, though, English was the primary language, and the EMs offered services comparable to those in mainstream congregations (Dhingra 2004). Still, members appreciated the ethnic character of the churches (see chapter 7). The first-generation services took place in Korean, with a Korean lunch served afterward. This is in addition to the cultural and social organizations that served the first generation of each group. Families encouraged maintaining customs and rituals as well, especially among Indian Americans, who often practice religion in the home.

Food is another symbol central to an ethnic identity. Although leaders did not explicitly mention ethnic food as something their children had to maintain, participants still associated it with their backgrounds, having grown up eating it. In addition, food is probably the most definitive representation of national cultures. Interviewees commonly referenced it when talking about their parents, their mothers in particular, and their interest in maintaining their ethnicity. Korean Americans and Indian Americans thus defined their ethnic social identities for the second generation in more or less comparable ways.

Internalizing Expectations

The pressure on the second generation to know their heritage meant that immigrants had effectively turned a social stigma on its head: second-generation informants felt ashamed if they were insufficiently attached to their culture, rather than the other way around. These cultural norms comprised the boundaries of who had real membership within the community and as such were policed (Barth 1969). Failing to uphold these characteristics meant failing in the moral order. Such a person did not simply lack ethnic traits but threatened the vitality of the diaspora by acting assimilated, and so he or she had to be critiqued by the community. For instance, Joanne grew anxious and leaned forward as she relayed her linguistic difficulties with elder Korean Americans:

> I've used [Korean] words before where I've used them incorrectly, and I've offended people, inadvertently of course. It happens a lot. My parents have to deal with that too because their friends say, "You should teach your daughter better because she said this." I feel bad because it makes my parents look bad.

Kithana similarly beat herself up over her weak cultural knowledge:

> Food, language, I wish I knew it. I don't know much about the religion or traditions. I wish I did. Because I'm Indian, I should know it.

A traditional culture became taken for granted as *the* way to be ethnic (Maira 2002).

Strangers too reinforced this expectation. For instance, I interviewed Mitch at a Korean restaurant. Mitch had recently become interested in his Korean heritage and felt ashamed for not knowing the language. Before the interview, a Korean immigrant waitress came to our table and started speaking to him in Korean. He said in very broken Korean, while smiling, that he did not speak the language. The waitress smiled back and then asked him if he was Chinese. Mitch replied in English that he was Korean and quickly assured her that he was learning the language. Just because one's parents were Korean (or Indian) did not mean that one gained full acceptance in the community.

Expectations from non-ethnics also reinforced the need to know cultural symbols. As Rajesh said of his co-workers:

> They ask a lot of questions. They ask about the red dot on the head and that kind of stuff, why the ladies wear what they wear and that kind of stuff. My only problem is, I'm not as knowledgeable about it as I should be.

The second generation also internalized cultural values and the need to take part in dominant institutions. For instance, they accepted the parental emphasis on education and hard work as means of overcoming discrimination (elaborated upon in chapter 4). During an interview with Judy, she humorously commented to me, "Especially in the Korean culture, first of all education is important and if you are going to get a master's or, like you, a Ph.D., your parents must love you!" Some found the pressure on educational attainment too intense. A Korean American man I spoke to who had not gone to college and who described himself as a "rebel" stated:

> A lot of Korean parents put pressure on their kids to succeed, and the last thing Korean kids want to do is disappoint their parents. Koreans are real chatty, and they say that so and so isn't in school. That makes the parents look bad.

He also mentioned a friend who dropped out of college because of the stress placed on the person by the "chatty" ethnic community.

The second generation received explicit and implicit teachings within and outside of their communities of what it meant to be Korean American and Indian American. Immigrants chose those elements that fit their status as margins within the mainstream. Their goal was to further their incorporation into dominant institutions compared to other minorities while still maintaining supportive values, customs, and symbols. They advocated this strategy rather than a reactive ethnicity or need for interminority solidarity, especially with non-Asian Americans. The second generation generally internalized this meaning of the ethnic social identity. I now turn to how the second generation developed their ethnic identities.

THE SECOND GENERATION AND DEVELOPING ETHNIC IDENTITIES

Ethnic identity development comprises a major emotional and social part of youths' lives and shapes the relationships they form as adults (Tatum 2002). The second generation grew up encountering from outsiders a racialized version of ethnicity that demeaned its worth, as discussed earlier, coupled with a general acculturation due to their residential and educational integration. At the same time their communities expected individuals to maintain a somewhat traditional cultural heritage as fitting their social status. What kinds of ethnic identities did they form in response? The second generation identified with other Americans but also wanted distinctive ethnic boundaries. The rest of this chapter focuses on how interviewees developed those ethnic boundaries. Their ethnic identity formation involves issues of race, but actors' racial identities (that is, attitudes toward being a minority relative to other Asian Americans and other races) and those identities' relationship to the first generation's prescriptions receive greater attention in chapter 4. Chapters 5–7 analyze how they managed the relationship of their ethnic, racial, and American identities.

On the one hand, the second generation often affirms an ethnicity in reaction to racism and may even build transnational ties to a homeland (Butterfield 2005; Chong 1998; Hurtado, Gurin, and Peng 1997; Levitt 2002; Min and Kim 1999; Portes and Rumbaut 2001). On the other hand, groups gradually lose distinctive ethnic practices and transnational commitments with increasing involvement in mainstream institutions and/or because they wish to avoid racism (Alba and Nee 2003; Child 1943; Chow 2000; Gans 1979; Kasinitz et al. 2002; Min and Kim 1999; Tuan 1998).[27] Often studies assess the second generation's trajectory by having individuals choose between "American," "ethnic American," and "ethnic" identity categories on surveys and measuring to what extent they maintain their communities' language, customs, and values. The vast majority of informants identified themselves as "Korean American" or "Indian American" and cared about similar aspects of their ethnic background: values of respecting elders and family, fairly conservative gender roles, religion, education, and symbols such as language, clothing, and customs. They appear, then, to be relatively homogeneous in their ethnic identities.

Yet, documenting choice of labels and cultural factors alone overlooks important variations in identity development. I find that actors approached their parental expectations in distinct ways, depending on how they connected to their background. To them, ethnicity meant one of three types of attitudes: (1) being part of a traditional ethnic community (referred to from here on as the "community" group); (2) being unable to fit in with their peers (the "fitting-in" group); or (3) feeling connected to one's family primarily in the home and with little relevance elsewhere (the "family" group). The meaningful events and feelings respondents associated with their ethnicity fell within one of these categories. Although these are not terms that the respondents used, they reveal differences in people's reactions to racism, sexism, trips back to the homeland, and other variations that usually have passed without comment in the literature but that guide identity development and its outcomes.

The three categories stemmed from a combination of (1) how much involvement informants had within their ethnic communities and transnational networks when young, in particular with both families and co-ethnic peers; and (2) their experiences within the mainstream, which included, on the one hand, racist treatment as physical and cultural "foreigners," and on the other hand, intrigue into actors' cultural differences given the popularity of multiculturalism (Lau 1989; Kim 2001).[28] Because these factors were not specific to an ethnic group, they led to divisions within rather than between Indian and Korean Americans. Adolescence proves to be a significant time period in the shaping of identity development (Adams, Gullotta, and Montemayor 1992; Bourdieu 1984).

Ultimately, most interviewees formed strong identities in line with their ethnic social identity, including a commitment to prescribed values and some proficiency in symbols. They adopted this more or less traditional definition of what being ethnic meant partly because of parental and community influence and partly because it suited their own needs in adjusting to the mainstream. (This is not to suggest that they did not frequently challenge parental prescriptions, as discussed in chapters 6 and 7.)

How Korean Americans and Indian Americans actually made sense of and developed their ethnic identities depended on their identity category. They hoped their identities would distinguish them from—but also allow a dialogue with—the mainstream. This identity development took place through a process of "identity work" (Field 1994; Hunt and Miller 1997; Snow and Anderson 1987; Stein 1997). Snow and Anderson (1987) define identity work as creating a personal meaning of a social identity that aligns with one's self concept. For instance, homeless persons who believed that they were on the verge of securing housing distanced themselves from the notion of being homeless, while those who thought of themselves as homeless accentuated their skills in living off the streets so as to affirm a commitment to that social identity. One associates oneself with or disassociates oneself from a social identity (i.e., ethnicity as defined by the first generation and others) depending on its fit with one's self-concept (i.e., one of three identity categories listed earlier). In Snow and

Anderson's model, people can accept or reject a social identity. I also consider how they select only parts of it to form their self-perceptions. Actors' definitions of their ethnic identities depended not only on which traits were prescribed (or institutionalized) in the social identity, but also on how the traits resonated with their self-concept and experiences growing up, that is, with their type of ethnic category (Schudson 1989). I elaborate on each category and members' identity work to develop ethnic American identities.

Community

About half of the respondents saw their ethnicity as making them part of a traditional community.[29] Unlike the supposed typical minority youth, these interviewees did not go through an intensive phase of rejecting or feeling distant from their ethnic background during adolescence (Cross 1995). Psychologists and sociologists argue that growing up with competing expectations from an ethnic community and from the mainstream leads to the "marginal man" dilemma, of feeling torn between the two poles and not secure in either (Park 1928; Stonequist 1937; Thai 1999; but see Green 1947). Instead, these respondents' upbringing grounded them in a supportive community that limited the effects of outside critiques of their background (Uba 1994). They actually had an easier time integrating with Whites thanks to their confidence in their ethnic culture, made up of prescribed symbols, values, family norms, religion, and so on. They learned this sense of community by growing up in a network of ethnic families and peers in their local area and transnationally (Fouron and Glick-Schiller 2002; Levitt 2002) (see Table 3.1).

Daily interactions with parents informed participants about their ethnic social identity, including such symbols as languages, foods, and clothes. As Judy said:

> Because you've just grown up with [your parents], and you've grown up as a Korean family, not even a Korean American family, I feel like, especially in the Korean culture, the bond between parents and children are [sic] very strong. Especially when communication is still there.

Respondents often looked down upon co-ethnics who were less knowledgeable than themselves of their ancestry, which in turn reinforced their own dedication to it. Involvement in ethnic institutions also taught them customs and values. Even in Dallas, with its smaller Asian American population, people

Table 3.1 Community connection

- Feel a sense of connection and responsibility to their ethnic community, including family, friends, and other community members
- Grew up with an ethnic community, both first generation and second generation
- Learned ethnic symbols, such as language and customs
- Participated in ethnic organizations while growing up
- Generally conform to behavioral expectations based on "ethnic" values
- Have consistently taken pride in their ethnicities

Thirty-nine participants had this connection: 11 Indian American men and 10 Indian American women, and 8 Korean American men and 10 Korean American women.

could grow up in a community atmosphere. For instance, Rupu lamented his peers' lack of involvement in temples:

> I think I was brought up a little bit differently [than other Indian Americans] because my parents were very religious from the beginning. Like I'm still pretty religious. I go to temple every Sunday and stuff like that. I don't find a lot of Indians that are even vegetarian, you know.

Temples also provide transnational links for members. Speakers from India give lectures. Some temples have brought over gurus to live in the United States and be spiritual guides.[30] A few Indian Americans, such as Samit, quoted at the start of the book, remembered educating their White friends about Indian cultural traditions. Instead of being ashamed of their foreign background, these informants knew enough to invite others to join in, making it easier to be comfortable with their ethnicity while they were young.[31] Korean Americans similarly referenced the church as a central site for the formation of community ties (Dhingra 2004).

Having co-ethnic peers in both public and private settings gave these individuals greater confidence in embracing their background, despite social stigmas against them. For instance, Ram reminisced over his childhood:

> I mean in my class there were I think four or five Indians, but because we saw each other outside of school, you kinda hang out. I mean there's a level of comfort there; we all grew up with the same type of parents. The same type of, you know—well, we all wore Adidas when we were kids, and we couldn't afford the Nikes. . . . My parents and most of the first-generation parents raise their kids with trying to keep certain Indian values or certain Indian commonalties. So they raised us with going to those type of events, going to certain functions or whatever it was. So as kids, those were things that we learned about, and we

kinda wanted to be a part of that because our parents were. Now if you were raised with Indians and Indian friends, you say, "Hey, what's wrong with Indians, and there's fun hanging out with them."

Peers played a central role in instilling contentment with one's background regardless of its minority status, instead of dwelling on "what's wrong with Indians" (Eder and Parker 1987). They helped turn a potentially shameful symbol—one's type of shoes—into a bonding feature.

Despite respect for their ancestry, respondents' narratives of their youth included difficult moments. For example, parental norms sharply conflicted with the typical Americanized upbringing that informants also enjoyed, which comes to be framed as "normal," making ethnic lifestyles "deviant." Such tensions are common among the second generation (Farver, Narang, and Bhadha 2002). Still, Vikram chuckled as he recounted his own series of experiences:

> I wasn't allowed to date in high school. So prom night is coming up, and I was allowed to go to prom night, but I didn't go because I don't know how to ask a girl. It was the scariest thing to me. . . . I know a lot of Indian music. I know a lot about Indian religion. A lot of my peers who are also Indian don't necessarily have that same knowledge. For them, I think, it is very confusing because on the one hand they are immigrants, and on the other hand they're supposed to be American, but they're different. I think for me, I was very lucky that I was given a very strong base in the whole culture. It helped me stand up just enough that I was different and people were interested in what I have to say. I think that might be what it is.

Instead of fitting a "marginal man" profile, actors still spoke in an overall positive tone about being comfortable within the mainstream. A traditional upbringing served as a resource and became a way of avoiding confusion about one's marginal status, despite friction between cultural expectations.

Identity Work for the Community Category   Because of their involvement in ethnic institutions, these participants had identities during adolescence that were already in line with their social identity. Their identity work consisted of reinforcing desired values and customs—those components that strengthened an attachment to a traditional community—instead of, for instance, popular culture. Laura grew up attending a Korean church. She wanted to practice and pass on customs that even her parents did not teach her:

> There's even that respectful level that you call your sibling, and things like that. We didn't do that. I think that it's needed because it brings a level of respect.

Of course, respect is also learned, but I think it brings a little bit more order to things, and it brings responsibility to me naturally, just because I'm older. And that's not how it's been in our family. . . . . I think that even though I was born here, I am still very Korean compared to someone else who was born here.

As Samantha said:

You can't lose your heritage because that is part of you. And I think people who say that they wouldn't want to learn Korean or learn about the culture, they don't want to learn about themselves.

For these individuals, ethnicity dominated their sense of self (Heiss 1992). To the extent that they did not practice significant rituals, they worried about losing their heritage. If people knew little of their ancestry, they would in effect know nothing "about themselves."

The prospects of marriage and having children also encouraged participants' identity work. Practically all of the second generation, regardless of the identity group, wanted to marry a co-ethnic and hoped to pass on their culture to their children, yet their reasons for desiring this type of life varied. For this group marriage meant continuing an investment in a traditional community and giving children a solid upbringing through participation in traditional events. For instance, Ram, who earlier stressed the role of community functions, imagined the kinds of activities his children would take part in:

You've heard the cliché "we had the best of both worlds." . . . I will take [my future kids] to garba. Oh yeah, I love that. I want to show them this is fun. He can twirl sticks and everything. I learned all that. So if it's important to me, yeah, then I'll show it to them. Because it makes—it just tells them who you are.

Respondents' type of identity category set the stage for how they assumed their children would experience their own ethnicity. Ram worried that if his children (though he had no children at the time) did not attend community events, they would not develop an ethnic identity, even though they could learn it from peers or from their own research in college as other participants did, discussed later. This quote, like Vikram's earlier, also illustrates that the second generation's ethnic and transnational ties may facilitate integration into the United States (Kivisto 2001; Levitt 2002). Youths' association with an ethnic community "tells them who [they] are" and thus heightens their self-confidence, which allows them to then mix comfortably with other groups and attain the "best of both worlds."

In addition to using ethnic institutions, these informants reinforced their ethnic identities by turning to co-ethnics. But not just any co-ethnic. Mary sat up straight as she outlined proper and improper ways of expressing Korean culture:

> I remember in one of my Asian American studies classes, I know these Korean Americans couldn't really speak Korean well. They were all proud that they could speak Korean and they would say, "Hey, let's go have a smoke" in Korean when there was a break time during class. Those kinda things. I said, that's not my thing. You have a choice as a Korean American to choose what values you want to pick to represent the Korean part of your identity. That has to do with respect for elders and certain other symbolic things I would like to take on. I didn't agree with it, so I didn't really hang out with that group.

Overall, those in this category had the strongest understanding of the social identity. Their identity work furthered a commitment to its more traditional elements, which allowed them to feel part of a strong community.

Not all actors grew up so attached to the ethnic social identity. Out of the seventy second-generation interviewees, just under half interacted more frequently with Whites when growing up. This latter set of persons fell into two groups, and their experiences varied accordingly. Most of them grew up unable to fit in with White peers because of their ethnicity. Psychological models of identity development predict that adolescents feel ashamed of their ethnic and racial differences and struggle with conflicting expectations between ethnic and American lifestyles. Youths gradually come to terms with their biculturalism (Cross 1995; Kim 2001; Phinney 1990; Tse 1999; Uba 1994).[32] This set of interviewees fits this pattern and makes up the "fitting in" category. The third set of participants also grew up without a strong ethnic community. But instead of feeling stigmatized by their difference, they have relatively few memories, positive or negative, of their background when young. They experienced neither a strong ethnic community with co-ethnic peers nor disparaging remarks from White peers about their physical and cultural "differences." They were not indifferent toward their status as second-generation immigrants (cf. Child 1943), but they often embraced their ethnicity as part of their families, primarily inside their homes. This is the "family" category. I first elaborate on the "fitting in" and then the "family" group. Both groups conducted identity work to develop ethnic identities in line with community expectations, with varying degrees of success.

Fitting In

Unlike the previous respondents, about a quarter of informants used Whites and not their ethnic community as their reference group (see Table 3.2). They

Table 3.2 Fitting-in connection

- Grew up feeling different and stigmatized from one's White friends
- Did not have many co-ethnic friends nor a broader co-ethnic community while growing up
- Did not participate in ethnic organizations while growing up
- Often developed stronger ethnic boundaries through befriending co-ethnics, typically in college

Seventeen participants had this connection: 4 Indian American males and 4 Indian American females, and 5 Korean American males and 4 Korean American females.

blamed their race and ethnicity for not letting them be "American." David summed up their childhood experiences when he said, "Being a little kid, knowing that you're different is the biggest thing. *That's who you are.*" These respondents' desire to appear American did not represent an acculturation, as framed within assimilation theories, but rather a racial strategy to appear less foreign. They could not feel comfortable around Whites, but they also lacked co-ethnic friends and did not participate in ethnic organizations because of the size of their ethnic community and/or the limited availability of accessible options. As a result, they did not fit in well anywhere. The most significant memories of their youth involved differences from Whites that reinforced the racialized image of their heritage as backward or strange. As Alex said:

> You have all the embarrassing moments with your parents that you—because in your eyes you look in the mirror and you don't see this Asian kid, you just see a kid like all your American friends. And so your parents still do things and act in a Korean culture manner here, and it's out of place. There is the issue of: Korean food was being cooked at the house, so when American parents would come over, the odor was certainly different. And it's not meatloaf and it's not potatoes, it's kimchi. Most of my Caucasian friends in college didn't have a curfew. They would come in two, three, four a.m., whenever. I'd have to be home at midnight, so that was difficult to deal with. Some of those stories from our childhood with the Asian friends at [university] we could sort of relate to.

Alex echoed Charles Cooley's (1902) "looking-glass self," of seeing himself as he thought others saw him, as just another "American." Problems began when he discovered more divisions from his friends because of his upbringing. This left him confused because he lacked co-ethnic friends to tell him who he was. In effect, Alex was asking: if being Korean American is not the same as being White, then what is it?

Beyond their social and cultural distinctions, the second generation, in particular women, frequently commented on their physical differences from White peers. Tammy said:

> Adolescence is such a hard time as it is, and then having to deal with the fact that you are different. I think that's the one thing I struggle with the hardest. All I wanted to do was have blonde hair and blue eyes, and that was so hard. You do; you want to look like all your friends. They don't understand why your eyes are smaller.

Racial distinctiveness not only could be an aesthetic annoyance but also could threaten one's safety. Cases of violence have been reported, including an incident in which an Indian American high school senior had her hair set on fire by a White male (Gibson 1988).

People gravitate toward or away from their ethnic group after experiencing racism, depending on if they had already taken pride or shame in it, respectively. This group moved away while the previous one moved toward its ethnic community. Those in the community category had an ethnic group to buffer them from at least some stigmas and promote more respected images. For instance, John said of racial stereotypes, "When I was growing up, it was the whole karate thing. If you are a geek, you just are, whether you are Korean or not." Those in the fitting-in category, on the other hand, internalized negative depictions. Rahul referred to the common notion of Asian American men: "They're geeks or nerds; they're big computer nerd guys that want to play on a computer. They don't go out and party." These interviewees wanted to befriend Whites, who were by definition more "cool," even though they felt uncomfortable with them. Without consistent exposure to an ethnic community, they rarely gained fluency in cultural markers, such as language and customs, during their youth. This furthered a distance from their group.

Lacking a positive association with their ethnic group, most avoided co-ethnics when the opportunity to socialize with them arose. Infrequent conversations with co-ethnics turned to their shared sense of difference from "normal" Americans, in order to find validation of their experiences. For instance, Andy recalled with a resentful tone the conversations held in the church that he occasionally attended while growing up:

> Usually I'll bring it up. I'll start talking about there's a Korean American baseball player, did you hear about him, he's from L.A. We talk about why there is no Korean American NBA player. They might be joking around but there is a lot of honesty. Like when talking about being a professional athlete and Korean

American, like are you kidding? Our parents would never let us do that. We had to study all the time.

Although chatting about sports stars is a common pastime, it takes on special significance here. These athletes symbolized the enviable ability to overcome racial and cultural differences and finally blend in, to be both a popular "professional athlete" and "Korean American."

Because of the emotional resonance of not fitting in, these actors viewed others, even non-Asian Americans, in terms of their degree of social acceptance. For instance, Meena, a teacher, projected her adolescent frustrations, still fresh in her mind, onto one of her White students:

> This boy probably took a bath once a week. He was really not clean and didn't take care of himself. I remember thinking, he probably thinks he has no friends, and he's just the oddball out. And, I remember thinking I would feel like that. I didn't pick to be Indian American, and I was the only Indian American in my class. And some of the kids wouldn't play with me because they thought I was different. Maybe the fact that I am Indian American made me look at it that way, like he's different and he could have different views.

Her type of connection to her ethnicity was so central to her narrative of growing up that it became a lens through which she interpreted the experiences of others.[33] As Douglas (1966) argues, falling on the wrong side of the "deviant"-versus-"normal" binary marks one figuratively as polluted and dirty, leading Meena to identify with the child who, literally, rarely took a bath.

Identity Work of the Fitting-In Category   These individuals grew up considering their ethnicity to be a stigma because of racism and cultural differences from Whites. As they grew older, they challenged the critiques of their ethnicity and hoped to fit in not despite but because of their group differences for once. They turned to co-ethnics for friendship as they met more of them in a supportive environment, often college. The prospects of marriage and parenthood made informants interested in learning more about their background, but not with the intention of passing on "the best of both worlds." For instance, Kithana said that she wanted to marry an Indian American and maintain her heritage, "Because someday I'm going to have kids, and I want them to know that they're Indian. I don't want them to be as confused as I am." For these people, teaching culture served more as a means of avoiding pain than sharing joy.

Though individuals in the fitting-in category were often motivated by notions of marriage and separation from parents generally, making co-ethnic friends served as the catalyst in actually performing identity work and shifting from shame to pride in their racialized background (Butterfield 2005). Because ethnicity mattered most in its effects on peer relationships, respondents focused less on its political elements and more on its symbolic ones, which had marked them as "different" and that suited the ethnic social identity. For instance, Richard said, "Growing up, I had mostly American friends; I didn't have many Korean friends, up until college." When I asked him what led to the change, he stared downwards and gave a lengthy response that demonstrates the felt significance of creating a personal identity that resonates with the ethnic social identity:

> I just sat down with a couple of Korean guys, and my Korean wasn't very good. And they were like, "Hey, let's speak Korean from now on." From there it just kind of started, hey this kind of fascinates me. I want to check out my roots and see what it's all about. That's what led me to go to Korea and be an exchange student, spend an extra year, take time off school and study. It really opened my eyes; I'm really glad that it happened. If I didn't go through that, then I'd be what they call "White washed" or "banana." I think I would have taken that path, just all American friends, possibly dating or marrying an American. I came at a crossroads.

His identity work consisted of learning the language from a friend and even spending a year in Korea to avoid being stigmatized as a "banana." As psychologists argue (Cross 1995), developing one's ethnicity often takes place in an extreme fashion.

Peers, rather than immigrant-led organizations or families as for the other two identity groups, served as templates for which aspects of one's background to learn within one's identity work. Having friends as models addressed these interviewees' particular needs for acceptance from a peer group *as* ethnic Americans rather than as pseudo-Whites. For instance, Meena, quoted earlier as empathizing with the student who did not bathe, learned traditional dances at her university:

> We do a lot of singing and dancing and show our clothes and stuff. We all like getting together and making up dances and doing the fashion show. Ever since I've gotten to college, I have seen other people do it and how involved they are, and it makes me want to be more involved. . . . I'm not the oddball out now.

She became an elementary-school teacher and recently put on a cultural show in order to educate the students, using those elements learned from friends. She described how she addressed the issue of "difference" in her class:

We did have a few Indian children in our classroom. And I had talked to one of the girls, and she told me she felt really out of place, that she felt like everybody thought she was different, and she just didn't feel comfortable. We did do a lesson plan in my class, on Indian culture, like the major holidays and things like that. We talked about Diwali and had some of our friends come in and do an Indian dance. We brought in some of our clothing and we wore that. And we kind of informed the kids about our Indian culture. . . . When I was little, I didn't want to be different. I wanted to look like everybody else and fit in, but now I think it's really cool, and I am proud that I can speak [other languages] and do Indian dances, and it makes me feel good. I feel sorry for my cousins that don't know any of that. They might as well just be White.

She hoped that others would not grow up feeling like an "oddball," as she did, by learning the same ethnic practices that allowed her to fit in: holidays, dances, and fashion, all practices she learned in peer organizations.[34] Knowing these aspects made one a "moral" person who fell on the "sacred" side of the binary, in contrast to her assimilated cousins.

This new pride in one's background allowed one not only to be "ethnic" in private but also to present a marginal identity to the mainstream, such as to Meena's students. Similarly, Veera commented on her shift in attitude regarding being an ethnic minority:

I used to be embarrassed because I didn't fit in. With dark hair and dark eyes, I didn't fit in. I changed my name to Veronica and other things because I wanted to fit in. There was a case where an Indian kid in North Carolina or someplace who was killed because she was different, had arm hair. . . . Having Indian friends gives you pride in who you are. If you only hang out with American kids, you always feel different. With [Indian Americans], I felt so much like them, I fit in. It gave me pride in who I am. Yes, I'm Indian, yes I'm different, yes I speak a different language, but that's an advantage.

Concerns over racism and shame regarding her "difference" have been mitigated owing to friendships that supplied a sense of "advantage" and allowed her to connect with outsiders.

Yet not everyone formed a peer community during or after college, and these individuals remained confused about their background. For instance, Kithana still had few Indian American friends, which hurt her self-esteem. She had a sullen look on her face as she said:

I identify as a mixed, confused, Oreo cookie. I have this one Indian friend who's straight from India, and he makes fun of me all the time. He doesn't see me as an Indian, and my White friends say I'm not like them because of my family or whatever. Then what the hell am I? . . . I hang out with White people, and I realize that I don't think exactly like they do. But, then I don't agree with everything my parents are telling me. So what the hell am I? I sometimes wish that if I was going to be born Indian, I wish I was born in India, that way I wouldn't know any better. If I had to be born here, I wish I was born White.

Without a peer group of significant others to give witness to her life as an Indian American, she did not conceptualize herself in those terms (Cooley 1902). Instead, her only identity options were as an Indian or American, neither of which fit entirely. As a result, she even regretted her ethnic status.

Visiting the homeland constitutes a common type of identity work to "discover oneself" (Maira 2002; Hall 1990). Yet Andy said that during his visit to Korea, he realized he did not belong there either:

I went to Korea in '94. It was one of the worst droughts, and I went there to do some farming. They have a term for Koreans who live in America—*kyopo*. Whether it's positive or negative it depends on the person. Some people think you're cool for that, and others could hate you. That's the first time I realized I really don't belong in Korea either. In the U.S. I knew from Little League that I was different. As soon as I moved out of the city into the hellhole suburb, it was apparent that I was different. In the city there was more diversity; it was great. I had three or four Korean friends in a class of thirty.

A few recalled intense experiences of rejection. For instance, Mark reported with shock of having been kicked out of a taxicab by the driver in Korea a few years earlier for not being fluent in Korean, which vividly demonstrated rejection by his own country. Most believed that they would find acceptance from peers in their *home*land as ethnic Americans but, not surprisingly, returned disappointed. Transnational ties, then, do not necessarily lead to a deeper connection to one's background, especially when one's expectations are unrealistic. Most of those who visited Asia often later found co-ethnic peers in the United States with whom they grew comfortable. Mark, for instance, married a Korean American and participated actively in his church.

Family

One fifth of participants fell into the family set as the connection to their ethnicity (see Table 3.3). Like those in the fitting-in category, these persons did not grow up within a community of co-ethnic peers and so felt a general sense of difference from others. Yet, they experienced neither emotional pain nor

Table 3.3 Family connection

- Grew up feeling a bit different, but not stigmatized, from Whites
- Made sense of their heritage through their families more than through friends or a broader ethnic community
- Rarely participated in formal ethnic organizations while growing up
- Felt a desire to get to know self through understanding parents' heritage more
- Often tried to research parents' background during college but had, on average, less success developing strong ethnic boundaries

Fourteen participants had this connection: 3 Indian American men and 3 Indian American women, and 4 Korean American men and 4 Korean American women.

an inability to get along with their White peers, as in the "marginal man" dilemma. They interpreted their ethnicity as connecting them to their families because they had the most exposure to it inside the home, rather than with a strong community or through derogatory remarks from outsiders. Because their background did not significantly shape their relations with others, some recalled few memories tied to it, in sharp contrast to the preceding groups. What these actors were *not* saying, however, is very telling. For instance, Scott believed that being Korean American had little if any relevance in his childhood. When I asked him if he preferred associating with Korean Americans or Whites when young, he said, "Honestly, I don't think that there was much of a preference. I was comfortable either way. . . . I guess I really just didn't care." While community leaders worried that not knowing their ethnic social identity would lead to anxiety, these respondents did not exhibit that.

A couple of participants had painful associations with their ethnicity while young, not in the form of a stigma from peers but within their families based on intergenerational tensions and often involving gender hierarchies. Alice spoke in a defiant tone toward her father:

In the Korean society, women and men are not at an equal level. I've had more challenges in my life because I'm a woman. At home everyone is a Korean, so I've had more challenges because I am a woman, the oldest daughter. When I'm at home and have to defend myself mostly to my parents, my dad mostly. Like to mow the lawn, because my dad says girls can't do it. I have to prove to them that being a woman doesn't prohibit me.

The gender double standard has different effects on the second generation depending on their cognitive category. Those in the community group had enough positive associations with their background to overlook these problems, while those in the family group wanted to assimilate.

Individuals in this category grew up knowing varying amounts of their ethnic culture, including language and rituals, depending on how much their parents taught them. Relatives may have visited from the homeland, and some interviewees would make occasional trips there. Many had inconsistent exposure while young. The results often were as Joanne described when talking about the demographics of where she grew up in Maryland:

> Ninety-nine percent Caucasian. It was a suburb. . . . I think my parents growing up were very busy working, and we weren't a typical Korean family. We didn't have a strong Korean social outlook. Whereas a lot of my friends grew up with the Korean church, my parents didn't. . . . Speaking the language is an issue. I couldn't read or write it. I could speak it but it was very slang. I had a friend that would teach me some of the words, and that is important to me. You can't really be a part of the culture if you can't speak it or read it.

Not being able to communicate in a native tongue distanced the second generation, especially Korean Americans, from an ethnic community because of parents' general lack of proficiency in English.

Identity Work for the Family Category   These respondents recognized the importance of ethnicity in their own lives as they gradually perceived greater differences from White peers. For instance, Rick had no Korean American friends when growing up because he did not attend a Korean church. He recalled without bitterness how he came to think of his ethnicity as he met co-ethnics with similar parents:

> I realized that in college, people went through the same way I grew up: emphasis on studying, way you see things, type of schedules parents had and not seeing them very often, you always helped out parents, asked what you did, and things that parents tell you [they] want from you.

His articulation of what it meant to be Korean American revolved entirely around interactions with his parents, not tensions with peers because of parents, unlike the previous group.

Those in the family category associated the ethnic social identity primarily with their family. So their identity work consisted of trying to comprehend more of their parents' background in order to better understand their own upbringing and identities. They did not seek out co-ethnic peers or community elders or activities, unless these were associated with their parents. As Sanjay explained:

The traits I get from my parent—work hard, family, [and] make money—are more important than the extended family. I'm not that close to them. So, it's more along the lines of emphasizing what I've learned from my family.

The prospect of marrying and having children made these individuals all the more aware of their lack of recognition of their ancestry, which in turn motivated them to perform identity work to develop a definition of it as performed by parents. Because they interpreted their ethnicity in relation to their parents, they assumed that their children would interpret it in the same way. So if they themselves were not conversant with their background, then their children would not learn of it, and their heritage would be lost (even though people can learn of it through organizations and peers, seen earlier). For instance, Usha paused as she reflected on why she recently started to attend a temple and practice dances associated with her family, and then said with an increasing sense of assurance:

> The ceremony ties you to family. If you go to garba, it is your aunts and your uncles, your nieces and your nephews all dancing. It brings you guys closer. . . . I am doing these [ceremonies] for my kids, and, secondly, I'm trying to find out who I am. If I don't know who I am, I can't tell my kids who I am. Now I can find out who I am.

Similarly, Rajeev experienced self-doubt after leaving his parents:

> Without my parents around me, I kind of wasn't sure what my heritage was. I always thought I knew, but as time passed further from age eighteen to twenty, I swayed wayward. During my last year [of college] I dated an Indian girl, and she was into the Indian scene. And I thought this was cool. I listened to Indian music again, practiced Hindi, took a couple of courses at [my university]. I got back into the heritage in that way, understanding my culture the way it was. . . . For me to understand my childhood, I have to understand where [my parents] came from and their childhood. I've researched it better, talked to people about it. Now I know who I am better because of how I was raised.

Identity work consisted of ritual dances and college classes, with the goal of forming a self-concept in line with the ethnic social identity outlined by families. This would then allow one the self-confidence necessary to be socially integrated away from parents, meeting their needs as the margins within the mainstream. These actors constructed a logical stepladder from learning about their culture to learning about their family to ultimately learning about themselves.

Some informants went back to Asia as part of their identity work in order to immerse themselves in the land that their parents came from. They often had more success than did those in the fitting-in category. Instead of looking for acceptance from peers, these individuals only needed to bond with family members and witness daily life there in order to feel that they had gained insight into their parents. Sangeeta discussed how the link between her parents and India led her to make frequent trips there:

> The line between family and Indian is blurred, but because it defines me, it is very important to me. I am going to India in a few weeks by myself to see family. But also I haven't been there in a few years, and I want to refresh my memory. I forgot what it is like to walk the streets. Not that I will get anything out of my week there. It is still something I want to do because it brings you closer and reminds you where you come from, even though you weren't born there nor brought up there. When my parents think of their lives growing up, it is not New Orleans [where Sangeeta grew up]. I know I think of New Orleans, but my growing up was Indian, which makes India somewhere I have to refer to [as] a home also.

Variations in reactions to visits back to the homeland have typically been overlooked in identity literature or explained as being due to personality or luck. But here we see that it depends on one's identity category. Because of their class status, they could afford to fly to Asia, even for two weeks, to nourish these transnational ties.

Because parents defined their background for them, those in this group rarely sought out co-ethnic peers in their identity work. When Tom attended an ethnic-organization meeting hosted by his second-generation peers, he did so "for the social connections, not because of my race. To be honest, I wouldn't feel comfortable hanging out with people only of my own race, or of any race." Those with the other types of connections, in contrast, explicitly joined such associations to be with co-ethnics. Rahul, in the fitting-in group, was a member of IANA because "it's kind of nice to go to a place where you are not the only Indian there; you are in a big group. It's comfort, something like that." Joining such groups, like visiting the homeland, springs from different motivations and has different implications depending on one's category.

Despite their efforts to learn more about their ethnicity, many in this identity category acknowledged that they were still unacquainted with their heritage. Even though Vinod took a course and visited India, he confessed, "I don't even speak an Indian language." They often had little success learning the ethnic social identity associated with their parents because they practiced it mostly on their own or in a classroom, and not consistently with co-ethnic friends or in ethnic organizations (Lave 1988). For instance, Joanne grew irritated when recalling an incident:

> There was this word [a friend] kept saying. And I asked him what it meant, and my parents kept saying it was another thing. I asked about four to five of my Korean friends and each one had a different answer.

> *Q: Why is one word important?*
> That's just one less thing that I can use. My parents speak with me in Korean and English, the combination. I would say not a day goes by when they say a word that I don't know the meaning.

Trying to learn Korean in order to better communicate with her parents constituted her identity work. Her Korean-language skills remained poor, and she resigned herself to not learning the accurate meaning of the word.

Not everyone wanted to learn their ethnic social identity. Given the centrality of their parents' role, if parents did not appear committed to it, then neither did respondents. Tom was one of only two participants who had little interest in maintaining his ethnicity, in part because of the model set by his family:

> Unfortunately I see more negatives than positives [in Korean culture]. The negative is the lack of the individual in the Korean culture. I've talked to my mother about this, and she's found her individuality later in life, and when younger she wasn't allowed; had to wear a uniform and not speak out.

In this case, identity work consisted of role-distancing from the ethnic social identity, which was facilitated by the weak demands placed on him by his parents. He described himself as a "regular guy." I asked how ethnicity tied into that self-definition. He replied, "How being Korean plays into being a regular guy? It really doesn't play much of a factor. I'm not shunning the culture away, but I'm not letting it define me. I'm defining myself." He defined himself, that is, he created his own personal identity apart from the ethnic social identity. Still, practically all the other interviewees wanted to learn more about their parents and thus themselves.

CONCLUSION

Members of both the first and second generations created identities that also allowed for some integration as the margins within the mainstream. Leaders and parents defined their ethnic social identities as supportive of dominant institutions while raising their status within the racial hierarchy. They framed cultural differences as comparable to mainstream practices, seen in the presentation of Hinduism. This relatively benign take on ethnicity does not bring to the forefront other possible components of one's background, such as types of marginalization and resistance struggles. Still, it fit groups' class, immigrant, and racial statuses, as explained earlier, and promoted greater diversity in Dallas. Given the influence of the ethnic social identity on the second generation, it follows that second-generation informants endorsed a comparable definition of their ancestry. This semitraditional, nonpolitical definition also fit with their efforts to develop ethnic identities that would address their needs within the middle-class mainstream, whether those needs be a cohesive community, acceptance from peers for their adolescent "differences," or deeper parental teachings.

Other researchers have argued that ethnic identities can coincide with, not take away from, an integration by promoting educational and occupational success in the public sphere (Portes and Rumbaut 2001) and by giving groups pride in their heritage so as to interact with others (Kurien 1998). Both of these arguments find support here. We also see another layer to this process of gaining pride in one's background. Second-generation Korean and Indian Americans strengthened their ethnic identities in ways that suited their particular needs within the mainstream, depending on their identity category. In addition, they integrated by publicly sharing their background, rather than only by taking pride in it privately. Far from integrating by becoming "post-ethnic," that is, having one's ethnicity be voluntary and not relevant in social relations (Hollinger 1995), they felt more comfortable in the mainstream by becoming *highly* ethnic.[35] Yet, this does not suggest a lack of tensions between ethnic and more American lifestyles for the second generation, discussed in chapters 5–7.

This analysis of identity work highlights individuals' agency in coming to terms with their background, as is currently popular in the academic literature (Cornell and Hartmann 1998; Flores 1997; Leonard 1992). At the same time it explains patterns of how they exerted their agency as they reached adulthood based on adolescent experiences (Adams, Gullotta, and Montemayor 1992; Bourdieu and Wacquant 1992). Missing from most models and literature on ethnic identity formation is how people make sense of their ethnicity, that is, how they feel it impacts their lives beyond the standard accounts of language, clothing, values, and so on, or whether they only felt shame about it or not. Depending on their identity category, second-generation respondents had different reactions to trips back to the homeland, racism, gender inequality,

and other experiences that shaped identity development. They also had varying interest in learning from co-ethnics. As Stein (1997) said, paraphrasing
Karl Marx, of certain feminists' attempts to construct identities as lesbians,
"Women make identities—but not exactly as they please" (p. 20). Similarly,
participants faced constraints not only because of their ethnic social identity,
economic resources, and cultural discourses (such as multiculturalism and
the depiction of Asians as perpetually Other), but also because of their identity
category, which in turn mediated the effects of other factors. In addition to
these ethnic identities, the second generation could develop a reactive ethnicity, as well as pan-ethnic and/or interminority connections, in direct response
to their racial minority status. I will take this up in the next chapter.

4

Model Americans and Minorities
Racial Identities and Responses to Racism

WE HAVE SEEN THAT RACISM AND SHARED EXPERIENCES, such as growing up with Asian parents, contribute to the formation of ethnic identities for the second generation. The same factors could encourage a reactive ethnicity as well. That is, the second generation may assert ethnic identities not merely to uphold a type of culture and community but also as critique of Whites and White institutions as inherently discriminatory (Bean and Stevens 2003; Portes and Rumbaut 2001). Informants may form pan-ethnic identities as well, linking with other Asian Americans and/or South Asian Americans (for Indian Americans) as racialized foreigners (Espiritu 1992). They also may bond with African Americans. It is assumed that the second and later generations, unlike the first, frequently develop ties with people of color because they have grown up within U.S. race relations as non-Whites (Lee 1996; Singh 1996; Tuan 1998). Some informants may even follow the path established by South Asians in Britain in the 1980s and self-define as "Black." Even if they do not befriend African Americans, Korean and Indian Americans may sympathize with their resistance to White oppression (Maira 2002). On the other hand, the second generation's privileged class status and distinct racialized stereotypes could weaken interracial and interethnic bonds, and affirm an apolitical notion of ethnicity in line with the ethnic social identity defined by the first generation, as seen in chapter 3. European Americans, such as those in the Irish, Italian, and Jewish American communities, gradually "became White" despite being treated as non-Whites upon arrival in the United States. Asian Americans may expect the same process: to not be seen as "White" but instead as "non-Black," and so as comparable to Whites (Foner 2005).

The question becomes, how did second-generation Korean and Indian American professionals make sense of being minorities? The previous chapter concentrated on how experiences with race and ethnicity influenced informants' attachments to their ethnic group and their definitions of culture. This chapter focuses on their race-based identities, that is how they defined themselves specifically as racial and cultural minorities relative to other races (see chapter 1). Rarely are actors' ethnic and racial identities analyzed together, yet both shape their adaptation.[1]

This chapter shows that as informants considered their status as minorities, they still were more likely to affirm their identity as ethnic Americans than to demonstrate either a strong pan-ethnic or person-of-color allegiance. Nor did they develop a reactive ethnicity. This does not mean, however, that they did not critique discrimination from Whites. They felt treated as racially distinct foreigners with an inferior culture and did not expect full acceptance. But they drew upon racial discourses beyond that of being non-White minorities, to make sense of their racial status. They adopted the figure of the model minority who fit within the immigrant history of the nation, albeit with physical and cultural traits that distinguished them from European immigrants. That is, they hoped to integrate as comparable (not equivalent) to Whites by accentuating a kind of racial and immigrant status that suited their position as the margins within the mainstream. Their views on race fit with an individual-level perspective on race and mobility, as is consistent with the United States' dominant ideology. This perspective frames economic success as being due primarily to hard work and acculturation, and considers discrimination to be an expression by prejudiced individuals rather than a system of inequalities that could link minorities together. Participants developed this perspective on race and mobility because of the stereotypes and treatment they encountered, the salience of ethnic culture and multiculturalism, their class status, and their location in Dallas. In addition, Indian Americans distanced themselves from other South Asian Americans, in particular after 9/11.

Groups form because of a number of factors, including racial and political conditions, transnational events, community organizing efforts, immigration laws, sense of common culture, and economic needs (Lien, Conway, and Wong 2003). These factors can be distilled into three major categories of influence— categorization from outsiders (such as racial stereotypes and discriminatory treatment), cultural ties, and common interests (Cornell and Hartmann 1998; Jenkins 1994; Lopez and Espiritu 1990; Spickard and Burroughs 2000). These categories explain why the second generation perceived racism as occurring at the individual level and thus developed primarily (not exclusively) ethnic rather than pan-ethnic or person-of-color boundaries. This chapter first explains how the dimensions of categorization, culture, and interests made interviewees feel attached to other minorities but then led to mostly an ethnic American identity for both groups. Differences between Indian Americans and Korean Americans are stressed. It then analyzes how interviewees wanted to battle racism.

PAN-ETHNIC AND INTERRACIAL BONDS

Research regarding pan-ethnicity has focused mostly on the political level (Cornell 1988; Espiritu 1992; Nagel 1994). For instance, Cornell (1988) argues that Native Americans in the 1950s and 1960s came together despite tribal differences because they were categorized as comparable groups in urban areas and shared cultural, political, and economic interests. Common political goals and being labeled as foreigners from outsiders led second- and later-generation Chinese, Japanese, and Filipino American students to rally together in the Asian American movement of the 1960s (Espiritu 1992).[2] Since then numerous pan-ethnic organizations and media sources have arisen, primarily in California, to reinforce their identity. This chapter first focuses on interminority bonds based on actors' sense of common culture and experiences with categorization.

As discussed in chapter 3, both Indian and Korean Americans shared a process of learning an ethnic social identity, which encouraged pan-ethnic sympathies (Lien, Conway, and Wong 2003).[3] As Deepa said of her connection to Asian Americans:

> Yeah, I think we can relate a lot of times with how our parents see things and how we should be, how we should generally strive to be the best. We can talk about our family in the sense that the whole family dynamic and the structure. I think they are [more] similar between me and my Asian American friends than my Caucasian friends. The whole respecting your elders. I see them talking about their grandparents and how it's important for their parents to take care of their grandparents. I mean, just the whole family plays an important role.

Although Indian Americans may have noted similar cultural experiences with other Asian Americans, few went so far as Deepa and developed such camaraderie at the interpersonal level. Korean Americans were more likely to have pan-ethnic bonds, but most still associated with co-ethnics or Whites. Alice had a mix of friends and spoke warmly of her pan-ethnic ties:

At first I would try to avoid other Asian Americans, but since I've been to college and realize how wonderful these people are, that we have things in common, I've created a bond with them. And, I feel comfortable to seek out or to meet other Asian people now. I don't try to befriend them more than others, but I try to befriend them, which I wouldn't have done before. . . . My friends are White and Hispanic and African American and Asian; I have a good mix of friends. . . . The focus on Asian American comes through being a forum sharing our commonalities: parents who are strict, make the grades, go to good college, and find a very good job.

The link between Asian Americans, in their opinion, was forged more at the personal than at the political level and was based on a level of comfort stemming from shared upbringings (Kibria 2002; Okamoto 2003). The lack of pan-ethnic political organizations in Dallas directed toward the second generation encouraged this interpretation.

Beyond cultural elements, participants noted a common categorization against Asian Americans as both the yellow peril and the model minority. For instance, about the latter stereotype Rajat said, in a resentful tone:

For one, [the image] is going to be thought of very highly. There's not a lot of Indians on welfare or things like that. On the flip side, it's like, we don't have to worry about their needs or take care of them. . . . The stereotype is [as] hardworking: they take nonthreatening jobs, they don't date your daughter, they don't talk to your son—things like that. They are good when you need them there. We can do whatever we want to them, and they're not gonna object. Let's say if there were ever any kind of police abuse or something like that, you couldn't be silent as the good minorities. . . . I think it applies to all Asian Americans.

Some pan-ethnic depictions were gendered, including notions of beauty, which also drew Asian Americans to one another. Asian American women complained of either greater sexual attention, because of an "exotic" image, or a lack thereof as dark-haired women in Texas, elaborated upon in chapter 7. Men felt ridiculed as nerds and as asexual.

Categorized as "all the same," many Korean American participants felt comfortable identifying as Asian American.[4] Tanya believed that Korean American was more a subset of Asian American rather than a completely different way of seeing oneself:

To a certain extent all Asians, they tend to see us as more the quiet people, the kind of people that wouldn't protest, or, you know, make a big uproar of things. I don't know if they really distinguish honestly. I think as an Asian, I might be able to distinguish more. . . . [There's] not a big difference, I think, between Chinese and Koreans.

Yet, such bonds did not lead to a salient pan-ethnic boundary that interviewees acted upon. They rarely joined pan-ethnic organizations, sought other Asian American friends, or spoke of wanting to pursue such engagements.

In addition to pan-ethnicity, Asian Americans can form solidarity with other minorities. Asian Americans' identification with other minorities has received surprisingly little attention (Dhingra 2003a; Lee 2000). The presumption has been that insofar as immigrant minorities complain about discrimination and economic disfranchisement, they disconnect from Whites. They are instead "people of color," even though they experience unique forms of racism (Flores 1997; Okihiro 1994). The second and later generations in particular supposedly develop such an identity because of having grown up within the racialized atmosphere of the United States (J. Kim 2001; Lee 1996; Singh 1996; Tuan 1998). Likewise, interviewees felt solidarity with African Americans on the basis of both groups' categorization as non-Whites. For instance, when I asked Ram if there was discrimination against Indian Americans, he said in a casual tone:

> I'm sure there is. There always will be, [due to] skin color. I think it's once in a while. It's 95 percent of the U.S. [that] is really good, but that 5 percent can be really screwed up. The whole Ku Klux Klan—how much do you hear about it? Well, not a whole lot. Well, it's there. It exists in the South, and it's not just against Blacks; it's against non-Caucasians.

When worrying about "5 percent" of the population—that was when interviewees felt solidarity with African Americans.

Vikram gave a concrete example of feeling categorized like other minorities:

> There was a specific instance with my junior high school band teacher, who was one of the most racist people I've ever met. The way he would level it against me was, we had this chair system—who is first chair, second chair, or whatever. He would always put me to last or second-to-last chair. I would get very high grades but I would always get last or second-to-last chair. He would help the other students more. If they would mess up on something he would give them a chance to correct it. I would get one chance, that's it. . . . My band director in junior high, Mr. Sanders was his name. I think in terms of minorities, we all had a Mr. Sanders along the way, whether it was a teacher or as a boss or as a neighbor. Somewhere along the way, we had that experience of being discriminated against and being made to feel different from everybody else.

His experience in junior high is reminiscent of complaints Asian Americans and other minorities make at work: they get good evaluations but few promotions and receive less supportive feedback (Cheng and Thatchenkery 1997).

Participants also connected with African Americans when they received vague stares and poor service. As Susan said:

> I have a good African American friend, and we experience the same thing, and we get treated in the same way. When we walk together into a restaurant, heads turn because there are two different minorities walking in.

Interviewees attributed such treatment to the lack of Asian Americans in the area and to a general anti-minority attitude from some Whites. A couple of Korean Americans even thought of African Americans and Korean Americans as having shared a similar past of slavery and colonization, by the United States and by Japan, respectively, although with different current realities. John said:

> Our backgrounds are similar because we are very oppressed. I think they do share common ground in that. Historically speaking, their time in America, the whole slavery issue, which carries on through today . . . I think Blacks have it a lot worse [than Asian Americans].

The second generation, overall, felt tied to other Asian Americans based on a shared culture and common stereotypes. Their connection to Blacks rested on lacking power relative to Whites and being fearful of those with strong prejudices. These pan-ethnic and interracial identities, however, proved symbolic rather than substantial, for individuals rarely went out of their way to act on them (Gans 1979; Waters 1990).

LIMITED INTERRACIAL AND PAN-ETHNIC BOUNDARIES

The dominant assumption in the academic literature is that minorities often challenge the racial status quo through oppositional practices and attitudes (Bonilla-Silva 2003). They recognize structural racism that marks minorities as inherently different in ways that support economic and social advantages of Whites. Portes and Rumbaut (2001) find that when members of the second generation experience frequent racism, especially as children, they tend to develop a reactive ethnicity or bond with other minorities and feel little connection with the majority or with dominant institutions, which are seen as strongly racist. This was rarely true in my sample. Even though Asian American professionals felt themselves treated like non-White minorities, they had other discourses and experiences to draw upon to make sense of

Table 4.1 Factors that encouraged an individual-level perspective on racism and similarly limited a reactive ethnicity as well as pan-ethnic and person-of-color identities.

- Categorization as model minority and as immigrants generally instead of as non-Whites
- Impression of poor African Americans as culturally stigmatized, along with criticism of affirmative action, especially for those informants who had not been labeled as similar to African Americans
- Discrimination against Asian Americans' cultural backgrounds as opposed to as non-Whites generally
- Popularity of multiculturalism instead of critical racial ideologies
- Lack of pan-ethnic organizations in Dallas
- The relative economic success of immigrants and the second generation despite racism, especially with greater acculturation
- Residential location in Dallas that limited interminority contacts and sense of problems impacting local Asian Americans

SOURCE: Interviews.

their margins-in-the-mainstream status. These included categorizations as the model minority and as distinct immigrant groups; the rhetoric of multiculturalism and the salience of ethnic culture; and limited interests in joining with other minorities because of their class status and residential location within Dallas. These factors drew attention to anti-immigrant racism but also limited respondents' concerns about it. Like the first-generation leaders (see chapter 3), respondents viewed racism as existing at the individual rather than the systemic level, which weakened the sense of reactive ethnicity as well as interminority solidarities (see Table 4.1). I discuss the effects of categorization, culture, and then interests, keeping in mind that the same set of experiences can fall into more than one category. I also elaborate on how Indian and Korean Americans experienced each category differently, which led to particular types of identity formations.

Distinct Categorizations

Stereotypes that distinguished Indian and Korean Americans from African Americans and that most notably characterized Asian Americans as the hardworking model minority weakened informants' person-of-color identity as non-Whites as well as a reactive ethnicity more generally.[5] This categorization instead encouraged an individual-level perspective on racism. The recognition that they were all potential victims of racism from Whites mattered little. The disengagement from Blacks could be seen as we conversed generally about what led to the second generation's socioeconomic status, a source of pride in their immigrant narrative. Most, though not all, actors perceived poor African Americans as culturally underprivileged and paid less attention to their social-structural constraints (Bobo and Smith 1998).

Asian Americans' stereotypical work ethic stood out as the main type of categorization distinguishing them from Blacks. Asian Americans felt as though they were known for succeeding through their own strenuous efforts, which fits the popular ideology of personal mobility and limited an oppositional stance toward dominant institutions more generally. For instance, Susan, quoted earlier, spoke of camaraderie with an African American friend in the context of encountering stares from Whites. Still, she grew more animated when she spoke of her ties with Asian Americans:

It's comfortable [being with Asian Americans] because they're from Asian descent. You have something similar. The commonality is that we're Asian Americans living in a White world [laughs]. Point blank. We have to work extra hard—not saying we have to be one step above everyone else, but that way we are not seen like another minority group. We have such strong work ethics, we don't want to be seen as just another minority group.

Rupu agreed:

I hate to be stereotypical, but most Black people are pretty lazy, man. They hate doing more work for less money, you know. This is, like, a generalization, this is not true for all, but they never want to go the extra mile. I think in general they're not as ambitious as, you know, we were brought up to be. I think they tend to settle for what they have or what's given to them. In general—I mean, that's not totally true, but if I had to generalize.

Living in a "White world" does not translate into identifying as a "minority," which could lower Asian Americans' social status even more.

Far from a person-of-color camaraderie, the Asian American work ethic made James express pride in a sibling relationship with Whites, in particular with Jewish Americans:

I think I am closer to Jews because of our work ethic. It is something that is within us. They really stress education. They really stress families. What the value of a dollar is and things like that. Because of that I have had Jewish people tell me that Korean Americans are a lot like them. . . . Maybe it is my belief in my own abilities that makes me think that I can excel. Because, financially, I come from a working-class family; my parents aren't very well off. All of my family is working class. Others have done very well for themselves because they have worked very hard. You will encounter prejudice along the way, but you can still work hard. There are minorities out there that believe they are not capable of doing something. Maybe it has something to do with my parents too, really pushing me that you can have anything that you want.

Kibria (2002) finds that Asian Americans felt a kinship with Jews as fellow immigrants who advanced economically but who remained apart from the mainstream partly by choice and partly by force.[6] This is in contrast to claiming, along with other minorities, economic and social disfranchisement relative to the majority. Because Asian Americans are racialized not only as non-Whites but more specifically as foreigners, actors could concentrate on this latter status and hope to challenge it as previous immigrants supposedly had done.

Interviewees also took comfort in the stereotype that Asian Americans excel in education relative to other groups owing to their supportive families. According to the dominant ideology, the effort to do well in school can compensate for poor environmental conditions, such as dilapidated buildings, untrained teachers, few or low-paying local job opportunities, and other social structural factors (Kozol 1991; Wilson 1987).[7] Lakshmi explained:

> Education is a big deal [in succeeding]. Behind education is discipline from your family, what your family expects from you in terms of how you conduct yourself and make yourself successful. . . . If your parents drive you and stress education, you can get through that stuff [i.e., a poor school environment].

Similarly, John, who stated earlier that both Korean and African Americans lacked power at the hands of colonizers, articulated African Americans' relative lack of economic success this way: "I think a lot of it has to do with the emphasis on education. It's probably not as high." Ogbu (1994) questions this popular type of categorization, arguing that African Americans care just as much as Whites about their children's educational gains. Among other factors racial inequalities in the school system as well as discrimination against even well-educated Blacks limits academic success. Parents' (and previous generations') educational level predicts educational attainment better than does interest in scholastic achievement. Although cultural attributes can impact school progress, these effects are mediated through groups' local and macro social structure and their history with the education system (Zhou and Bankston 1998). Missing from these interviewees' accounts of their success are the high educational levels and human capital with which their parents immigrated, which in turn facilitated economic achievement (Rumbaut 1994).

How hard one works, how hard one studies, and, with that, how hard one acculturates to middle-class norms dictate socioeconomic progress. Such an impression among interviewees further limited the relevance of a reactive ethnicity as well as reduced their impetus to identify with other minorities. Ram, quoted earlier as connecting with African Americans due to the prejudices of the Ku Klux Klan, became dismayed when elaborating on the reasons for many Blacks' economic conditions:

> I think what it really comes down to is adapting to the American culture. And if you want to be a part of it, then there are certain things that you should try to do, as in learn the language, speak it properly. And I don't mean just Indians. I mean if you look at African Americans, some of them, whether they're from the ghetto, you know, they don't speak the same way. Because they're not proper.

As the contexts shifted from concerns over extreme racists to the gradual success of Asian Americans through acculturation, so did interviewees' solidarity with other minorities. Asian Americans' ability to move from "foreigner" to "native" placed them within an immigrant trajectory, in their eyes. This distinction between "ghetto" and "proper" African Americans was key to the perspective that racism could be overcome through individual effort and that it was not inappropriate to criticize certain (though not all) Blacks (Bonilla-Silva 2003; Subramanian 2000).[8] Speaking standard English, along with working hard and becoming highly educated, fit the model-minority categorization of Asian Americans and so are discussed in this section, even though these traits ostensibly refer to cultural attributes.

Most of these Indian and Korean Americans disapproved of affirmative action because it prioritized race, rather than effort and merit, in allocating resources. That immigrants had been able to succeed without set-aside programs demonstrated to them that the United States, if not completely accepting of minorities, still had an open education system and labor market. For example, Meena was adamant in her belief that

> just because you are a different color or a minority doesn't mean you should ever get precedence over anybody else. I think it should always be based on qualifications and how you perform.

In respondents' opinion, poverty could be overcome through hard work, family guidance, and acculturation rather than by deliberating about racism, which would actually handicap Asian Americans. Tom was incredulous that some Asian Americans would endorse affirmative action:

> If you look at affirmative action, and if Asians are looking out for Asians, and I tend to think a lot of them are, then getting rid of it has increased the population

of Asians in [universities] . . . . Asian Americans don't raise as much hell about being impoverished as African Americans and Latinos do. That's because we realize that we're poor because we're poor. And to get out of that, you have to work hard. African Americans and Latinos say, "We're poor because the White man is keeping us down."

Participants were right in that dismantling affirmative action has led to increased admissions for Asian Americans in some states (such as Texas and California). Some Asian American activists have supported affirmative action while condemning restrictions on Asian American enrollment, such as through informal quotas, higher standards on verbal SAT scores, and the claim of "overrepresentation" of Asian Americans despite their large number of applications (Takagi 1992; Woo 2000).

Other participants, such as Jason, were supportive of yet felt ambivalent toward affirmative action for equally qualified minorities, even as they criticized some African Americans for not working hard enough:

> If you're working with someone who is Black, and he has no skills compared to you, and you're getting the same pay, of course that would make you upset. But I mean, if he's Black, and he has the same skills as you, then that's good. You know what I'm saying? It all depends on the individual and who hires him, and that kind of idea. It's good. Without that, there would be so much less progress in society in general.

Jason noted the general hardships faced by African Americans and hoped for greater racial equality. He saw affirmative action as tolerable for those who deserve it, namely those Blacks who attained adequate skills regardless of the resources in their environment.

Although most participants felt that they stood apart from other minorities, about a quarter did not distance themselves from African Americans when discussing their economic and social status. They took pride in their categorization as the model minority but believed other minorities faced harsher racism that limited their mobility. Still, these individuals did not endorse a person-of-color unity. It is more accurate to consider them as simply not judging other minorities as much as the previous respondents had. For instance, Joanne had a nuanced account for the relative successes of Asian Americans, Latinos, and African Americans:

> I think part of it is family. Very rarely are Asian American families broken apart. They are usually typical families with husband, wife, and children. There seems to be a stronger support network, not necessarily a work ethic that's different but

the ability to figure out how to make things work. My parents came with absolutely nothing, and they were able to be successful and provide for their children and all that. Similar with Hispanic families and African American families—a lot of them have started with nothing, but somehow they're not able to get to a higher level. I do think there is a lot of discrimination for people in those races, and I've seen it on the job. I've seen it happen, like, no matter what, they are held to different standards.

This did not mean, however, that she perceived a strong connection with other minorities. When I asked her which racial group Korean Americans had the most in common with (besides Asian America), she did not hesitate in replying:

Whites. I'd say because it's never about our abilities that we are discriminated against, it's more so our appearance or maybe even by our accents. I have had a lot of times clients speak with me over the phone and when they meet me they say, "I had no idea you are Korean," or they will think I am Chinese at the time. They say that.

She stressed Asian Americans' particular treatment as potential foreigners, which distinguished them more from other minorities than from Whites, in her opinion. As seen here, documenting only Asian Americans' critiques of racism would misrepresent their racial identities.

Members of the second generation criticized other minorities less frequently and extolled an inherent "Asian" culture if they knew of immigration patterns and compared their ethnic groups' success to people in their homeland. Vikram gave a thorough response to whether a distinctive work ethic accounted for Indian Americans' general achievements:

Work ethic would be to me, I think, an ironic way to state it because in India, if you look at some of the people that are working there, the work ethic isn't really that great at all. I don't know if it is [a] work ethic [that] infiltrated into the culture as much as I think it's the situation in which immigrants came here. If you look for example at the Latino community, [they] were coming here a lot of times because they were trying to escape something very terrible. So when they come here, they are not thinking, let me get a college education then go to America. . . . A lot of the Indians that came here, from what my understanding has been, is that back then [the U.S. government was] only taking certain types of people. They were only taking the doctors and the engineers and people with computer skills or whatever. Because of that, when they came here obviously they had a skill set to give them earning power. I think that had a lot to do with it.

Unlike those who mostly distanced themselves from other minorities, one-fourth of informants had ambiguous reactions to affirmative action. For instance, Rajina, a doctor who felt "more comfortable with a patient base [that] is very multicultural," said:

> It has some advantages because African Americans and Latinos don't have as good primary and secondary educations. But, for certain professions you want the most competent person possible, as in the medical field. To a certain degree you are compromising that profession.

These respondents recognized socioeconomic differences from other minorities but still felt a bond with them, and so they evinced qualified support for government programs targeting those races.

Yet even as some participants spoke of their similarities with other minorities, their interminority allegiance proved more discursive than observable, as discussed later.[9] In other words, interviewees noted their greater similarities with Whites than with other minority races, but not all perceived other minorities in the same way. After explaining these divergent attitudes toward Blacks and the unique types of categorization experienced by Indian and Korean Americans, the chapter goes on to discuss the effects of culture and interests on participants' racial identities, which further discouraged solidarities with other minorities.

Explaining Variation in Relation to African Americans

Why informants had varying impressions of African Americans is not clear on the surface. Both those who had more and less sympathy toward Blacks experienced discrimination directly when young and as adults. They also reported that their parents encountered similar types of racism. There was no variation by ethnicity, gender, age, occupation, class background, or any other factor. One difference, however, was the extent to which each group had been categorized as like other minorities or as distinct from them in day-to-day interactions.[10] Those who had more contact with other minorities and/or who felt labeled as similar to them were more likely to feel sympathy for those minorities. For instance, Rick said:

> I grew up with some [Blacks], so I understand a lot of their concerns and see how hard it is for them. . . . In high school I was friends with everyone. I played football and had Black friends. I played lacrosse and that's a White sport, and then I took honors classes and knew those students.

Rajish also noted that at his workplace, African Americans had a special interaction style with him. "They talk to you a little differently than they would a Caucasian. They feel friendlier toward you, more open." Mediratta (1999), a second-generation Indian American, similarly acknowledges that having close Black friends and reflecting on the writings of African American authors, such as Toni Morrison, helped her form a person-of-color identity.

On the other hand, Susan, a teacher, had been labeled as distinct from African Americans:

> With students, I was accused of being racist. An African American mom said I was not treating her daughter equally to the White kids. And I said [sarcastically] that makes sense since I'm not [White] either. A lot of the blond teachers at my school encountered the same thing.

Despite her protests, she came to be painted in the same strokes as the "blond teachers." Overall, Indian and Korean American experiences with racism were not enough to create a solidarity with other racial minorities, even though such experiences created a felt distance from Whites (Dhingra 2003a).

Other factors besides types of categorization contributed to informants' opinions of African Americans. A couple of Korean American women who had taken Asian American studies courses in college felt greater solidarity with Blacks. As noted earlier, having more historical knowledge of Asian immigration also diluted an embrace of the model-minority stereotype. Class status and experiences with racism influence but do not determine perspectives. Notable, however, is that even when interviewees had distinctive attitudes toward other minorities, none articulated a marginal identity at the expense of observing ties with the mainstream.

Yet, Asian Americans share commonalities with African Americans within a structural racism that their distinct racializations as foreigners obscure. Both nativism and anti-Black racism stem from the same source: the intersection of White privilege and capitalism that leads to the use of minorities to sustain racial (and other) inequalities. African Americans serve as surplus labor who received lower wages within the split labor market (Bonacich 1976). Asian Americans solve contradictions within capitalism, for they are recruited to fill holes left by a lack of attention to social welfare, such as in the medical field, in the academy, and so on (Ong, Bonacich, and Cheng 1994). At the same time they remain marked as either too passive or too aggressive and so do not threaten institutionalized hierarchies. An immigrant framework on race relations, while appealing and accessible at the micro level, neglects systemic power differences between Whites and non-Whites that acculturation and socioeconomic mobility rarely overcome. Yet, the everyday tools that

Asian Americans have to combat discrimination often consist only of avoiding ethnic-specific attacks, as seen here. Informants were busy navigating racism and had limited resources with which to fight it. Historical allegiances between Asian Americans and African Americans have appeared only on occasion.[11]

Actors concentrated their discussion of the model minority stereotype in relation to African Americans instead of to Latinos, despite the latter group's significant presence in Dallas. Interviewees reported encountering neither Blacks nor Latinos often but commented more easily on Blacks because they made up more of the popular discourse on race relations. Informants had vague images of Latinos as falling in between Blacks and themselves, for Latinos struggled with poverty and low education but were still hard workers who cared about family. They supposedly cared more about working than about succeeding in school and, like other minorities, needed to acculturate further in order to lift themselves up. Little camaraderie existed with Latinos because they generally occupied separate occupational categories, did not share the Asian American categorization as the model minority, and had a seemingly distinct set of issues, according to the Dallas mainstream media. Referring to African Americans was easier because they represented a clearer position in the racial imagination.

Distinct Categorizations of Indian Americans and Limited Pan-Ethnicity
Surprisingly little research has investigated Indian Americans' degree of Asian American pan-ethnic identification (Shankar and Srikanth 1998).[12] I find that they encountered unique types of categorization (and culture, discussed later) from other Asian Americans, which limited a camaraderie. For instance, the historic racialization of East Asian Americans as "Orientals" restricts a pan-ethnicity. East Asians and Filipino Americans fought against such references in the 1960s during the Asian American student movement. Yet, they remain defined as a physically distinct, Mongoloid race apart from the Negroid and the Caucasoid (Kibria 1996). Many Indian Americans referred to East Asians as "Orientals" without realizing its racist connotations. For instance, Gautum said, when asked if he identified as Asian American: "Technically we are Asians, we are from Asia. But I tend to think of Asians as Orientals. If someone says, 'I saw an Asian,' I tend to think of an Oriental." References to Asia rarely mean South or Central Asia. In addition, the term "Oriental" evokes depictions of "yellow face": the exaggerated caricatures of East Asian Americans

with "slanted" eyes, bucktoothed, pigtailed, and wearing straw hats.[13] When I asked Kithana if she identified as Asian American, she insisted:

> No. I hate filling out those forms. You fill in Asian and they think you're Chinese or Japanese. When they say Asian, they don't mean Indian. I've just noticed that when they say Asian, I filled that in, and on my school report it said Oriental. So after that I'm like, I'm Indian, and quit checking that box.[14]

Because of their physical appearances, geographic origin, and culture, Indian Americans have become targets of life-threatening attacks, as discussed in chapters 2 and 3 (Khandelwal 2002; Lessinger 1995; Misir 1996). This reinforced their ethnic identities in regards to race. The image as possible terrorists has further weakened a pan-ethnic identity. Post-9/11, South Asian, Arab, and Muslim Americans find themselves increasingly targeted as threats to the nation—with general tensions, threats, verbal abuses, and physical—even fatal—attacks.[15] The yellow peril has become the brown peril, with religion and geographic origin as major components. The increased suspicion of Indian Americans has led to some anxiety for these participants, but less so than if they were Muslim or turbaned Sikh. Many said that if asked if they were Muslim, they responded no and no tensions ensued. After 9/11, Aditi's concern grew for her male relatives and for South Asian American men generally, but she gradually felt consoled by the comparatively few stories she heard of hate crimes:

> I was just really sad [upon hearing of the attacks of 9/11]. But, I know one of the issues that I had, particular with being Indian, was that I was very fearful for my husband, my brother, and basically a lot of young Indian men. The fear of retaliation. I was really scared about that. Overall, I think people did very well. Yeah, I know there were issues here and there and, unfortunately, there were some victims of that kind of retaliation. But when I think about what happened and the extent to the retaliation, I mean, I'm always very impressed with America when it comes to racial issues. When I see other countries and the issues they have, I think given the diversity we have, I just think it's really impressive how well we all get along.

Many interviewees echoed Aditi's sentiment that the United States had relatively more tolerable race relations, which limited a reactive ethnicity for informants still after 9/11. While that was comforting in theory, Indian American participants, particularly men, paid special attention to their public image after the attacks so as not to appear un-American, even anti-American. For instance, Rahul began to worry about his safety:

I was careful how I dressed. I probably wore my American flag around a few times just to let people know I wasn't one of the quote unquote "enemy." I sent emails to some of my friends letting them know that you should just be careful about going to certain places, like dressing in ethnic attire and keep a low profile, and things like that. Yeah, so I guess it did affect me. . . . The dry cleaner I go to, he's from South Asia and there's another one I go to who's East Asian. And the South Asian dry cleaner, as soon as 9/11 happened, had flags all over the place in the store. The actual plastic that covered the coats had a U.S. flag on it saying "We care," and they had a pin. Meanwhile the Chinese dry cleaner, or an East Asian dry cleaner had none of those things. I haven't done any studies and haven't done any sampling or run any regression analyses, but I bet you if you went to all the Indian dry cleaners in D/FW, and all the Chinese ones, you'd see that sort of thing.

South Asian Americans have put patriotic bumper stickers on their taxi cabs, draped American flags on their store windows, cut their hair and stopped wearing turbans, and monitored their dress. In times of heightened threats to national security, Asian Americans must actively perform an "American" identity so as not to become the "enemy." Who the supposed enemy is, however, further divided Asian America, for some felt under threat while others did not, seen in how both dry cleaner owners responded.

Nowhere has the stigma of being a possible terrorist been more pervasive than in airports and on airplanes. "Flying while Brown" has joined "Driving while Black" as another popular form of racial profiling. After 9/11, news reports circulated of passengers being asked to de-board planes, trains and buses, and of men in particular being subject to stricter security searches. Vikas noticed a milder form of prejudgment:

Well, I got on an airplane on October 11 [2001]. That was an interesting feeling; you had several definite stares. Let's see, October 6 I was on a plane to Florida and there were definite stares.

Actors used caution when traveling in certain areas around Dallas/Ft. Worth after 9/11 and the violence that took place in the area. Local events included a Pakistani American store owner being shot and killed in a retaliatory hate crime in Dallas (National Asian Pacific American Legal Consortium 2001). Vikas went on to say:

I was more cautious about where I went [after 9/11]. In Plano I wasn't worried. Okay in Richardson. In these suburbs I wasn't worried because they're mainly educated, and they understand that there are differences between someone who looks like me and someone who looks like me and that's Arab. Now, does that mean that I was going to go down to some parts of town where there are a whole bunch of rednecks, like, trailer-trash area? And I say that in the nicest way. Heck no! There are people who don't understand differences still.

As attitudes about suspected terrorists grew sharper, so did respondents' characterizations of Whites, in particular of those in poorer geographic areas. They felt safe among "educated" populations because they worried about misperceptions of their ethnic background rather than about endemic hostilities toward Asian Americans. Later in this chapter I will discuss how class status influenced understandings of racism. Overall, the unique forms of categorization impacting Indian Americans reinforced a nonoppositional ethnic identity. Participants also commented on the distinct racialization of their ethnic cultures, including religions, discussed in the next section as cultural divisions. I will also examine Indian Americans' interests in solidarity with other South Asian Americans.[16]

Categorizations of Korean Americans and the 1992 Los Angeles Riots
Korean Americans often face unique types of categorization from other Asian Americans as well, given their ownership of businesses in inner-city neighborhoods. Yet, most Korean American informants did not articulate a distinct sense of interminority relations. The 1992 Los Angeles riots as well as tensions between Koreans and Blacks in New York City have made both first- and second-generation Korean Americans more politically active and sharpened their differences from other Asian Americans (Kibria 2002; C. Kim 2001; Min 1996; Park 1999). These participants, however, had a more subdued reaction to the riots, and only a few expressed a deep distrust of African Americans or a politicized response. Andy was one of those few. When I asked him what the major needs were of the Korean American community, he replied:

> Leadership. Awareness within the Korean community that we need to become more integrated. What happened in L.A. is horrible. It totally misrepresented Korean Americans. There are definitely political needs. There is awareness that we need to be more united. . . . I mean, African Americans have vocal leaders, people like Jesse Jackson who are very charismatic and vocal. Asian Americans—the L.A. riots showed that we have no real leadership.

Andy grew up in a suburb of Chicago and had no direct connection to the Los Angeles riots, but he still saw them as a defining issue for the community. However, he neither joined nor contributed to a political or community organization that dealt with interminority issues. He belonged to KAP, in part because it "requires minimal commitment, which is good."

By and large most other participants were relieved that nothing happened to people they knew, and the event became a memory of the past rather than a turning-point event in their lives. As Peter, a small business owner in Dallas's Koreatown, said:

> I was worried about what was going to happen here. There were a few outbursts in downtown, but nothing here. You can't blame the Black person for being upset that someone's selling merchandise and then taking all the money out and going somewhere else. But then you can't feel sorry for them, because they have the same opportunities as anyone else and they're not taking advantage of it. But what I think they did is retarded. If you are going to loot, why loot yourself? It's like burning down your own house. Go loot somewhere else and bring the goods back.

Many expressed frustration over the disaster and the negative media coverage of their communities, but they also understood, even if they did not agree with, the frustrations African Americans felt. Some reported that the second generation did not care about the event. A couple even critiqued Korean American immigrants for looking down on Blacks. Alex, a lawyer who dealt with Korean American clients, said:

> One of the problems that I see is there is a great deal of friction between Asians and other minorities. I'll give you a very quick and extremely graphic example. There was a convenience store and they were in a sort of predominantly Black area of town. What I heard was that a lot of the Korean women and clerks would all wear gloves. They did not want their hands to touch the same money or item that Black people touched. They were considered like they were dirty or something. To me that was astounding! That was the level of lack of respect that they had for these people. First of all . . . there is no way you can get a first-generation Korean to talk to you in English and [have] it sound soft and smooth. Everything is "no," "yes." Couple that with this complete lack of respect and it builds up a great deal of resentment to me. What was astounding was, here are your clients—these are the people who put your kids through school, that let you drive your Mercedes, and let you live in an $800,000 house. Yet you treat them like less. Then you get really surprised when they come and burn down your business. I don't get it.

Given that some saw Korean Americans as being the ones at fault, the riots did not increase interminority tensions. Even though the riots mark divergent types of racial experiences between Korean and other Asian Americans, it did not significantly contribute to the lack of pan-ethnic and person-of-color identities.

In sum, the types of categorization facing Indian and Korean Americans relative to other minorities encouraged an individual-level as opposed to a structural-level view on mobility and race and weakened ties to African Americans, even among those who felt sympathy toward them as fellow people of color. It also curbed a pan-ethnic identity for Indian Americans, in particular after 9/11.

The Racialization of Culture and Multiculturalism

The centrality of culture in the racialization of Asian ethnic groups, and in actors' interpretations of racism, further limited the interest of these "margins in the mainstream" to develop either strong ties to other minority groups or critical ethnic identities. Interviewees, in particular Indian Americans, did not focus on discriminatory experiences shared among Asian Americans. Dallas has also historically lacked either pan-ethnic political organizations or a broader culture that would encourage an Asian American consciousness. Instead, informants noted prejudices toward their unique backgrounds, which curbed a person-of-color and pan-ethnic camaraderie and strengthened ethnic boundaries. This discussion refers to cultural attributes brought from the homeland that were felt to deserve tolerance. It is a separate issue from cultural notions within the categorizations of Asian Americans discussed earlier, such as the model minority. The resonance of culture in informants' upbringing, as explained in the previous chapter, contributed to this perspective.

Beyond the standard symbols of language, food, dress, and customs that all immigrants claim as distinctive, Indian Americans noted religion as a common source of derision from others, particularly in a highly (Christian) religious state such as Texas. This further distinguished them from other Asian Americans. Rupu shrugged his shoulders in frustration over some people's reaction to his Hindu faith:

> As far as Christians are concerned, I don't see the point [of trying to educate them] because they're just trying to look at cults and our religion. Christians are die-hard, dude. If you're not Christian, you're going to hell. It's the most annoying thing.

Vikram, on the other hand, believed that his religion opened up avenues of conversation with others:

> I feel like if somebody wants to ask me something, I am very ready to tell them. We don't eat meat for the following reason, we don't do this for the following

reason, here's what we believe in, here's why we do it. A lot of times they are very interested and are like, "Can I go [to the temple] sometime?"

Regardless of whether Indian Americans had positive or negative interactions, religion contributed to their image as culturally separate from other Americans, which their racial status as non-Whites often aggravated.

Korean Americans also felt racialized based on stereotypical cultural differences as "Orientals." Judy was in disbelief over a set of encounters at her workplace:

> I think a lot of people there didn't have exposure to a lot of other cultures. I had a lot of experiences there that were surprising. Like, vice presidents would run around the hall, one of them in particular making those Chinese noises for fun without realizing what she was doing. Things like that, but it was mainly out of ignorance. One time I got a comment from someone, because I had to go home early, about how my husband must control me or something. And then I had another incident where a girl was talking about a Korean guy she had met at one of the trade shows, and she didn't know how to say thank you to him. So, she did one of the Buddha moves, like one of these things [puts her palms together and bows her head], and it was like she didn't realize she was doing it.

She blamed the tensions at work on others' lack of "exposure" to and "ignorance" of different "cultures," as opposed to people's misappropriation of non-White culture generally. Despite the pan-ethnic nature of the stereotypes, she explained her more meaningful attachments to an ethnic identity:

> I identify myself as an Asian American. But that's an interesting question because I think the reason I do that is because that's how I've been identified. That's how people have identified me ever since I was a little girl. You were Chinese or Japanese. It's kind of interesting, even though we are seen as one group, we [Korean Americans] don't have any kind of relationship with any of [the other ethnicities] within the Asian American grouping. We are still separate. None of us really do anything together as Asian Americans. I think it's because everybody has a lot of pride in their own culture.

Emotional ties to one's ethnic community far outweighed those to an amorphous pan-ethnic group, despite the type of cultural disrespect encountered. The types of civic organizations generally available in Dallas reinforced an ethnic culture rather than pan-ethnicity (see chapter 2).

The salience of culture in experiences of racism not only limited interminority bonds but also promoted an individual-level view on racism more generally, a view that what Asian Americans faced was mostly ignorance of their ethnic backgrounds from prejudiced persons, rather than institutionalized racism. Tammy said:

> I don't think there's that feeling of "Oh, you're holding us down" that other
> minorities have. Our cultures are so different. I don't know much about Black
> culture, but on the outside it looks more like Whites'. Asian Americans are
> viewed more as an ethnicity, I think, immigrant. African Americans are viewed
> more as a race.

Similarly, Gautum said:

> I think we come from such a different background [that] biases are definitely
> going to exist, and I think that has to do with education and ignorance. We come
> from a different religion, different culture, different sense of what we want out
> of life—it's kind of broad to say that—we just come from that background where
> we do things differently. And whenever something different from the status quo
> happens, it's looked at as different and looked down upon.

Although critiques of one's culture could lead to a reactive ethnicity and
a resistance of hegemonic discourses, such was not the case here. Actors recognized intolerance toward their marginal status but framed it as being due
to the ignorance of "less educated" individuals and thus not indicative of systemic barriers that significantly divided them from the mainstream. This view
of discrimination, which is especially strong in the era of multiculturalism, has
helped Asian Americans reconcile their status as a minority ethnic group that
is nonetheless part of the American middle class. Ironically, anti-immigrant
discrimination actually bonded Asian Americans to Whites. It appeared more
comparable to what immigrants who are currently part of the mainstream had
encountered historically than to what other minorities faced.

This multicultural perspective contrasts the cultural mood of a generation ago. During the 1960s, second- and third-generation Asian Americans
became politically active to assist their own groups and Asian Americans
broadly. They drew from both the working and the middle classes. Those
activists sought a greater understanding of themselves in an atmosphere of
protest and racial awakening (Espiritu 1992). People of all colors protested
the Vietnam War, which had special relevance to Asian Americans given
the geographic proximity of their homelands to Vietnam and the image of
physically similar Vietnamese battling fellow Americans. The civil rights
movement, the Chicano movement, and the Black Power, Red Power, and Yellow Power movements fused people's quests for learning about their ancestry
with issues of race and hierarchy. Instead of only wanting to study their native

language or traditions, native-born Asian Americans also wanted to challenge histories of external and internal colonization. Of course, those are the Asian Americans whom we remember. Many did not engage in social movements, and we find a great deal of variation among the second generation today as well.

Key differences in current national culture influence the ethnic identities of many in the second generation. Movements in the 1950s, 1960s, and 1970s called not only for changes in individuals' prejudices, but also for changes in social structure regarding the distribution of resources. Although there have been many notable improvements, the goal of interracial camaraderie and justice for the poor has turned into a push for identity politics. This places each racial, ethnic, gender or sexual group in charge of its own—and only its own—interests. The discourse on civil rights and government intervention to promote racial justice has become that of multiculturalism, with its emphasis on cultural education as a means to equality (Davis 1996; Marable 1995). Although many students in the late 1960s and early 1970s pushed for ethnic studies programs, today many seek Asian studies in an attempt to understand their history and themselves. The political culture also has become more conservative, as seen in the appropriated rhetoric by the conservative right of "color-blindness." Self-esteem and open-mindedness, not material resources, have become key tools to social advancement (Glazer 1997). Programs designed to assist minorities and the poor, such as affirmative action, Aid to Families with Dependent Children, and others, have come under sustained political attack. Along with critiques of social programs have come limits on the rights of illegal immigrants, seen in the passage of Proposition 187 in California and similar proposals in other states. The rhetoric on immigration separates "legal" from "illegal," "good" from "evil," and encourages immigrants to divide and conquer one another in pursuit of political and cultural favor, especially since 9/11. These shifts promoted ethnic-specific identities for Korean and Indian Americans, in particular for those who have obtained a comfortable class position, rather than creating a need to join intergroup coalitions to secure racial and economic parity. I will discuss the influence of multiculturalism in more detail later in regard to actors' responses to racism.

Weakly Shared Interests

Actors' interests joined with their categorizations and cultural discrimination to further an ethnic American identity and a critique of race relations on an individual as opposed to a systemic level. The emphasis here is less on depictions as the model minority, views toward other minorities, and cultural critiques and more on how informants understood the severity of racism that they and their families did encounter. Participants downplayed their racialization as foreigners because of their apparent trajectory of upward mobility in tandem with greater acculturation, such as previous immigrants had achieved.[17] This characterization accompanied the model-minority categorization. Given such achievements, racism appeared to be inevitable, because it was due to prejudiced persons. But it did not seem like a defining condition of living within the mainstream. This limited interests in supporting pan-ethnic organizations, demonstrations, or political candidates in reaction to racism, a perspective that residing in Dallas also contributed to. Interviewees formed this opinion without assuming that they could fully assimilate, at least in the near future.

Racism appeared mostly as xenophobia, which meant that with acculturation the second generation worried less about it. Because they felt critiqued for their cultural differences, as those differences decreased over a generation, so did concerns over discrimination. As we sat in the study of his parents' well-appointed suburban house, Vikram reflected on his parents' achievement in the face of the prejudice they encountered:

> Well, I think that generally [racism] divides itself amongst generation lines. My parents have been more subjected to that kind of bias and prejudice than I have been. This very neighborhood that we live in, I know people that act very different around my parents than they do around me. They kind of treat me more like an American, with them there is a little bit more of a distance. And, I know that in my parents' business, they have come across people who think, Here are a couple of dumb immigrants. They're not going to know what they are doing. Then later on [they are] surprised that these "dumb immigrants" are a lot smarter than they are and they can hold their own. I think my parents come across that initial prejudice more than I do.

Informants compared their relationship with Whites to that of their harassed immigrant parents rather than, as expected for the second generation, to native-born Americans.

The fact that interviewees deemphasized racism did not mean that they had not felt its sting. But, they and even their parents had achieved educational and financial success despite whatever discrimination existed. No need, therefore, to fret over its long-term consequences, regardless of one's skin color. For instance, Richard recounted with a resigned instead of a bitter tone an incident he and his girlfriend experienced while trying to enter a church service about a half hour late:

> We saw a couple of people going in. I would say it was about 99 percent Caucasian. The usher stopped us and pretty much kind of showed us the door in a very subtle way. He was basically saying we weren't welcome. That's what I perceived it as. We couldn't even go into the back and sit. That kind of bothered me. If they want to do that it's fine. It goes both ways because when I was in Korea and I would see foreigners, the natives would do the same thing. I understand. . . . Back in grade school they were poking fun, I guess it's just ignorance on their part. Obviously we look different. I guess [the discrimination stems from] just being uneducated. And it really bothered me back then, but now it's no big deal. I'm here to make a living, work hard, and I guess you can't please everyone. Not everyone can accept you for who you are.

The ability to "make a living" limited interviewees' interest in responding to individual ignorance. Usha explained away anti-immigrant episodes as being due to prejudiced persons and spaces that she could effectively "ignore." She recounted an incident:

> I went to a very private, religious college. There was one instance where a lot of us Indians hung out at lunch together, and there was a White guy that was saying something bad about Indians, like they were always causing trouble and they need to go back to their own country. My friend overheard him and he was like, "Hey, what do you think you are doing?" And they just had a fight right there in the cafeteria. This guy was Caucasian and was not very open-minded. I think in the South, like in the major part of South Texas, I think you find less open-minded people because there is less cultural diversity there.

Still, Usha did not consider racism as severe when she left that university and that part of Texas:

> I think if I were to really look at [racial discrimination] yes, I think I would see it. But if I just don't look at it and I don't know it's there, that kind of ignorance, then I won't feel as bad. I know it's there, but I am choosing to ignore it.

Some racist encounters, however, one could not ignore. Rahul recalled:

Three, four times people would actually vandalize our house. Threw toilet paper at the trees, wrote, you know, "fuck you" on the cars and with shaving cream, "go back home." I would say it happened three times.

Q: How did that affect you?

Well, it's just unnerving, you know, growing up in that whole environment where you don't really fit in culturally with people. When I say culturally, I mean kind of in a broader context. Like, I think I would be much more comfortable in a upper-middle-class community, where people are more focused on education and less violent, less aggressive physically, and things like that.

Even incidents like the ones Rahul describes did not create interest among Asian Americans in joining other minorities because it targeted them as foreigners and aligned them with highly educated Whites who presumably would not be so anti-immigrant. The lack of concern over racism contrasts with assumptions about its everyday effects. For instance, Feagin and Sikes (1994) found that African Americans worry about racism in the work and leisure spheres and often respond by critiquing the racist individual, especially when racism seems obvious, and demanding equal rights as guaranteed under the law.

Of course, not all in the second generation brushed aside racist episodes. For instance, Susan, who had stressed Asian Americans' work ethic relative to Blacks, grew visibly angry as she recounted an incident that took place at a fabric store a few years ago. A service agent, after Susan complained of not receiving assistance, said to her, "In our country we wait." The agent finally served Susan and tossed Susan's fabric back at her. She talked to the manager:

> And I told the manager, it is racist, just because we're Korean. I made this big thing about being born in this country. And, I don't even sound Korean; I'm totally Americanized. And [the service agent] whispered something underneath her breath about "in this country." And I said I'm going to sue you guys. I called the director of the region, and he apologized and said, "Are you OK," and I said no. And, they gave me $50–$100 in credit, and I won't go back there. I made sure the whole store knew she was racist, and I told people when they walk in not to go to her because she's racist.

Depicted as a non-American even though she has no foreign accent, Susan asserted her native roots.

Yet, even as some critiqued racist behavior, neither Korean nor Indian Americans became highly politicized to challenge it. Because respondents downplayed the severity of racism from isolated bigots, they had little interest

in joining (the few available) pan-ethnic organizations or in actively supporting Asian American political candidates, two measures of pan-ethnic boundaries (Espiritu 1992). Hardly any were active in pan-ethnic social, religious, or
economic organizations. Even when public forums for activism were available, interviewees rarely joined. For instance, a few months before my fieldwork, an open meeting was held at a university in Dallas for Asian Americans
to discuss the fact that for a couple of weeks some local nightclubs had not
been allowing Asian Americans inside. The situation resulted from an Asian
American shooting another Asian American outside one of the clubs. A half
dozen participants, mostly Korean American, mentioned the event.[18] Still,
none attended the public meeting; some claimed the exclusion policy was an
isolated event that these Asian Americans may have brought on themselves.
As Samantha recounted resignedly:

> There was a club that wouldn't let Asians in because they thought they would
> be in gangs. It's unfortunate, but it's reality. I didn't participate in [the protest]
> because it hasn't touched me personally, because I wasn't with that group that
> was denied entry.

Interviewees considered such incidents to be isolated and to stem from particular circumstances rather than from pervasive stereotypes that would limit
them in a significant way.

Respondents did not advocate pan-ethnic political alliances either. Political ties often serve as the strongest catalyst for groups to join under a pan-
ethnic umbrella (Nagel 1994). Some first-generation leaders, as seen in chapter 3, advanced political and financial causes within the Asian American Small
Business Association. Most in the second generation preferred voting for a
co-ethnic if they completely agreed with the person's policies, but they had less
enthusiasm for other Asian American candidates. Kithana's response, when
queried whether she would vote for someone who was Indian American, was
typical for that group:

> Not just because he's Indian, but if the people were equal, then yeah, because
> the person is Indian.
>
> Q: Would you vote for a Chinese American?
> Only if what the person was saying was smarter. The same logic wouldn't
> apply. No, it's Indian versus the rest. I think that's because I'm Indian, I guess.
> I don't care if you are Chinese or Mexican or White, but I get a little prejudiced
> when it comes to Indian, because I'm Indian.

Korean Americans expressed some inclination to vote for an Asian American candidate per se: less than if the person was a co-ethnic but more than if he or she were a separate minority. This generally fits exit polls found in California, which have found that Asian Americans would vote for an Asian American over another candidate assuming that the two were equally qualified (Fong 1998). When I asked Susan if she would more likely vote for a Korean American candidate, she replied:

> It would make a difference, but platform is more important. If the political views were totally against mine I wouldn't do it. Same for an Asian American. For Black, no. The difference is that they are Asian. Asians need to be represented more. There are none in politics. I think we need to have a voice in something. We don't get that voice. I don't know what topics we need that voice in, but I feel we're underrepresented.

The response reveals a common stance among participants. Because they lacked political interests tied to their ethnicity or race, they could not articulate a need to have ethnic candidates. Still, in today's multicultural era, which is shaped in part by identity politics, a group's prestige is tied to having someone of the group's background in office rather than recognizing commonalties with other groups and working together for shared gains. Others also had difficulty explaining the reason for political representation even though they advocated it. For instance, Tajind served as IANA's liaison from the Dallas chapter to the national organization, one of whose goals is to unite Indian American professionals. He had trouble, however, articulating the relevance of such unity:

> We don't need that same type of voice. There are some who think we do need a voice, I don't know why. I think I'm living the American dream. Maybe there are things that are affecting us that I don't understand.

Later in the interview, he said he would vote for an Indian American political candidate:

> We need a voice, a representative in the political arena, political awareness. Most people don't know the power that we could have, in the political world or in corporate America. If every Indian in America quit working in the techie world, that could have a huge effect. To harness that power.

Yet, when questioned why, if Indian Americans did not need a voice (as he had said earlier), it was important for them to consolidate their power, he hesitated and struggled for a response:

> I don't have an answer for you, to tell you the truth. Maybe not today we're discriminated, but in 10 years, who knows? We may become slave labor to the tech

industry. That is going on now. Companies bring over Indians, have them work, and then send them back. They may offer them a green card, but then you have to work for that company. That is very white-collar slavery. That affects Indians coming from India. How does that affect you, as someone from America? Maybe the image of Indians will be negative.

When pushed, Tajind came up with explanations for why Indian Americans should join together, but the political issues remained vague or removed from the current lives of U.S.-born professionals. The contradictions and ambiguities in actors' thoughts on this topic illustrate their margins in mainstream status: they wanted better representation as other minorities have, but did not know why that was important, because they felt significant ties to the majority. The desire for a co-ethnic political representative did not signify interests in combating political disfranchisement at the hands of Whites, but a belief that co-ethnics simply would know more about one's issues. Overall, respondents downplayed the effects of racism and planned on gradually attaining economic and social equality with the support of their own communities.

Influence of Dallas on Shared Interests

The setting of Dallas had little effect on participants' concerns about significant discrimination, their links to other Asian Americans, or their interests in forging interminority ties. In fact, their location could have encouraged their milder views on racism. This is despite the stereotype of Texas as a racist, ultra-conservative, uneducated state. Understanding the effects of Dallas on identity formation elucidates, by contrast, the dynamics in areas with more Asian Americans. The second generation worried slightly more about racism in Dallas than if in metropolitan cities in California and the East Coast. Although most considered Dallas racially mixed, they still recognized greater diversity elsewhere in the country. An Indian American who had recently moved to Dallas from New York City said during a dinner organized by IANA that she was struck by how often she was the only non-White in a public place.[19] A couple of informants were surprised when they learned that Asian Americans in Los Angeles easily made co-ethnic and pan-ethnic friends while growing up. Some also reported more stares here than they got in the Northeast or on the West Coast (Dhingra 2003b). A few went further and described Dallas as made up of Whites who had been in Texas for generations with "old money" and who carried prejudices against all people of color. Tanya described a series of problems in Dallas, including possible racial segregation in a wealthy section of Dallas:

Just hearing from other people, I think they feel going to restaurants or things like that, maybe they'll seat them somewhere else where it's more of a hidden area, not, like, right by the window. I've heard [that] places like Highland Park won't let anyone in [to buy houses], even if you have the money. It's more like, you know, all White. And if the town has that much power, they'll do anything to not let people in that they don't want.

Forced residential segregation, not typically a problem for Asian Americans (Alba et al. 1999), may be informally sanctioned in some areas of Dallas. Only a few interviewees considered Dallas highly diverse.

In general, respondents noticed less racial diversity in Dallas than in other major cities but still felt generally safe there. Sanjay voiced a more common concern:

Texas is that kind of state where you meet a lot of rednecks and hillbillies. I've met these people in these [smaller] towns I go to. And you can shield yourself from it, but these people hold down jobs and try to bring you down.

The ability to avoid rural terrain and its stereotyped inhabitants—not the possible racism itself—mattered most to interviewees. This indirectly limited Asian Americans' interest in bonding with African Americans as fellow victims of racism.

The type and size of the Korean American and Indian American populations that the city attracted also lessened their interest in joining other Asian Americans to combat racism. Although Dallas has welcomed a number of Korean American and Indian American professionals, only recently has there been an increase of those in lower-status occupations who would need assistance, according to community leaders (see chapter 2). Gautum also remarked:

I think there are some differences from [the] East Coast and South. I've been to a lot of places. The East Coast tends to be where the boat lands, and you have a denser Indian population in New York and New Jersey than here. And the people in Dallas, or Houston, or on the West Coast, you have to think how these people ended up here. A lot of it boils down to education and job opportunities, so a lot of the people who come here are educated. If you ranked the Indian education level of Dallas, Chicago, [and] New York, Dallas would be higher. It narrows the population you have, and you are selecting out the pick of Indians to a narrow group of educated Indians.

Supporting this anecdotal evidence, in 2002, two-thirds of Asian American men and women in Dallas, more or less, had at least some college education, as referenced in chapter 2.

Exposure to community problems (or lack thereof) also influenced racial opinions. Judy said as we sat in a Barnes and Noble bookstore:

I've never met Asians that need help. I talked to my father about that, actually. I asked why in this country there aren't a lot of Asian Americans who are poor or whatever, and they said because one of the reasons is if you are poor, because families take responsibility for other members. So if you are, someone is always going to take you in and make sure you are taken care of.

Informants did not witness economic exploitation or unfair living conditions in Dallas, such as the kind Chinese American activists found in Chinatowns in the late 1960s, problems that suggested a need to mobilize with other Asian Americans (Wei 1993). They did not live through the animosity toward Korean Americans in New York City and Los Angeles. Nor did they live in proximity to the "dot busters" of Jersey City, New Jersey, or communicate with taxi drivers who encounter public and police abuse and commercial exploitation. This is not to suggest that the Asians in Dallas lacked problems, for the first generation listed a number of issues that migrants faced, such as hate crimes, legal needs, small business development hurdles, lack of accessible health care, poverty, and others, as discussed in chapters 2 and 3 and further in chapter 7. Yet, these issues did not directly impact second-generation professionals employed in white collar occupations who already had U.S. citizenship. In effect, leaders of the first generation had stronger pan-ethnic ties than did the second generation, in contrast to the dominant assumption within immigration studies. Also, the kinds of Asian Americans who migrated to or stayed in Dallas frequently entered business careers and therefore had little contact with those who targeted social-justice causes, especially given the few community organizations dedicated to that effort. These factors made Dallas residents less likely to pursue pan-ethnic social justice work, even though they cared for their communities and for social equality generally.

The size of the ethnic groups, the lack of pan-ethnic culture in Dallas relative to that in other cities, and members' residential geography also limited one's interests in forming interethnic bonds. There were not enough Korean and Indian Americans to support a diverse set of organizations, but their numbers were sufficient to meet individuals' most pressing needs, namely avenues to socializing with co-ethnics and support for a group culture. Although Asian immigration to Texas is growing, it lacks the history and infrastructure found in California that promotes a pan-ethnic consciousness. Los Angeles, San Diego, San Francisco, and other cities that have historically served as hubs for Asian immigration (and still do) have numerous pan-ethnic associations focused on the arts, religion, social services, politics, and the labor market. The plethora of such organizations, along with activities on university campuses and local politics, make residents more aware of pan-ethnicity and shared interests. The associations and general discourse on Asian America also offer residents avenues to critically examine structural racism. Participants rarely attended the few pan-ethnic religious, business, or social/professional organizations that existed in Dallas. For instance, at an Asian American church in Dallas, a vast majority of attendees were Chinese American.[20] The Asian American Small Business Association has a pan-ethnic staff and membership but, with its focus on business owners, serves predominantly the first generation.[21] When IANA and KAP tried to outreach to other Asian American social groups, many members expressed little interest because they could already meet their social and networking needs within their ethnic group. Susie, president of KAP in 2000, remarked that KAP had met with a comparable pan-ethnic professional organization in the past, yet members said they had received little benefit: "There was negative feedback about hanging out with them before: 'Why hang out with them, we have a fine group.'"

Informants also rarely encountered other minorities because of their overall residential integration with middle-class Whites (despite some possible barriers) within the urban sprawl emanating from Dallas, in contrast to Latinos and especially Blacks (see chapter 2). Many were surprised by how frequently they saw other Asian Americans in cities in California, as opposed to Dallas.[22] Second-generation professionals also reported rarely seeing other minorities when they went out to restaurants and bars except as work staff (most often "backstage" as cooks and cleaning crew, rarely as wait staff, bartenders or hosts/hostesses). As Rajeev said, "You go to a club and see White, White, White." Informants rarely patronized clubs frequented mostly by Blacks and Latinos. So, although being in Dallas was not necessarily a problem in terms of their racial treatment, it did little to promote interethnic or interracial alliances among minorities or to challenge participants' opinions of other minorities.

Actors' own political ideology also influenced whether they considered joining with other Asian Americans. Edward Park (2002) argues that those Korean Americans who identified themselves as politically liberal were more likely to support African Americans following the 1992 Los Angeles riots than were self-proclaimed conservatives. Lien, Conway, and Wong (2003) found, on the other hand, that people who are politically involved, either Democrat or Republican, identify more readily with other Asian Americans. Like Park, Korean Americans and Indian American interviewees who self-identified as liberal noted a stronger political affiliation with other Asian Americans and other minorities than did conservatives, even though they still did not act on that affiliation. The conservative culture of Dallas and the South relative to the West Coast and the Northeast also could have contributed to the more conservative racial attitudes generally, even though those raised in Dallas had opinions comparable to those of recent arrivals. More research is necessary on how political beliefs map onto racial identities for Asian Americans.

Indian Americans' Weak Interest in a South Asian American
Pan-Ethnic Identity

Although South Asian American organizations have been growing in number nationally, how much the second generation identifies with the term South Asian American in daily life remains understudied (Kurien 2003). We find that Indian American participants were not interested in identifying with other South Asian Americans despite, and at times actually because of, the tendency for the majority culture to label all South Asian and Arab Americans as the same (see Table 4.2). These informants assumed that distinguishing themselves from other South Asian Americans, especially Muslim Americans, after 9/11 would alleviate misguided hostilities against them as supposed terrorists.[23] This is comparable to informants' belief that by associating with educated Whites, they could avoid discrimination as foreigners. Even before the tragedy some Indian Americans reported little sympathy toward other South Asian Americans, despite having certain characteristics in common such as physical appearance, geographic origin, and general culture, because of the emphasis placed on Indian and sub-ethnic heritage within their communities. For instance, when asked whether she considered herself South Asian, Veera replied, "Not really. You look like them, so probably a stronger connection to them than to Orientals, but not much."

The September 11 attacks and the aftermath of racial profiling and war on terrorism furthered this momentum. Most preferred avoiding association with Muslims from both within and outside India. Transnational ties with the homeland fueled tensions between these groups in the United States. Rahul stated:

> Probably because my dad was such a strong hardened Hindu and all that, I have
> a bias against Pakistanis, Bangladeshis—Muslims, basically. I'll be very frank
> with you: I don't go into a situation hating anybody, but I go in there feeling very

Table 4.2 Factors that limited South Asian American identity for Indian American informants

- Interest in avoiding categorization as terrorists, especially following 9/11 (affects mostly Muslim Americans and turbaned Sikhs)
- Transnational conflicts between Muslims and Hindus in South Asia
- Religious preferences that create division from Muslim Americans

SOURCE: Interviews.

cautious and guarded having a friendship with a Muslim, because I'm prejudiced too.... [Racial profiling is] probably excessive.... Those terrorists [of 9/11] have attacked many countries, many people, including India, you know, including other places in the Middle East, you know. If you can eliminate a group of people that are doing bad things, you should do that.

He went to a Hindu youth camp one summer but claimed that the experience had no impact on his attitudes toward Muslims.[24] Support for the war on terror further limited any camaraderie.

Nor did Anu form a South Asian American identity. She resented the continued communal violence in South Asia and endorsed an aggressive approach in Afghanistan by the United States in retaliation to the September 11 attacks. When asked whether she worried for her own safety, she replied no:

[The hate crimes] were isolated incidents, and most of these things were going on because people had certain outfits on or appeared to be.... I mean, if I see a Sardarji [Sikh] walking down the street, there's no way—how can you mistake him to be Muslim? My opinion is how can you retaliate against somebody if you don't even know who they are? I was embarrassed again [about] how stupid Americans are and how narrow-minded. They just don't have a clue.

Q: *If they were upset at Afghanis in America, that would make sense?*
    Yeah, absolutely.

Q: *But being that it's someone who's Sikh . . .*
    Right, that doesn't make sense to me.

Like many non-Muslims (she was a nonpracticing Hindu), she emphasized the differences between Muslim and non-Muslim Americans rather than the more challenging (and unlikely) goal of persuading people not to retaliate in the first place.

Most Indian and Korean Americans, like many other Americans, felt a stronger bond to the United States after the attacks and endorsed the "war on terror." Such nationalism, while commonplace, could have furthered participants' distance from Muslim Americans. Patriotism toward the United States often mixes with distrust over racial profiling, the Patriot Act, immigration restrictions and deportation, and a foreign policy that frequently undermines Arab and Muslim populations abroad. Participants felt more allegiance and sympathy toward the United States, yet at times still tempered this with their awareness of tragedies affecting other nations, including their homelands. This in turn mitigated some persons' adverse stance toward Muslims. As Akash said of his response to 9/11:

> I guess I was relatively proud to be the person that I am in this country, as far as the freedoms that this country has offered and opportunities that it's offering. So after 9/11, somebody came in here and took away what people had built up for hundreds of years. . . . I had less outrage about 9/11 because I had seen it. I consider myself somewhat educated about parts of the world. I'm not so ethnocentric that this [event] is all I see. I see outside the borders because my parents grew up outside of the borders. I have experience outside of the borders. So because of that, I see what's going on. So when something like this happens, it's [not] a big deal. Don't get me wrong—those people didn't deserve to die. But that many people die in two days in other parts of the world and nobody bats an eye. So where's the outrage, where's the support, where's all the help for these folks?

The contrast between Akash's and Rahul's statements demonstrates the unpredictable effect that transnationalism can have on diasporic attitudes. One thing clear is that the second generation does not need detailed knowledge of a homeland to still be impacted by it in reaction to national events (Levitt 2002). Akash evinced the effects of transnational ties even though he was not familiar with Indian politics. When I asked him if he knew much about Indian politics, he replied, "Not too much. I probably couldn't speak about the parliament, the government, the whole process of the way things work there."

Vikas's international exposure also made him more sympathetic to Muslims and more critical of the United States and its policies in the Middle East:

> I probably had a different view on [September 11] than most people did here. They were thinking it was all the whole Arab thing and so forth. You have to look further past that. You have to look at American policy toward Israel and the fact that we have sold arms to that area. They don't remember the mid '80s—we were funding [Osama bin Laden] to help keep Afghanistan free from Russia. And why did he get upset? Because we put troops on Saudi land back in 1990 when we did Desert Storm. Why else was he upset? Because America was selling arms to Israel. And what was Israel doing? Bombing the hell out of Palestine.
>
> I should have just said it's the Arabs and the Muslims, and they're bad and

all this stuff. They all should be shot and they should all be killed and that. And that's not the case. India suffered more from that thing than anybody here ever has, with the war and things like that, as well as Pakistan and Bangladesh. [My] judgment [is] based on, let's analyze what we have today.

This last statement—focusing on current politics as opposed to historical and cultural events—provides insight into his amenable attitude toward Muslims and Muslim Americans. Still, he, like practically all Indian American partici-pants, prioritized ethnic and even sub-ethnic commonalities when discussing marital partners and friendships (this will be discussed in chapter 6). So, inter-religious and interethnic bonds, even when articulated, are highly situational.

Overall, although many Asian Americans in the middle class promote pan-ethnic and/or interminority strategies in response to racism (Espiritu 1992; Prashad 2002; Wei 1993; Zia 2000), these actors did not. For the most part, Korean American and Indian American participants believed that racism targeted primarily cultural and social differences as it did immigrants gener-ally, distinguished them from other minorities, and could be dealt with (not necessarily overcome) without forming a reactive ethnicity or interethnic and interracial alliances that would prioritize their marginality over their main-stream status. They adopted this framework because of their distinct types of racialization from other minorities, the centrality of culture, their economic accomplishments, and their location in Dallas. The question remains of how they advocated responding to racism if not by joining with other groups.

RESPONDING TO RACISM

To combat their racialization as foreigners, participants adopted a comple-mentary strategy of highlighting both their acculturation and their cultural distinctiveness. They had learned middle-class, mainstream norms, as pre-scribed by the first generation, and also believed in respecting physical and cultural differences, as endorsed by popular multicultural ideology. Actors reasoned that if the majority continued to recognize their acculturation and hard work, their image as passive or as competing foreigners would dissipate. Samantha believed equality was a matter of time:

> There are more [Korean Americans] growing up in Western society, [who] know the language. So, as time evolves we can be as successful as the rest of them, and [the] same status would be accorded. If you look at [the] status of Caucasians here, they're all CEOs, but look how long they've been working here. But, you look at Koreans, it's just starting in Dallas in our generation.

In their opinion minorities could succeed if they played by the normative rules popular among the elites of the nation, as discussed in chapter 3 (this topic will be further treated in chapter 7). Because they had been model players under those rules, they deserved a status equal to that of Whites.

At the same time, informants recognized that they still would be treated to some degree as un-American, given their physical appearances and cultural differences, on which prejudiced individuals were sure to focus. In response, they hoped to integrate *based on*, not despite, their minority standing. They endorsed a multicultural approach to battle racism. As James summed it up: "Multiculturalism is a function of race. It's a way of saying, if you are not going to accept us, then let's enjoy what we are. That's how I do it." These Asian American professionals believed that prejudice stemmed from ignorance of their background rather than from a refusal to accept it, and that their backgrounds should be appreciated. As discussed in chapter 3, groups hoped to integrate partly through public acceptance of their ethnic background. Even those who felt sympathy with other minorities endorsed this tactic rather than interracial solidarity. As Sylvia commented:

> I think [Asians] are more similar to Blacks because they're still seen as minority. They don't get as much respect. . . . [To combat discrimination,] I think if we emphasize, if we talk about the differences, that helps to explain why a certain culture acts that way. So I think if you understand that, it's easier to get along with them, to know why our culture is that way.

Practically none of the participants were active in organizations that addressed discrimination through political means. Only one person had joined an organization to address issues of occupational mobility. Gautum belonged to a group for American physicians of Indian descent. Yet, he still emphasized a multicultural outreach to dismantle prejudice. He explained why he joined the organization: "As far as the physician organization, I've gotten (a) contacts, and (b) interactions with physicians who are farther along than I am, as far as advice about the roadblocks that are there for Indian physicians." The association could help him deal with any obstacles stemming from being Indian American. Notably, he joined not in order to confront or dismantle prejudice against Indian Americans, but to learn how to handle it. He believed public statements intended to mitigate discrimination should be cultural:

> I was extensively involved in the India Day Parade in New York City in 1991. That was great because it was an open exhibition on India, and people of all races came in. It was great to educate people about India. We talked about the beliefs.

It was mainly of Hinduism, a religious festival, of nonviolence, peace, love all humanity, that kind of stuff. It opened a lot of eyes.

Asian Americans can support affirmative action for Blacks but multiculturalism for themselves because they see each group as dealing with distinctly different types of issues. A multicultural stance, in their opinion, applauded cultural diversity and broadened the definition of "American" to allow immigrants to be part of it.

Even those who felt connected to African Americans did not adopt customary "racial" tactics, such as actively pushing for political change. Wendy complained of racism and thought others saw Asian Americans as a threat but said:

I don't see any reason for us to get political about. It is not on the top of the list. We came here for one reason. It's not that we shouldn't. I think that there is a lot we should be heard on, but the priority for us as a group is trying to settle in.

Nor did the interviewees quoted earlier who supported co-ethnic or Asian American political candidates suggest it was a pressing issue. Trying to settle in and be quiet is a common Asian American strategy for attaining equality. Unfortunately, it rarely works. Asian American communities often become politically active after encountering major civil rights violations, such as the Vincent Chin murder case, the Los Angeles riots, the Wen Ho Lee affair, post-9/11 hate crimes on Arab and Sikh Americans, and so on (Espiritu 1992; Zia 2000).[25] The second generation did not turn to public programs, did not demand the enforcement of civil-rights legislation, and did not seek government intervention to fight against racism, as middle-class African Americans often do (Feagin and Sikes 1994).

CONCLUSION

Actors overall were in a difficult position as margins in the mainstream, for despite having achieved significant attainments educationally and economically, they remained maligned by stereotypes and at times hostile treatment as supposed foreigners. Because they do not fit into clear categories, interviewees formed seemingly contradictory racial identities. They encountered racism from Whites as perpetual foreigners and non-Whites generally, but as they acculturated they experienced less prejudice, as have European immigrants. Depending on the context, individuals claimed greater or weaker solidarity with other Asian Americans and with African Americans.

Still, interviewees stressed some attitudes more than others. They adopted an individual-level rather than structural-level perspective on racism owing to the kinds of categorizations they faced, the role of culture, and their group interests. This encouraged them to accept that when they were treated as unwanted immigrants, it was by prejudiced, less-educated persons, and it limited interviewees' solidarity with other minorities. Blacks, not Asian Americans, ironically became the real cultural foreigners owing to their lack of acculturation into middle-class White norms, which would reduce anti-Black prejudice and accelerate group mobility. Participants hoped to integrate as Korean Americans and Indian Americans, that is, as the middle-class model minority and as culturally rich immigrants, rather than either to ignore their marginality or to embrace it with "oppositional views" toward Whites (Bonilla-Silva 2003, p. 8). Simply examining people's critique of racism at the hands of Whites, as was done at the start of the chapter and as is normally the case, would lead to mistaken conclusions regarding intergroup solidarity and a reactive ethnicity, in which Whites were generally resented and ethnic attachments were defined as hostile to the dominant group. In-depth interviews that target groups' impressions of multiple racial groups and their class status offer a more telling portrait of racial identities. The impact of actors' racial identities on race relations will be examined in chapter 8.

Korean Americans intimated a symbolic pan-ethnicity. That is, they felt tied to other Asian Americans because of their shared experiences and the tendency in the United States to place people into racial categories but did not act on the identity in meaningful ways. Although researchers, in particular those using quantitative methods, often find that the second generation claims a pan-ethnic identity, we see here that actual pan-ethnic boundaries, which depend on observable practices, may still be weak. Indian Americans did not even endorse a meaningful South Asian American identity owing to a lack of a common culture and shared interests, in particular after 9/11. The assumption has been that the second generation, unlike the first, is uniting as Asian Americans and people of color in response to the continued racism. Although some vocal Asian Americans promote an activist agenda and push for greater curricular and personnel representation in universities and in community organizations, they often represent a small percentage of the population.

This and the previous chapter explained actors' identity development based on their status as the margins in the mainstream. Although we know why, how, and to what extent interviewees developed "ethnic American" identities, this is only half of the identity puzzle. To understand actors' adaptation, it is necessary to analyze how they actually lived their ethnicity and race in daily life and in their life-course decisions. The second generation makes sense of ethnicity and race in ways that connect them to the mainstream, and so they have little inclination to limit expressions of these identities in the public realm. In addition, second-generation migrants have acculturated identities because they have grown up as part of the U.S. middle class. The remainder of the book will examine how actors dealt with multiple identities across four major domains of daily life: work, home, leisure, and civil society.

5 Multiculturalism on the Job

The Work Domain

THE SECOND GENERATION'S EXPERIENCES as ethnic and racial minorities reinforced individuals' ethnic identities and consciousness of race. Yet only knowing how much persons care about and how they define their identities reveals little of how they form group boundaries with or distinct from others. How Korean and Indian Americans actually enacted their ethnic and racial interests in daily life and in their life-course decisions shaped their adaptation and stratification. The central issue here is how second-generation professionals attended to their multiple identities in this sphere and what impact that had on their comfort and sense of long-term mobility. How did they construct themselves as "good" or "normal" employees despite an ethnic minority status that marked as other? We often consider the white-collar workplace to be a mainstream space legally prohibited from discriminating on the basis of race, ethnicity, gender, religion and other categories. But in what ways might it judge people based on group differences and treat them as minority workers? To what extent does the second generation try to hide its ethnic and racial background, as expected within the literature on immigration and as prescribed by the first generation (see chapter 3), and to what extent does it integrate that background into the workplace? Addressing this involves understanding what is expected of ethnic minority employees, that is, the domain code. As explained in chapter 1, a cultural code, or schema, refers to an agreed-upon way of processing information and behaving among individuals that is judged "proper" within a given context, regardless of whether the individual personally prefers it, (Fiske and Taylor 1984; Friedland and Alford 1991; Swidler 2001).

In brief, informants' experiences indicate that the workplace cultural code expects both mainstream and multicultural practices, not just the former. It allows for a narrow set of expressions of diversity and even rewards groups for acting on their ethnic ties when that furthers profit gains, and so uses them as minority workers. Yet the domain code also counts on day-to-day conformity to a mostly Anglo, masculine set of norms, which in effect frames Asian Americans as foreigners (Cheng 1996). Participants noticed ethnic, racial, and gender differences from others at work despite their acculturation. This resulted in discomfort and some concern over their mobility, while also offering opportunities to get ahead. Informants responded to this domain culture by censuring their ethnic and racial identities at times. But, they also brought these identities into the workplace in ways that still affirmed a status as respectable white-collar professionals, efforts that remain overlooked in the literature on minority employees. These efforts involved both recognized, rewarded displays of one's background and unexpected, unrewarded displays. In other words, informants hoped to gain equality as *Asian American workers*, and in the process they at times created a lived hybridity. Their use of ethnicity and race, however, could cause long-term problems for their own and other minorities' success. I distinguish between those informants who preferred to integrate and those who wished to segregate their identities (Brekhus 2003). Few interviewees, though, chose either one or the other preference as their sole strategy. My main emphasis here is on how people primarily integrated identities while negotiating their workplace cultural schema. Respondents' first encounters with the schema occurred in diversity seminars.

DEFINING THE WORKPLACE THROUGH DIVERSITY SEMINARS

Although the workplace has traditionally been characterized as a cold space that treats individuals as numbers rather than persons, growing research has documented that organizational cultures can give meaning to employees' daily experiences (Fine 1996; Martin 1992). Some organizations are small enough to form their own "idioculture," with distinct norms that employees create themselves; but participants mostly worked in larger spaces, such as national corporate firms, hospitals, manufacturing companies, schools, law firms, and so on.[1] The employee is to fit into rather than create the norms in such spaces. Historically, the workplace has been devoid of company-endorsed recognition of "difference." Even as the number of minorities entering traditionally white-collar occupations increased, many left relatively quickly as a result of an unwelcoming company culture. As James Preston, chairman and CEO of Avon in the late 1980s to late 1990s, said, companies brought in more minorities but failed to retain them. "In hindsight, we were making a fundamental error. We were not *valuing* diversity, merely *recognizing* it. We were not *managing* diversity, merely *tolerating* it" (1996, 3; emphasis in original). "Diversity appreciation" and "management" have become popular programs in both the for-profit and not-for-profit sectors (Fong and Gibbs 1995; Wise and Tschirhart 2000).[2]

Diversity management encourages employers to recognize cultural differences to varying degrees, depending on how thoroughly leaders practice it. A multicultural, tolerant environment can limit conspicuous employee tensions but may still not question the White male privilege that undermines desired employee unity. The company also becomes more competitive globally with greater diversity recognition, and its managers (who are presumed to be White) learn how to tap into workers' unique talents instead of treating everyone as the same (Coleman 1994; Knouse and Dansby 1999; Thomas 1991, 1999). The expectation that diversity advances a company's financial goals is a major rationale for multicultural programs. In practice, managers can learn to talk to minorities differently, such as telling Asian Americans explicitly that they are not being criticized when their work is, so as to avoid a cultural misunderstanding (Wu 1997; Young 2000). This lesson fits within diversity management's platform of recognizing a group's culture in order to produce effective communication and organizational output. Such interpretations of diversity programs perpetuate the state's framing of immigration and race, that minorities are beneficial when they sustain the economy but that their differences must be contained rather than deeply explored (Davis 1996; Lowe 1996). Still, from the minorities' perspective, this kind of recognition can facilitate mobility and limit discomfort because they are not penalized for their differences (Cox 1991; Cox and Blake 1991; Jackson 1992). The extent to which the white-collar labor market is a mainstream space, in which ethnic and racial differences dissipate in relevance, remains in doubt.

Diversity seminars are often the first time employees encounter the workplace's explicit approach to group differences. A handful of participants had attended diversity seminars, which they felt defined the workplace cultural code in the way the literature suggests: as prioritizing organizational productivity and attempting to limit conspicuous employee conflicts based on group differences. This meant, in practical terms, encouraging the expression of diversity when it promoted company profit but otherwise only cursorily acknowledging elements of marginal cultures. There was no detailed account of particular group differences, nor was there any questioning of dominant values and assumptions within workplace infrastructure that could threaten White male privilege and lead to full employee unity (Gallos 1997; Golembiewski 1995). Some respondents found the seminars relatively ineffectual, though most saw them as valuable. Samit, who worked for a national accounting and consulting firm, said:

> You go to training and they have a multicultural session, but that's just to cover their asses. They teach you to love one another, why can't we all get along. It's more along the lines of people of different backgrounds or beliefs, you don't want to offend anyone, and people may take things out of context given their various backgrounds.

The lesson, in effect, was less to speak about group differences than it was to understand them.

Tammy received a similar message, although she had a more favorable opinion of her company's multicultural efforts:

> They encourage diversity. I've only been there a few months, but I've been told they have special programs to educate people on how diverse our particular office is compared to other offices in the company. They make a special effort to make sure no one feels isolated. There is an open-door policy, that if you ever hear anything or see anything that's derogatory toward your race or ethnicity, they reward you on making the environment a more comfortable place. I know they make a special effort at Christmas time not to say "Christmas." They try to have a holiday party. They try to be open-minded that not everyone there is going to be White. I haven't been there for the other holidays yet, but I know at Christmas-time they made an effort.

The narrow goal of actual diversity management—not to allow practices that disrupt employees' work—becomes clear here in the decision to report offensive behavior and even to rename a Christmas party as a "holiday" party. Yet this tactic does not encourage real unity and instead affirms dominant culture as normative, for only clearly offensive actions are to be reported and the party continues to correspond with the Judeo-Christian calendar. In practice, multiculturalism did not lead managers to embrace employees' unique backgrounds. Nonetheless, it still carried an important message in today's white-collar workforce, and employees often appreciated hearing it.

As we sat in Samantha's office after work, in the human-resources department of an insurance company, she eagerly discussed the company's diversity efforts:

> Before, there wasn't as much awareness about diversity. Now, everyone has gone through a sexual harassment class, which should just be called harassment since it talks about race, religion, ethnicity, etc. That's the way our company is being very proactive and saying, they're people too. . . . There is an African American

organization and a Hispanic organization, and they want to make sure that they are treating [clients] fairly, and I think they are doing a much better job than before. They go out to predominantly African American communities and tell them what we have to offer. Networking is basically what it is. It's a networking thing.

People of color were not simply employees but instead ethnic employees, for their color shaped their responsibilities on the job and "networking" expectations. Yet outside of such opportunities to assist the company, people of color are expected to act like everyone else. We only need to know about group differences so as not to offend members of the group, for diversity training occurs within a "harassment" framework. In line with these norms of the practice of diversity management, she informally conversed about generic customs of Korea with co-workers, but not about any detailed matters. She said, "People ask questions about the culture, and I'm happy to talk about it." Yet she did not share her lifestyle with co-workers. Her personal life involved "not people from work. [I] leave work at work." She hid personal aspects of her ethnicity even within an "open" and "tolerant" environment.

Organizations appear particularly progressive when they not only give anti-harassment trainings but hold diversity programs designed to educate the workforce on cultural differences. Laura, for instance, was asked to lead a diversity exercise at her company one year during the Asian American month of May, which she enjoyed doing but the benefit of which she had trouble articulating:

> One thing that I was involved with was the Asian network, and they did Asian awareness, which was last month, and each week was something else. One week was a guy doing karate demonstrations, and the next week was different traditional outfits of each country, and another week we did a panel discussion where every country was represented. I think it's great, but at the same time there just weren't enough people who showed up. It was mostly Asians.

> Q: *What is the goal of this event?*
> I'm not sure. I don't know, I guess. I don't know, really. I think it's just awareness, just to let you know that there are these different groups out there, and there is a difference between them.

Although she hesitated in formulating the goal of such demonstrations, she decided that it was to make people aware of group cultures, which theoretically could lead to an admiration of differences that then would translate into respecting all co-workers. Because there were no non-Asian Americans to see the performance, she deemed it ineffective. Yet such displays, when attended by non-Asian Americans, may do more harm than good. These performances depict Asian American employees as more "Asian" than "American" and as embodying common stereotypes: as karate experts, dressed in traditional clothing, and tied to countries across the globe. In addition, having people don ethnic attire did not mean that all types of differences would be allowed. Still, most actors enjoyed having at least some representation of Asian backgrounds present since it let them feel at least somewhat represented at work. Their endorsement of the diversity seminars and performances signals how eager they were for positive recognition of their background. In fact, Laura mentioned her participation in this event at her EM church during a singles meeting, and people applauded her effort.[3] Regardless of whether respondents liked diversity seminars, a consistent theme involved references to stereotypical group images so as to deter harassment and to assist company profits, without questioning mainstream norms or allowing for a free exchange of diverse lifestyles.

This schema of diversity recognition, focused primarily on productivity and on not offending others, fits the way in which such programs fall within the social structure of organizations (Morrill 1995). Diversity management often takes place either in human-relations or public-relations departments, as training for employees in how to avoid making insensitive remarks, or in strategic planning sessions and as part of managerial responsibilities when clearly connected to productivity. Workplaces mostly deal with diversity when it causes conflict, such as having procedures to handle derogatory remarks. Exercises in exoticizing cultures appear preventive, even enlightened measures intended to ensure smooth relationships within the company. Also, companies expect minorities to express their ethnic or racial background as a representative of the organization in order to accrue more profit, such as by networking.

WORRIES OF DISCOMFORT AND MOBILITY DUE TO ETHNIC DIFFERENCES

I now turn to the tensions informants felt owing to mainstream assumptions within the workplace despite the presence of diversity seminars. Actors' discomfort and anxieties regarding their ethnic and racial differences at work elaborate on the domain code and demonstrate minorities' dilemma of finding acceptance as regular employees. The workplace's intent of mostly treating everyone the same meant, we see here, an expected conformity to bureaucratic

norms that supported a White, masculine culture and that marked participants as separate from other employees. I first discuss informants' concerns
with cultural disrespect and then with the model minority stereotype and
glass ceiling.

Surprisingly little research investigates how minorities experience their
marginal identities within the workplace (Prasad and Mills 1997). That which
exists finds that African Americans consider such environments insensitive
to their differences, which makes them both uncomfortable day to day and
nervous about their long-term mobility (Cose 1999; Feagin and Sikes 1994;
Gilbert and Ones 1998; Soni 2000). For instance, Soni (2000) finds that minority and female employees at a federal agency discern a lack of respect for their
communication styles, a sense of being disliked, and an overall discomfort,
which leads to concerns over not being promoted. Standing out because of
one's race, gender, or other social identity often hurts one's status at work by
creating distance from managers and other employees (Kanter 1977). Second-
generation Asian Americans are fluent in American norms and already have
integrated into mainstream institutions, and they supposedly consider their
ethnic culture primarily in the home. Yet, as seen in this section, they continued to sense cultural distinctions from co-workers. Participants recognized
lifestyle preferences, such as a prioritization of family and leisure tastes, that
differed from bureaucratic expectations. This is not to suggest that only ethnic
minorities face such tensions at work or that they were victims of targeted
intolerance; rather, respondents interpreted experiences through an ethnic
and racial lens, which affected how they displayed their background and what
kinds of workplaces they preferred.

According to interviewees, co-workers rarely tolerated meaningful cultural differences, namely what were referred to as "Asian" family norms and
interests, because they did not support productivity.[4] Women especially noted
the value of honoring family, which contrasted with the workplace code of prioritizing the company over the family. Actors remarked that Asian Americans
stereotypically had more responsibilities toward their family than did most
other Americans.[5] Sangeeta, who worked at a manufacturing firm, lamented
the stark disparities between how she felt toward her family, who lived in New
Orleans, and how she assumed her White co-workers felt toward theirs:

> Sometimes it's uncomfortable [at work] because of some of the beliefs I have from
> being Indian American and the way [co-workers] approach things. An example
> being, I go home so often. I organized a surprise twenty-fifth anniversary party
> for my parents and took it very seriously. It was my parents. And the problem

was that this was so important to me, and they wouldn't let me take that Monday off after the weekend. And I had all my family members there. To them it was just another family get-together that you don't want to go to. I was like, "No, you don't understand, I like my family." They were like, "Yeah, that's great, but no." They don't understand what is important to me. I feel like I have to explain everything.

Although many people, regardless of their ethnic background, want more time off from work for family events, she thought a more multicultural workspace would have a more open-minded staff that would recognize the cultural assumptions built into bureaucratic norms. Her current setting "is uncomfortable. It makes it not pleasant at times."

Perceived different approaches to family not only made interviewees uncomfortable but also caused concern over their mobility. Laura complained of the trouble involved in securing time away for family responsibilities and referenced her luck at having a supportive manager:

> My sister is pregnant. This is going to be the first baby in the family. First great-grandchild, first grandchild, first niece, everything. And my issue was that I wanted to take time off for this, and coming up to managers and asking them if I could take time and work remotely or something has been something that I have been really hesitant about in asking. One of my managers—he's really, really laid back—was like, "Yeah, I think that would be okay." So, yeah it does pose a problem. My dad turned sixty, and it was a big deal. I had to ask them if I could not come in. That is a big issue about family. My roommate—her mom went to Korea, and they own a sushi-to-go place in Manhattan. She needed to be there to help out for two weeks. I went to visit her one weekend when she was away, and she had her laptop logged into the computer, working both jobs at the same time, and it was crazy. But I think she hesitated, and I would hesitate, to ask for vacation time. Even though I have vacation time to spend, but to ask for it is a little. . . . So, we would work both jobs.

Women, regardless of race, face a conflict between home and career expectations, so we would be mistaken to read these comments as referring to an Asian American or even immigrant dilemma per se (Blair-Loy 2003). Still, Asian American females felt a heavier responsibility for attending to parental and other family needs, as prescribed by the ethnic social identity, and read these experiences as marking them as separate from others in unwanted ways.[6] In the example of Laura we see the intersection of ethnicity and gender. Women generally avoid confronting supervisors, especially when promoting their own needs (Tannen 1994). Even when some second-generation Korean and Indian

American women had time off or found an understanding manager, they did not want to leave work for family since doing so suggested a lack of commitment as an employee (Moen 1992). The culture of the setting influenced actors apart from the significant others in the interaction. Laura had even led a diversity exercise at her company, yet she still was wary of expressing certain elements of her ethnic lifestyle, which demonstrates the limited effectiveness of such seminars in addressing employee issues (Holvino 2000). In this case she dealt with the tension between a proper worker and being ethnic by going out of her way to show dedication to the organization. By doing so, she also fulfills the stereotypical expectation of Asian Americans workers as dutiful and willing to put in as many hours as requested.

Other than family dynamics, both men and women encountered explicit and subtle tensions over lifestyle differences that further revealed their organizations to be only selectively open to diversity.[7] Interviewees noted unique experiences and leisure interests that marked them as distinct from the standard profile of the young American adult implicitly endorsed at their workplace. Rajeev spoke of a previous job interview:

> At a financial institution, it was obvious that it was a Caucasian place. He slaughtered my name on the interview, and when I corrected him, he said, "Whatever." So I knew this was going downhill. He didn't like the fact that I didn't keep up with my high school football; I didn't know if they were state champs. I'm like, it was eight years ago.

Lacking an all-American name and interest in an all-American pastime of high school football reinforced Asian Americans' status as outside of hegemonic masculinity, even though the exchange contained no clear racism and its effects cannot be quantitatively measured. He did not get that job but eventually brushed off the incident.

Ram, a computer engineer, revealed in measured tones as we sat in his office that subtle differences in tastes created distance from his boss:

> I know there's already a step back, whether it's his view or my view, because I can't see myself hanging out with him, and I don't know if he can see himself hanging out with me. Because we are Indian driven, because I am, and I choose to hang out with Indians. That means, in that statement, I'm limiting myself with the certain type of friends I can have. . . . Business is always who you know.

The fact that White men often hold positions of power influences the culture of the workplace, in particular smaller ones. Ram's (and maybe his boss's) hidden discomfort did not stem from any negative bias but from a natural interest in associating with those most similar to oneself (Kanter 1977). Getting ahead is as much a function of talent and skill as of social networks, cultural capital, and one's fit with company leaders (Bourdieu 1984). So, even if ethnic minorities are acculturated, they can still be at a disadvantage, having grown up in immigrant households. Even studies that document a glass ceiling can overlook the subtle ways in which group differences may increase minorities' anxiety. The possibility that this would limit mobility did not preoccupy actors' thoughts but often rested in the back of their minds. As explained in the previous chapter, they rarely responded actively to subtle or even extreme acts of prejudice, and instead concentrated on securing their own status.

Women encountered ethnic and gender barriers in day-to-day interactions at work, further suggesting a homogenous culture despite a rhetorical commitment to diversity and to make each employee feel welcome. The stereotypical masculine culture of sports and drinking, though not determinative of one's experiences at work, created a ritual mode of socializing that many male respondents found acceptable but which made some females feel conspicuously out of place. Rajina, a resident at a hospital in Dallas, explained her dilemma with White male doctors and with her professors when in medical school:

> They talk about sports and hunting, and you're not in that clique. So, you may think there is some subtle discrimination because you don't fit in. You sense that the doctors would feel more comfortable hanging out with [other] White doctors, having a couple of beers. There's always that thought in the back of your mind of being discriminated against in terms of a promotion or salary, but you hope the professors are more open-minded than that. The best way to get past that is to have more interactions.

This is similar to, yet a different spin on, the dilemma facing recent immigrants whose cultural norms, inability to speak "un-accented" English, and social interests sharply differentiate them from Whites (Wu 1997). Although women, regardless of race, can be uneasy in such an atmosphere, some attributed their anxiety to their upbringing as socially conservative women of color. Men often can build a stronger rapport with other men who hold advanced positions in the organization and gain access to information to get ahead more quickly (Tannen 1994; Williams 1992).

A more ethnically mixed demographic created correspondingly different cultural norms and degrees of comfort. For instance, Jennifer contrasted how she reacted when interviewing with a law firm in Dallas with one in San Francisco:

Maybe I picked up some kind of vibe, you know; it was very subtle. I picked up on their discomfort. There's a law firm here in Dallas, and I went to lunch with this guy, a partner. He was wearing a cowboy hat and boots. And he took me to this very, very Texas ranch-themed restaurant, with animal stuff hanging on the wall. I don't know—he was just too Texan for me [chuckles]. . . . When I want someone to see me, I don't want their first thought [to be], "Oh, she's Asian." You know, I just want to be Jennifer, you know what I mean? I don't want my ethnic identity to be my sole identity 'cause that's really not. When I was in California, with everybody I interviewed, I felt like they were not seeing me just as an Asian person but as any other candidate. Because there's so many Asians there. And it was so refreshing. That's why I think I really liked working there, because I didn't feel like I had to do anything extra or had to work harder to prove myself. . . . I think it was just because in Dallas or Texas, Asians had entered the law so late.

In a diverse setting she felt culturally and physically unmarked, so she did not feel as though she was required to "prove herself" so much. This contrasts to her sense of not belonging in a stereotypically Texan steak house replete with men in cowboy hats and dead animals as trophies. Although such symbols may be more cosmetic than meaningful, Jennifer declined the position at the Dallas firm to work in San Francisco, only to return to Dallas a few years later to join a different firm and be near her family.

Ethnicity mattered in implicit ways as well. Cultural values that informants learned in the home or in ethnic communities carried over to the workplace, and not necessarily in productive ways. As Alice said:

My first job, I wasn't outspoken. I would just do my work. The boss was always correct. I know at home you don't ask a lot of questions to your parents, and that is basically submissive. I am more challenging now, and that is more American.

Men reported a similar pattern. Said Rajeev, "Like respect for elders, even in the workforce, including your superiors and managers. I'm less confrontational than most Americans would be." Participants referred to the assertive style as "American," but a more specific interpretation could be as more in line with the work domain code, which expects a certain kind of worker that some Asian Americans may not have been raised to be. They had to learn to switch between value sets as they moved between institutional contexts (DiMaggio 1997).

Not all in the second generation complained of discomfort and prejudices. If Asian Americans felt that they appeared fully "American," given their acculturation, they worried less. About a quarter of informants referred to the direct questions about their backgrounds as the only times that ethnicity came to their minds at work. In fact, those in the family category who developed little knowledge of their heritage (see chapter 3) hoped to limit even these kinds of interactions because they felt little commitment to their ethnicity outside of the home sphere. When I asked Sanjay, who notably went by "Sam" at work, what relevance ethnicity had there, he replied, "You try not to make it an issue. You try to make it the most remote part of your résumé, of the conversation. It's not applicable." He did not recount feeling uncomfortable in the workplace and thus having to avoid ethnicity. Instead, ethnicity did not come to his mind.

Similarly, Samit saw no barriers to mobility for those Indian Americans who could communicate well, and he sensed little cultural difference from co-workers:

> The only thing I can really talk to is my experience; I don't see a lot of problems. Despite the fact that 90 percent of the people who work there are White males, I don't see it as a hindrance. In my field, no. Well, qualify it: being able to communicate and get your point across and being able to interact with a client effectively. If I'm a guy with a thick accent straight from India, he might not have the aura, style to carry himself well. . . . [Overall,] I don't see [being Indian] as an asset or a detriment either way. . . . Generally, I'm more worried about the fact that I'm short. You notice all the bigwigs are tall. [We both laugh.]

Although committed to maintaining his ethnic ancestry, he considered it a private issue that only mattered when in a clearly defined ethnic space. When I asked him whether he found ethnicity relevant at work, he replied:

> I didn't experience discrimination or prejudice really at school. I think that one social situation, even here at work, is the fact that there's a majority of one race; they have a lot of things in common. I don't think it's that big of an issue for me. . . . [My Indian activities include] going to garba or a temple or someone's place to eat, that is, with Indians.

These informants naturally preferred to segregate their ethnicity into the private sphere, because that is how they had experienced it while growing up.[8] But we will see later the influence of the domain cultural code for respondents. Practically all liked to bring in some elements of their background, namely those that fit within the domain schema.

Overall, the diversity seminars and actors' encounters of ethnic differences illuminate the domain code. It allows and may even encourage group differences that further company profits but mostly expects conformity to norms supportive of a White, masculine lifestyle, even as the goal is to encourage full employee unity. Most informants felt like ethnic employees instead of fully standard ones. The lack of either full tolerance or intolerance of group differences raises the question of how actors manage the external treatment and internalized expectations that come with being Asian American. To some degree they tried to minimize intergroup tensions, as seen in their tepid approaches to managers to request time off for family needs. I discuss other strategies of handling multiple identities after examining respondents' concerns over explicit racial stereotypes, which further inform the domain code.

THE MODEL MINORITY AND MOBILITY

Research on Asian America concentrates on the glass ceiling and the model-minority stereotype, especially for immigrants and with little mention of the second generation (Cheng and Thatchenkery 1997; Fernandez 1998; Hurh and Kim 1999; Tang 1997; Woo 2000). Asian Americans appear as hardworking but deficient in communication skills, and as accommodating instead of aggressive. They may not socialize informally with upper-level managers and so lack access to internal job ladders. As a result they can hit a glass ceiling, meaning that they receive some promotions but rarely enter upper management. Therefore, they do not threaten the status of White men even as they help uphold the nation's economy (Friedman and Krackhardt 1997; Wu 1997). Kibria (2002) finds that second-generation Chinese and Korean Americans also worry about the model-minority stereotype. In response, they often avoid other Asian Americans and act in an assertive manner. As mentioned in the previous chapter, many participants considered the stereotype to have helpful and harmful characteristics: marking them as hardworking and technically competent, which they mostly agreed with, yet as passive and lacking communication skills on a par with those of "real Americans," a view they resented. They worried that they would be seen as foreign and incompatible with the culture of the workplace because of these negative aspects, which eventually could have economic consequences. The workplace outlaws explicit discrimination, but informants remained concerned over the subtle effects of stereotypes, which further illustrates the primary labor market's narrow degree of racial acceptance.

The assumption that interviewees were passive concerned them because it contrasted with the workplace's cultural image of a "manager" (Woo 2000). Andy said that upon closer investigation, the model-minority stereotype did more harm than good:

It's a long way from Charlie Chan. I would like to complain about it, but it's better that than something else. But, it's probably equally as bad in the sense that it's a stereotype. It might seem positive but it's not. It paints us as passive. How many people want a passive leader? You're not going to get the leadership roles. I rather have someone who's a risk taker, and that's the opposite of that stereotype. . . . [Being Asian American is] neither going to hurt you or help you in getting an entry job and middle management. You're not going to see the old-boys' network kick in until upper management.

Joanne agreed that despite any positive connotation associated with the model-minority myth, it still marked Asian Americans as being like other minorities:

I think there are some similarities [with other minorities]. For example, you are not White and no matter what, you will be denied certain privileges that I think White people, particularly White men, have always had. I think that minorities are not necessarily seen as assets. I think they are seen as minorities, in terms of the workforce, before they are seen as employees. The minute you see a minority, whether it be Asian, Hispanic, [or] African American, there is this standard that just sets you.

Most of these individuals were new to their jobs, having worked at their companies for less than two years. As a result, the glass ceiling seemed like a distant concern. As Tammy replied when asked if she worried about discrimination at work:

Maybe later on as I try to work my way up the corporate ladder. I'm just now starting to feel it out. You hear all the time about the glass ceiling, and you wonder if it will happen to me. As of right now, I don't feel like it's affected me.

Although many respondents believed that the image hurt Asian Americans' chances for promotion, it is important to note that most had done well so far.[9]

Participants had to overcome not only others' perception of them as passive, but also the common racial imprint of them as uncommunicative and socially inept foreigners, which handicaps career tracks into management. Mohit, an engineer, observed:

I think we have such a certain mold that people look for, and the White male fits that mold of being energetic and being charismatic. I think that the other thing is that people don't believe that Asian Americans can relate. I mean, I have been told that if I go work in a plant, that most people don't think I can relate to them because the only thing they have ever seen is some stupid *National Geographic*. You know, the same old story, they see a woman who popped out a baby in a village and they think that is what the entire country is like. So that is what they think I am like. Then they listen to me talk and all of sudden they are like, "Oh, you don't have an accent. Oh, wait a minute. You've grown up here all of your life?" Then you have to take a step back because I am breaking the stereotype of theirs. They assume that I was going to be a technical person because I was Indian. Then, they started talking to me and all of a sudden the reality got them. "Oh my God, you want to be a manager?"

Media images and even diversity seminars exacerbated this foreigner impression by highlighting participants' Asian "roots." As seen in previous quotes, "charisma" in the workplace culture referred to the ideal Texan, a strong White male who walks with confidence and tells it like it is.

The combination of racist stereotypes and cultural differences could have impeded the mobility of some already. Rajesh, one of the oldest interviewees at age thirty-three, wondered as we sat in his house if he was already hitting the glass ceiling as an engineer at a global food production company:

> I think it is tougher for an Indian to make it up the management ladder versus a Caucasian or anyone, just from what I can see. Just that there aren't as many Indians in the management ladder that people know about. There are people who think Indians are good workers and hard workers and that kind of stuff, but as far as management. . . . I've seen more Caucasians get promoted quicker than I have seen myself, after I have reached a certain point. I'm still trying to judge to see why. If it's like a barrier or whatever, I still haven't figured it out.

Although he did not know what was causing this potential barrier, the reasons could have been the combination of the model minority image as technically smart but uncommunicative and the potential cultural barriers noted earlier. Indian Americans in other science-based fields recount a similar dilemma (Fernandez 1998). Rajesh's experiences are not uncommon among second-generation men. For instance, in 1989, U.S.-born Asian American men in the Los Angeles region earned less than native-born White men when controlling for education, occupational history, and family and individual characteristics (Cheng and Yang 1996; but see Sakamoto and Xie 2006). Both actors' experiences and secondary data suggest that the workplace may see Asian Americans as racialized workers rather than as individuals.

Women can face an even thicker glass ceiling than men because of racial and gender stereotypes that distance them from the assumed standard employee (Federal Glass Ceiling Commission 1995; Fernandez 1998). Even compared to other women of color, Asian American women are more likely to have a graduate education but not be in top management (Woo 2000).

Female professionals in general appear as either passive or emasculating (Epstein 1992), and the same false binary applies to Asian American women as well. Female participants worried about seeming too passive for the Western workforce. Judy relayed a lengthy personal experience at her former workplace as an account executive:

> They label Koreans and Asian Americans no matter what as being quiet, being submissive, even in the workplace. I just remember some of [my] annual reviews, saying you need to be more outspoken. Things that were part of my culture that they couldn't understand and they couldn't accept, they wanted me to change. A lot of people there didn't have exposure to a lot of other cultures. . . . [My supervisor] was one of those "let me take care of you" personalities, thinking I couldn't do it myself because I was a woman, but on top of that because I was Asian. I think a lot of promotion and stuff is biased in a lot of ways. . . . I think what they do is promote diversity in terms of the look and feel of an organization but not the promotion of somebody. Look at just the workforce and stuff—there still aren't a lot of Asian Americans who are in pretty high positions in the business world. [Companies are] just kind of saying, look how many Asians we have in this building and how many African Americans, but still it remains.

She felt critiqued for having a work style that did not fit a corporate culture, even in an era of multiculturalism—a common phenomenon among Asian Americans (Young 2000). Her impression that she was a tokenized minority made her want to quit that job, but she did not expect other environments in the South to be better.

Many women complained of possible barriers based less on race and more on gender. The old-boy network, which both female and male participants felt was active, offers more openings to Asian American males than to females. Anu, like Sanjay (or "Sam"), quoted earlier, had limited exposure to Indian culture:

> I thought that I was Indian because people saw me as Indian. And, you always think that [being Indian impacts you] in some aspects or in some way. It's just the blood that you have in your veins. Well, it doesn't! Hello!

When I asked her if, as a management consultant for a computer corporation, she worried about the glass ceiling, she replied:

> All the time. The fact that I'm the only female there lots of times, certainly there's a glass ceiling. Without a question. But I'm not the only one who's whining about that. Every other female whines about that. You know, I stand out more as a female than I do as an Asian.

Q: You don't worry about anything based on being Indian.

    No. I haven't seen evidence of it. But I've seen it happen to other Indians. I'm talking about my parents because of the way we [the second generation] approach things and way we speak. They still think like they're from India, whereas since I grew up here, I don't. My father would handle something differently than I would. He's more, "Do things the right way." Whereas I do whatever it takes to get from point A to B [laughs]. I approach things the same way as my colleagues do. I can assimilate better than he can—that's what I'm saying.

The second generation thought that parents faced more problems because of a lack of acculturation, and they focused on culture as a key cause of discrimination, as seen in chapter 4. As a result, those individuals who sensed few cultural differences and who had not encountered strong prejudices from co-workers worried less about an ethnic-based glass ceiling. They fit within the culture of the workplace. However, this did not erase gender-based boundaries.

    Respondents also looked to the experiences of other employees to assess a possible glass ceiling. Seeing co-ethnics who were already in upper-level positions or knowing of friends who had done well in similar occupations assuaged concerns over discrimination. For instance, John worried little and reported, "Well, I guess because I haven't really experienced a whole lot of [discrimination] myself and . . . I'm trying to think of an instance that might have happened to a friend," but he could not. In contrast, Joanne herself had not encountered troubles at work but expected to, given the anecdotes of her friends:

> I think that a lot of times, we [Asian Americans] are passed up. And, [Whites] think that just because we've managed to do well and managed to go to the good schools and get an education, we're still functioning high. But I see a lot of people that get lost and are denied opportunities because they are not seen as having had to deal with any hardships.

Q: Denied what kind of opportunities?

    In terms of jobs, and a lot of antidiscrimination policies don't cover Asian Americans. They cover Hispanics and African Americans. Even my Indian friends say, "Look, I get screwed all the time but no one cares because they see [that our] parents are successful engineers, they are businesspeople, they are executives. They don't think that anyone does this to me."

Participants hoped that their American sensibilities would offset any implicit or explicit cultural differences and the image of them as passive and uncommunicative. Some actors had more confidence in this than others, depending on their own degree of ethnic attachments, their encounters with co-workers, and the experiences of other Asian Americans.

The second generation's experiences with ethnicity and race, then, show that the workplace maintains stereotypical images that are expressed in sometimes subtle fashion. The point is not whether Korean Americans and Indian Americans definitely encountered inequality. Interviewees had done well so far at their jobs, and none had faced extreme racism or sexism, although most were new to their careers and studies have documented a glass ceiling for Asian Americans. The point is that ethnicity and race often marked them as possible foreigners and as outside of the normal workplace culture, and that caused, if nothing else, some concern for most. They responded to their prioritizing of family by contritely asking for time away, if at all, while stressing a commitment to the workplace. They also brushed off racially loaded incidents as inevitable, especially in the South, and concentrated on what they could do to get ahead. Next I elaborate on what other strategies interviewees used to advance their comfort and mobility at work. Informants employed two types of boundary work to accomplish their interests: censuring certain expressions of their background so as not to appear as too distinct from Whites, and performing aspects of their ethnic and racial identities in ways that conformed to the workplace schema and so would hopefully not threaten, and would potentially even advance, their mobility and comfort.

CENSURING EXPRESSIONS

Minorities in the workplace frequently handle their marginal status by segregating their identities, that is by behaving like other employees when at work and displacing one's ethnic and racial identities to the home (Anderson 1999b; Bell 1990; Kibria 2002; Pattillo-McCoy 1999).[10] Many first-generation Asian Americans also feel uneasy at work because of cultural differences in language, customs, popular culture, and religion (Wu 1997). They segregate their identities, acting "ethnic" at home and "American" at work, because the workplace is seen as a "rational" space where ethnicity is not pertinent (Saran 1985). Interviewees similarly tried to censure displays that could exacerbate a racialized ethnicity. As discussed in chapter 3, they generally hoped for acceptance based to a degree on their ethnic differences. Yet this did not mean that they expected acceptance at all times. The decision to hide one's background stemmed partly from some persons' preferences to segregate their identities, but also from the domain code.

Most notably, participants did not condone wearing ethnic clothes or speaking an ethnic language because these symbols carried little benefit for workplace productivity and were highly visible to other employees, and so only exacerbated their image as the other (Gherardi 1994). Gautum, a doctor, worked in a self-defined multicultural environment with other Asian Americans but still interpreted that to mean an Anglo-dominated space. As we sat in his parents' home, where he and his wife resided, he contemplated the divide between work and home:

> If I choose to go to [the] grocery store now wearing chuppels [i.e., sandals], then that's fine, and I'm not ruffling any feathers by doing that. But in the workplace that's inappropriate. You wonder what the person's real motives are for doing that. You're definitely making a statement. Doing that in private is honoring culture and not making a statement.

Few people of any background wear "private" attire in the workplace, so wearing standard shoes may simply represent a common separation of home and work. Still, important here is that respondents read such clothing as not simply regarding home but making a cultural "statement" contrary to the domain code. Donning chuppels in private is "honoring culture"—and not welcome at work.

Gautum's perspective stemmed partly from his inclination to keep his private and public identities separate:

> The Indians in Dallas that I know tend to be more inwardly focused. You have your outside world of work or school, and you have your home life, and that does foster a sense of schizophrenia almost. We go to work Monday through Friday, and when it comes to weekends we stay with our own kind. That is slowly getting better as far as extending out to different cultures, different races. But with our parents, they hung out with other Indians more.

Yet the decision to segregate identities also stemmed from the domain schema, which prioritized employee unity over group-based identities, especially if their relationship to work goals is not clear. Gautum went on to say that he did not mind being seen as an "Indian American" doctor in ways that suited the expectations of the workplace:

> [Being Indian American] for the most part is an asset. If you walk into a situation and people are looking at you and already have you pigeonholed with others who are highly successful, then it's opened up some doors, but it's [up to the] individual to live up to those expectations. And I think it's harder to meet higher expectations. But I think those expectations are good, it will open up some doors. . . . I personally believe that in public roles, just because someone wears a dot on her head, is she ruffling feathers, is that a bad thing? Maybe not. I don't know. It shouldn't necessarily be a bad thing.

The decision to self-segregate stems in part from implicit cultural rules, not only from personal preferences, which must be accounted for in order to explain ethnic boundaries. He began to wish he and others had the freedom to express a cultural background "in public roles." When he could appear as ethnic while fitting the workplace code, such as being a competent doctor, he considered that appropriate.

Respondents also criticized speaking in public in an ethnic language as disruptive to interpersonal unity and not beneficial to company goals. As Sylvia, a nurse, said:

> I think when you're in a professional environment, like at work, I don't think you should be speaking [Korean] because you have other people around you that don't speak that language, so I think stick to English. . . . I wear professional attire, and if that's required you should stick with that.

Akash elaborated on other reasons to avoid using a non-English language:

> Other people get uncomfortable when you're speaking another language, and they don't know necessarily what you're saying. They might think that you're talking about them. I mean, you have to have some sense of professionalism when you're at work, and I think part of it is not to speak another language when you're in an English-speaking environment. You end up segregating yourself with the Indians that you're associating with, and that there is some bond there that they have with you that you don't [with others], and so instead of just creating that sense of bias, I just don't prefer to do it. I'm not here as an Indian supposedly, I'm here as just an employee. I should act the way they want me to act and behave in a proper way.

Participants believed that in some respects (as opposed to others, discussed in the next section), they had to choose between an ethnic and American self-presentation, and that the choice was clear based on how "they want me to act," as "just an employee" rather than as an "Indian." "They" does not refer to anyone in particular but instead to the domain schema. Akash brought other aspects of his personal life into the workplace, but in a manner that fit the organizational culture. I interviewed him at work, and atop his cubicle were stuffed toys (such as Godzilla) and in his cubicle were figures from the movie *Star Wars*. This affirmed his cultural citizenry as a consumer of Hollywood rather than further racializing him as a potential foreigner.

In addition to censuring cultural symbols, interviewees avoided conspicuous interactions with co-ethnics even when speaking English, in contrast to their behavior in the private sphere, so as to preempt a glass ceiling (Kibria 2002). Tajind, a software engineer, described how he carried himself on the job:

They have the image of Indians in software as being immigrants, hardworking, not going to complain, and not being able to socialize. I speak English well, and when I meet someone, they see that I can speak like them. I want them to know that I'm not like [the immigrants]. My way of thinking is very different from people straight from the motherland. The way you're raised is very different. The topics of conversation we choose. You also see that Indians hang out with Indians from their part of India. I don't hang out with those guys.

These workers, then, carefully managed what impressions they gave to which people so as to maintain the identity of a "regular" employee as defined by their "multicultural" workplaces. To fit within the workplace culture, they denied an interest in ethnic solidarity. As will be seen later, this denial was partly ineffective and selective, for participants both remained framed and presented themselves as ethnic workers when this was helpful to workplace goals.

EXPRESSING ETHNIC AND RACIAL DIFFERENCES

In addition to censuring displays that could mark them as foreigners, these margins-in-the-mainstream actors sought ways to appear equal to Whites without denying their status as Asian American. Most felt as though they were treated as ethnic employees by co-workers and by supervisors and wanted to express their backgrounds as well. Their boundary work consisted of affirming a commitment to their ethnicity and race through both private and public displays that they hoped did not paint them as "too Asian." They accomplished this strategically so as not to violate the code at work, which at times required creative manipulation of how and where they used cultural symbols.

Private Expressions

Participants enacted their ethnic identities, keeping in mind the racial implications of appearing inherently "Asian" rather than "American," by choosing with whom to share their background and with whom to have only cursory conversations. Some had private conversations with co-ethnics in which they expressed more personal concerns than they did with other co-workers. Women were more likely than men to cite such conversations. Joanne in effect code-switched when talking with White and Asian co-workers. With the former she limited topics to

random things, sometimes movies, books, restaurants—in Dallas that's a big thing. Some of my women colleagues are like, "Where did you go shopping, what are you wearing." Those aren't what I want to talk about with my Korean colleague because both of us share a similar background. We would share political conversations and women's issues.

Meena, an elementary school teacher, had found the workplace more comfortable as a result of such exchanges:

> Last year we had three other Indian Americans on staff. It was kinda nice because I was doing cultural stuff, and I could actually talk to other teachers about [this] and tell [them] this is what I am doing. Now I don't share my personal life with anybody because they don't understand it.

Although it is rare for people generally to form personal ties at work, notable here is that ethnicity played a role in shaping types of dialogues.

The second generation also invoked cultural symbols when conveying clearly private matters. Akash refused to speak in an ethnic language with co-ethnic employees, as quoted earlier, but did so when talking with his mother at times on the phone.

> My mom's English isn't as strong as her Gujurati is. So, if I'm on the phone with her and I think she's not quite getting my point, then [I would speak Gujurati]. When I'm talking with a co-worker [who speaks Gujurati], I wouldn't, just because I don't think it's appropriate to do that in a work environment.

He used different languages for the phone call and the public conversation, even though both took place as he sat at his desk at work and were directed to only co-ethnics. He did not rule out speaking in Gujarati when at work, indicating that decisions to do so or not to do so depended partly on the domain schema rather than purely on a personal policy.

Public Expressions, One on One

Korean and Indian Americans enjoyed talking about their ethnic culture and did so in an increasingly public manner because that let them bring their personal interests into the workplace despite its mainstream-oriented informal rules. They thought that they spoke more often about their background to peers in Dallas than they did elsewhere. Actors attributed this to Dallas's open atmosphere and to the fact that Texans had less exposure to Asian Americans. People's questions served as opportunities to dispel false impressions of the homeland. Rick said about a Latino co-worker:

> He started asking me about Asians, and I told him that he could ask me anything he wanted. How to tell if someone is Korean, Chinese, or Japanese, and [I said] that you could tell who was who by the name, and the meanings of names and different marital arts, and foods. So, he would ask questions.

Only on occasion did they get annoyed with such conversations, when assumed to know all about Asia, an assumption that carried with it the implication that they were not Americans. For instance, Andy frequently enjoyed talking to co-workers about Korean culture but commented:

> It depends on how they ask. If they say, "You're not an American, what are you," then it's offensive. If they say, "I'd like to learn more about your culture" or "This food is really good," sure, I like that.

Everyday conversations actually required strategic decisions about with whom to share what information, so as not to appear too ethnic for the domain cultural frame. In the process participants hoped to appear simultaneously as diverse and as full employees, in fitting a lived hybridity. They confined conversations to benign and stereotypical elements of their background, such as their homeland's customs, foods, and so on, which fit the multicultural norms of the diversity seminars. Co-workers often saw the second generation as informal tour guides. Usha, who worked for a telecommunications company, recalled:

> People are always asking me questions. Like food—they are very interested in trying Indian food, or interested in our dresses. Like, we are not going to bring up religion, obviously, unless you are really good friends with that person. It's more ethnicity, culture, where you're from and what you do.

Actors rarely ventured into possibly contentious issues, especially in cities such as Dallas with a strongly religious Christian population that made Indian American informants stand out.

Although normally swearing at work is frowned upon, informants found that sharing curse words in their native language to be another acceptable fashion of expressing ethnicity in one-on-one conversations. Like food and dress, exchanging profanity fits the multiculturalism articulated within the domain code. Acknowledging superficial differences is permissible and actually brings us closer together by helping us know the other group better. Said Rahul:

> There's a guy I work with, he's constantly saying, "How do [you] say elephant shit?" "How do you say" all these different curse words. Then he goes and tells other Indians. He calls them "mofo" or whatever in Hindi.

The second generation found these exchanges humorous and innocuous. Yet here, co-workers again referred to stereotypical elements of Asian Americans' backgrounds, in this case an India as full of elephants and therefore littered with "elephant shit." On occasion respondents also would speak in an exaggerated ethnic accent to make co-workers laugh. They found no harm in such behavior since they felt everyone knew that they were simply having fun and "playing" ethnic. These exchanges affirmed stereotypical and therefore non-threatening images of a group without challenging dominant practices or privileges.

Interviewees had to be strategic in their choice of whom they shared their background with, not only in what they said. Conversations about diversity often are framed within a harassment or "problem" framework, as seen in the seminars. Communicating about difference could suggest tensions at work. For instance, when asked if she spoke about her heritage to co-workers, Jennifer said:

> Yeah, they ask questions, you know. They might want to know a couple of phrases in Korean or something like that. I wouldn't tell them how mean people were. I probably wouldn't share that with the manager. I would share that with someone who was equal to me, like level-wise.

> Q: Why wouldn't you share that with the manager?
> You just don't want to come out distinct. I don't want them to feel extra cautious when they're trying to promote me, or feel that "What if she thinks that this is discriminating against her" or whatever. I want it to be based upon my work, not because they're scared. I don't want them [to] be feeling different toward me because of something in the past that I shared with them.

Overall, interviewees expressed ethnicity in ways that did not challenge the White-dominated culture of the domain code, allowing their marginal background to coexist with their status as employees.

Public Expressions to Groups

Given their already public image as Asian employees and their own commitments to their identities, interviewees did not feel satisfied with one-on-one level references of their background. Expressing group differences more openly required creative efforts to still conform to the domain schema and not impede their mobility. Participants' agency in accomplishing this again demonstrates a lived hybridity. This possibility of openly acting as ethnic minorities in public spaces remains underinvestigated and unexpected (see chapter 1). Actors creatively altered cultural symbols so as to convey a desired meaning without drawing heightened attention as foreigners. Mohit was a chemical engineer, and one of his co-workers was an elderly Indian American man. It is customary in India and for Indian Americans to call older men and women "Uncle" and "Aunty" as a sign of respect and surrogate kinship. Mohit explained how he negotiated referring to the elder co-worker during a group meeting:

> You know you are supposed to call them "Uncle." I was talking to Nadeen and he was like, "You can't call me just Nadeen. You have to call me Uncle." And I am like, "You're right—if I see you outside the workplace, I will call you Uncle." But when we are in the workplace, that does not work. People are going to be sitting by me and hear me go, "Hey, Nadeen Uncle." They are going to go, what? It just does not work. I am like, it is not a lack of respect. He is like, "No, we have to come up with something." So I call him "Prof" because he used to be a professor.

People have leeway in how tightly they enact roles, and by using "Professor" instead of "Uncle" Mohit was able to avoid breaching standard norms (Heiss 1992). Ethnicity entered the public sphere of work but, as seen in these examples, in carefully worked out ways.

Informants also used the times and spaces at work reserved to oneself, although still publicly visible. For instance, Vikram, a vegetarian, served as a law clerk for a judge in Dallas and took advantage of the lunch hour:

> I'm at work, I'm in a business suit. I'm not thinking about religion all day long the way they are at the temple on that same day. I'm at work in a business suit, talking with attorneys, dealing with everything, thinking during the morning hours, man, I'm hungry, I'd really like to eat something right now. And then come noon, I go and heat up my Indian food, and I'm eating that for lunch, in my business suit, in the middle of chambers in the middle of the U.S. court building. So the two worlds come together.

The choice of foods and the setting of the lunch hour made such displays acceptable because cuisine is a standard ethnic item within multiculturalism, and the lunch hour is one's own time.[11] Enjoying Indian food in a public space did not necessarily threaten his image at work.[12] Respondents also made use of their cubicles by hanging up pictures of family (Nippert-Eng 1996), which reminded them of a bond that they had difficulty expressing in more public ways, such as taking time off.

Participants worried that freely expressing ethnic symbols might limit their mobility. When they had achieved positions of authority or did not feel constrained by workplace culture, they changed their behavior to make their workplace more comfortable for them. For instance, Jyoti was a doctor who had her own small office with a personal staff. She had strong attachments to her heritage, but no more than some others who hid such vocal displays given their different workplace environments. She wore ethnic clothing at home and at work:

> [I wear a salvar kamis] five or six times a month to work. I wear the subdued colors, like a lemon yellow or light peach, none of the bright pink or blues, but I will wear them here. People love them, say they are beautiful. There are just days that I'll feel Indian when I wake up. Or, I know that I'm going to my in-laws' or I'm going to a music lesson that evening, and I'll want to wear something Indian just because I feel like it. Or, it's a particularly special day or religious day or something like that. On Diwali I think I wore one.

When I replied that others refused to wear such clothes, she went on to say:

> I am my own little island here. I've got my nurse, my medical assistant, my receptionist. And, it's me. I disagree—I think that we all bring a lot of ourselves into the workplace. I love sharing my culture. That's not the reason I wear it. I wear it because I'm comfortable in it. I try not to be offensive. That's why I don't wear the really bright colors. You don't want to stand out and be flashy. But, there's no reason why you can't wear a lemon yellow and look just summery.

> *Q: Would you wear it to an IANA event?*
> It would depend on what the event was. If it was at a bar, no. It doesn't go with that kind of scene. I wouldn't wear it to the baseball game. Going to a Western bar to socialize in a Western manner, no. Work doesn't feel that "American" to me. It's my profession, but it's still who I am; it's not what I'm doing. This is part of what I do everyday, all the time. If I only came here once in a while, I doubt I would wear something Indian.

Jyoti was the exception that proves the rule of conformity to domain codes. Even though work is a "Western" space for most interviewees, it was not for her. Indian Americans have a public status as competent doctors, and so by wearing ethnic dress she was not necessarily threatening her professional image. Because of her particular institutional setting, she had the authority to define the workplace cultural code as she liked, in a non-Western way, and so publicly to assert her heritage (Fine 1996; Nippert-Eng 1996).[13] A bar, on the other hand, was a different story (i.e., code).

Sylvia criticized the notion of wearing ethnic clothes or speaking an ethnic language to co-workers, yet she displayed her ethnic values in the workplace in other ways that seemed more natural to her. She worked in an ethnically diverse hospital, with first-generation immigrant nurses, and was in charge of her hospital floor. She spoke of her unconscious "personality change" when addressing Asian Americans:

And the very fact that when I see an Asian, I have a tendency to bow when I say hello or goodbye. And especially if they are Korean, I even respond to them in Korean. And it is very unusual for my staff to see me do that. And I was, you know, questioned, "Do you notice that you bow when you move around." I was like, you know, I wasn't intending to, but it just happens because I'm just accustomed to doing that. And my personality changes when I am talking with an Asian than, say, an American, even in the workplace. I respond in the very fact that he's an older person or she's an older woman. I am not going to talk to them like I talk to a Caucasian friend or even a woman of the same age.

Q: *Do you ever get concerned that you should try to be more like other co-workers.*
No, because [the other nurses] see me as more Americanized than Korean, because maybe they know that I was born and raised here. They feel like I've assimilated or I've become . . . I'm American. So it's a little different in the very fact that they can't judge me in that same way, not because I'm lacking in my English or lacking in my experience, because I grew up here. I'm more so than some of the others who've immigrated here.

With more authority and American cultural capital than her peers, she had more leeway in how she presented herself and so could switch to a Korean style of interacting without repercussions. Her status at work protected her from the negative implications of acting ethnic in a public yet subtle manner.

Public Expressions and Mobility

Expressions became even more overtly public as actors found ways to advance their mobility within the multicultural workplace. Because Asian Americans already appear as ethnic employees, informants hoped to use that to their advantage, rather than presenting it only in benign ways. Interviewees believed that elements of the model-minority stereotype, in particular Asians' work ethic and head for numbers, and the current push for diversity at work could benefit Asian Americans and possibly help break the glass ceiling. So they hoped to be read as racial employees in this manner (Ho 2003). They felt that they had to come across both as properly "Asian"—that is, as intelligent, hardworking employees—and as "American"—that is, communicative, up to date with current styles, and not passive. They accomplished the latter by censuring ethnic displays and public interactions with co-ethnics that would further their image as cultural foreigners. To achieve the former, they highlighted the "Asian" qualities of a strong work ethic and their ability to bring in co-ethnic clients. The ability to act on one's marginal status while supporting an employee status represents another instance of a lived hybridity.

Because they were in Dallas, a disproportionate number of Asian Americans worked in the telecommunications and computer industry. They have stood out as competent yet may still encounter a glass ceiling (Fernandez 1998). Nevertheless, interviewees believed that they would face fewer handicaps in this field than in others given Asian Americans' strong representation. As Laura said:

> I think it might even be a plus, just to be Asian. In an environment where it's especially IT, they automatically assume sometimes that Asians are good programmers or whatever because predominantly, you go into that major and you will see predominantly Asians there, you know. So, it could probably work for the best.

Sanjay even commented that he likely received an easier time getting hired because he was seen as an ethnic employee:

> The educational background is known. And I think that [in] the overall industry I'm in, technology, Indians are seen as the forefront. You got a whole lot of talent out there: software developers, hardware, entrepreneurs. Indians go across the ranks. People attribute some competence [to you] without looking at [your] paper résumé. The managers and directors see that I will see it through, and I think being Indian may have something to do with that.

Respondents prided themselves on having attained their success via merit (as opposed to those who supposedly rely on set-aside programs), yet many were happy to receive assistance based on the model-minority stereotype because they saw it as well-deserved for Asian Americans generally. Samantha commented:

> Most people know Asians are hardworking. My parents could have gone on welfare, and they didn't. You have to admire that. The stereotype will follow you. The stereotype of being smart, work hard, always valedictorian of class. If that image follows you, you can't help it. [*Laughs*]

Worth noting is her choice of words: that most people "know" rather than "think" that Asian Americans work hard.

Asian Americans have tried to use stereotypes to their advantage and to demonstrate those "Asian" traits that suited organizational goals and thus advanced their own mobility. James illustrated this effort with a quote in chapter 1: by wearing glasses as props to portray himself as "Asian" and as "good with numbers," and then donning contacts on the weekends. In the process he acted on multiple identities simultaneously despite their assumed contradictions. He in effect reversed the expectation and acted Asian at work and American at home. Gautum, quoted earlier, enjoyed appearing as an Indian American doctor while he avoided other displays of his ancestry. This image may continue to mark actors as racially apart but it did so in a way that fit the workplace goal of promoting productivity as well as the capitalist role of Asian Americans as high-skilled laborers (Ong, Bonacich, and Cheng 1994).

Along with positive racial images, individuals considered the current stress on diversity in the workplace to help them and other minorities (Kim 2004). Many were glad to benefit from this trend. Alice said she and an African American co-worker spoke of the shifting impact of being a woman of color today:

> Historically ethnicity has been a constraint, but now we see it could benefit us because the business world realizes that to be successful, you need to integrate a diverse group of people in terms of ethnicity and gender.

Anu typically avoided an "Asian" image at work unless she could benefit from the cultural capital that came along with being "ethnic" in some circles, referring not to the model-minority stereotype but to her cultural ancestry (Bourdieu 1984). She was quoted earlier as not finding ethnicity relevant at work and said that she would not discuss her ethnicity with co-workers. She even skipped the question on surveys regarding ancestry:

> There's a rule, an unspoken rule that you do not discuss your personal life [at work]. I think it's different in Dallas, and I think it's different in New York City. Especially when you're in a fairly senior, high-profile position, you do not discuss your personal life [in New York City]. . . . When I fill out applications at work, I do not fill that out. Well, I mean, why are you putting more variables into play if you don't have to? As a businessperson you're focused on the bottom line, and you're focused on business [, not ethnicity].

She would not accentuate her background

> unless it benefits [me] in some way. I mean if you're working at a firm and one of the partners is a man, and he's very much into his Indian culture, and he talks about it because you have something in common and that can open the door for you, yeah. But I certainly wouldn't do it for any other reason.

Her decision of whether and how to display her heritage rested partly on the domain schema. In a twist of the informal network that keeps minorities out of management, Asian Americans could imagine using ethnicity to connect with certain managers. Although respondents are often emotionally commit-ted to their ethnicity, their decision to act on it at work could stem also from an interest in obtaining resources.

Informants believed that they could advance their mobility by acting "Asian" outside company doors as well. Organizations framed Asian Ameri-cans as explicitly ethnic workers when they could tap into niche markets, as seen in the diversity seminars, or draw upon special talents. Because the Ko-rean American and Indian American communities are growing segments of Dallas, Asian Americans often were hired to break into them. Richard, an insurance salesman to small businesses, said his firm expected him to take over the Korean American market in Dallas, given the group's dispropor-tionate number of small businesses. He spoke proudly of how the company had recently hired an Indian American manager and given money to Asian American events:

> Just a cultural thing where they pursue that market, the Indian market in Dallas–Fort Worth. I think some of my trainers and managers, they want to know more about how they could help me better, how to better get out in the community. They want to see me get better. I guess. Like last night, there was an Asian Small Business Association awards banquet. Our manager paid for half of the table, and we had to pick up the rest. He didn't have to do that. He did it to get our name out there and [create] more awareness.

At a job fair hosted by the Asian American Small Business Association in Dallas, national companies actively solicited bilingual and bicultural Asian Americans to serve as ethnic ambassadors. Recruiters expressed hope that such individuals could earn more business by building trust with their ethnic group in the region.[14] One even handed out chopsticks with her company's name printed on them. Ethnicity and the model-minority stereotype, then, could help Asian Americans to gain a foothold in the workplace, although not necessarily to break through the glass ceiling.

Participants did more than promote the image of Asian Americans for themselves. They wanted to hire Asian Americans when possible and go into business with them because of their minority background. Joshi worked for an Internet start-up:

> The one person I hired is a Vietnamese gentleman from Kansas. . . . [He] offered a kind of fresh perspective, and that is what kind of attracted me to his capabilities. The people that come to the table, the Caucasians, they are not used to dealing with limited resources. When I look at people succeeding in Silicon Valley, it's no

surprise to me that it is all the ethnic groups, because they have grown up with having to make do, to create a lot. Every company is going to be led by an Indian or Korean or Chinese.

Mahiya managed a clothing store:

> You know, Asians work a little bit harder. I see my Vietnamese girl, and my Filipino girl, even my Hispanic girls, they work hard. I mean, my Vietnamese girl actually can, will work nine to nine, and she never gets tired. The reason I hire them is because they have the same ethics as me. Because I've been in other stores and I've seen, you know, laziness.

The fact that their ethnic-minority stereotype suggested a higher productivity allowed them to publicly act on it at work, by hiring Asian Americans, without breaking the domain schema. Importantly, they did not say that they wanted to work with Asian Americans because of shared cultural preferences, such as placing priority on family, enjoying spicy foods, and so on, which is a basis of public camaraderie that many avoided, unlike when in the private sphere (see chapters 6 and 7). Like the companies that actors worked for, these informants saw other immigrants as ethnic workers, that is, as people whose ethnic and racial background would influence productivity. Framed in this way, participants strategically brought their ethnicity and race into the public realm rather than compartmentalizing it to the private domain.

As we go from the corporate sphere to more creatively oriented occupations, actors' displays change as well. Individuals fit their expressions of diversity (or lack thereof) to the domain schema. Teachers and others whose job responsibilities include relaying culture face different institutional expectations than do those in the for-profit sphere (Lamont 1992), and they were both more expected and had more opportunity to express their ethnic identities publicly while supporting workplace goals. A few teachers used public cultural shows to introduce students to their ethnic backgrounds. Meena, as quoted in chapter 3, dressed in ethnic clothing to commemorate Diwali. Her willingness to wear this attire publicly contrasted sharply with Gautum's attitude toward publicly displaying even sandals. Similarly, Mary frequently discussed the benefits of multiculturalism with her mostly White junior high school students. She told students that people may have surface differences in skin color, language, foods, and so on, but all are Americans and should unite as such:

> I wonder if my kids will be sick of the topic [of multiculturalism]. I think it is good that they are exposed to it, though. I always present it in the sense that "this is America." It is the whole idea that we are Americans and we are all in this

together. Last year I had a saying that we all smile in the same language. I think it is neat that the kids are exposed to someone of color teaching American history.

These teachers are rewarded for appearing not as standard employees nor even as "bridges" between two cultures, but as "ethnic natives," the image those in the corporate sphere wanted to avoid for fear of hitting the glass ceiling. Yet, instead of talking about substantial differences or tensions between countries, popular multiculturalism frames intergroup differences as only skin deep and assumes that everyone ultimately has the same beliefs (Fish 1998). Although Meena put on a cultural show, she still avoided talking of more personal aspects of her background to most co-workers, as quoted earlier, because they do not fit the standard multicultural norms of acknowledging groups' superficial differences only.

CONCLUSION

The workplace is changing to encourage more diversity, with increasing numbers of seminars and anti-harassment trainings. Despite these efforts, it can remain a White, male-dominated space. Workers of all backgrounds face tensions, yet Asian Americans noted ethnic, racial, and gendered types of resistance.[15] In addition to perceiving their background as relevant, they also encountered frequent questions about it. Asian American professionals' deviance from the established workplace culture made them somewhat uncomfortable and concerned about their mobility (Cheng 1996). At the same time, the white-collar workplace actively, not only subtly, framed minorities as ethnic employees in narrow ways when such a point of view supported company goals, which makes the workplace not a true "mainstream" arena either in practice or in theory (Waldinger 2003). Social-structural integration, then, is a far cry not only from acculturation, but also from full occupational assimilation.

In reaction, Korean and Indian Americans did not simply compartmentalize their identities into separate spheres and hope to totally avoid being recognized as ethnic minorities, as is commonly assumed. They constructed themselves as "proper" workers not only despite but also partly based on their marginal status, while staying within the domain code. They found ways, at times unanticipated, to express their marginal identities while conforming to the workplace's mainstream-oriented assumptions. Their efforts often resulted in a lived hybridity in which contradictory identities were attended to simultaneously rather than only in separate spheres or times (which participants also did). It is helpful to see how everyday behaviors constitute a lived hybridity because that indicates actors' agency in moving past dichotomous notions of place and identity to create more comfortable lives that blend private and public elements. As the domain code changed, so did their displays. Participants' efforts involved more than endorsing the model-minority stereotype and required sensitivity to local conditions. A domain-based analysis sheds light on the cultural and social constraints causing tensions for minorities at work and on how they decide on remedies.

Korean and Indian Americans furthered their integration as employees while still maintaining salient ethnic and racial boundaries, which has a number of implications. The effects on respondents' adaptation and stratification of their ability to manage multiple identities with a lived hybridity are discussed in chapter 8, as are the implications of Asian Americans' experiences at work for our conceptions of the significance of race and of how race functions. Standard measures of inequality do not necessarily capture the effects of race. In addition, Asian American professionals succeeded in promoting their ethnic and racial identities in an often unwelcoming space rather than assimilating, yet it is important to note that they were not resisting the hegemonic values in the capitalist workplace of prioritizing company productivity or corporate-sanctioned multiculturalism. They saw little reason to oppose the domain schema given their investment in the white-collar workplace and the belief, discussed in chapter 4, that hard work would lead to success, as they had seen in their communities, heard from popular discourse, and experienced in school. They acted, at times boldly, within this cultural logic to advance their need for comfort and mobility. In other words, they hoped to appear as Asian but not too Asian. Yet simply by conforming to the domain code, they could exacerbate their chances for mobility (this will be discussed in chapter 8 as well). The need to balance identities was not simply a matter of bringing their ethnicity and race into the "American" sphere of the workplace. Their adaptation depended also on how they acted on their identities in private. I will take this topic up in the next chapter.

6

Aspiring to Authenticity
The Home Domain

GIVEN THE CHALLENGES that the second generation faced in feeling comfortable at work, one would imagine that they would express themselves as they wished in their homes. But even there identity displays are rarely the sole choice of agents. How did the second generation conceive of this "marginal" space and balance identities in the home? The chapter addresses the broader point of how people attempt to attain the "best of both worlds" when those worlds feel as if they collide, a particularly salient problem in the home sphere. Also, how do their race, class, and, in particular, gender shape their experiences in this realm? I discussed in chapters 3 and 4 how Korean Americans' and Indian Americans' racial and ethnic status contributed to their interest in a strong cultural identity. It is important to see how people actually experience and respond to the ethnic social identity in context.

The home is an especially significant site of identity management. It supposedly offers a space where individuals can reveal their "true" selves, in privacy and away from the gaze of others (Somerville 1997). The search for a sense of home, a sense of support, also has been well documented in Asian American fictional literature and theater (Kondo 1996). Because Asian Americans appear as perpetual outsiders, they need a space of belonging. In addition, the politics of family forms a backdrop to the tensions actors felt in this domain. Children's economic attainments measure the moral worth of a family, notably of the mother. A poor economic showing signals a poor upbringing, as seen in the now infamous "Moynihan Report" and its critique of the Black family and mother in particular (Steinberg 1989). Asian American families, because of their image as a model minority, have received the opposite criticism of being sometimes *too* smart (see chapters 2 and 3). The image of the Asian American home, much like that of the ethnic enclave, suggests a private, mysterious space with dubious "smells" and potentially suspicious cultural practices and motivations. Asian Americans, especially women, feel pressured to facilitate the economic success of the next generation through a strong ethnic environment, while appearing sufficiently American in order to avoid the racialized impression of their homes as *too* Asian.

I argue that instead of informants' homes (both apartments and houses) being a shelter from others' demands, informants felt obligated to create a "proper" domestic environment, even when living on their own. What "proper" involved depended on the home domain code. This code, based on respondents' experiences, meant reproducing an ethnic setting, guided by the examples of one's family. This would set the stage for one's own "ethnic family" and so assure both moral and economic achievement for the next generation, fulfilling the politicized role of the family. It was not despite but rather because of their integration that participants wanted to maintain a semitraditional home life. Far from being a natural or organic process, interviewees—women especially—went out of their way to construct such a space. At the same time, they remained committed to what they defined as contrasting "American" interests that could prevent them from being "too Asian."[1] They accomplished this within both cognitive decision-making processes and in physical actions. Although the notion of "Asian" as traditional and constraining versus "American" as liberated and autonomous masks the heterogeneity and contradictions within cultures, respondents read their preferences in a dichotomous manner. They felt guilty when they sacrificed one identity for another, in particular when they did not live up to the home cultural schema.

This chapter explains the tensions interviewees, in particular women, felt between their self-defined ethnic and American lifestyles. It gives significant attention to how they made these categories overlap both psychologically and in practice, even at times simultaneously, as suiting a lived hybridity. The result is an inventive definition of adulthood that accepted many (not all) parental preferences and the domain schema but also self-perceived American interests. Actors did not fit into one box or the other, even as they spoke of the "Asian" versus "Western" dichotomy as real. The ability to psychologically blend lifestyles together can have unexpected implications on individuals' adaptation and actually create a deeper perceived commitment to a group identity than is exhibited in practice. I explain this forging of a distinct "ethnic

American" adulthood by first discussing the cultural objects and symbols that informants used, or wanted to use, in their homes, which helps illustrate the cultural schema of this domain. I then discuss how individuals tried to reconcile various lifestyles as they made major life-course decisions.

OBJECTS AND LANGUAGE

This section begins to establish the code of this domain and informants' reactions to it, which other sections elaborate on, by referring to the cultural symbols expected in the home. One's decorations signify much about a person, including one's membership in a wider community and one's upbringing (Bourdieu 1984; Gram-Hanssen and Bech-Danielsen 2004). Home became a "front stage," that is, a space for participants to publicly display to others and to themselves an environment reminiscent of how they grew up (Goffman 1959).[2] To accomplish this actors needed to construct a proper theatrical set composed of objects from their homeland, even if they did not understand their significance. They blended together the expectations of the home code and other aesthetic tastes shaped by their upbringing in the United States.

The older and farther along a participant was in his or her life course, the more thought he or she had given to an ethnic family and the more ethnic decorations he or she had. I visited three single men's apartments, both Korean American and Indian American, to conduct interviews, and none of them had visible ethnic markers. There were sports paraphernalia, such as a poster of Michael Jordan, non-ethnic artwork, kitchens with a few supplies, couches, chairs, televisions, video games, and stereos. Still, many who were recently married or single and lived on their own had one or two ethno-national items and claimed to want more. For instance, James and his wife had few decorations of any kind in their home.

> Just pictures of families. We went to Cancun for our honeymoon, so there is Mayan stuff. My father actually has a room in his house that is decorated definitely Korean, from making it look like it has paper doors. It is like a traditional Korean home. I thought it would really look great. Maybe have one room in my house.

If and when James purchases ethnic items, he wants to replicate what he grew up with rather than choose just any set of cultural objects, as suiting the domain schema. I also visited the homes of three male interviewees who were married to co-ethnics and who had children. Fitting their life-course position, they had numerous ethnic items. For example, the home of one such Indian

American man had wall hangings of framed woven Hindu religious scenes and an Indian rug. He and his family had just finished eating Indian food for dinner (and offered me some of it). A Korean American married father had a Korean dining table, vases, and artwork. The few homes I visited of participants who lived with their parents, all Indian American, had Indian rugs, woven wall hangings of religious scenes, pillows with miniature mirrors sewn into them, and other ethnic decorations. One such individual, Gautum, complimented his parents' tastes and wanted to replicate them when he and his wife eventually bought their own place. "My parents have done a good job of not decorating their house too Indian-y and not too Westernized where there are no representations of our culture. Our house will be a mixture like this."

Participants did not keep everything in their culture that they had been exposed to, but prioritized that which connected them to their upbringing and fit their personal preferences. As Lakshmi said:

> Cultures overlap all the time in nearly everything. In how you dress, such as dressing American but wearing Indian jewelry. In the way you handle yourself, how you speak. There are different words in my vocabulary. That's just who I am. I can express myself better with this jewelry. American jewelry—I haven't found anything that captures me. Gold bangles are much more me than a bracelet. Because, I don't know if this is totally it, but this is how I grew up, this is how my mom dressed me. I had all that American jewelry at some point, in high school, but then threw it away.

Interviewees did not imagine having total freedom in this domain. But they still did not need to adopt a prepackaged notion of how to construct an ethnic lifestyle and so sacrifice their other interests, in this case Lakshmi's preference for Western clothes to accompany Indian jewelry, resulting in a lived hybridity. Commonplace symbols such as bracelets represent a type of identity in this domain, especially when contrasted with "how my mom dressed me." The consumption of cultural objects serves as a common way of affirming a group identity (Purkayastha 2005).

Informants also picked up implicit cultural habits that they saw in their ancestry. Alice stressed the importance of eating Korean food, following the practices from her upbringing.

> My parents didn't really share or express Korean culture with us often. . . . When we ate dinner, we ate together as a family. Now that we've grown up we eat at different times, but growing up we ate together. It's fun—you share what was going

on during the day. Time spent with your family. . . . [Eating Korean food is] the same way that my mother and grandmother did it.

Actors' choices, then, represent a confluence of multiple interests that still attend to the domain code.[3]

Although participants had some flexibility in which symbols they displayed in the home domain, practically all believed that speaking their parents' native language was essential to affirm ties to parents. Otherwise, communication with one's ancestors, especially for Korean Americans, would be limited, which in turn would negate the home domain as a space to pass on a sense of family. Many spoke in their ancestral tongue with their parents or grandparents, with varying degrees of proficiency. Peter, a married father, said, "My wife and I speak Korean at home. Both [sets of] in-laws are Korean, so [the children] get Korean bombarded on them all the time." Sanjay, on the other hand, said of his Hindi skills, "I don't know it. I used to know it but it's gone downhill." A few others had no knowledge of their parents' language at all.

Those informants who did not speak their parents' language felt guilty that they were losing ties to family. They used "identity talk" to redefine the essential meaning of their ethnicity, so as to still uphold the home schema despite their acculturation. Identity talk, through what one says, is a form of identity work, that is, one's rejection or embrace of a prescribed social identity.[4] I use this analytical tool in a slightly different manner than that of boundary work. Identity talk refers to statements people make to affirm identity commitments psychologically, while boundary work refers to physical behaviors that indicate an observable, not simply (or even necessarily) articulated, difference between groups. What we find here is that participants stated a commitment to certain elements of their ethnic background instilled by their parents and engaged in boundary work to affirm those elements. The result allows them to stay committed to multiple lifestyles rather than feeling that they must sacrifice one for the other. Tammy felt guilty for lacking proficiency in Korean and having limited communication with her parents. When I asked her what cultural elements of her heritage she cared about, she replied:

Language, especially because that's how I communicate with my parents. There's a lot [of] stuff that they say that I don't get the gist of. When they talk to me they use a lot of English so I can understand. And again, my parents watch Korean videos, and I can't really do that because there's so much that I miss. Being able to write my mom a Christmas or birthday card in Korean and not "Happy Birthday Mom" [would be nice]. And you know, that's ridiculous.

Yet, as she discussed her ethnic identity further, she went on to say:

> No matter where I am, I'll always be Korean. Some of the things [about being Korean American] I won't lose [if I move away from home]. I would lose my language, but I wouldn't lose my work ethic, my respect for elders. There are certain things my parents have instilled in me that are part of my character.

As Swidler (2001) argues, we choose between cultural repertoires (i.e., sets of knowledge, skills, and symbols) so as to pursue our needs within specific settings and situations. Within the "tool kit" of what being Korean means, Tammy used identity talk to select a definition that she could practice, namely the generic values of working hard and respecting elders. For her, this addressed the problem of not speaking Korean. It is not a coincidence that she highlighted those elements that her "parents have instilled," since these are central in recreating an ethnic family. She brought her identities together, albeit not simultaneously, in a way that attended to the domain schema. At the same time, the ability to choose among possible cultural repertoires with which to define her ethnicity arguably facilitated her integration. She felt attached to an ethnic boundary despite her limited knowledge of its symbols. For instance, she may not have found it necessary to learn Korean because she considered herself tied to her community through adherence to desired values (to be discussed further in chapter 8). As the rest of this chapter demonstrates, identity talk along with boundary work was a strategy many actors used to feel that they had satisfied the expectations of a certain lifestyle.

We see the impact of the home code on how informants decided to use cultural objects and talk about symbols. The chapter goes on to explain how they dealt with the code as they considered the need to behave "American" by acting as an independent individual with personal autonomy (Hasnat 1998; Kang 2002). They brought their marginal and mainstream lifestyles together despite the perceived incompatibility between them. In the process they continued their own version of adulthood, even as they understood the binary between "ethnic" and "American" as real. To be a "true" Indian or Korean, one must live with one's parents, marry someone one's family prefers, and maintain traditions as one rears one's own children. These expectations, as well as others placed principally on women, were the most emotionally resonant for informants in the domain.

LIVING WITH ONE'S PARENTS

Parents trusted unmarried interviewees, even as adults, to live at home if they did not need to move out for employment or marriage, as is common in

Korea and India, especially when the first generation grew up. Most of those respondents whose parents lived in the Dallas area resided in their parents' homes. A few framed this decision as both ethnically distinctive and similar to moving out, which kept them from appearing un-American and resolved any contradiction between their value sets. John explained why he lived with his mother, brother, and sister-in-law:

> Even if I had the money, I don't think I would move out. That really is a cultural thing. I don't really mind living at home. It's not very restricting and what not. It's a lot cheaper.

His articulation represents a lived hybridity, in this case reconciling contradictory identities through subjective reasoning rather than physical practices. The living agreement provided him with practical and emotional advantages without entailing a loss of the freedom considered central to the American definition of adulthood.

Others, however, did not so easily bring these lifestyles together. As Rajina said:

> I've definitely gotten grief from other cultures, Caucasians, "Why are you staying at home, you're not a kid." But it's worked out for everyone. I think a lot of the things we as Indian Americans have to deal with are projected images, like you have to leave home at eighteen, you have to go out and drink and be in a frat/sorority. You know what I'm saying? And we internalize these things. But later we realize that you don't have to live your life like that. *There are other ways of being an adult.* (emphasis added)

Certain ethnic norms that challenge deeply held mainstream notions of adulthood, namely to live independently after a certain age, become stigmatized as non-American. This exacerbates a bicultural conflict for the second generation. Rajina responded to this by strongly endorsing the home cultural frame and then stereotyping the alternative as almost juvenile—linking leaving home with partying rather than as a possible mature way of performing adulthood. Because moving out signaled the privileging of an American identity over an ethnic one, a few chose to stay with their families despite wishing to live elsewhere. Kithana already felt guilty about not being "Indian" enough because she spoke only English, had few co-ethnic friends, and knew little of her ancestral history. Her face was sullen as she moaned:

> I would like to move out of my house. I know if it got bad enough, I [would] move out. Indian parents give you a lot of guilt. Last night my dad was talking to his brother, and my cousin moved back home, and my parents were like, "He has given up his whole life to take care of his mother. It's about time the son moved

home." And like, why? You had your youth, let us have ours. And you make us feel guilty about that. If I [could] overcome the guilt, I would move out.

Only a few individuals who were single and whose parents lived in Dallas had moved out. They read such a decision as fitting a mainstream lifestyle, fulfilling a rite of passage as "normal" Americans. In order to solve the problem of threatening the domain code, they accentuated certain meanings of their ethnicity that they did fulfill (Swidler 2001).[5] They formed a distinct sense of adulthood by reconciling contradictory interests as Tammy had done. This was not the product of a single action, decision, or symbol, but came about by attending to various types of practices. Samantha was proficient in Korean, had many Korean friends, and followed cultural holidays, yet decided to live on her own:

My parents weren't going to have one of their daughters moving out, but I was like, "sorry." I didn't put it in those terms, but this is my life and you have to accept it. And, the longer they live here, the more they realize there are things they're going to have to accept.

Q: *Why did you want to move out?*

All my life my parents took care of things. Even when I was living at home working, my grandmother did my laundry. Learning who I am, gaining responsibility, learning how to live on a budget, freedom. You live at home [and] you don't pay for rent, food. You don't really realize living [with]in your means. I know I hurt my parents when I moved out, but it's something I have to do and something I need to learn. But, they learn[ed] to accept it. . . . The Koreanness is something I hold on to. I still talk to my parents, still do things for them. I don't do as much because I'm not there all the time. I still take my mom to the grocery store, read some mail for them, go home for birthdays.

She insisted on "learning who I am" in an American manner, defined as "freedom," but she affirmed her ethnic social identity in other ways. As was common for informants, she engaged in identity talk to accentuate certain meanings of being ethnic that tied her to family, as well as boundary work to act on those meanings.

Some who moved away from their parents relied on future hopes rather than on current actions to balance perceived conflicting roles. For example, David seemed trapped in frustration between his current way of life and a traditionally Korean one:

The way to get rid of that tension is that I should be doing things that are Korean, and I seem instead to be doing things that are American. But I am doing Korean things, but in a different way.

He elaborated on this "different way":

> Some people could argue that [look] how American he is, he left home. Yeah, that shows I'm American, but [it] doesn't take away from the point that when I have a family, I'll provide for them. I moved out [of my parents' home] because I'm an adult. If my parents were in dire straits, then I would consider living at home and using my money for rent. But they're OK, they're getting by. If it boiled down to something like that, I would move home. . . . I prefer to marry a Korean. It would keep at least some of my culture together. We'll both be Korean and know what our backgrounds are. Plus, my parents can always teach the kid Korean.

Participants drew a line in the cultural sand, such as out-marrying or not taking care of elderly parents (Pyke 2000). As long as they did not cross that line, they would satisfy the home script. Such intentions moderated fears of being assimilated. David's psychological bridging of identities, however, could further his integration, because it rationalized his departure from home.

Those interviewees who left their parents' homes in other cities to move to Dallas did so for work and, to a lesser extent, educational opportunities. Such decisions did not suggest a disregard for family, because parents had pushed both their daughters and sons to gain advanced degrees and white-collar employment.[6] In fact, leaving one's parents' home for a good job could represent a belief in, rather than disrespect for, the ethnic culture and the racial strategy to mitigate against racism by attaining a respected class status (see chapter 3). Such an interpretation allowed individuals to stay cognitively and emotionally committed to an ethnic lifestyle even as they left their family. As seen in these examples, respondents did not always affirm either a purely Americanized or a purely ethnic profile of adulthood, but often sought ways to accomplish both.

MARITAL EXPECTATIONS

In signifying one's commitment to the home code, decisions over how to decorate one's house and where to live paled in comparison to whom one married. Marriage shapes future ethnic boundaries more than do other measures. A quarter of respondents were married, all to co-ethnics. Heterosexual marriage was expected within both ethnic communities, with gay unions considered antithetical to the dominant image of both ethnic groups (Lee 1998; Shah 1995). No one in the second generation, all professed heterosexuals, claimed a desire not to get married. Marriage fits within the home domain because couples form homes together and also because actors viewed it as a family issue, not simply a personal decision. Diasporic communities often have rules about how to create an ethnic family: one should give birth while in wedlock to a co-ethnic in order to produce not simply a child who reflects one's nationality but to affirm an ethnic boundary: a community comprised of "moral" individuals who abide by set norms of behavior (Anthias and Yuval-Davis 1989). This section explains, first, why most individuals wanted to marry a co-ethnic, and then, how they pursued that while maintaining a sense of biculturalism.

Why Choose a Co-Ethnic

Practically all in the second generation wanted to in-marry in order to be with someone who would be racially similar, who would get along well with their families, who cared about education, and who grew up balancing competing identities.[7] Such a marriage also would facilitate recreating a semitraditional setting within which to start their own families and raise children proud of their "marginal" status. Yet, actors who were fluent in their culture, often those in the traditional-community category (see chapter 3), wanted more than simply a co-ethnic partner. Linda spoke without regret of her friends' collective decision to narrow their dating circle to someone proficient in Korean as they began to consider marriage:

> Up until we graduated from college we felt it was okay to date other nationalities, but once we graduated college and we knew marriage was coming up, we decided never to date another nationality except Koreans. I was even told dating and marriage is totally different from being friends with somebody. Therefore, you can be friends with anybody and be open to anyone, but when it comes to dating and marriage you shouldn't. It's for good reasons. Children. Parents were a huge issue. If my parents don't speak English, how am I going to have my wife or husband relate to their in-laws?

"Parents were a huge issue" in this domain, as fitting its schema.

Indian Americans, unlike Korean Americans, have regional differences of language, religion, food, and customs, which many considered when making marriage decisions. Samit noted:

> Ideally I'd like to marry a Gujurati. Language is a big deal, but that's not the biggest deal. I think all of the aspects of the culture are slightly different: language, religion, whatever other things go with it.

Mohit similarly prioritized language in choosing a partner:

> Like, for instance, like my dad's brother, he married an Italian lady, so I have three cousins I hardly know. They don't speak a word of Gujurati. So even, like,

little things they just don't get. Like, this is not just for me. Because when I am in a family, it is family. Everyone knows how to speak Gujurati.

A group of people united by blood still would not be a "family" for Mohit, who grew up speaking Gujarati and expected the same for his children.

Although they were interested in a prospective spouse's ancestry, the second generation also cared that partners expressed "Americanized" interests. As Rick said:

I couldn't marry someone from Korea who wasn't Westernized. Language—my language skills aren't great; Westernized mindset—more independent and ambitious and sarcastic sense of humor.

He wanted to maintain a sense of heritage but still stereotyped recent immigrants as lacking social skills, being too conservative in their tastes, wearing unfashionable clothes, and not understanding American colloquialisms. The marital decision brought to the forefront the desire to balance contending interests. These challenges, and participants' attempts to resolve them, speak to the broader issue of how to satisfy competing sets of expectations in regard to a highly emotional issue.

Negotiating Expectations

Second-generation Indian and Korean Americans entertained what they saw as two competing philosophies of marriage: a traditional ethnic perspective of finding the most appropriate match in terms of ethnic and class statuses, versus the more Western, romanticized notion of falling in love with someone regardless of either background or parental opinion (Dasgupta 1998). Interviewees interpreted their experiences in this binary manner, even though these notions are social constructions (Swidler 2001). Women in particular felt stricter parental expectations and so more possible tension. Yet, interviewees also broke down this supposed dichotomy and negotiated between these expectations.[8] When research focuses exclusively on the marital decision itself, as often is the case, actors' real identities may be misrepresented because more complicated cognitive processes may be obscured. We first see this in how actors decided whom to marry.

Whom to Marry   Most participants said explicitly that they wanted to satisfy their parents, as suiting the home domain. Practically all parents told the second generation to marry a co-ethnic, though some had stricter expectations than others (Purkayastha 2005). Parents were central actors within the home domain and therefore had more influence on marital decisions than on other life-course choices, such as one's career. Deciding to follow parental wishes often feels like giving up something and can be a painful process (Maira 2002). Participants used two tactics to satisfy their multiple preferences. They maintained self-defined "American" interests by speaking of their readiness to pursue their own marital choices, even as they sought ways to satisfy their parents. They also broadened the boundary of their ethnicity while staying within its general meaning, so as to allow more flexibility in their options. The act of talking itself created a lived hybridity because it simultaneously provided an outlet for an American identity without leading to behavior that likely would violate the home schema. This helped actors forge their own path to adulthood, for they satisfied their parents as a first priority but in ways that gave them more freedom and so could be communicated well to other Americans and not appear foreign.

Jennifer kept open the possibility of marrying a non-Korean American, even as she dwelled on reasons to in-marry, especially as a minority in Texas:

> When I was growing up, my father was adamant: "You must marry a Korean." He's like, "Better not marry a non-Korean." I really took it seriously, like I felt like if I didn't marry a Korean guy, I would literally break my dad's heart. . . . You know, I'll tell you right now, I could totally marry someone non-Korean. I could totally marry this blond-haired guy and be like, wow, what happened? I'm open to that, but I would say I want to marry some Korean, and I want him to look like me, and I want my children to look like me. In California you see many, many, many, many interracial couples. It's not even a big deal, you know? I think [in] Texas—you see that too, but people stare. I think there are a lot of uphill battles even now to marrying outside your race. I think you should marry the person that's your soul mate, you know, regardless of race. . . . I want to marry a Korean because it's sort of natural, and I'm more inclined that way anyway. Plus, it would make my parents happy. I've never had to face a situation where I was in love with somebody that my parents objected to, and I wonder how love conquers all. Would I be able to stand up to my parents? I don't know.

The tension between parents and children in choosing a partner is clearly not limited to Asian Americans, as witnessed in countless Hollywood movies. Still, the second generation interpreted it as an ethnic issue as they entertained "standing up to parents" if they fell in love with "this blond-haired . . . soul mate." Although Jennifer intended to in-marry, the act of talking about the possibility of not doing so entertained her various interests.

Participants also redefined what an "ethnic" partner meant. They broadened the meaning of the category to allow for more choice and control over the marital decision, but without necessarily threatening parental preferences. For instance, Ajay's knowledge of Indian heritage "isn't too much," but he still wanted to marry a co-ethnic, partly to satisfy his family:

> There are two reasons I'd marry an Indian. One, just because I'd probably feel more comfortable with it. But number two, to appease my parents. As far as my parents are concerned, they'd prefer a Gujarati Hindu. But for me, because I have different Indian friends, that doesn't bother me. . . . I don't know what type of Hindu I am. You know there's like the different levels. Because personally, for me, that's not a big thing. I don't even know, if somebody asked me, "What are you?" I'm not even a practicing Hindu, so I don't know why I call myself Hindu.

This articulation of ethnicity in terms of hard-to-measure values rather than strict religious practices allowed for more possible mates and thus more control over the marital decision, yet without threatening the ideal of in-marriage. Most Indian American informants thought religion brought them closer to their nationality, and they intended to marry within their religious boundary. Yet, variations within that boundary mattered less to them.

Religion had a potentially different impact on Korean Americans. For devout Christians it served as an additional limitation on whom one could marry, but it also gave them another dimension besides ethnicity to focus on when choosing a partner. James believed that his ethnicity intensified his faith, and vice versa, which made marrying a non–Korean American Christian an unlikely scenario. When I asked him if as a Korean he felt an even stronger bond to Christianity, he said:

> I would agree with that statement. I think a part of our culture, especially Korean Americans love that stuff. [Christianity] talks about Christ being the head of your family. That is really traditional in Korea. Americans stress individualism, where Korean Americans want to be a part of a group. There is a purpose behind it.

Laura spoke of a similar intersection of ethnicity and faith but gradually honed in on the latter:

> I am Korean American, but I am Christian as well. So, for me I can't separate the two because that's who I am. . . . I think being Christian influences me more than being Korean American. I can name several people who are not Christian, but their thoughts are different, you know. So, it's different. I think that [the] Christian part of my life is a lot bigger, you know. I would be the same type of

person if I was not Korean American. I have a lot of Christian friends that are not Korean, that feel a lot like me. So, I would probably relate better if you were to ask Christian or non-Christian.

Broadening the category of acceptable partners to include Christians generally gave Laura more control and independence in the marital decision but did not threaten the domain code of satisfying parents because so many Korean Americans attended church. Still, if faced with needing to defend a non–Korean American Christian, or a Korean American non-Christian, to one's parents, these informants could articulate a rationale. In order to encourage co-ethnic marriages, the EMs had "Singles Night" on Friday nights.[9] While I saw no obvious flirtation between individuals—most people associated with friends—one man confided that he attended in order to meet women.

Anu also stressed non-ethnic criteria that similarly extended the boundary of possible marital choices without challenging parental inclinations. She eventually married an Indian American systems engineer.[10] When I asked her if she had preferred to marry a co-ethnic, she replied:

Well, yes and no. I'm kind of flexible about that, and I guess my parents kind of influenced that part. What was important to me and what was important to my parents and my family: somebody who's educated and somebody who has values and [a] family orientation. And, to me personally, what was important was somebody who was driven. If it was non-Indian then, I don't know. It would have been fine for me in the long run, but. . . . [My parents would] not completely freak out but yeah, be concerned about it.

She could have her cake and eat it too by marrying a co-ethnic as encouraged by her family while prioritizing her own preference of financial potential in a partner, given the average education level of Indian Americans.[11] Actors' articulations in regard to selecting a partner allowed them to appear as following both parental prescriptions and their own independent heart and so illustrates a lived hybridity. In their approach to adulthood, they deconstructed the binary of "ethnic" versus "American" even as they felt that binary to be real.

How to Meet Someone   Given that parents had influence over whom one married, it followed that they gave input on how to find someone as well. Interviewees wanted to have authority over this process but again did not want to shut out parents completely, because doing so would violate the accepted role of Indian and Korean parents as guides in the selection of a spouse. Informants attempted to resolve this issue more or less the same way they decided whom to marry. They either talked of their agency while still seeking to fulfill the ethnic social identity, or framed the ethnic and mainstream cultural norms in finding a spouse as complementary rather than contradictory. Participants first sought to circumvent their parents' involvement by selecting a spouse on their own. As Radha said:

> I joined IANA because I thought I would meet other Indian people. I'm finally in a big city—how do I begin meeting Indian people? I won't meet them at work; my neighborhood won't have that many. And my parents were pushing me to get married, and the arranged marriage thing is hard to do from across the country.

Some interviewees who attended IANA and KAP and even EM events did so with the express purpose of meeting co-ethnic partners, which was more relevant in Dallas than in cities with larger concentrations of co-ethnics and so with more venues to meet them.

Yet, a few individuals, in particular those in the traditional-community category and who lived near their families, agreed to their family's assistance in meeting a spouse. Parents wanted a strong role in guiding the marriage of their daughters, especially, and expected daughters to marry soon after graduating college. A variety of formal and informal institutions for Asian Americans to find co-ethnic spouses have arisen, including magazine and newspaper advertisements, family connections in the homeland and in the United States, professional meetings, and recently Internet dating services. Most women objected to having ads taken out in ethnic publications and to traditional arranged marriages, since these tactics fell far outside the American norms of courtship. Yet, ethnic differences between Korean and Indian Americans surfaced again in regard to how to meet a spouse. Even though Mary had been introduced to her husband long-distance through her pastor and had met him only six times before their engagement, she remarked:

> With the Korean community [arranged marriage] happens amongst the first generation, and you will see that with the first generation that's coming over recently. But, with the second generation a lot of them seem to be very against it.

Indian Americans had a more ambivalent reaction toward such arrangements.[12] Veera spoke in a protective manner about arranged marriages even though she did not anticipate having one:

> Divorce is so accepted here. All my friends have stepbrothers and stepsisters. It's not as common [in India] as here. Arranged marriage works. You're more willing to work at it than end it. More and more people are doing the arranged marriage.

You can post a personal on sikhnet.org. I don't think it's me, but I'm not averse to it. I think a lot of kids are like, I'm twenty-four and I don't have a significant other, and I'm going to go for the arranged marriage thing. Arranged marriage is being introduced to someone by parents, and if I like it I take it from there. It's not meeting the spouse on the wedding day.

When Indian Americans highlighted their final authority in how to meet someone and an ability to take time in making a decision, they framed this strategy as relatively comparable to the standard American way and thus as acceptable.[13] Only a few participants had met their spouses through such introductions, but hardly any criticized it as the wrong way to meet someone. One participant, Jyoti, met her husband after placing an ad in a magazine, but she knew him for a year before their engagement, communicating mostly via the phone. Gautum met his wife, who lived in England before moving to Dallas to marry him, through his parents' social network. He knew her for a couple of months before the wedding. Women articulated the potential benefit in such marriages; many of their parents had met under such conditions, and they appeared happy. Few felt that arranged marriages would be detrimental to the wives.

Overall, we find that an inclination to in-marry does not constitute an unquestioned commitment to one's ethnic group. Most actors went out of their way to please their parents in choosing whom to wed and how to meet that person. Still, the second generation maintained a sense of ultimate control over the pursuit of their own personal preferences and so succeeded in psychologically balancing their divergent types of adulthood, while still prioritizing the domain code.

DATING OUTSIDE ONE'S ETHNIC GROUP

Having seen the seriousness of marital choices, it should not come as a surprise that dating, especially outside one's ethnic group, provoked strong emotions as well. Dating rarely served as a topic of conversation with one's parents, even dating a co-ethnic, because, according to interviewees, parents considered it a morally suspicious practice. Although dating is becoming more commonplace in Korea and India, parents often viewed teen relations through the same lens in which they grew up, and so they framed dating, especially for girls, as an "American" sexual practice antithetical to "ethnic" ways (Gibson 1988; Min and Kim 1999). Dating, especially dating a White person, signifies attaining a higher racial status as "normal Americans." Yet, as interviewees became more serious with partners outside their ethnic group, namely Whites, they felt that they were violating expectations to reproduce an "ethnic family." How did those informants who dated, especially outside their ethnic group, reconcile that with the domain code?

One tactic in effect denied the problem by keeping it out of the home sphere. Informants occasionally lied to parents, especially to those who most strongly disapproved of the practice. They physically kept dates away from the domain boundaries. As Tammy said:

> I have a really good White friend. Indian culture is the same way [as Korean culture]. [The White friend] can't understand why I was dating a mutual friend and he couldn't come and pick me up. He would have to bring a ring! It's just different. And she couldn't understand that. I was talking to my Korean friend, and she said, well, it's just different.

A backstage-versus-frontstage difference in self-presentation to parents served as a common boundary work strategy to maintain dual identities, especially when dating outside of the ethnic group (Dasgupta and Dasgupta 1998; Goffman 1959). This tactic also served as a means for them to maintain power over their lives relative to their parents (Leonard 1999). The second generation often bonded with one another over these experiences. According to Judy, "One of the commonalities of being a Korean American [is] having to struggle with some of the dating issues, some of the things that Caucasians didn't have to deal with." Most participants had dated by the time they had finished college.

Some hoped to resolve this tension rather than struggle through it. One strategy involved identity talk, redefining the social identity so as to allow dating. This occurred in two ways. The first was reframing parental restrictions less as a cultural divide and more as a generational one. Joshi observed:

> Our parents came here. They bottled up India and brought it here in 1950 or 1960. They have taken those values and tried to make them apply to a revolving American culture. India moved on and our parents didn't. In India everyone is dating, everyone is doing things that you would say, oh my gosh, what are you doing? It is not Indian anymore.

Dating, from this perspective, did not equal assimilation but signaled a contemporary Asian American, even Asian, mentality that had incorporated Western practices. Such interpretations let the second generation feel both comparable to "real" Americans and committed to an ethnic boundary.

The second involved stressing attributes that parents would approve of beyond ethnicity, a tactic similar to that used when interviewees were trying to gain control over their selection of a spouse. For instance, Rajeev, who was seriously dating a White woman, acknowledged that his parents would prefer he marry an Indian, but that they also valued educational achievements, which he defined as an Indian American trait. When I asked him if his parents cared more about ethnicity or education, he said, "My parents, I don't know. I think their preference is education, but I don't know." When I asked whether they would be happier with a highly educated White person or a less-educated Indian, he reflected, "That's a toss-up, but I think the well-educated Caucasian." These individuals may not be affirming the domain code in their minds, but at least they are not rejecting it. Their identity talk illustrates a relatively weak lived hybridity, for they acted "American" with their dating choice but interpreted it as somewhat—not fully—satisfying ethnic norms. The level of education a person has attained is a key predictor of marital choices (Kalmijn 1991), which means that an emphasis on scholastic achievement in order to justify interracial marriages may become more common.

It is difficult to redefine the ethnic social identity in regard to marriage that would make an out-marriage acceptable. Respondents also used identity talk to spin their actions in ways that allowed for a continued commitment to the ethnic community. For example, Joanne had been dating a White man for a few years, did not know Korean, and had few Korean American friends. She worried about being too assimilated. I asked her if she preferred not to date Korean American men. Her voice rose as she said defensively:

> To be honest it is because Korean men have never asked me out! My parents are always, "Why don't you date a Korean?" and I say it's because they never asked me out. What am I supposed to do? It wasn't a preference at all.

Rather than take full responsibility for her relationship, she pointed to external circumstances.

Not all interviewees preferred to marry a co-ethnic. If their parents did not push for such a marriage, then participants could out-marry without seriously violating the home schema. Tom was one of only two people whose parents did not strongly encourage an in-marriage or many practices of their heritage. He felt less pressure than his Korean American peers. He said of his parents:

> They would like me to marry a Korean, then if not then Asian. The pressure is less than most Korean parents. I will probably marry a Caucasian. That's the major thing; I don't know how that will go. Other traditions I won't likely keep, like mourning my grandmother every year. I didn't know her, so I don't know. I do see some significance of it. I don't know.

Women faced greater expectations in terms of dating and going out because of the symbolic and material importance of their sexuality, which led a couple of women to prefer an out-marriage. Sexually active girls, especially those involved with people outside their ethnic group, threaten the religiosity and "cultural authenticity" of their community (Alumkal 1999; Maira 2002). Parents gave daughters earlier curfews and monitored their daily behavior more often, although sons also faced restrictions. As Deepa said of her male cousin: "My cousin does not have to deal with it. He's younger to me but he gets to do a lot more than I do. Just going out in the wee hours of the night." Alice reacted against these kinds of gender hierarchies, which she witnessed in her family (Chow 2000):

> Growing up I didn't want to marry a Korean American, because my dad is so biased because that's the tradition he grew up in. Now, I would marry someone based on personality, Korean American or whatever.

One way to reconcile conflicting identities is to prioritize one over the other rather than bring them together (Heiss 1992), which she had done earlier but had recently tempered.

As discussed in chapter 4, participants expressed weak pan-ethnic and even weaker person-of-color identities, and this is seen also in their comments on marriage. They felt connected to Asian Americans because of their shared racial characteristics and (presumed) shared values of hard work and concern over family, but that did not translate into a clear inclination toward them rather than Whites as marital partners. As Samantha said about her preferences, "Everyone's equal after Korean." Other Asian Americans did not speak their native language or know traditional customs and so did not fulfill most parental preferences. Also, living in Dallas encouraged less of a pan-ethnic identity than living in California (as discussed in chapter 4), which has high rates of Asian American intramarriage (Shinagawa and Pang 1996). Still, a few Korean Americans noted that having a general physical appearance in common with Chinese Americans made them a better option, so that the children would look monoracial (Kibria 2002). Indian Americans often reported little if any interest in other Asian Americans over Whites. Indian Americans also had little interest in marrying other South Asian Americans. For instance, when I asked Radha if she would marry someone from Sri Lanka or Nepal, she gave a response I heard frequently: "No, they're no different than an American. Because of the customs and the language." Tensions following 9/11 and general prejudices against Muslims, as seen in chapter 4, also limited interest in interreligious marriages from informants (none of whom were Muslim). Even those who had little knowledge of religion, such as Ajay, quoted earlier, expressed hesitation at considering such a union. Parents often had strict restrictions, especially in regard to relationships with Muslims.

Although interviewees claimed that all groups were equally undesirable outside of their own ethnic community, they still formed a racial hierarchy in their marital leanings (Pang 1998). Korean and Indian Americans said that they would more likely marry someone who was White than either African American or Latino. Many of their parents would disapprove of bringing home members of a different minority race. As Akash said of her mother:

> To her, unfortunately, African Americans, Hispanics are not . . . she just still has
> a bias toward them. I think [my parents] would prefer, if I was going to marry
> a non-Indian, that it would be American, just because I think their bias is still
> there.

The ethnic groups equated "American" with White, that is, with the majority, with which neither native-born minorities nor other immigrants fit. Given the influence of family on marital selection, as well as their own attitudes on race, participants rarely considered marrying into another racial minority group. Even those who felt somewhat tied to other people of color, as explained in chapter 4, did not feel comfortable with the idea of marrying one. The bond was more theoretical than personal.

Overall, participants mostly tried to explain behavior that challenged the home schema in ways that still affirmed a commitment to an ethnic family. This is not a story of simply contesting parental expectations that felt too constraining, as often portrayed. This serves as a caution to standard assimilationist interpretations of intermarriage as signaling a lack of ethnic attachments. Asian Americans have a higher rate of intermarriage than do other minorities, but when controlling for group size, they still prefer to in-marry (Fong and Yung 1995–1996; Qian 1997). These findings help explain this seeming contradiction. We see how individuals with emotional commitments to their background make sense of a decision to out-marry. From the previous section we also find that decisions to in-marry are not simply an embrace of an ethnic community, for many spoke of possibly out-marrying as part of how they came to accept an in-marriage. The line dividing most of those who in-marry and those who out-marry is finer than is usually assumed.

MARRIED WITH (ETHNIC) CHILDREN

Tied to second-generation Asian Americans' and their parents' interests in marrying a co-ethnic was the desire to pass on an ethnic culture to the next generation. Knowing one's heritage seemed necessary for dealing with one's marginal status. As explained in chapter 3, informants wanted themselves and their offspring to understand their "origins," in part because they would never be accepted as full Americans. Said Wendy:

> If that connection with my parents wasn't there, it would be very difficult. I have never thought of any other way of maintaining that. My peers are not as tradi-tional. I always think of Korea as being traditional. My language. Respect[ing] elders is very important.

> Q: *Why are you invested in a Korean identity?*
> I am Korean American. I don't look American, not what people think an American looks like. I will never be really American. I don't look American. I think my appearance makes the biggest difference.

Learning an ethnic culture allowed one to define one's racial and ethnic back-ground rather than have others define it in a stigmatized manner, as seen in chapter 3. Although the desire to avoid racism encouraged a few to embrace an American identity, those who had developed salient ethnic identities affirmed that boundary in response.

We see the effects of the home cultural code quite clearly on how the sec-ond generation planned on raising their children. Participants felt obligated to perform rituals and traditions in order to recreate an "ethnic" environment for the next generation which otherwise might not occur given interviewees' own integration. Whether they understood the rituals or not was less relevant. For instance, Rupu smiled as he spoke of his intent to perform rituals that he considered eccentric for his future children:

> Shave their head, yeah, I'll probably do all that stuff. I mean, it can't hurt, right? Like there are some customs that you just think that some idiot just made up and people just started doing it. And nobody knows how it started and why they're still doing it. You know, maybe some of those customs I'll probably fall back on. I actually am afraid my children won't have the same culture that I grew up with, and that's where I really want my parents to be involved in my kids' upbringing. I think your culture does make you who you are. Your ethnicity, your back-ground makes you who you are. And, you know, religion is a major part of your culture, defines what is right and wrong and stuff like that. And then I look at

Caucasians' 60 percent divorce rate, you know. There's less family problems in Indian families. It's because it's their culture that keeps them together.

Rituals represent a historic, static notion of culture that you can "fall back on" because they are always there to catch you. The inexplicability of some adds to their historic nature, and so makes them seem all the more effective in transferring an ancient culture. They link individuals to a sense of established social relations and meaning (Wuthnow 1987). Not adhering to them risked raising wayward children who would be "too American," that is, involved in drinking or drugs, disrespectful to adults, and likely to get divorced.[14]

The desire to recreate an ethnic setting for their own children led participants, even before they had children, to engage in practices that they did not understand in order to familiarize themselves with the heritage. Rajeev, who was in a serious relationship with a White woman, started up again some of the practices learned in his parents' home when he considered having children and worried about their possible full assimilation:

> We were exposed to Indian music, food. We went to India every two to three years; went to temple, puja; my parents spoke Hindi to me; my parents are really into the puja scene, jagratas and stuff like that, a lot of prayer in the house. . . . As I was getting older, I was thinking, are my kids going to have any idea of what being Indian is, especially if I marry a non-Indian? What's that going to do to a kid? Also, as you get older you have conversations about religion and are questioned on it, and you realize you didn't know as much as you thought you did. . . . I still keep fast on Tuesdays simply because of the fact that I don't do anything religious. Tuesday is something to do with Hanuman—don't eat meat. It's religious. I pray once every two weeks, out of guilt, in my head.

Other Indian Americans, as mentioned in chapter 1, also carried out home rituals that they confessed to not understanding but that they found appropriate, even necessary, in the home sphere.

Religious rituals performed outside the church made up less of a Korean American ethnic identity, but they also performed cultural, secular customs. Those who lived with or near their parents engaged in more. Korean Americans, such as Samantha, referenced poorly understood holidays with their families:

> [We] celebrate Chinese New Year; it's not just Chinese. We celebrate it because it's another holiday to eat, I guess. I don't know. We go home and celebrate with our families. Holidays that we celebrate: a parent's sixtieth birthday is important, [celebration of] a child's [first] one hundred days is important, [the] first birthday

is important. My grandmother is turning ninety this year, so that's important in any culture. My mom is traditional about these things.

She went out of her way to enact a satisfactory ethnic identity, which involved rituals that signified family.

Even when actors made their home life feel ethnic, they decided also to pass on "American" norms to their children, such as greater freedom in dating, gender equality, and communication, because these issues had caused them conflict during their upbringing (Shrake 1998). Their selectivity about what they adhered to furthered their "ethnic American" approach to adulthood. Enacting an ethnic identity in the home realm did not mean mimicking one's parents but instead following their examples when those were seen as helpful in creating a healthy cultural environment. When those examples seemed detrimental, informants planned to do otherwise. Korean Americans in particular, like Jason, often remarked on the need to be more communicative than their parents:

> I think more American families, Caucasian American families, are very open.
> I think their parents talk to their kids more openly about more personal things.
> My parents never talk [about] anything personal [to] us, my brother and me.
> They ask us questions, but they're not really prying into my business.

Relaxing, but not abandoning, these restrictions also could make one's children more open and comfortable. Mary, for instance, distinguished between timeless attributes that made sense to pass down and more generational practices, namely strict hierarchies between family members:

> Some of the holidays I would pass on. [Also worth keeping is] respect for elders, not in the sense that you need to back down on your own views because you are giving in to your elders, but in the sense that you are acknowledging that they are older and they might be more wise. Definitely something I would not teach them is the sexism that exists, for example, the way a man would treat his wife.

She also interpreted the value of respecting elders in a manner that allowed for personal autonomy. Critiquing sexism within one's ethnic community and homeland has often been equated with a pro-assimilationist stance.[15] Yet, diasporic women have written on and denounced sexist attitudes and practices within their communities without advocating the assimilation of their groups (Abraham 2000; Anzaldúa 1987; Song 1996). Most participants, both women and men, felt comfortable with slightly traditional gender roles but not with roles that were as highly differentiated as in their parents' generation.

Participants also did not mind losing those elements of one's culture that were not stressed in their own homes while they were growing up, because the home schema prioritized replicating one's ethnic family rather than one's general heritage. When I asked Sylvia which parts of Korean culture she wanted to maintain, she said:

> I guess respect for the elders. The value of hard work. The importance of the family.
>
> Q: *Are there traditions you want to maintain?*
> Not really.
>
> Q: *And that's because . . . ?*
> My parents didn't really focus on the traditional things.

Like many in the third and later generations (Tuan 1998), a few interviewees had not only modest knowledge of their ancestry but also little motivation to learn more, given their upbringing. They could fulfill their particular home script without knowing as much as others in the second generation. They had grown up in the fitting-in or family category (see chapter 3).

Even those respondents who hoped to maintain rituals did not assume that the third generation would form such salient attachments to an ethnic community as they had. They recognized that despite their intentions to practice customs and rituals, they had "lost" some of their parents' cultural norms and assumed this acculturation would only accelerate for their own children. Although rituals can teach someone what it means to be ethnic, on their own they do not sustain that connection. The third generation tends to lack contact with immigrant grandparents, that is, with "real" Koreans and Indians. Alex, who married a Korean American, said in a resigned rather than fretful manner:

> But eventually . . . the same thing that's happening now with Korean Americans is what's happened to the Catholics, the Irish, when Europeans first settled here. When I have kids, my kids are in essence going to be no different. I think in the next twenty to thirty years, there is going to be a ton of interracial marriages and offspring, and so really, over the next two to three generations, everyone is going to look alike. They are not going to be this distinct Asian face versus a Caucasian face.

When cultural barriers with Whites dissipate, intermarriage will increase. Actors' class status facilitated both this perspective, as discussed in chapter 4, and the higher rates of Asian American intermarriage with Whites than with other minorities. Class did not figure much into how actors talked of their home sphere or of their intentions for raising children, but it has implicit effects, for they credited their own economic achievements to their ethnic heritage, as seen in chapters 3 and 4 (Rudrappa 2002).[16] With such efforts interviewees hoped to raise ethnic American children who would have the best of both worlds and be able to handle their marginal status.

GENDER DIFFERENCES AND CONFESSIONS OF A "FAKE FEMINIST"

As seen already in this chapter, gender differences are paramount in the home domain. Women have the primary responsibility for making the home an ethnic setting, in contrast to men, whose encounters with the outside world of work, laws, and Western culture supposedly threaten their ethnic character and that of the family (Anthias and Yuval-Davis 1989; Chatterjee 1989). Instead of gender inequalities being simply a holdover of homeland norms, some immigrants reinforce them as a reaction to their newly racialized status within the United States (Bhattacharjee 1998; Espiritu 2003). Gender hierarchies also can result from a conservative religiosity in the United States, not simply an ethnic ancestry (Alumkal 1999). Regardless of the source, immigrant women often face stronger familial expectations than do their mainstream peers. As women attain more economic power as immigrants than in their homeland, gender relations become increasingly (not totally) egalitarian (Jo 2002; Pessar 1999). Still, women—both immigrant and otherwise—typically must perform or oversee most domestic duties regardless of their employment status (Hochschild 1989; Hurh, Kim, and Kwange 1978; Kim and Kim 1998), even when second-generation men assist in the home more than their immigrant fathers (Coltrane and Valdez 1997). This meant that female participants had to put in a greater effort than men to balance the duties of the home code with a sense of autonomy over their private lives. This involved deciding where one lived before and after marriage, how one carried out one's role in the house, and how one balanced work and family.

As mentioned earlier, parents often guided children's living and dating arrangements. Which home one lives in marks one's allegiance to the moral order, in part because of concerns over sexuality. Because women have historically been the purveyor of culture, their virginity serves as a symbol not only of their family's moral integrity, but also of their ethnic ancestry. Mothers too, not only fathers, want daughters in particular to be socially and sexually conservative (Mukhi 1998). Ailee Moon (1998) finds that Korean American parents expect more conservative sexual practices from their children than do even Koreans in Korea. Parents also expect a daughter to move in with her husband's family or at least to be more accessible to his family than they expect of the husband in return (Kang 2002). Abandoning these duties could distance them from their community. Female informants frequently bonded over these expectations. As Mary said:

> We moved in with my mother-in-law, and I joke about it. Part of it was [for] financial reasons and part of it was cultural. Because my husband is the oldest son and my mother-in-law is a widow, it is assumed that he would take care of his mother. In our church we have quite a number of only sons or oldest sons that are married and we (the married women) say that there is a "first son" or "only son" wives' club. We will talk about in-law issues and tradition, should we follow or should we not follow. I have my frustrations. [My husband has a younger brother (in his late twenties)], and traditionally there are things that the wife of the older brother will do. When I refer to him, I refer to him by a certain title, which is a title of respect. I have to use that term, and there are certain things I do for him even though I may not want to. When my mother-in-law was sick, I packed his lunch for him. On Saturday I will be throwing him a birthday party.

She had constructed an informal female community based on the double standards faced in the home. While none of these women preferred to live with their in-laws, they had agreed nonetheless to do so.

Mary's tensions at home were mild compared to Mahiya's, who separated from her husband after living with her in-laws. She spoke with great heartache of her time with her husband and his parents, which she called a "disaster":

> Disaster in the sense that they were home all day. I couldn't really have people over. We couldn't really have a social life. And they were just mean. They were very typical Indian. Like I should be cooking, which is fine. But, if I'm working all day, and she's sitting home all day, then she should cook, right? They just expected things of me that I couldn't deliver. They wanted me to speak Sindhi, which I couldn't. I tried a little bit here and there, but if I couldn't, I couldn't. I said [to my husband] why don't we just get our own place? I think everything will be fine. I was totally Americanized, you know. I'm the way I am. . . . They didn't assimilate. . . . My father-in-law didn't speak to me for ten months, not a word. And he did this in front of other people who came over, he didn't talk to me. . . . I started saving money. I think I was getting a little bit more confident in myself again. I was working [and] everybody likes me. I have money now, I don't care. I have enough to get me started. And I walked out.

Mahiya's story illustrates the troubles that result from abiding by the home code when its expectations are too severe. As she earned money, she adopted a different ideological framework that had rested in the back of her mind, not as a wife or daughter-in-law but as an independent, employed woman. Luckily, her parents and their friends and relatives accepted Mahiya back rather than blaming her for her domestic problems.

These quotes also illustrate that women were measured not only by where they lived but also by how they conducted themselves in the home. Chores, customs, rituals, and responsibilities pass from one generation to the next, so that the daughter-in-law picks up where the mother left off. As Judy said of teaching ethnic traditions to children: "I think women in general, women know more of it because it's the women that have to do most of the work in terms of tradition." Taking care of the home also meant raising the children to be middle-class citizens, as prescribed by families, religious institutions, and the broader discourse of women as caretakers. This has a special impact on minority women. Many of these college-educated women dealt with this situation by deeming it appropriate to some degree. They believed they should be able to have careers yet still be in charge of the domestic sphere. Kithana said:

> I think the man should get up and help in the kitchen a little bit, and a woman should be able to have a job. I think some differences are OK. I would laugh if I was working and the man took care of the kids.

Usha also commented:

> I think more so women, we're very nurturing people, much more than men. It's a stereotype, but that's what I believe. I think a lot of Indian men that I speak to, they want to instill those beliefs to pass on to their kids.

While some considered this imbalance appropriate because of internalized gender roles, others resented any double standard. Wendy noted: "If I was a guy I could do anything I want. If I got married, then I would not have to worry about taking care of kids, the home life." With their high employment rate and high earned incomes, many Korean American and Indian American women demanded a more (though not completely) egalitarian set of norms within the home, which men may not accept to the same extent (Park 2000).

The fact that ethnicity impacted the home domain in gendered ways meant that men and women faced different duties, not only that women faced expectations. Men felt that, in contrast to Wendy's comments, they could not "do anything" they wanted. As Richard said, being the "head of the household is very big. That's just our culture. One thing I've picked up is [that] a man has a lot of responsibilities. He picks up the family or he can bring the family down, I think." Men expected their wives to work but identified themselves as the primary breadwinners, a description with which most women agreed.[17]

Even when women and men had specific roles, women clearly had more responsibilities, which caused tensions in balancing work and family. It was not always easy to create the best of both worlds. They felt encouraged by their families to work but still had fewer options while growing up and even as adults in terms of dating, sex, and related choices (Agarwal 1991), not to mention a possibly thicker glass ceiling because of both their race and their gender (Fernandez 1998). Radha noticed that there was

> kind of a double standard: you want to raise Indian American women to be assimilated to the culture and get ahead career-wise, but when it comes to a personal level, you don't want that. Catch-22. From a career standpoint, a lot of Indian men think it's OK for you to have a career as a hobby, and that's unfortunate. Some people who are impressed that you have a career are the same ones threatened by it. And Indian men tend to be more threatened by an Indian woman who's successful than an American man [is] by an American women.

Parents' encouragement of advanced education for their daughters with the simultaneous double standard in terms of freedoms was not contradictory, at least in theory. Many women said that their parents wanted them to attain a high level of education so that they could take care of themselves if something happened to their husbands. Also, a good education made the women more "marketable" to prospective spouses and so did not take away from their duties within the home (Zhou and Bankston 1998). But women noted tensions in both pursuing their careers and being a traditional wife and mother, roles expected not only by parents but by partners to some degree. Women often bore the brunt when these two ideal worlds collided.

Those women whose mothers had worked full-time worried most about sacrificing an image as American when they considered having children, and they engaged in identity talk to reconcile this. The tension most clearly manifested itself in whether to work or stay at home after having children. According to these women, Indian and Korean women had little problem with being stay-at-home mothers, while American feminists (and White, American women generally) did not accept such roles. Even though many "American" mothers struggle with this same tension and many immigrant mothers work, interviewees conceived of it as a bicultural conflict. Actors balanced their competing expectations by searching for a meaning of feminism that fit with a decision to stay at home, at least for a short while. Even those who were not in a romantic relationship spoke of this dilemma of "career versus family" as waiting for them. Sangeeta listed various ways of being a feminist and decided upon one that she deemed "fake" but that allowed her to be a future stay-at-home mother, as fitting her impressions of her ethnicity:

> Coming from that background, it molded me. Having a mother who worked longer than my dad caused any stereotype to be shot. He himself had a demanding job, but it was reversed. He is the one who went grocery shopping. . . . Friends of mine call me a "fake feminist," and the reason is that, sometimes, I feel like I have to portray this more independent image, because I don't ever want to be viewed as a weak individual. Because whether or not people mean it, they say things like, "Don't worry, your husband will take care of you." That's the last thing I want. I mean, I don't mind if he does. I just want to be able to take care of myself if I have to. I can only appreciate that now. A year ago, even six months ago, I was very, "I am never going to stay at home and watch the kids; I am always going to work." . . . I think women are good at being mothers and men are good at being fathers. There are differences. I am more open to it now, and it is because I appreciated where I come from. The only thing I can't stand is men who are like, "She can't do it." Respect her, respect her independence! You shouldn't be told not to work. . . . If I have children and I have to give up my career, that will be hard. That will be really hard. But it is definitely something I would consider seriously. I think some of it has to do with being Indian. I think my mom would have given up her job if my grandmother didn't live with us. I had a mother figure to come home to.

Through defining feminism to mean making one's own decision, even if those decisions reinforced traditional gender roles, Sangeeta created a psychological lived hybridity and balanced her competing identities.

Similarly, Judy was married and pregnant when I interviewed her. Unlike the stereotype of Korean women, her parents raised her to be very "career oriented," which fueled her own cynicism regarding gendered roles. I asked her if she thought that she would stay at home with her child. She became tense and responded:

> I struggle with it because that's not how I was brought up. I was brought up to very career, even from my parents, I was brought up to be very career oriented. I think it's going to be a struggle for me for a while. . . . I noticed even between myself and my friends, we have very different views on roles of the husband. I consider myself a feminist, but that doesn't mean I believe everything that all

feminists believe. Feminism is being able to give women choices. But because of that, certain things, like the role of a wife is to be the cook and to do the cleaning and all that stuff, it's very different from the way that I was brought up. Even though my parents were Koreans, they taught us not to be that way, not to be weak.

By the time I conducted my follow-up fieldwork, she had quit her job and given birth. She saw her Korean American friends who stayed home "to cook and do the cleaning" as not feminists, and in effect, "weak." She talked about starting to work again, as her own mother had done but in sharp contrast to other Korean American women she knew. She had not committed to a time frame or type of occupation. In the meantime her decision to stay at home temporarily did not violate her mother's precedent nor her definition of a feminist because it was her choice and so fit one of her definitions of feminism. As seen in these examples, the actors used identity talk to choose from among popular definitions of an American collective identity, in this case feminism, that could be reconciled with other cultural norms.

CONCLUSION

Participants expressed their identities differently in the home than outside of it and went out of their way to recreate domestic spaces reminiscent of their upbringing. Rather than see this domain as one of respite from public stereotypes and rules endured in the workplace, it had its own strict cultural code of behavior that was connected to the public realm. Informants hoped to support the next generation through supplying an ethnic atmosphere reminiscent of their own upbringing, which would encourage appropriate moral choices and economic achievement. As long as the home schema continues to exert pressure on interviewees and on women in particular, which increases rather than decreases as they progress through their life course, they will continue to stay committed to their ethnic social identity to varying degrees. Yet, informants' manner of going about this often depended on their self-defined "American" interests as well, at times beneath the surface of their actions, to which a margins-in-the-mainstream perspective draws attention. Korean and Indian Americans did not simply segregate their identities to distinct realms, as the literature suggests (see chapter 1). They upheld a moral family while not appearing *too* Asian and foreign.

Actors drew together their multiple cognitive categories by performing a biculturalism in various ways. The second generation frequently accounted for their multiple identities simultaneously within a single practice or deci-sion, that is, through a "lived hybridity." They accomplished this in how they articulated decisions—such as where to live, whether to date outside one's group, and whether to work as mothers—and not only in physical actions. We see that the cognitive process entailed in decision making attended to di-vergent expectations, which actions alone may conceal. At other times and as fitting recent formulations of how individuals use culture (Swidler 2001), participants selected meanings of their groups' identities that fit together and then acted on those meanings, such as when choosing one's partner or dealing with being English-monolingual. This, in turn, addressed the problem of con-tradictions between the identities. This is comparable to a lived hybridity in that opposing expectations are reconciled within the same domain, albeit not in a single action or decision-making process. The possible impact of actors' identity talk and boundary work tactics on their adaptation receives attention in chapter 8.

This linking of diverse commitments is in addition to the most commonly cited way of balancing multiple interests, which is to compartmentalize them into different settings and hide disruptive practices. Informants engaged in this as well. A selective assimilation, for instance, involves acting ethnic at home so as to facilitate social structural-assimilation in the public sphere. So, actors adopt multiple strategies to handle the challenges of their home life's varying expectations. Regardless of strategy, negotiating identities does not take place in just any fashion. It is guided by the home code, and so a domain-based analysis furthers our understanding of people's agency and constraints in constructing meaningful lives.

By addressing more than one lifestyle in their daily life and life-course deci-sions, informants formed their own approach to adulthood that could trans-late well to more assimilated and traditional versions. They thereby created an adulthood that maintained an ethnic family without necessarily appearing to outsiders as culturally and racially inaccessible. This is not necessarily a per-fect, harmonious resolution to diverse expectations. Tensions within and be-tween these worlds, most notably a gender double standard prominent in both American and Asian cultures, are addressed but not necessarily resolved. Fe-male participants seemed committed to satisfying the expectations of the home code but wanted to do so in their own way, which was still unclearly defined.

Nevertheless, informants broke down the binary notion of ethnic and American lifestyles while enforcing ethnic boundaries at home. Academics assume that to contest the contradictory definitions of "ethnic" and "American" means to comment on their overlapping and contingent nature. Such is not necessarily the case. The issue is not just that a hybrid lifestyle shows "American" and "ethnic" to be constructed categories, for we already know that (Hall 1990). It is also that actors considered these identities as mostly contrasting, reified ways of life, but nevertheless frequently brought them together in daily life. The emotional and social significance of marriage, language, and related matters discussed here makes actors' accomplishments all the more noteworthy. Although work and home are central to individuals' daily lives, the leisure and civil society domains also deserve attention in gauging immigrants' adaptation, as will be discussed in the next chapter.

7 Becoming Cultural Citizens
The Leisure and Civil Society Domains

THE PREVIOUS CHAPTERS have shown that second-generation Korean and Indian Americans did not segregate identities to specific realms, nor did they rely on liminal spaces to enact a hybrid sense of self. Instead, actors found ways to display, or at least remain psychologically committed to, competing interests while attending to work and home domain cultural schemas. To understand the second generation's adaptation and stratification, we need to move beyond these most commonly studied arenas. Leisure and civil society are important sites since they offer a bridge between public and private. They remain overlooked even though people spend so much time in them, in activities that they choose for their own enjoyment and that further their interests. Both spheres offer the opportunity to interact with co-ethnics or with other groups under less stringent rules than at work or at home. So, actors have more agency here than elsewhere to create group boundaries as they choose.

At the same time, these domains carry their own cultural frames that can influence how actors felt they were expected to behave and how they negotiated their margins within the mainstream status. These arenas have particular importance not only for identity management but for their continued implications for the racialization of Asian Americans. Claiming citizenship depends not only on one's legal status but also on one's social and cultural image as a "true" American (or not). One's career and domestic norms help establish one's public worth, but one's use of free time indicates one's degree of socialization into White middle-class normativity. These domains impact the second generation's ability to challenge Asian Americans' image as foreigners.

This chapter explains how informants constructed group boundaries first in the leisure realm and then in civil society. The kinds of leisure activities that people engage in have implications for identity development because they supposedly manifest our intrinsic interests. In this chapter, the term leisure realm will not pertain either to those events considered by participants to be domestic duties or to sponsored programs by civic associations. Because leisure is a more individualized space, it lacks as strict a cultural script as the other domains. Still, institutionalized leisure activities exist that make up the mainstream domain code and include eating at restaurants; attending Hollywood movies and sporting events; going on dates; drinking at bars and coffee shops; going to friends' homes; and visiting museums, shopping malls, and boutiques.[1] Actors engaged in these activities partly as a racial strategy, not simply as lifestyle preference, to overcome the image of people presumed to be foreigners on the basis of their physical and cultural backgrounds (Park 2005). But trying to overcome their racial stigma with these pursuits, even with co-ethnics, threatens a commitment to their ethnic group. Leisure practices presumably challenge the moral order of ethnic communities because they can involve drinking, dating, and disregard for ethnic language and culture. We see that informants did not simply mimic the patterns of White Americans. This is not a story of assimilating culturally while still associating with co-ethnics. Informants performed dominant leisure options and asserted a cultural citizenship as "American" while affirming an ethnic American identity, through enacting a lived hybridity at times. Yet, participants' success in converting leisure activities into "ethnic" endeavors can actually weaken their group ties, for it furthers their investment in mainstream spaces and blurs the boundary between "ethnic" and "American."

Much has been written on the changing nature of civil society in America, especially in terms of concerns over declining or altered styles of participation (Putnam 2000; Wuthnow 1998). Civil society, including volunteer organizations, religious associations, and others, can strengthen our private ties to public institutions, such as the government. Yet, the rise of ethnic organizations has made social conservatives anxious over the "balkanization" of the country into specific identity categories (Schlesinger 1992; Woodward 1998). This can apply even more to Asian Americans, given their image as perpetual foreigners. The ethnic associations of both first- and second-generation Asian Americans in Dallas attract members who seek ethnic-exclusive bonds for both emotional and instrumental reasons. As a result, Asian Americans could fail to live up to the prescribed schema of civil society, which is to link groups of people to one another (Alexander and Smith 1993). Association leaders and members attended to concerns over balkanization by affirming an ethnic solidarity both publicly and backstage, but in different ways (Goffman 1959). In the process, these Asian American professionals continued to construct themselves as cultural citizens while attending to conflicting interests.

THE LEISURE DOMAIN

The leisure domain represents more than a space of relaxation and entertainment. Because engaging in leisure activities is typically a self-motivated behavior, they represent and help create people's identities (Dimanche and Samdahl 1994; Kelly 1983; Shamir 1992). According to Shamir (1992), leisure practices can be so salient that we create a "leisure identity" in addition to identities based on home and work, especially when those practices require intense effort, time, and financial contribution. This realm offers more opportunities for one to act on one's own interests than does the work sphere, which makes the chosen practices, even when approached casually, influential on self-conceptions and images presented to others. Although the leisure realm does not strictly regulate behavior, it is not free of normative actions. Race, class, gender, geography, life-course stage, and other social categories shape the kinds of activities people engage in (Fischer 1994; Hochschild 1997; Jeffres, Neuendorf, and Atkin 2003; Wilson 1980). For instance, cooking styles have come to signify class differences (Hollows 2003).

Unfortunately, information is lacking on how immigrants, minorities, or marginal groups generally participate in the leisure realm (Stodolska 2002). Existing research has investigated the different types of activities that minority groups perform, as opposed to the manner in which they go about them. This bias in the literature fits the presumption, discussed earlier, that one's type of activities indicates one's identity. In general, scholars analyze ways in which minorities access leisure opportunities because of differences in income, acculturation, and interests, such as African Americans' greater historical engagement in social activism (Floyd et al. 1994; Gitelson, Bernat, and Aleman 2002; Hylton 2003). Hylton (2003) finds that immigrants' identities not only reflect but also are influenced by their leisure choices, such as how unemployed African Caribbeans' turn to the arts to fuel a positive conception of their community. In a similar vein, Kivel and Kleiber (2000) argue that lesbian and gay youth's choice of leisure activities shapes their sexual identity development—for instance, playing drums helps girls break out of gender stereotypes. The youth also interpret commonplace activities in personally resonant ways, such as enjoying how comic-book heroes are able to live dual identities as gay and lesbian youth must often do.

The literature suggests, then, that individuals' choice of leisure activities depends on their social position, and that the activities in turn influence identity formation. This raises the question of how Asian Americans maintained commitments to their ethnic lifestyles while engaged in mainstream leisure spaces. Being in Dallas constrained leisure options because of the dearth of casual places frequented primarily by the second generation.[2] Respondents mostly took part in mainstream activities as fitting the leisure code, which affirmed their "American" status but could challenge their standing in their communities' moral order, even if performed with co-ethnics. This chapter first elaborates on the tensions that second-generation Korean and Indian Americans felt within this sphere based on racial and ethnic differences. Then it examines how they took part in mainstream activities, partly in response to those tensions, while containing threats to their ethnic social identity posed by those activities.

Tensions within Leisure Spaces

Indian and Korean Americans complained both of stereotypes from out-group members and of cultural tensions with their ethnic lifestyles when engaged in mainstream leisure activities. In other words, they felt challenged in being accepted as full participants in this realm as *Asian* Americans. The second generation experienced frequent prejudice in the leisure domain, such as in bars, restaurants, and stores, ranging from unwanted attention to a lack of attention. The social sphere, unlike the workplace, lacks strict roles and regulations of behavior, leaving people to act more freely on stereotypes and prejudices. Actors received more stares than usual when they entered restaurants accompanied by co-ethnics. It occurred so frequently as to become humorous for some. Susan laughed as she remarked, "We make jokes like 'Asian Invasion.' Because when we go to a restaurant, and of course a crowd of ten Asians, it's the 'Asian Invasion.'" Vikas spoke of mistreatment in a restaurant and how he "proved" it was racial, with more satisfaction in his response than resentment over the event:[3]

> There were ten of us, three [White] Americans and seven Indians sitting at a table at a restaurant, but the American guys would sit with their backs to [the rest of the restaurant], so all [the waiters] see is an Indian table. We waited for

twenty-five minutes for somebody to give us service. I'm like, just for grins, let's see if this is actually the case [i.e., due to racial prejudice]. Why don't you [White] guys go sit over there facing the crowd or facing outward, and these [Indian] guys come and sit over here? Two minutes, less than two minutes, right away [we were attended to]. We stood up, said we're not eating here, and walked out. My American friends were appalled; they couldn't believe that was the case. The Indians, we were like, "OK, let's get the hell out of here, we don't care." [The White friends] actually went up to the manager and stated that that was wrong. The manager was like, "Why don't you come here and we'll take care of your meal and everything on the house," and they were like, no. They couldn't believe it more than the rest of us. We were just like, whatever, they don't deserve our business.

Such occurrences reinforced informants' ties with co-ethnics familiar with such discrimination.

Beyond the generic image as a minority, actors encountered sexualized stereotypes in this domain, more pronounced than in other arenas, that again constructed them as outsiders. Women were exotic while men were ignored. Tammy spoke mockingly of White men approaching her at bars. Typical pick-up lines consisted of, "'Oh, I know someone who's Korean.' And they speak a few words of Korean. And I'm like, 'That's great, buddy.'" If not seen as exotic, then women were perceived as deviant from the normative sexual image, especially in the South. Judy, who grew up in New York, said:

I think Korean women are seen as not being very pretty compared to Caucasian. Especially coming down south I noticed. They have this set way of viewing beautiful women, and Asians aren't a part of that. The big hair, the blonde, blue eyes, that kind of thing. It'd be different if I was in New York or I was in California or whatever.

Along with racial marginalization based on physical appearance, Korean and Indian Americans noted a dismissal of their ethnic social identity as abnormal owing to the culturally normative expectations in this sphere. Participants encountered this in regard to obligations to prioritize community and family rather than personal interests. As Samantha recalled:

My roommate [in college], who's White, didn't understand why I went home every Saturday, but my Korean friend did. It's that sense of severing yourself from your parents that [my roommate] wanted. Part of why I needed to go home is that I need to do things for my parents. My mom doesn't drive, so I have to drive for her. And if my mom and I get into a disagreement, my Korean American friend could say she understands where I'm coming from, but I also have to understand where my parents are coming from. And my White room-mate would say, "Your mom's being irrational!"

Feeling that one had responsibilities to one's family contradicted the self-gratification motivation of the leisure sphere, especially pronounced on weekends.

To the interviewees, a difference of priorities seemed like a minor obstacle to acceptance compared to family restrictions on dating and drinking. Popular culture presents parental support for dating as natural, and schools formally promote it with dances, parties, and other events. Drinking also is framed as a youthful practice that should be limited rather than forbidden, especially as one enters college. Yet according to parents, these were borderline-immoral "American" practices that youth, in particular women, should not get involved in. Some participants had been ridiculed by White and even co-ethnic peers for their abstinence. Aditi had as a child internalized her parents' restrictions on drinking:

> My parents would use this phrase a lot or they would somehow always distin-guish, like, oh, that's something that American kids do and you don't want to. You don't ever want to drink because that's something that American kids do.

Knowing that some co-ethnics were partyers and that many in the first gen-eration drank, Laura attributed her and many of her friends' choice not to do so to their religious rather than their ethnic background:

> You know, there is a way in which other Koreans go to happy hour, other Kore-ans drink and smoke. I don't think just because they're Korean or Asian they're not gonna do that. I think, for me, it is more because I've been growing up in a church, and so most of my Asian friends are from a church background.

A number of interviewees, mostly women, did not drink or drank very little. Many who did worried about failing in their community's moral order, dis-cussed later.

The common parental caution against acting too "American" represented a racial, not simply a moral warning. Participants hoped to fit into American youth norms partly to overcome their image as the racial foreigner. Parents counseled against assuming that such endeavors would bestow a White status. As Kithana commented:

> If I want to move out or go on a date, [my parents] say, you're Indian, don't try to be American and White. Don't try to be White because no one will ever see you as American. You'll always be Indian.

As seen in chapter 3, the first generation considered its heritage as a means to help children deal with their minority position. Eschewing assimilated practices represented not only a cultural boundary, but also a racial response to chasing (in vain) acceptance by Whites as full cultural citizens.

Along similar lines to concerns over drinking and dating (discussed in chapter 6 with marriage), a few in the second generation, notably women, felt discomfort in viewing the sexual explicitness of standard television programs and movies, which violated their communities' conservative approach to sexuality. They responded by distancing their personal preferences from what they saw on the screen. Rajina said, "I don't put as much stock in a lot of the shenanigans of promiscuity—like in *Seinfeld* there is a lot of promiscuity—because of how I was raised." Similarly, Veera said:

> I look down on more stuff, on movies that are so into sex. You would never see a couple kiss [in Indian movies]. Yes, we have pornos, but in the mainstream movies it's not there. America crosses the line; the sensationalism is too much.

This tension, like that originating from proscriptions against drinking or dating, results from having a lifestyle considered "deviant" with respect to the normalized dominant culture. In that regard its effects are related, albeit not equivalent, to those of active discrimination at restaurants in that they challenge informants' sense of full acceptance within the domain code as *Asian* Americans.

Upholding the Moral Order in the Leisure Sphere

As befits their margins-in-the-mainstream status, actors wanted to feel comfortable as ethnic Americans and at the same time to feel accepted within the leisure sphere, rather than either remaining in ethnically isolated activities or fully assimilating. This is a different predicament from the situation of the workplace, in which both parents and workplace culture expected Asian Americans to mostly assimilate, and from the home domain, in which ethnic-based routines were normative. Participants dealt with this tension by presenting themselves as fully part of the leisure domain but also as ethnically distinct. This represented not only a desire to blend ethnic and acculturated lifestyles, but also a racial strategy to appear comparable to Whites while maintaining a group solidarity. They accomplished this in three ways: actively compartmentalizing or bringing together ethnic and mainstream friends and endeavors; "ethnicizing" and re-framing mainstream activities, that is, engaging in them in self-perceived "ethnic" ways; and performing ethnic-oriented options that took place within dominant institutions.

Actively Segregating or Joining Activities and Friends   A common strategy of separately taking part in both "ethnic" and "American" leisure events (Danico 2004; Hall 1995; Hurh and Kim 1999; Maira 2002) in effect denies the problem of how to maintain a community's moral order while in integrated environments. Those participants who were familiar with the Dallas community and its infrastructure used this tactic most often. Sangeeta had an uncle and aunt who lived in Dallas, and she took pride in listing the various activities that kept "who I am" in balance:

> You ask me what I like to do. I went to a Lenny Kravitz concert last night and to the temple tonight. It is because of who I am. One doesn't take precedence over the other. One isn't more fun than the other. It's who I am.

Along with segregating activities, the second generation commonly segregated friends. Joining co-ethnic and White friendship sets seemed like crossing a boundary, often fraught with anxiety, instead of simply interacting with individuals who happen to be of the majority culture. Informants had mostly co-ethnic friends. Many had longtime White friends from college or earlier but felt distant from Whites in general. Lakshmi elaborated on the gap with other groups:

> When you're at a bar, the people come up to talk to you, and everything is different. When you're with Indians, it's more homogenous. You feel more the same. When you're with Indians, it's less effort, less effort to have fun. Being comfortable and having fun, having a good night. When you are with Caucasians, you are more nervous. Not really nervous, but when you make a little more effort, you discover new things, have different experiences. . . . The way we treat people, [the way] we think, maybe that's what separates us.

Despite any discomfort, informants felt it necessary to occasionally integrate their friendships. They felt they were in a catch-22 situation of wanting ethnic solidarity, owing to external prejudices and cultural dissimilarities, but feeling it necessary to break down that solidarity to feel "American" because of that status's hegemonic association with Whites. As Lakshmi suggests, associating with Whites often was a conscious decision rather than an organic development. Similarly, Andy said as we sat in his living room:

> I thought I was being a bit closed off. I had Caucasian friends, but I'd only do certain things with them. They weren't close friends. I thought I could

identify better with Korean Americans. I think it's part of getting that Korean identity.

Similarly, Ram and his wife had gone out of their way to form friendships with Whites, even holding a Christmas party, despite being Hindu, as part of a racial strategy to appear equal to them. He commented with some frustration:

> So we want to have non-Indian friends, and we do have a few, but nobody that at least at this point that is, you know, tight. And we've tried to build a relationship with certain non-Indians, and it's just not developing yet. I don't know, maybe in time it will. Like we moved into our house now, but coincidentally across the street is an Indian. So, I mean that's the first person we're gonna know probably in our subdivision. . . . In a large party or in a non-Indian function, Sonia and I both say we can't hang out in [Indian American] cliques. That's not good for how we are viewed. When we actually held a Christmas party a couple years ago, the biggest thing we wanted to do was make it a good mix of people, and not be just an Indian thing, so that the non-Indians wouldn't feel out of place. We worry about that.

Being exclusive in their friendships was not a problem within the home schema but could damage how they "are viewed" within the leisure frame, since it challenged the local leisure domain's expectation to mix with the dominant group's spaces or persons. Since American "means" White, associating primarily with co-ethnics reinforces Ram and Sonia's image as perpetual foreigners even though they own a middle-class home and speak fluent English. It was rare that the second generation integrated their friendships and, as seen here, often required intentional effort.

"Ethnicizing" and Reframing Mainstream Leisure Activities   The tactics just described either kept participants' lifestyles apart or put them together in the same room, but without linking them in a manner that dealt with the tensions. The second generation also went about or conceived of normative leisure events in self-defined and overlooked "ethnic" ways. Their efforts made them comfortable as ethnic Americans while allowing them to conform to the same leisure code as Whites. Respondents integrated their ethnicity into commonplace activities through a variety of means: by invoking a community-oriented feeling when out socially, by referencing ethnic symbols and customs in public, by commenting on leisure practices in the homeland, and by keeping in mind socially conservative values.[4] These efforts demonstrate a lived hybridity, for they allowed the second generation to reconcile identities often within a

single course of action. The practices also show that how one pursues an activity, not only the activity itself, shapes identity formations in the leisure sphere.

Informants frequented the same leisure establishments as Dallas's young White professionals, thus conforming with the domain script. Such an association helped bestow on them a sense of cultural legitimacy. They still affirmed an ethnic boundary through how they interacted with co-ethnics, not merely by having co-ethnic friendship circles. According to Mohit, Indian Americans express a "more the merrier" attitude, while White Americans prefer groups in which each person has a clear connection to the others:

> I think any kind of group activities, I feel like I am always left out when it comes to the White group. When they go out as a group to a club, they only invite me, I think, because I work with them and not for any other reason. Whereas, an Indian group is like, yeah, you can invite whoever you want. It doesn't really matter.

In fact, John referred to Korean Americans' community orientation as appealing to certain Whites:

> It's funny, you always have a few token non-Koreans in the group, because I think they really enjoy that sense of unity. It's not just a group of people that formed a community. I think it has to do with the dynamics of the community, which I think are a little bit more warm, I guess.

Having Whites as the outsiders in a group of Korean American friends turns the standard minority-friendship dynamic in the United States on its head. The majority, not the minority, is the one who sticks out in this case, even in Dallas, with its smaller Asian American populations.

How interviewees routinely spoke with (and did not speak with) co-ethnic peers also supported a group boundary as they consumed standard leisure activities. Those in the traditional-community category (see chapter 3) cared most about practicing ethnic symbols. Laura said that language was important in choosing friends. "I'll speak Korean anywhere, just about anywhere. . . . I feel I can express myself more fully in Korean than I can in English." Very few participants spoke in Korean or an Indian language when with co-ethnics. They occasionally inserted an ethnic boundary by making jokes in an ethnic tongue. Co-ethnic friends also gave interviewees an opportunity to converse about news events in their homeland, which other Americans may not have considered in depth.

Less observable of an ethnic boundary involved what actors did not say. As Chad remarked about his co-ethnic peers:

I don't talk to them about anything "Korean." It's just general things. But it's assumed when you're talking, you don't say things because you're Korean. You try not to swear, for one thing. Try not to talk about other people in the group. I think when we talk, we try not to be more like Caucasians or Americans. When they talk, they make a lot of noise. Maybe they don't. They don't pay their share of the bill. A lot of that goes around 'cause we think Koreans are not stingy with the money; we tip. We'll take care of the bill for the girls and things like that.

In addition to conversation styles, Chad, like other men, "ethnicized" leisure practices such as eating out by being chivalrous, which rested on a patriarchy that limited women's authority. The practice of paying for others rather than splitting the bill also could reflect the social exchange principle that with frequent contact, one can be confident that one will receive back what one gives (Lawler and Thye 1999). Still, participants read it as drawing a line between themselves and the mostly Whites sitting next to them in restaurants (Thai 1999). In the process they reimagined commonplace pastimes—going out to eat—as ethnic ones. Although they enjoyed such interactions, they still had to worry about associating too often with co-ethnics rather than with Whites, as discussed earlier. This was not a solution, but only another tactic for fully participating in this realm as ethnic Americans.

Interviewees displayed ethnic symbols and customs not only when with co-ethnics but also when with White friends. In particular, some Indian Americans expressed a desire not to eat meat or drink alcohol based on their religious convictions. Vikram conveyed confidence in his ability to do so publicly:

Being Indian has been somewhat of an asset because I think when people first meet me, they hear an American accent, they see somebody wearing American clothes, and suddenly they realize things like I don't drink, I am a vegetarian, something that intrigues them. When we go out to a bar, I am raising my ginger ale while they are all having Long Island iced teas or whatever they drink at these bars. I can't identify. I think eating and drinking is the way people bond. On the other hand, I think that people see—wait a minute, here's a person who's also got that tie to his culture and is able to strike that balance. I think people respect that a little bit, where this is a person who is able to be himself. In that sense it's been an asset. It also gives me more to talk about.

In Dallas and elsewhere, eating meat represents a standard dietary preference, as is drinking alcohol during happy hour. Actors developed boundary work practices—raising a glass of ginger ale while wearing "American" clothes—to allow for participation in these rituals despite cultural differences that could mark them as foreign.

More effort, beyond just being in assimilated spaces, was required to bring participants' ethnic social identity in line with some popular endeavors. These included drinking and dating. In chapter 6 I discussed dating and sexuality as they relate to marriage. As mentioned there, one strategy to deal with dating involved identity talk, reframing parental restrictions less as a cultural divide and more as a generational one. Participants invoked a similar method to reconcile drinking with an ethnic lifestyle. As Sanjay said:

> Even in India you see people pushing back and becoming more Westernized, more mainstream. I've seen my cousins, and [by] leaps and bounds they've gone past what is traditional.

Veera also commented:

> [Indian American young adults] don't drink and smoke and have lived a sheltered life. They've always lived at home and haven't gone out much. My cousins in India are more advanced. . . . a lot of my cousins married their boyfriends.

Interviewees framed drinking or staying out late as antitraditional but not anti-ethnic.

Depicting their decisions to drink as not violating an ethnic lifestyle, however, did not fully resolve internalized tensions, since many parents' message in this regard was clear. Because redefining the social identity is a difficult task, actors also engaged in other minor boundary work to feel comfortable as ethnic Americans while drinking. Informants believed that they drank and went to parties, if at all, to a controlled extent, which marked them as American while acknowledging—if not necessarily following—community and religious preferences. They "ethnicized" drinking, in their opinion, by going about it in somewhat tempered ways, especially relative not to Whites but to some co-ethnics. David elaborated on his balanced approach to drinking during college compared to extreme positions:

> My Korean friends were conservative; they didn't drink. They would break out the Taboo and other board games. There were Korean sororities and fraternities, and I would hang out with them, but they were punks. My Caucasian friends were punks too, but it seemed that the Koreans were worse. It seems like since they were Asian they took it to a higher extreme than the Caucasian friends. You can be on extremes: a conservative or a goofish party animal. I was pre-med and knew I needed to keep it together.

Rajeev also looked down on Indian Americans who got carried away with their freedom from their parents as they started college:

> They're into the drinking scene, and that's cool, but they try to push the limit. This is because they were so repressed at home, when they finally got their taste of freedom, they went AWOL. It's sad.

Going "AWOL" suggests that such individuals abandoned their membership in a group. These informants, on the other hand, appeared comparable to Whites while still affirming a sense of group boundary. Although it is possible to assert one's place within an ethnic group by distinguishing oneself from Whites, differentiating oneself from "goofish" co-ethnics affirms an adherence even more strongly, for it positions one as superior to those who otherwise could claim group membership.

The second generation believed that some co-ethnics drank so much because they were denied that opportunity within their culturally conservative families. Yet, a number of individuals, often women, did not drink or drank little. Usha offered a different theory that highlighted the relevance of race:

> It seems like my Indian friends, they go out to get drunk. That is like their purpose. And my purpose and [that of] my American friends, it's not going out to get drunk, it's to go out and have a good time. Drinking is involved, yes, [and] in the process we do get a buzz or get drunk. It's not the purpose, and I don't think it should be the purpose. But a lot of my Indian friends say, "How would you like to get drunk tonight?" It just seems like we have to prove ourselves to a broader society and say, "Hey, we're not nerds, we're not geeks. We could go out and have fun just like the next AKO or a frat or somebody." They are trying to prove themselves to broader society.

Drinking served as a racial strategy, not simply an instance of acculturation. Asian Americans face the challenge to "prove themselves" as Americans, instead of as racialized foreigners, while also blending in seemingly contrasting commitments to their ethnic community. Not all succeed in this, including those who "went AWOL." As seen in chapter 3, interviewees would occasionally not associate with co-ethnics in order to avoid being racially stereotyped as "nerds" or "geeks." As they developed salient ethnic identities, concerns over the stereotypes did not automatically disappear.

Ethnic Practices, American Institutions   Participants invoked another lived hybridity strategy to integrate an ethnic identity into the mainstream leisure sphere: engaging in those ethnic-oriented pursuits that took place in or were comparable to those in popular American institutions. Anu listed her and her husband's ethnic outings:

> We eat Indian food sometimes, and I drag him to a movie, like we saw *Monsoon Wedding*. I will support films like that. I'll also go to Sotheby's when I [am] in New York. Sotheby's had an Indian exhibit and stuff like that. But I wouldn't go to an Indian bhajan or something. You know, some kind of like musical concert like that, it might bore me.

Being Asian *American*, many found traditional events uninteresting in their leisure time as opposed to the home domain, where they took pride in their adherence to such events. Ethnic-oriented activities within mainstream institutions proved more accessible and comfortable. Such entertainment, including the films *Bend It Like Beckham* and *Monsoon Wedding* and the television show *All-American Girl*, often dealt with culture clashes of traditions and conservatism versus individualism and independence. This dualism fits with many interviewees' own impressions.

Similar to an ethnic-focused museum or film were nightclubs that catered to particular immigrant communities. Although these options were limited in Dallas, actors spoke of such spaces in major urban areas with fondness. For instance, Jason said:

> Like a restaurant or a club—not so much here, but like in New York—if I went to a club or a restaurant, it was probably Korean. It's only Korean music. They might throw in a couple American songs, but it's mostly Korean.

Korean pop music has become increasingly popular overseas. Such venues offered more than just co-ethnics to socialize with; they also offered aspects of Korean culture that still let one be part of standard leisure routines.

Victims of Their Own Success?

The ability to blend an ethnic lifestyle into common leisure practices or to find mainstream institutions that catered to one's ethnic group caused some to worry, however, that the second generation would in fact lose its culture. The distinction between what is "ethnic" and what is "American" blurs as popular institutions become more multicultural. In other words, the easier it becomes to assert a cultural citizenship as American while maintaining ethnic distinctions, the weaker those distinctions possibly become. Radha commented in an agitated tone:

> It's easy to get cultural pieces, like movies, food, clothes, [and] music, than it used to be. I think it will continue to be a global economy, and people will be

much more comfortable with different groups. Then [Indian culture] becomes one of the many. It's like, do you want to go out for Thai food tonight or. . . . It's not something you own or relate to you as yours so much as you have access to.

The diaspora's growing strength within a global economy can actually hurt ethnic retention even as it provides the tools to facilitate it.

The consumerist attitude toward culture is not isolated to such obvious transactions as eating at a restaurant. The second generation approached ancestral traditions and customs in the same way, as something one could turn to in order to acquire a traditional set of values and lifestyle (see chapters 3 and 6). Still, the more conspicuous use of their native country's popular culture caught actors' attention (Purkayastha 2005). Wendy noted the irony of a more culturally Korean, yet simultaneously more assimilated, second-generation youth:

> Actually, I see the second generation becoming more . . . I was going to say more assimilated. More Americanized. Kids in high school and junior high know more about Korean culture, Korean music, Korean fashion. I don't think it is being lost. [But] it is more materialistic. They aren't more into the culture, the history or anything. It is more material, like fashion and music.

These youth enjoyed ethnic leisure activities and products but are still at risk of losing their ethnic culture. John hoped that superficial interests among Korean American youth would deepen later. He believed that teenagers in the second generation had a firm grasp on Korean culture, but not of the traditional sort taught in churches or community organizations:

> Just pop culture. I mean, there are some positive residual effects, like Korean society is truly hierarchical, like certain titles when you are older, and a lot of kids are into that. Like if you are older, and they are calling you by that title. I don't know if they truly understand what's behind all that, but it is a start. Hopefully later on they will get more interested in it or learn somehow.

Youth may find referencing Korean popular culture appealing since doing so marks one as both unique and interested in current trends. The notion of popular culture itself suggests an ephemeral attachment to ethnicity. Korean culture has become a type of fun, so it may lose relevance for this younger cohort as other entertainments take its place. A similar trend is taking place for Indian Americans with the growing popularity of henna, a yellow-to-brown dye made from the leaves of the henna plant (Maira 2000). Though seen by some Indian Americans as a positive recognition of an ethnic practice, the increased attention could threaten henna's relationship to historically significant celebrations in India. Indian Americans begin to consume henna in a manner leaning toward cultural appropriation, in which groups sample multiple customs without attending to their contextual significance.

Concern that increased access to national culture ironically weakens ties to one's heritage appears warranted based on some participants' attitudes toward ethnicity. Tammy commented on reading materials that referenced her ethnicity:

> One time in *Glamour* they had an article, a Korean American person in general, [on] how her life was and such. It was interesting just to see that viewpoint. In *Newsweek*, they bring up national crisis type deals, like nuclear weapons, North Korean infants are starving, dah dah dah, that kind of stuff.

She referred to issues on the Korean peninsula (albeit North Korea) as generic world news but the article on the individual life of a Korean American as "interesting." Her reference to the North Korean article illustrates Radha's point of the rise in available ethnic references as a possible threat to strong group attachments. The story falls into the category of general world news and loses any distinction that could connect to a sense of ancestry, which Wendy lamented. The availability of information and events becomes a double-edged sword, on the one hand giving people a link to their ethnicity and a public recognition of its worth, yet on the other hand making one's background generic and of less personal significance.

Overall, the second generation asserted cultural citizenship by taking part in this public sphere despite tensions that grew out of their ethnic-minority status. They accomplished this while attending to an ethnic social identity, often with a lived hybridity, so as to be comfortable as Asian Americans in mainstream spaces. The implications of this for their group boundaries are discussed in the conclusion of this chapter.

THE CIVIL SOCIETY DOMAIN

The final major domain of individuals' lives that I will discuss is civil society. The term refers to the set of institutions and organizations, rather than individuals, designed to accomplish goals that persons alone cannot achieve as effectively. Examples of civic organizations include churches, soup kitchens, Alcoholics Anonymous, and bicycling clubs, to name a few. Civil society carries a stricter cultural code than does the leisure sphere. According to the civil society schema within a liberal democracy, it is important for members of a group to pursue the group's collective goals in ways that do not infringe upon the freedoms or privileges of other groups. To the extent that an organization encourages members' interactions with those outside it, it fulfills civil society's expectations about "bridging" groups rather than simply bonding members to one another. This bridging can be along ethnic/racial, class, geographic, or other lines that people would not cross normally in their friendship circles. By linking individuals together, civic organizations create social capital that encourages concern for others and interest in participating in the nation's democracy (Putnam 2000). Organizations that do not further such connections only build internal solidarity without promoting democratic gains (Alexander and Smith 1993). Such criticism has been applied to ethnic groups as sites of narrow interests unassociated with, and even hostile to, national unity.

The main question for this domain is how ethnic and religious associations—which members join in order to be with their ethnic community, apart from other groups—fit within the logic of civil society. Do the organizations simply bond members to one another, and thereby only reinforce a marginal identity, or do they also bridge communities and so help construct Asian Americans as full citizens? If the latter, how do they form that bridge given that members often prefer ethnic exclusive spaces?

Emotional and Instrumental Motivations for Joining Ethnic Organizations

Immigrants have a history of starting ethnic or religious associations upon arrival, including ethnic churches and synagogues, newspapers, social clubs, men's and women's organizations, labor associations, and others (Gamm and Putnam 1999). Such organizations replicate the sense of solidarity immigrants had been accustomed to in their homelands. They also facilitate adaptation to the new country. Members gradually adjust to their environment and form identities more conducive to their new lives, often moving across sub-ethnic lines to develop ethno-national identities. Newcomers learn from co-ethnics about job opportunities, government regulations, immigration opportunities, and other issues that help them navigate bureaucracies. Ethnic associations also encourage assistance for local civic needs, such as beautification projects or care for the elderly. Such organizations, then, lead to involvement in mainstream ones. Ethnic associations gradually lose relevance as immigrant communities acculturate, find acceptance in mainstream groups, and have their needs met in those groups, which take less effort on the part of the individual to run (Kamphoefner 1996).

Later generations' involvement in ethnic clubs is more limited because of their increased acculturation and mobility. Continued membership by later generations has been due to a lack of social acceptance based on physical, occupational, or residential distinctions (Gans 1962; Kitano 1969), political interests gained through ethnic mobilizing (Glazer and Moynihan 1970; Takahashi 1997), and/or cultural particularities (Fugita and O'Brien 1991). Although it is not unusual of the second generation to join ethnic associations, the fact that most interviewees do not belong to mainstream associations, such as local book clubs, volunteer associations, and so on, either instead of or in addition to ethnic ones, calls for an explanation. I found that most actors participated almost exclusively in ethnic organizations not despite but rather because of their integration.

Searching for a Safe Space   Individuals join civic associations for both emotional and instrumental reasons (Wilson 2000). Emotional reasons consist of a desire for social support in the face of general racial and cultural marginalization. Mohit referenced this in explaining his participation in a ras garba dance festival held in a high school gymnasium in Richardson, a suburb north of Dallas, and sponsored by local first-generation Indian associations:

> I think for me sometimes, it is like when I go to a dance, I feel like I am not a stranger anymore. I feel like everyone around me is like me, and there is this monkey off the shoulder that is kind of gone. And it is a level of comfort that I don't get anywhere else. I know when I am going in there what to expect. I know that there is going to be a mass crowd. People are going to push. But I also know that the music is going to be there. They are going to stare at me, but it is all Indians so there is this whole kin thing. I think for me, that is a part of the culture that I enjoy, and I don't like to lose things that I enjoy.

At least a thousand people had shown up for this event. I saw a few of the second-generation informants standing in the entrance and dancing on the stadium floor; most were wearing traditional attire. Interviewees had achieved mobility and residential integration, yet they participated in events sponsored by the first generation primarily for emotional reasons, namely a felt commitment to their ethnic culture and a desire for acceptance among surrogate kin. The suburban high school gymnasium became an Indian cultural setting with people pushing, a distinctive type of music and dance, food, and people in ethnic clothes.[5]

Most Indian Americans who visited a temple did so primarily to bond with their community despite their re sidential dispersal and affirm cultural ties to their homeland. The temples supply a fossilized "authenticity" as much as, if not more than, religiosity for attendees. People—women in particular—dress in traditional attire. One hears Hindi or Gujurati used more as a means to convey culture than to communicate information, since most people also speak English. Cultural centers attached to temples also physically demonstrate the connection between religion and ethnicity and affirm a separation from other groups (Ebaugh and Chafetz 2000; Kurien 1998). Race also played a role in membership, for Asian Americans' cultural backgrounds often come to be labeled as suspicious, as discussed in chapter 4. When I asked Rajat if being non-White buttressed his interest in maintaining his heritage, he responded:

> Yeah, in that I think that because we're not White, we are a little more driven to do that. We'll always be different in physical appearance and also in name appearances. . . . [The temple] kind of reinforces—hey, I'm a Hindu, I have roots with this culture. It kind of reinforces this group. . . . I think it gives the community here in Dallas a center. I think it gives them like a spiritual center to go to. Hey, you may be this, this, and this, but you are all still Hindus. That kind of gives everybody a sense of identity. That would give [us] a little more strength or a little more leverage.

Leaders similarly saw the temple as a means of affirming their community's self-esteem in response to a racialized ethnicity. They positioned themselves apart from, and even above, the mainstream in private, internal conversations. For instance, Kuba stated that members of the first generation built a Hindu temple in part to teach the youth that they can be superior to Whites, for "there is nothing they can do that we can't do better." The exclusively ethnic nature of the organizations was a central element in their emotional appeal. Even though relatively few second-generation Indian Americans attended temples regularly, many valued having access to such an institution.

First-generation Korean American elders ran various cultural organizations, while second-generation pastors, for the most part, led the EMs that informants attended. Both types built up an internal solidarity that members appreciated. Park of the OKA explained that the first generation's organizations hosted Korean events, with which KAP members sometimes assisted:

> Several times a year, we have our own festival: Korean's day, year-ending party, art festival, a few holidays, like Korean national holiday. We get together and show our traditional art. This year, at the Korean festival, we also had a traditional Korean marriage. When young guys are curious and ask questions like "What's going on?" we explain it, and they always talk about it later.

He even attended a KAP monthly dinner and spoke of his desire for more partnerships between the two organizations.[6]

Although second-generation Korean Americans went to events sponsored by elders only on occasion, they frequently attended services in or near the church buildings of immigrants (Chai 2001). At the EMs pastors spoke mostly on religious topics that would be addressed in any conservative Protestant service; they made little reference to ethnicity (Dhingra 2004). Still, most members frequented these rather than mainstream churches because of the camaraderie they found there (Chong 1998). James commented on the need for ethnic churches for racialized groups:

> If I *have* to be something, I want to be Korean American. I *want* to have something like apple pie. If you are not going to let me have that, let me do that with whatever is associated with Korean Americans. I am more comfortable with Korean Americans because they have been discriminated against. Why would you feel more comfortable with that group otherwise? (emphasis in original)

Actors also preferred Korean American congregations because of a shared culture. Judy remarked:

> In our Korean church, we have a Korean American group that primarily speaks English and the Korean group that primarily speaks Korean, and because we are in that church setting on Sundays and whenever, we will hear Korean spoken. I think that does influence—it reinforces our Korean Americanness, or our Koreanness, even.

Although pastors considered it the parents' responsibility to promote an ethnic heritage, the EMs promoted "ethnic values," which fit with their conservative Christian values of respecting family, being deferential to elders, and having semitraditional gender norms (see chapter 3). EMs also offered a few structured opportunities for the first- and second-generation congregations to interact, in joint services hosted twice a year on average.[7] These services, conducted in Korean and translated by the EM pastor into English, exposed the congregation to the Korean language.

Attendees considered the EMs to affirm their connection to their community, even though, after repeated visits to the EMs, I rarely saw members speaking Korean with the first generation and never to one another. Interactions between members of the first and second generations, even when they were the same age, were infrequent. For instance, during a singles ministry at World Gathering, the EM members entered the gym to play volleyball, and soon afterward young adults from the first-generation ministry, around the same age as the EM members, also arrived at the other side of the gym.[8] Due to a scheduling error, both groups believed that they had access. For the few minutes before the second-generation members realized their error, only a few people of either group crossed the court to greet one another; most talked only amongst themselves. In addition, KAP did not sponsor any events to commemorate Korean holidays. Instead, it offered more social events, such as volleyball games and Christmas parties. Also, none of the EMs had any physical Korean markers inside their congregations. Overall, these associations brought co-ethnics together, took note of some major holidays, and allowed individuals an opportunity, if nothing else, to practice cultural symbols. The churches thereby offer members the potential to explore their interest in and increase their knowledge of their heritage. Members appreciated the Korean American identity of the churches and the ways that Christianity and ethnicity intertwined, and so they went out of their way to attend them.

Dating and Networking with Co-Ethnics   Members' instrumental goal of finding co-ethnics to befriend, marry, and network with joined with their emotional interests in a racialized safe space or in an ancestral culture to make ethnic associations popular. I now turn to how KAP and IANA bonded people together, with some reference to the EMs. Informants' acculturation could have encouraged membership in mainstream organizations but instead furthered interest in community-based ones as a means to meet similarly educated and successful co-ethnics. These organizations were for Dallas the only way co-ethnics could interact with each other in large numbers. In bigger cities, one sees Indian and Korean Americans at film screenings, clubs, bars, theaters, museums, lectures, readings, community or political events, and other sites that cater to a particular group. Yet in Dallas, even though it is the ninth largest city in the nation, there was little opportunity for interactions with peers on a regular basis outside of formal associations.

Because people joined IANA and KAP primarily to meet co-ethnics, the organizations had the image of "meat markets." When attending not just larger parties, but also IANA's informal networking events, it was clear that many people were interested in meeting potential partners of the opposite sex. Men rarely approached other men whom they did not know, and a woman often had more than one man standing near her. I witnessed the same scene at KAP's larger parties. Yet at KAP's smaller monthly dinner meetings and social gatherings at a bar afterward, as well as at IANA's meetings, people mingled more easily across and within gender lines.[9] Even the EMs became known as spaces to meet partners. A few Korean American men said that they attended churches because that is where Korean American women were. A few women said that they had met their spouses at church.[10] Only a few non-ethnics attended events sponsored by KAP or IANA. No informants mentioned that they or anyone they knew had turned to these organizations as a means to find same-sex partners. The president of the only independent gay Asian American organization in Dallas said that his group had more contact with other gay associations than with other Asian American ones, owing not to any notable tensions but to members' preferences.

Samit stressed another reason why members wanted to meet co-ethnics:

> This is a key point: we have been one of the most successful groups of immigrants, and this is all done on our own, completely on our own. There's never been a concerted effort to make this network, and this can augment our group. It's just inherent. It's easier. You have something in common. I see you and already I know it's easier to build that network. And honestly, Indians are so fucking successful that when you want to network, you want to network with successful people. And put a group of highly successful people together, who knows what they can do.

Contrary to common assumptions, actors' professional integration into the white-collar workplace stood as a reason to come together rather than stay apart. To help capitalize on this, IANA hosted an investment club with monthly meetings on such topics as how to build a successful investment portfolio and how to buy real estate. This section of the organization had its own Web site within the group's Web site and is often mentioned in the weekly e-mails of upcoming events. It also held a seminar on e-commerce and a monthly "business-card-exchange" happy hour, which gave attendees an opportunity to network in a casual atmosphere. The efforts of IANA Dallas chapter efforts won it the award for best professional development in 2001 and 2002, over all the IANA chapters nationwide. IANA also held cultural events, which members appreciated as well. KAP and IANA appealed to professionals almost exclusively, bringing in people of a single "ethno-class" (Gordon 1964; see chapter 6). A few in working-class professions and/or without a college education felt uncomfortable in those settings (Dhingra 2003b). The groups' titles explicitly referred to professionals and networking, and practically all the members had finished college and worked in the corporate or medical sphere. KAP was primarily a social group that gave members opportunities to network informally. They held a seminar on investing in the stock market a year before my fieldwork, according to members.

Bonding and Bridging in Civil Society

Organization leaders and members affirmed ethnic boundaries among members. Yet, organizations that only bond attendees to one another can actually limit the effectiveness of civil society in the long run by not encouraging the formation of bridges between these groups and others. Civic organizations can connect people outside their category of ethnicity, class, religion, gender, politics, and so on with whom they otherwise would not have sustained interactions (Eliasoph 1999). This builds social capital across a variety of social statuses, which in turn contributes a number of social benefits, such as helping mobilize local communities, keeping possible social deviants from feeling abandoned, and supporting the nation's democracy by giving people insight into others' needs (Putnam 2000). More diverse spaces also help members overcome prejudices and unify the nation (Gutmann 1994). Given the promise of such organizations, those that are inclusive and fit within the democratic ideals of the country receive greater social approval (Alexander and Smith 1993; Brettell 2005a; Kurien 2003).

The concern over whether organizations fulfill democratic ideals takes on an even greater politicized importance for ethnic and racial associations. The rise of multiculturalism and the growing acceptance of ethnic identities have worried conservatives that attention to particular groups sacrifices national unity (Glazer 1997; Gleason 2001; Schlesinger 1992). According to these critics, ethnic minorities are focusing too much on their ancient histories, at times relying on spurious facts. The presumed goal is to position themselves as apart from and even superior to Whites, and/or as "victims" of oppression (Ceasar 1998; Woodward 1998). Civic organizations can encourage this "balkanization" of the United States by positing their group as exclusive and uninterested in others and by criticizing the government and the racial majority. Identity-based organizations can further group-based mentalities that undermine the supposed liberal democratic basis of our government (McWilliams 1998). From this perspective, ethnic associations that prioritize exclusive memberships threaten the nation, especially when their members consider themselves better than other Americans. Asian Americans in particular already appear as exclusionary groups. This concern over national disunity is all the more relevant for these informants, given that few took part in mainstream civic institutions that would establish them as full citizens.[11]

This conservative critique of pluralism and civil society is not only highly popular but fits with the perspectives on race and power offered by participants in chapter 4. They emphasized their belief in meritocratic institutions that would facilitate overcoming most racism, especially given their own hard work and educational achievements. This attitude contributed to their ethnic American identity and lack of pan-ethnic and person-of-color alliances. Most actors did not want to address racism by criticizing the state and promoting group-based initiatives, such as affirmative action. Instead, they agreed with the liberal democratic image of the nation that people should be measured and treated as individuals (Gleason 2001). As a result, they could not justify exclusive civic organizations as necessary for resisting racism and giving needed resources primarily to their own groups, even though they protected self-esteem. Respondents would be contradicting their own attitudes toward combating racism and toward group mobility by dismissing concerns over their ethnic-exclusive format.

The question becomes, to what extent did the organizations serve members' interests for racial, ethnic, and religious support, often in exclusive settings, without creating schisms between groups? Group leaders performed boundary work to appeal to co-ethnics, yet they did so in ways that reached out to other Americans as well. They reached out through creative and openly visible efforts that denied group differences at times and at other times framed their ethno-national ties and their racial and class statuses as actually making them accessible to Whites. In this way they helped their members gain acceptance as cultural citizens who contributed to a liberal democracy rather than remaining foreigners. These efforts are in line with the lived hybridity documented in the other domains. In particular, groups welcomed others as members and publicly demonstrated a complimentary relationship between their groups and the government, dominant institutions, and local charities. I focus less on the practical goals and accomplishments of organizations' efforts and more on how those efforts connect to the domain schema.

Open-Door Policy   As explained earlier, members joined homogenous spaces for emotional and instrumental reasons, and both they and leaders often referred to their preference for associating with people like themselves. Still, they thought of their ethnic organizations not as contradicting American ideals but as actually furthering them. In their opinion, their ethnic associations followed in the footsteps of those created by previous immigrants and were permissible as long as no one was excluded from joining. America was an immigrant nation that gave people choices of how to be, and as long as the organizations accepted others, as America does, there was no problem. This was more of an issue for Korean Americans as Christians in a predominantly Christian country. Pastor Kwon described his impression of multiculturalism as he explained why it was all right to have a mostly Korean American, highly acculturated membership:

> I've heard it this way: salad bowl. You have all these different tastes in this big bowl. I don't know if [the Korean church] creates distance. People have choices. You can go to a Korean church, but if you don't want to, you can go to whatever church you want to. That's what America is. I don't think that takes away from America, since America is all these diverse things. It doesn't create distance from the mainstream since there is so much diversity. There is a mainstream, but there are all these other parts. . . . Basically, the Korean identity, their willingness to identify with the Korean culture, is stronger than their willingness to identify with their denominations, among the churches. For example, the Korean Presbyterian church, Methodist church, and Baptist churches are more willing to communicate with each other than with[in] their denominations. Even among the [second-generation] EMs.

Pastors eschewed the melting-pot analogy, as feared by critics of multiculturalism, and instead accentuated the preference, even the right as Americans, for groups to maintain ethnic differences over and above religious denominations. Yet, pastors and informants noted proper and improper ways of exercising their rights and insisted that they did not close their doors to others (Newfield and Gordon 1996; Taylor 1994). Mary made a similar point in defending her EM as part of America:

> I think that there is no real American culture. I think America in itself is all of these different groups coming together, and somehow some of these values were formed. America is just being able to embrace all this diversity. It also depends on how the institution approaches it, of course. If they are going to be very exclusive, that is a problem.

Mary and most of the other interviewees did not mind their religious and secular organizations encouraging a restricted ethnic boundary. Sylvia was the rare exception in questioning the outcome: "When we are in church and we are in America, but with all Koreans it feels like we are isolating ourselves." Though worried about the "isolationist" nature of the EMs, she still attended one.

Although it made sense for Hindu temples to be ethnically exclusive, it was still important for them similarly to convey a welcoming attitude to others.

Gautum questioned but ultimately felt comfortable with the dual rhetoric of his Hindu temple, whose open-door public face belied its preferred exclusivity backstage.

> The temple is funny because there are two types of meetings, the weekly Sunday meeting and general festivals. The festivals are for everyone, and the rhetoric is, "We shouldn't step on anyone's feet." And on Sundays, it's more, "We're Indian and look at our culture, it's better than their culture." Like family, divorce rate, our kids don't drop out of high school. It tends to glorify the differences. I think it's OK. If the end is to belittle the other culture, then no. If the end is to make one's own self and family better, that's fine.

As explained in chapter 3, for instance, Hindu representatives framed their religion and culture as comparable to Christianity, working alongside other faiths to create a more spiritually nourished city. Backstage from the civil society domain code, it could be a different story.

Demonstrating Support of the State   In theory the associations conveyed themselves as open to others, but they had almost exclusively ethnic memberships. In practice the organizations gave back to the nation by publicly demonstrating their allegiance to it. Organizations linked their members to the state by explicitly signifying a complementary relationship between the U.S. government and India or Korea at the cultural and symbolic levels.[12] Such demonstrations not only satisfied the domain code but also brought needed attention to group concerns and could possibly break down discrimination against members, as discussed in chapters 3 and 4.

The interest in backing the state defined what kinds of cultural displays the members preferred and the organizations sponsored. Rajat distinguished between practices that properly and those that improperly demonstrated one's background within civil society:

> It's okay to have an Indian Day Parade, a little India, a little China. But I don't think you should have [government] forms only in Hindi or only in Chinese or only in Spanish. Indian Parade is okay because you are stressing diversity. "Hey, I'm an American but I'm from India." The other one is, "Hey, we are going to cater to your needs and satisfy just you and forget everybody else." I think what they should do is make English the official language. That's a common thread that everybody's going to have.

The need for a "common thread" conforms to the democratic ideology of honoring the unity of all groups over that of any single one's interests

(McWilliams 1998; Wolfe 2000). Becoming accepted as American does not mean abandoning ethnicity but instead framing it in ways that suit the state, or more specifically the domain code (Rudrappa 2004).

In addition, the main Indian American organizations employed religious events in response to 9/11 to ameliorate possible racial or cultural tensions, as discussed in chapter 3. Gauruv, president of IANA in 2002, could not explain why no secular public or political discussion of 9/11 took place within IANA (he was not president at the time), even though a Pakistani (not Indian) American was shot in Dallas in a hate crime following the terrorist attack:

> I, unfortunately, do not think anything happened as far as IANA was involved. If I'm not mistaken, one Indian was killed in Dallas. There might have been a discussion or fundraising effort. But in terms of IANA, nothing that I'm aware of. I think it was being talked about so much in the press and talked about so much with their friends, so that talking about it at another forum [did not occur].

The organizations did not see themselves as making political statements regarding the communities so much as defending their culture against explicit critiques and as promoting economic and political interests. The lack of action, by default, contributes to Indian Americans' implicit support of the state.

This implicit support is furthered by the lack of overt political conversations sponsored by organizations that challenge the state. The leading Indian American organization did not sponsor debates on the role of South Asia in the war on terrorism or on U.S. foreign policy. It invited elected officials to gatherings in order to demonstrate their commitment to the democratic process and to make sure their concerns were heard (Brettel 2005a). Korean American organizations, while fewer in number, similarly concentrated on cultural elements and local business needs rather than on controversial political dimensions. Possibly contentious parts of a Korean background, such as the continued military presence of Americans in South Korea and its accompanying tensions, were downplayed. A national Korean American civil rights organization that encourages the political participation of Korean Americans by sponsoring citizenship and voter registration recently started a chapter in Dallas.[13] Another recent addition to the local Asian American landscape is an Asian American advocacy organization. How they add to the strategies of the existing organizations that informants and their families participated in will become clearer over time.

Informants' concern over pushing their ethnicity too far into the public consciousness, and thereby seeming to demand public recognition over other groups, also shaped their organizations' aesthetic and symbolic choices. Actors believed that their associations could demonstrate that they were not "forgetting everyone else," as Rajat said, by publicly presenting themselves in an inclusive manner. The EMs' boundary work included changing their names to non-Korean titles and physically separating their congregation spaces from their parent churches (Dhingra 2004). Hindu Americans faced stronger challenges because of their religious minority status. Gautum complimented efforts by certain temples not to appear atypical:

> I've seen temples built across the country, and they are extravagant, and they may give the wrong message. We're not trying to say, hey, look at us, we can build a temple in your neighborhood. . . . If it's a Hindu temple that looks like a Hindu temple, it's going to stick out like a sore thumb.

In effect, it was all right to be Hindu as long as one is not too Hindu. Both Korean Americans and Indian Americans tried to walk a fine line between satisfying their communities' interests and appearing divisive. As communities grow and gain more political power, more elaborate displays of their ethnicity may follow.

In addition to self-censorship, organizations publicly used selective, symbolic displays to demonstrate their political dedications. IAA hoped to help members adjust into mainstream institutions, as noted in chapter 2. Its cultural and social events made explicit reference to a complementary relationship between India and the United States. For instance, at a secular Indian American youth camp in 2002, children posed for a photo while holding signs reading "God Bless America" and "USA and India Love Freedom and Democracy," along with both the Indian and American flags.[14] In August 2002, at a Dallas event honoring India's independence, there were also American and Indian flags, waving side by side, along with booths offering bank accounts, insurance, and samosas.[15] Such signs demonstrate not only to out-group members but also to in-group members that what it means to be Indian American is to be part of a patriotic and consumerist nation, thereby linking their multiple identities.[16]

These examples demonstrate the power of domain schemas. Signs and slogans indicate the influence of the domain cultural frame, for these props were not necessary in the leisure or home realms when co-ethnics came together. Asian Americans appear mostly as "model" cultural citizens: proud of a heritage that complements that of their adopted nation. They may need assistance in becoming full members of the state, which the organizations are facilitating. The United States and India or South Korea become siblings based on their purchasing power and democratically elected governments. This selective public presentation served as a practical response to both the racialization of Asian Americans as potential foreigners and members' desire for greater political voice. The organizations' efforts suited the domain code and gained its members more attention and assistance at the local level (Brettell 2005b).

Demonstrating Support of Dominant Institutions   The ethnic associations also conformed to the civil society code by integrating members in key social-structural dimensions, namely media and corporate representation, residential location, and attainment of a high level of education, while still affirming internal solidarity. The organizations' events helped gain members local recognition and general mobility and portrayed a commitment to the mainstream based on members' ethnic or racial status as supportive minorities. We also see that leaders consider pan-ethnicity as either an aid or a liability in claiming citizenship. It is an aid when it sustains a model-minority image, as in this section, but a liability when it suggests a prioritization of one's race over others, seen in the next section.

For instance, the Asian American Small Business Association hosted a meeting with representatives from the local NBC television station, mostly from its news program, to gain Asian Americans more recognition.[17] Personalities both in front of and behind the cameras were present. The meeting took place in the association's building, located in the small-business district of Dallas, half a mile from a small nucleus of Korean American–owned stores. Shah started the meeting by telling the NBC staff that the audience represented "Asian America." The audience of mostly first-generation Asian American businesspeople asked for the sports section to cover prominent Asian Americans in the area (such as the Vietnamese American linebacker for the Dallas Cowboys National Football League team), for the station to hire Asian Americans, and for greater coverage of international issues. When one NBC respondent said that there were currently no Asian Americans working for their news division, but that it was interested in hiring some, the audience nodded their heads in satisfaction. Many questions, like the use of HDTV and the progress of the Dallas Cowboys, had no connection to Asian America per se. No association members asked about possible negative portrayals of Asian Americans in the media. Asian Americans appeared as interested viewers who were supportive of the corporate media and desirous of helping it fulfill its stated mission of covering local issues and attending to diversity.

The organizations also facilitated the second generation's involvement in other social institutions in an indirect manner, which informants noted as important in justifying their groups. Rajat did not consider IANA as too exclusive:

> I think [IANA] strikes a balance between the two. Because, yes there is IANA, and yes, we are celebrating our ethnicity, our difference. [But] a lot of things we do talk about are in the cultural mainstream: buying a house, buying a car, a college workshop for kids, and stuff like that.

The financial seminars noted earlier further this economic function. The organizations construct individuals as social citizens who can consume middle-class markers, such as a preferred residential neighborhood, type of car, and school system, in implicit contrast to those who cannot (Park 2005). The fact that Rajat justified IANA's existence in this manner also indicates the effects of the domain schema. In the home or leisure realm, individuals did not feel the need to rationalize co-ethnic friendships by referring to what they talked about to their friends and in fact stressed that they often had conversations with co-ethnics that would be impossible to have with outsiders. Hindu Americans also defended their religion and temples by arguing Hinduism's overlap with Christianity, as discussed in chapter 3.

Demonstrating Support of Local Charities   The organizations also engaged in charitable activities both for Dallas residents generally and for their own communities in Dallas and abroad. Doing so not only assisted others, as was important to members, but also furthered the groups' image as ethnic Americans, that is, appealing to co-ethnics yet supportive of other Americans. Outreach to charities indicates a commitment to the prescribed civil-society code (Alexander and Smith 1993; Putnam 2000). It is by coming together as co-ethnics that they were able to assist others, thereby integrating because of, not despite, their marginal status. Their giving also furthered a stereotype of model minorities as financially successful and contributive to the public welfare. First-generation leaders, such as Jain in chapter 3, took pride in donating to local organizations because it helped combat the image of scheming foreigners. Second-generation organization members similarly felt strongly that their volunteering should not be focused strictly on their own community, for doing so would negate their role as Americans. As Kithana said, "You shouldn't try to hide your traditions or how you go about doing things. That doesn't mean you should only help Indians or be an Indian society. You should go to India for that." Whom one volunteers for represents one's national allegiances and so suggests either committed or uncommitted citizens (Wilson 2000). The second generation applauded organizations' charitable efforts and believed that associations had a duty in this regard.

IANA had a strong record of donating to charities both in Dallas and in India. At one of IANA's volunteer planning meetings, suggestions involved working mostly with institutions that served the less fortunate in Dallas, including Habitat for Humanity, soup kitchens, charity walks for medical research, children's shelters, and clean-ups of local parks and highways.[18] IANA offered a significant amount of outreach, so much so that it earned community service awards in 1998, 1999, 2000, and 2001 from the IANA national board. As Gauruv said of IANA's charitable focus:

> It's mostly those [organizations] that have branches in Dallas. We have done stuff, donated funds to charities in India. But our goal, in terms of spending time, you don't want to do that when you're in Dallas. So it's mostly Dallas driven. For example, we are doing the Habitat for Humanity on Saturday. It's locally driven.

Second-generation Indian Americans also reached out to their own community, both in India and in Dallas.[19] This internally focused volunteering provided needed support to individuals and required significant time and money from group members and leaders. Their choices of ethnic-oriented volunteering often served people in their homeland, such as following a natural disaster. At an IANA community service meeting, a couple of suggestions included helping the impoverished in India through such activities as sending medical supplies to needy clinics. Involvement with the Dallas Indian American community often centered around assisting the first generation in promoting educational success for their children. This included volunteering for the ethnic groups' own spelling bees and career fairs for youth. Indian American children have created for themselves an image as spelling bee masters and have won a disproportionate share of National Spelling Bee championships, a status that such efforts aim to maintain. The Dallas Indian American community also assisted on occasion with health fairs and other social service offerings sponsored by IAA that gave needed support to co-ethnics, often elderly, who might not otherwise know how or where to receive adequate health care.

Gauruv also proposed an ambitious program for IANA to help Indian Americans who lacked the financial means for college:

> One of the goals is to start a foundation for people who are Indian who are financially strapped. We haven't developed the prerequisites yet, but we're trying to start a fund where you consistently have a fund out there. This is at the Dallas

level. Dallas [chapter of IANA] has been aggressive in forming this foundation. Only two, three other chapters—New York and San Francisco—have formed it. We may help people that are here and are in high school and want to go to college. But they can't afford to go to college because of financial needs. But they are very intelligent and have qualified to go to college. So we'd like to give some kind of assistance. Not necessarily a large donation but some kind of funds where they can buy books or get something small out there. We don't have the funds right now, and our goal is not to be a $100,000 asset-based organization. It's to have a few thousand dollars to have money to give some assistance but not full assistance. It's difficult with the transition of the board every year.

This significant and altruistic endeavor addresses a growing problem in the Indian American community: those in the lower and working classes who cannot afford the increasing tuition and costs associated with college. While alone this ambitious program does not dislodge any disadvantageous stereotype of Indian and other Asian Americans, it draws attention to the economically underprivileged within the community.

Given that KAP was a smaller organization than IANA and lacked a national association with branches across the country, it had fewer resources to donate. Still, members took pride in their assistance to the needy within the Korean American community, mostly elderly who needed language and medical assistance. Samantha discussed the charitable works sponsored by KAP and by first-generation Korean American associations, in which KAP also occasionally assisted in:

We had a day [for those] who didn't speak English; [KAP members] would translate whatever they needed. When our Korean Small Business Association had a party, we would volunteer, like a New Year's party. One thing I like about KAP is that they have a $1,000 scholarship. They choose the winner based upon how well and thorough an essay is by someone who applies. It is advertised in newspapers. Other issues include taking care of our elderly. I know a lot of families do that anyway, but sometimes there are elders out there who can't do anything. Also, there is a language barrier on knowing what their rights are. Also, they give advice, like free medical or legal advice. They try to get different occupations to come in, like medical or legal.[20]

The organizations' choices of which causes to support suggest communities comparable in some respects to other Americans, namely with elderly who lack insurance. They also highlight immigrant-specific needs, such as legal and language assistance as immigrants deal with small-business and real-estate issues, how to acquire necessary visas, how to navigate bureaucracies, and so on.

KAP's college scholarship for a Korean American high school student would be administered based on merit without consideration of financial need. At a monthly dinner meeting, members continued to plan out how the scholarship would be advertised and what to ask in the applications, so that high school students would enjoy the process as much as possible.[21] While much of the EMs' service was internal to the church, they also offered missionary work in other countries as well as local assistance, including visits to homeless shelters and soup kitchens.[22]

The charitable programs of KAP and IANA that served their communities reinforce an ethnic American image acceptable to outsiders, one of being distinct from the majority primarily in degree of acculturation rather than by race or class. This in turn allows the organizations to continue their outreach without drawing possible criticism for violating the domain code by prioritizing social differences. This approach also suggests that problems facing group members remain internal to the community, without requests for public recognition, and so are relatively minor although still worth noting. Those served appear primarily as lacking acculturation, such as in English-language ability or in knowledge of the medical system. After adjusting to the rules of America, they potentially can make it on their own. The proposed scholarships also demonstrate a recognition of actors' economic privilege relative to co-ethnics. Neither draws off public funds, as government assistance programs like affirmative action do. As a result, they would not violate the widely held aversion to competing for public resources as a group rather than as individuals. So, the organizations are able to reach out to their ethnic communities without their standing as proper civic associations being challenged.

In addition to charity to their ethnic community, leaders also considered whether to volunteer for other Asian American groups. Their goal of being recognized as ethnic Americans meant not prioritizing a racial identity. Claiming the model-minority stereotype did not suggest racial interests so much as accomplishments as a racial group. For instance, KAP had been planning to work with Habitat for Humanity. Yet Susie, president of KAP in 2000, said that KAP would not sponsor activities to help Asian Americans who were not Korean, such as Vietnamese Americans, who have a large community in Dallas. When I asked her why KAP would do Habitat for Humanity and not assist Vietnamese Americans, she replied:

> I would push for things like Habitat for Humanity, things that benefit humankind. We are professionals and that is a professional thing to do, to help others.

> It would have to benefit the Korean community or a general cause. Things for the
> Vietnamese community are too specific.

Informants could have promoted the civil-society schema while embracing
their racial status, such as by joining with Vietnamese Americans as fellow
Asian Americans and petitioning the government for greater assistance despite the supposed lack of economic and social challenges facing the model
minority (Zia 2000). Yet, by prioritizing their role as ethnic Americans who
help local Dallas residents regardless of background, Korean Americans fit
within liberal democratic ideals and so avoided the criticisms of privileging
group-based, in particular racial, identities (Ceasar 1998). The selective boundary work of the organizations was deliberate. Susie commented that volunteer
work primarily "is important for us as PR."

The organizations' outreach assists groups, but the ethnic image of populations primarily marginalized due to a lack of acculturation and knowledge
of group institutions worried some. OKA's Park warned against imagining
Korean Americans as the model minority:

> It sounds like we are one of the successful community, but I don't want it to
> sound like that because we have our own problems in the community: senior
> citizens, language, abuse, and between Korean competition in business.

Domestic violence continues to be a serious problem in both Korean American
and Indian American households (Abraham 2000; Campbell, Masaki, and
Torres 2002; Song 1996); the main organizations had not drawn explicit attention to it as of yet. In addition, Asian American women work in low-paying,
gendered service occupations, such as in garment factories in Dallas (Um
2005). The concentration of small businesses and the interminority tensions
that often ensue also will not go away with acculturation (Abelmann and Lie
1995). As referenced in chapter 2, Indian Americans in Dallas live in poverty
in numbers just below the Dallas average of 13.4 percent and Korean Americans just above it, suggesting economic needs for each group, in particular
the latter. Continuing problems facing all Asian Americans, such as the glass
ceiling, receive little notice. This is not to critique current organizations, but to
note the number of issues facing the communities. It is extremely difficult for
social, cultural, or religious associations to effectively address problems rooted
in cultural mores, racist assumptions, and macro socioeconomic shifts. The
organizations did quite a bit, especially considering that they are completely
voluntary. An image as mostly productive citizens in pursuit of greater acculturation, which allowed these organizations to comfortably do outreach in

line with the domain code in the first place, may ironically and inadvertently further the image that worried Park—that their communities did not need to attract public attention to their concerns. Overall, the associations found ways to fit the domain schema that allowed their members to form bridges with other groups rather than staying internally focused, while still attending to a variety of ethnic-specific concerns.

CONCLUSION

In the leisure realm the code is to engage in mainstream practices that may conflict with the ethnic social identity. In civil society they found themselves in ethnic-specific environments while needing to assert a commitment to mainstream groups. The predicament across both is the same: trying to demonstrate a cultural citizenship as Americans by conforming to a domain code, while at the same time hoping to bond with one another due to external maltreatment and cultural preferences. Informants frequently engaged in a lived hybridity and used selective public and backstage presentations in order to satisfy various sets of commitments. A margins-in-the-mainstream perspective draws attention to people's agency in handling competing interests. By following the domain codes, they made themselves into good citizens who prioritize dominant consumption patterns, types of social engagements, and civic practices while still furthering group needs.

Participants' experiences across the spheres further demonstrate the salience of domain cultures in identity management. How individuals made sense of symbols and practices depended on the relevant cultural schema, even when with the same people or in the same location. For instance, actors worried about appearing too ethnocentric at parties or in their conversations in civic organizations, but in other situations they took pride in such activities. There is no internal contradiction between such emotions, simply a difference in cultural context.

These findings comment on the often-studied topics of acculturation and pan-ethnicity. The second generation's decisions about engaging in mainstream behaviors, such as dating or drinking, do not necessarily represent a natural acculturation and the irrelevance of race, as argued by assimilation theory, but can signify a strategy for resisting racialization as foreigners.[23] Race shapes the leisure choices people make, even (and especially) when they are adopting popularized options. And so race, along with gradual acculturation, in part creates the tensions participants felt between acting "American" and acting "ethnic." Informants' efforts also shed light on pan-ethnic formations. Organizations did not follow a single approach to pan-ethnicity and instead eschewed or embraced the identity depending on the meaning it would suggest. Rather than asking whether organizations are pan-ethnic or not, as is normally the case, we should ask when and why they are, and with what effect. As seen here, their answers depend greatly on their role within the domain code.

These findings also offer insight into the literature on leisure and civil society as relevant to assessing immigrant adaptation. We normally determine the preferences of groups based on the kinds of leisure endeavors and civic organizations in which they engage. These are useful devices but alone do not capture the adaptation process. As symbolic interactionists argue, meaning is created in interactions, and the meanings different people assign to the same task vary. We capture group boundaries better by examining subtle differences in how actors both interpreted and performed leisure and civic events. There is not a clear, linear relationship between partaking in mainstream popular culture, for instance, and ties to one's ethnic group, as suggested by assimilation theory. The manner in which one engages in various pursuits, not only how many such pursuits are performed, reveals commitments to an identity more clearly.

At the same time, the integrating of identities could have unintended consequences in the leisure and civil society spheres, discussed further in chapter 8. Their lived hybridity in the leisure domains could contribute to a greater integration than anticipated. Also, as multiculturalism and globalization make ethnic spaces more popular and the second generation makes mainstream spaces more ethnic, the division between groups diminishes even further. "Ethnic" endeavors may become only those that occur in explicitly defined private spaces. In other words, their success at integrating lifestyles in the leisure sphere could contribute to a segregation of identities over time.

In addition, acting as cultural citizens in both realms could carry unexpected implications. The claims of full citizenship represent a political act, in much the same way acting as a proper worker and domestic family does (Park 2005). In the leisure realm this depends on the second generation's economic ability to mingle in White middle-class spaces and their cultural capital in conveying ethnicity in socially acceptable ways. In civil society, organizations' public efforts embraced a liberal democratic multiculturalism and a model-minority image. These politicized frameworks present their marginal status as supporting the mainstream. The implications of this on their and others' mobility and acceptance within the nation's supposed liberal democracy are discussed in the next chapter. Suffice it to say here that the reliance on liberal democracy could unintentionally create a longer-term challenge to Asian American professionals', as well as to other groups', hopes for acceptance as equal citizens. Still, informants created an affirming, supportive place within these domains without furthering the "balkanization" critique, which required intense effort. This will also be explored further in the next chapter.

8 Conclusion
Reconciling Identities, Recognizing Constraints

IN THIS BOOK I HAVE ANALYZED how Asian American professionals make sense of and enact their ethnic minority status. I conceive of these Korean and Indian Americans as margins within the mainstream in order to move past the dichotomy of majority versus minority in identity formations. Though minorities, in particular those in the middle class, occupy both sets of spaces, they are portrayed as permanently outside the mainstream. While useful, such a perspective when taken alone may misrepresent minorities' fully intended boundary formations. Overall, second-generation Korean American and Indian American informants developed an "ethnic American" identity in response to their various social locations. They critiqued assimilation and discrimination but also hoped to integrate as highly ethnic and as a model minority, instead of developing a reactive ethnicity or hiding their group differences in the private sphere. They accomplished this while attending to a self-defined American identity, but which conflicted with an ethnic lifestyle. Their daily identity choices and practices depended largely on the differing cultural codes of the domains of work, home, leisure, and civil society. By displaying both marginal and mainstream identities, at times simultaneously, actors broke down the practical binaries of immigrant versus native and minority versus majority, while still considering those binaries real. They also defined themselves as equal to White workers, as moral families, and as cultural citizens without denying their status as ethnic minorities. Yet they remained constrained by ideological and practical expectations at the domain level that limit challenges to the basis of their unequal status. This study has examined micro-level processes of identity management and linked them to both group- and macro-level constraints and implications. The findings build upon and add to dominant models of identity development, identity enactment, immigrant adaptation, multiculturalism, and race relations.

DEVELOPING IDENTITIES

The notion of being ethnic, racial, or American fails to represent how people can form multiple identities, nor does it articulate how these identities can both support and contradict one another. Korean and Indian Americans defined and shared their background in ways that made them part of their host society. The first generation prescribed a selective assimilation that included those cultural elements that promoted economic mobility despite discrimination (Portes and Zhou 1993). The categories of traditional community, fitting in, and family elucidate how second-generation participants actually developed identities relative both to their communities' moral order and to their particular middle-class environments. Interviewees were not waiting for a post-ethnic America into which to fit publicly (Hollinger 1995), but instead hoped to integrate as highly ethnic. An identity-work perspective draws attention to informants' agency in developing ethnic identities that fit their needs, but without suggesting that identities are completely fluid. Informants could not assert just any definition of a background because they were constrained by their ethnic social identity. The salience of these three categories for each individual can be traced back to adolescent experiences and so were not totally variable.

It is by framing people as margins in the mainstream that we also understand their racial identities as ethnic Americans. Much like classical assimilation theory, the Black-White paradigm frames groups as either minorities or part of the majority and overlooks how people can create notions of self that serve their needs as members of both groups. Although Asian American and ethnic studies have deconstructed the Black-White paradigm in regard to understanding what racism means and how race works, it still dominates in making sense of racial identities. Looking solely at informants' attitudes relative to Whites would suggest a reactive ethnicity or pan-ethnic identity, commonly assumed in both immigration and ethnic studies scholarship. Yet their types of categorizations, cultural pulls, and interests as professionals in Dallas supported an identity as a model minority and as multicultural immigrants. They adopted an individual-level perspective on race relations, believing that they could attain equality gradually despite some people's prejudices. These margins-in-the-mainstream actors remained marked by race yet without its strong stigma, which limited its felt significance. Given their ethnic and racial identities, it made sense that they reified as real and relatively static the cultural and social differences between their groups and others.

Research within ethnic studies and immigration should continue this analysis on groups' variations in adolescent experiences that guide their path of ethnic identity development. An analysis of the first generation also offers deeper insights into identity development, for it gives better context for the second generation's perspectives. In addition, we also should consider groups' multidimensional racial positions. Doing so demonstrates how identities result from groups' statuses relative both to the majority and to other minorities, for together these varying statuses lead to a complicated, nuanced set of attitudes. Informants' goal to integrate as *Korean* Americans and *Indian* Americans is a bold stance, especially in geographic areas without a long history of Asian immigration. They noted the challenges they faced in developing such a perspective, but they also remarked that doing so was personally and socially meaningful. Furthermore, we see variation not only between Korean and Indian Americans, especially in regard to religion and physical appearance, but also within each group, which otherwise would remain overlooked in research on individual populations.

COMBINING IDENTITIES, NOT ONLY SEGREGATING THEM

It is not enough to just measure the content of the second generation's identities, for the ways in which these are expressed also created distance from or integration with others. The binary notion of being either ethnic/racial or American also carries over into the standard thinking on identity enactment: that we supposedly express one role and then the other, depending on place and time. This study demonstrates the constructed nature of this binary while accounting for its felt significance. Chapters 5–7 accounted for the tensions actors felt between their various commitments and then how they dealt with those tensions. We better assess identity performances and adaptation by seeing (1) that actors could perform their identities within the same space, frequently within the same action, as opposed to only segregating them, and (2) that they performed their identities relative to the domain cultural scripts.

In regard to the first point, the prevailing notion within academic and popular discourse, discussed in chapter 1, is that people segregate conflicting identities to discrete realms in order to maintain a cognitive and emotional

balance. We certainly see that members of the second generation at times separate identities to distinct spaces. This meant going out of their way at times
to please outsiders or parents and confining disruptive practices away from
others' view. Still, Asian Americans chose both to bring their ethnic minority
status into the public realm and to bring their Americanized identity into the
private realm. Their ability and desire to do so move us past the conventional
notion of living in two worlds, which governs our thinking about the second
generation. Informants' boundary work and identity talk at times resulted in a
"lived hybridity," in which they attended to multiple sets of interests simultaneously, often creating a new course of action. It is helpful to see how a single
action, such as putting on glasses at work or reconceptualizing dating, for
instance, represents a hybrid moment. It draws attention to how actors went
beyond the static notion of one identity versus the other in daily life. One
could be both a racial minority and a star employee, or a dutiful child and a
hip American. Although segregating identities is common, as demonstrated
in this study, the combining of them receives the most emphasis because it
remains overlooked and informs various fields of study.

Normally, conversations about hybridity within cultural studies refer to
cultural products or to liminal and elusive third spaces that are fleeting and
hard to pin down (Gray and Thumma 1997; Lavie and Swedenburg 1996; Zhou
and Lee 2004). Examples include dance scenes, music, plays, and race cars,
which symbolize the reconciling of self-definitions (Gross, McMurray, and
Swedenburg 1996; Kondo 1996; Namkung 2004). Outside of those moments
identities seemingly remain separate and in tension (Maira 2002). Taking
the analytical tool of hybridity and applying it to daily life, I suggest another
way of thinking about commonplace actions and psychological processes that
highlights individuals' agency (Certau 1984). There is no liminal or third space
in this case. The notions of boundary work and identity talk give us a means
to see how people affirm, both consciously and unconsciously, social expectations with their day-to-day behaviors. Yet this linking of identities does not
break down in actors' minds or in the broader imagination the notion of static,
dichotomous roles that remain embedded in cultural and political discourses
and in the rhetoric of communities, families, and peers. The act of combining
lifestyles in daily life has implications for groups' adaptation and racialization,
discussed below.

The ability to bring together identities illustrates interviewees' agency. In
addition, this analysis sheds light on how people actually exercise this agency.

Informants' boundary work and identity talk were guided by both the ethnic social identity and the domain schemas. The ethnic social identity, itself shaped by immigrants' racial, class, and migrant statuses, served not merely as a reference point for the second generation but comprised a moral order of "proper" versus "improper" behavior. Understanding how and why first-generation immigrants defined their backgrounds as racialized professionals, along with the community sanctions on behavior, explains the various pressures placed on informants to act in a certain way. The second generation's own identity formations, discussed in chapters 3 and 4, reinforced their felt need for an ethnic boundary in daily life.

Informants also dealt with domain schemas as they exercised their agency, which pertains to the second point of identity performance. Informants could not bring their lifestyles together in any way that they liked but instead had to conform to various codes (Caplow 1982; Swidler 2001). As respondents moved from one stage to the next, from the corporate sphere to schools, from talking with co-ethnic peers as friends versus talking to them as organization members, and so on, they shifted the meaning of their background to suit the variety of contexts. Contradictions in what people say and feel often are attributed to personal ambiguities, but they may in fact signify the influence of cultural spaces, such as when informants praise the value of respecting family when in the home sphere and criticize it when in the leisure sphere. Identities are more "positionings" than static entities one turns on and off (Hall 1990). In this dance of ethnic and racial expressions, actors illustrate that there is no stable ethnicity or race that they simply live, but instead, that they perform in diverse ways to satisfy particular audiences, including themselves (Goffman 1959).

Participants' agency in integrating identities into spaces from which they are normally absent, such as acting on an ethnic identity at work and an American identity at home, remains overlooked and even unexpected because of the emphasis in the sociology of culture literature on the power of cultural codes. Research on culture and place typically considers the codes to be active almost regardless of individuals' location, and to determine individuals' behaviors and attitudes (Caplow 1982; Lamont 1992; Lichterman 1999). For instance, gay activists frame their gay identity differently based on their organizational context, even when each organization has a number of the same core members (Lichterman 1999).[1] Agency is seen in people's ability to create the cultural norms that a group then follows and to choose a cultural "tool" or "repertoire" that fits an institution's culture and advances their needs (Eliasoph and Lichterman 2003; Swidler 1986, 2001). I am not pointing to deficiencies in these studies; I refer to them simply to demonstrate that the major focus of research up to now has been to establish the power of culture. This study accounts for that while showing how actors also negotiated cultural codes, as seen in chapters 5–7.

Of course, informants also conformed completely to domain scripts at various times, as mentioned above, even though the analytical emphasis here has fallen on the ability to handle conflict. In fact, informants went to great lengths simply to act as expected within a cultural space, without trying to create a hybrid lifestyle. Some informants were more interested in integrating identities than were others (Brekhus 2003). But it is important to note that all participants wanted to do so to varying degrees, and their ability to do so remains overlooked.

Highlighting the significance of domain codes is not meant to suggest that micro-level conditions did not influence identity choices at the interpersonal level, as indicated by social psychological research in both sociology and psychology (Alexander and Wiley 1992; Stryker 1992; Tajfel and Turner 1986). Yet other people in a setting did not easily offset the perceived domain script, which indicates the importance of focusing on group boundary performance through a sociology-of-culture lens. Still, interactants influenced respondents' approach to their identities. Laura, for instance, would not have considered taking time off from work if her boss had not allowed it. When they felt control over their environment, they altered the domain schema to act more as they pleased, as seen in Jyoti's approach to her office (Fine 1996; Sewell 1992).

The second generation's boundary work and identity talk were thus influenced both by a domain's cultural schemas and by others who were important to them, with emphasis here placed on the former. By conceiving of these professionals as margins within the mainstream, we see how they actively brought their two worlds together across diverse spaces, and gain insights into identity performance. Without downplaying individuals' agency, we also see the power of culture.

MULTICULTURALISM AND INTEGRATION

The fact that participants are able to construct ethnic and racial identities and to bring their various identities together in daily life helps elucidate their adaptation. Adaptation has two components: to what extent the second generation is assimilating into or distancing itself from the mainstream, and to what extent it is furthering a racial/ethnic equality or a stratification.

The first question pertains to whether Korean and Indian Americans are promoting multiculturalism or assimilation. I am less interested in if informants are assimilating or not because group boundaries, as seen in this study, are malleable (Cornell and Hartmann 1998). I concentrate more on how the findings offer new means to evaluate adaptation, which bridges these two outcomes. Informants furthered a multiculturalism with their embrace of ethnic boundaries, and this makes multiculturalism's relationship to integration a central issue. I define multiculturalism in its most popular form and as practiced by participants, as expressions of cultural (as opposed to political) differences and social solidarity among group members. Whether multiculturalism not only differs from but contradicts assimilation is debated (Alba 1999; Kivisto 2005; Kivisto and Rundblad 2000; Salins 1997). Conservative critics of multiculturalism, as discussed in chapter 7, see it as antithetical to the history of the United States, a country supposedly built on the ability of groups to get along and promote a common cultural core (Ravitch 1990; Schlesinger 1992; Woodward 1998). On the surface, then, informants' expressions of group boundaries not only in private but also in public spaces would further multiculturalism and limit informants' integration.

According to leading philosophers on multiculturalism, however, maintaining ethnic interests is not harmful to the nation (Nash 1992; Parekh 2000; Taylor 1994). Multiculturalism allows for significant cultural variance but does not contradict integration if it fits within a liberal democracy, that is, if expressions of difference overlap with a dedication to principles of democracy, core values, and individualism. Multiculturalism should not prioritize individual ethnic groups over intergroup unity, nor should it prioritize group identities over the rights of individuals (Nash 1992). Integration, from this perspective, does not necessarily entail acculturation or complete social structural assimilation. It instead depends on civic incorporation. As long as individuals become citizens and contribute to popular institutions as members of the majority—for example, participating in politics or working in the primary labor market—they are contributing to the essential tenets of the state and so are integrating (Kymlicka 1995; Newfield and Gordon 1996). A shared culture should loosely link groups but need not result in a melting pot, for each group has the right to maintain its identity (Taylor 1994).[2] Those group differences that compliment the core culture should be encouraged as offering new, safe ways of (re)considering key ideas (Alexander 2001). According to this view, the overall effect of mainstream multiculturalism on the nation is similar to that of full absorption: both outcomes accentuate what ties groups together rather than what makes them unique, and both prioritize national allegiance over an ethnic one (Wolfe 2000). Inclusion of immigrants' differences, rather than a more narrow assimilation, is the multicultural goal. The question then becomes whether Korean and Indian Americans are furthering national unity, and thereby integrating, as they express group differences.

Yet it is unclear how to assess whether a group violates a common culture of broad ideals and so is integrating or not (Outlaw 1998). This is easier to determine in some settings than in others. In terms of revisions to public school curricula, such as in American history textbooks, school boards have battled over how much and in what manner to include ethnic diversity (Glazer 1997). The result has typically been a revision of standard accounts of U.S. history to demonstrate that minority groups played a major role in the construction of the nation even as they faced discrimination in the process. Running through theses accounts are themes of democracy, individualism, the work ethic, and other neoliberal principles on which the United States prides itself, rather than the reliance of the United States' economic success on the continued subjugation of, for instance, minorities and women (LaBelle and Ward 1996; Ravitch 1990).

It is not clear how to measure the extent to which people's expressions of multiculturalism contribute to or challenge the unity of the nation in their daily lives. What would group members need to do in order *not* to uphold the values of democracy, freedom, and so on? When are group rights overemphasized? Movements such as Afrocentrism arguably pursue ideals of equality and democracy, even though they are considered separatist and highly critical of the state. It is necessary to move past the question of whether group slogans or broad principles promote national unity or the uniqueness of a group (Sollors 1998) and toward understanding how individuals actually enact multiculturalism and are integrating (or not).

Sociologists also have changed positions on whether multiculturalism can connect with assimilation and national unity. Assimilation originally had been defined as the loss of ancestral cultural symbols and the exclusive entrance into mainstream organizations, friendships, neighborhoods, marital unions, and self-identifications (Gordon 1964). Scholars critiqued this definition as too strict, for according to this measure even European Americans have not fully assimilated. Instead, cultures were seen as changing with circumstances and as becoming salient to achieve shared interests (Glazer and Moynihan 1970; Yancey, Ericksen, and Juliani 1976). As a result, assimilation came to be defined more broadly to allow for some multiculturalism, so that immigrant communities could keep group boundaries in private or in occasional cultural displays (such as ethno-national parades) but still be integrating (Alba 1990; Gans 1979; Waters 1990).[3] Even recent immigrants who build robust boundaries have been framed within an assimilationist paradigm, broadly defined. Portes and Zhou (1993), along with other scholars of segmented assimilation theory, astutely argue that groups use ethnic social, cultural, and economic capital to assist members' upward mobility. As long as immigrants learn to participate like other Americans in mainstream institutions, including the educational sphere, popular civic organizations, the primary labor market, and so on, then affirmation of group boundaries in private coincides with national unity, as argued above (Gibson 1988; Zhou and Bankston 1998). Alba and Nee (2003) extend this compatible relationship between multiculturalism and assimilation by defining the latter as immigrants' entrance into mainstream spheres and a voluntary approach to their ancestral cultures in private. In contemporary mainstream, public spheres, ethnicity has little relevance for social relations in part due to laws prohibiting discrimination. If groups' access to resources does not depend directly on their ethnic or racial background but instead on their human, social, and cultural capital, then multiculturalism does not disrupt national unity and is compatible with assimilation. One should be "cosmopolitan," that is, voluntarily appreciative of cultures but not necessarily bound to one (Alba 1999; Hollinger 1995).

In other words, scholars have brought multiculturalism and assimilation together through determining how many ethnic versus mainstream practices people engaged in and whether they can be accepted as Americans instead of as members of ethnic groups. To the extent that individuals perform a seemingly distinctive ethnic/racial identity in the public sphere or an American lifestyle in private, they are avoiding or encouraging assimilation, respectively. This leads to measures of integration in terms of how much English immigrants (and their descendants) know, how many work for white-collar establishments, how many live in integrated versus segregated neighborhoods, how many belong to mainstream civic associations, how many have non-ethnic friends, how much discrimination they face, and so on.

Yet we find in chapters 3 and 4 that second-generation Asian Americans valued their group differences and did not consider abandoning them in order to integrate. Furthermore, although they entered middle-class institutions, they did not consider their ethnicity voluntary, nor did they decide to leave it at home, as seen in chapters 5–7. They were seen and saw themselves as ethnic minorities in private and also at work, during leisure time, and in civic associations. As they grew older, they rarely joined White-dominated associations or made close White friends. They also asserted ethnic differences across various spheres in response to their racialization as foreigners. According to current adaptation models, these professionals would not be integrating but would instead be threatening to balkanize the nation by consistently acting on their group differences in both private and public, even if they identified as ethnic American instead of Asian American or as people of color and even if they went out of their way to display camaraderie with Dallas locals in public. Many also did not support government intervention on behalf of particular groups, such as affirmative action programs or bilingual government forms. In other words, the conclusion that they are not integrating appears mistaken, given their embrace of liberal democracy.

This apparently mistaken assessment of the second generation's adaptation indicates a possibly misplaced conception of the practical relationship between integration and multiculturalism and of how to bridge them. Instead of weighing only *how much* groups express their identities, we also need to know *how* they do so. Indian and Korean Americans did so in ways that supported mainstream institutions and a liberal democracy because they did not prioritize ethnic or racial interests over those of the individual, *even as* they promoted group differences in public. This is seen not through a group's broad values or through individuals' degree of ethnic community versus mainstream institutional involvement and cultural knowledge. Instead, qualitative analysis elucidates how actors furthered their integration even though they drew ethnic and racial boundaries in daily life, such as with a lived hybridity. The important point indicating their integration is that they made sense of and expressed differences in ways that supported the cultural codes within each domain, and so they fit within the institutionalized logics of each space that reproduced dominant patterns of social relationships (Friedland and Alford 1991).[4] Examining how groups handle conflicting identities in daily life and locating that process in cultural spaces offers a revised way to assess the relationship between multiculturalism and immigrant integration.

Because this is a case study, more research needs to be conducted to see how other groups promote group boundaries while either conforming with or upsetting the cultural schemas of public and private spaces. It appears too simplistic to suggest that advancing group boundaries across public spheres necessarily weakens integration. Also, the governing assumption that immigrants and their descendants segregate their identities to distinct realms or bridge them only in liminal or hybrid spaces is false.

UNINTENDED IMPLICATIONS FOR ADAPTATION

I have highlighted the second generation's ability to integrate identities and explained how this resolves the tensions between assimilation and pluralism. Yet informants' efforts could lead down the path of either greater or lesser integration, at least temporarily. Informants blended identities through boundary work and identity talk. As an example of the former, they expressed their ethnicity at work, "ethnicized" how they went about common leisure practices, and so on. In ethnicizing how they went about common leisure practices, for example, they redefined the meanings of both the ethnic social identity and their actions in order to psychologically reconcile discrepancies, such as dating outside their community or deciding to stay home as a mother. We should not see all of these hybrid techniques as equivalent. The blending of identities through boundary work and especially identity talk can unintentionally weaken distinctions between identities, thereby making it hard to distinguish an "ethnic" from an "American" practice (Alba 1999). For instance, drinking in moderate amounts in the leisure sphere conveys little if any cultural marker, no matter how actors talked about it. In addition, touting one's sporadic or even frequent rituals at home can unintentionally weaken ethnic boundaries if customs become repositories of ethnic heritage, allowing one to feel deeply ethnic even if one is otherwise highly acculturated. All of this applause for the second generation's affirmation of group boundaries does not mean they have not lost some of their distinctions from the mainstream.

But boundary work and identity talk do affect group boundaries and adaptation in significant ways. Regarding boundary work in the leisure realm, for instance, ethnicity is not just symbolic: many informants had mostly co-ethnic friends, felt committed to community norms to some degree, and faced sanctions, at times administered by peers, for violating the moral order. They engaged in ethnogenesis by incorporating mainstream activities into their ethnic boundaries (Tuan 1998). The fact that the second generation brought ethnicity and race into the public sphere also demonstrates a commitment that will not dissipate in the near future. Identity talk, while not necessarily demonstrative of a visible group division, is also important to consider when assessing adaptation. For example, group boundaries change when a member marries, whether inside or outside the ethnic group, regardless of how actors make sense of these decisions. Still, identity talk indicates that the single decision, such as whom to marry or where to live, does not represent the total sum of one's ethnic identity or intended future actions. Actors take into account multiple sets of interests while making such a choice, as revealed through a qualitative, in-depth account. Participants affirmed their status as "ethnic-Americans," living not only on the hyphen between the words but feeling deeply committed to both sides of it as well, even for those with less knowledge of their ancestry. Furthermore, informants' desire to pass on their culture to the third generation, the support of diversity within multiculturalism, and the popularity of community organizations signal the motivation and the long-term infrastructure necessary to continue some forms of ethnic boundaries. The role of race in reinforcing group boundaries will continue as well, discussed below.

EXPLAINING DOMAIN CONFORMITY

Respondents abided by the domain codes, rather than contradicted them, because of their economic and social mobility within mainstream institutions and their corresponding adoption of an immigrant narrative. Having already achieved financial stability within two generations as racial minorities, they had a general faith in the rules of popular national discourse that hard work and civic responsibility lead to economic mobility and gradual acceptance. Asian American professionals have a generally positive racial image as the model minority. They work in the primary labor market, live in residentially integrated settings, enjoy popular leisure environments (albeit with some hassles), and send their children to satisfactory public or private schools. At the same time, they could benefit from voluntary organizations that offer interactions with the first generation, networking with trusted professionals, and opportunities to converse about their ethnic experiences. These individuals enjoyed the "best of both worlds", as many said. What encouraged conformity to domain codes was this attitude, joined with their perspective on race relations, explained in chapter 4, that ignorance of difference rather than systemic inequalities mostly hindered full acceptance.

This does not mean that the second generation did not experience barriers in the institutions or that they believed everything would take care of itself. Instead, they assumed that they had to put extra effort into securing their advancement as Asian Americans. They pushed hard in the workplace, selectively drawing on their ethnic and racial status. At home they constructed a setting that would promote continued public success. They also accomplished a cultural citizenship as ethnic Americans in the leisure and civil society spheres. They considered these efforts successful and so were able to work within the domain codes.

DOMAIN INTEGRATION AND STRATIFICATION

Asian Americans are both immigrants and physically distinct minorities. The second generation fits an immigrant trajectory of gradual integration into the public sphere while maintaining ethnic community ties. But this does not erase their marginal status, for their immigrant and minority statuses coexist. They remain racially separate from Whites, as explained in chapter 4. Informants recognized this continued racialization as foreigners and tried to offset it both by presenting themselves as "American" and by framing cultural and physical differences in a positive light as like other immigrants. They ultimately hoped to fulfill the "Asian American dream" of being accepted as Americans (Zia 2000). Yet this social acceptance via selective self-presentation could be short term. We need to ask: what are Asian American professionals integrating into?

In chapters 5 and 7, I discussed how informants integrated into domains as employees or cultural citizens by bringing in their ethnicity and race in select ways. Such an integration represents a racial project and shows the continued effects of race on them (Omi and Winant 1994). This is instead of the more common framing of their integration as an assimilation or a benign multiculturalism based solely on skills and acculturation. Race does not necessarily restrict the short-term mobility of Asian Americans at work but may in fact facilitate it, for their use of the model-minority stereotype could help them get certain jobs and connect to the state. In addition, the general tolerance of certain cultural differences in public domains suits the dominant ideological conception of racial groups as either hardworking and "sacred" or lazy and "profane," with Asian American professionals as the former (Ong 1996). As Shah said in chapter 3, Asian Americans have benefited from a racial hierarchy that places African Americans and Latinos on the bottom both in Dallas and nationwide. Conceiving of African Americans as being on the lowest rung in the racial hierarchy fits their economic role as a labor pool that can be exploited and whose stratification becomes morally tolerable (Bobo and Smith 1998). The Black/non-Black divide gives Asian Americans some racial privilege, such as making their integration as immigrants rather than as racial minorities more acceptable (Bean and Stevens 2003; Foner 2005; Yancey 2003). Their integration into the domains indicates the power of race, not its declining significance and therefore could impede their acceptance as full equals.

We normally measure the effects of race by documenting a minority's distance (economically, residentially, in social status, etc.) from Whites. Yet here we see that race matters all the time, not only when one is experiencing clear racism. Research in Asian American studies critiques the Black-White paradigm but continues to assume that race matters when Asian Americans are unlike Whites. It is necessary to move beyond this prevailing conception of how race works in order to assess its relevance. There is rarely a time when race does not have influence. It is more important to ask *how* actors deal with ethnicity and race, not *if* they do.

This framing of integration as a racial project fits recent scholarship on Whiteness. Assimilation supposedly occurred for European Americans over generations as they gradually took advantage of labor market opportunities and entered educational institutions and mixed neighborhoods (Thernstrom 1973). Yet this narrative misses the roles of race and racism in shaping immigrant adaptation. European Americans overcame ethnic barriers and assimilated into the White race not simply because of their acculturation and entrance into dominant institutions, but also in reaction to the growing (free) racial minority presence in United States from the early 1900s onward (King 2001). There were psychological and material benefits to joining the White race, and the dominant groups also benefited from greater numbers politically and economically (Ignatiev 1995; Roediger 1999).

The fact that Asian Americans' integration into the domains represents a racial project suggests that they are reinforcing their own racialization. By conforming to the domain codes, informants may unintentionally hurt their own long-term prospects for equality. The state reproduces itself and social hierarchies through people's adherence to its logics at the local level, seen here within the domains. Abiding by the codes, even in creative ways, does not challenge their racial assumptions, for instance that Asian Americans are productive workers or that "good" citizens are those who contribute financially to the welfare state. In fact, their lived hybridity may make informants feel as if they already are challenging the domains, thus leading them not to question any implicit injustices. An acceptance of a liberal democracy does not address head-on the fact that we rarely interact with one another as individuals and interact instead as members of physically marked groups. Such tools of stratification as institutional racism; social networks along racial, gender, and class lines; and others are not dismantled or deeply questioned (Park 2005). As a result, groups further equality mostly for those who fit into the dominant norms and images of each domain. But their minority status will continue to mark even those most assimilated as apart from the majority and paint them as possible threats, physically, financially, and morally (Lee 1999). Although participants did not mind a certain amount of racism, in the long term they could face more problems that limit their acceptance and status. The Black/non-Black divide works with—it does not replace—the White/non-White one to confer some privileges but also place some limits on Asian Americans. Assessing domain codes explains how minorities' efforts to resist marginalization can in effect reinforce it. This is most clearly seen in two supposedly "mainstream" arenas, the workplace and civil society.

The workplace treated informants as ethnic workers. Their attempts to use that image to their advantage, while itself a bold move, may handicap them at some point. Asian Americans serve primarily as labor to uphold the U.S. capitalist economy (Ong, Bonacich, and Cheng 1994). They were rewarded as the model minority who have networks within the community and for multicultural displays, as endorsed by diversity seminars. These rewards, however, can be short-term. Attempts to work with co-ethnic clients attract revenue but gradually can limit the advancement of minorities, who are not seen as representatives of the entire company (Collins-Lowry 1997). Being the "model minority" can lead to their gradual exploitation as obedient citizens who are willing to put in more hours than others despite the possibility that they will encounter a glass ceiling (Cheng and Yang 1996). It also can cover up the needs of other Asian Americans and other groups who encounter language barriers, gender hierarchies, lack of social networks, poor schools, and discrimination that impede access to the primary labor market, not to mention mobility within it (Kwong 1995; Zhou 1992). First-generation immigrants, for instance, appear all the more foreign within the domain codes. It cannot look good for recent immigrants when members of their own ethnic group avoid talking to them, even in English. Too much success also can fuel the yellow-peril image for the second generation. To the extent that capitalism depends on racial divisions among labor pools, informants will have difficulty being perceived as individuals analogous to the majority, regardless of their acculturation (Bonacich 1976; San Juan 2002). The result of these trends is that Asian Americans remain framed as non-Americans. This allows other (majority) citizens to see themselves as "real Americans" despite the growth of immigration and of multinational corporations who no longer rely on U.S. labor, only on American dollars (Lowe 1996).

Time will tell if this latest second generation is successful in displaying its "Asian" and "American" styles to get beyond a possible glass ceiling, and how they will deal with a ceiling if more members believe they have encountered it. Also, women in particular found their comfort limited when they felt pressured to endorse workplace norms that deprioritized family.[5] Having these concerns heard becomes more difficult under diversity guidelines that prioritize productivity and group unity, guidelines that Asian Americans support overall. It is unfortunate that the workplace institution has created this racial and gender dynamic with its bureaucratic norms that privileged White males and that individual informants lack the agency to openly critique these pressures. Instead, they must work within them to advance their own interests, as fitting the capitalist logic in which they (we) work.

Similarly, in civil society organization leaders and members strove to bridge public and private interests. As a result they displayed support for the state in order to create a public profile as "good citizens" rather than as "foreigners" who prioritized their own agenda. Their ethnic-exclusive organizations, like their leisure practices, ironically promoted their integration. But their integration is not likely to occur within the liberal-democratic ideal of the state. As in the workplace, despite their efforts, they did not come across as simply "ethnic Americans" comparable to other Americans but with a different immigrant origin. Instead, as mentioned above, they appeared as the model minority. Race and class allowed for their claim on cultural citizenship as being the right kind of people, who consume middle-class leisure activities and do not take resources away from the state or challenge White privilege. Although helpful in the short term, a shift in race relations, often due to trends outside of Asian Americans' control, can challenge this cultural citizenship. This approach to seem like the majority leads to a narrow definition of Asian American rather than a more open meaning of American. Such a logic also limits acceptance of cultural differences that cannot be translated into Anglo or Christian traditions (Wolfe 2000). In addition, it unintentionally draws attention away from group needs of both Asian Americans and non–Asian Americans—which may require state intervention, such as poverty, minority educational assistance, and so on (King 2001). Gender and sexual-orientation rights within the ethnic communities also come to be glossed over with such outward presentations of traditional communities (Bhattacharjee 1998). There are other ways of fulfilling civil society's role of linking individuals to the state, such as joining with other marginalized groups to protest undemocratic and un-meritocratic practices (Okihiro 1994; Zia 2000).

It is easy to critique minorities in general for not resisting racialization more forcefully or for accepting the ideological sway of broad discourses such as multiculturalism. But a domain-based approach that uncovers the power of local cultural expectations gives a clearer explanation for people's actions. The analytical level of local institutions provides a picture of how hegemonic assumptions within capitalism and the state both gain force. This, in turn, leads to an appreciation of the interventions actors were able to make that opened up the work, leisure, and civil society spheres to greater ethnic expressions.

This discussion of domain-based stratification also helps us rethink what we mean by mainstream spaces. There is no such thing as a space where race and ethnicity have little or no relevance (Waldinger 2003). The white-collar workplace not only tolerates diversity but expects it, as does civil society. But this does not mean that the mainstream does not exist or that it allows ample expressions of diversity. It is more accurate to define it as having strict guidelines for how to express one's marginal status. The guidelines are shaped by corporate capitalism and the liberal-democratic state, as seen in chapters 5 and 7. To fit into the mainstream, Asian Americans must act not "White" but "American," in line with the state. As minorities convey their background in an acceptable manner, they make the mainstream more multicultural, but in controlled ways that offer limited real acceptance of difference. For example, informants could make jokes about elephants and curse words at work, but they could not freely discuss religion. They are likely to remain lodged in middle management given their statuses as almost White, at least not Black, and potentially too foreign.

Private spaces differ from mainstream ones, but not to the extent typically portrayed. Private spaces offer more latitude for the expression of elements of one's background considered antithetical to parts of the public sphere, such as religious rituals, ethnic language, and so on. Yet as seen in chapter 6, such spaces have their own expectations on how to express ethnic identities so as not to disrupt hierarchies within the ethnic community based on gender, race, sexuality, class, and life-course stage. In addition, the private sphere has responsibilities to the public that informants, especially women, try to uphold. The state depends on a "functional" private sphere to train youth to accept their place within the capitalist market. The home is where "culture" supposedly is passed down and good citizens are formed, measured by groups' crime rates, economic class status, and so on. African Americans are critiqued for failing in the public sphere, for which the Black family is blamed. As long as Korean and Indian Americans maintain a generally high economic position, in particular for the second generation of the post-1965 wave of immigration, they have more freedom to create marginal spaces as they like. Still, they must be mindful of appearing too foreign. What divides marginal and mainstream spaces is the roles associated with each in perpetuating the state and corporate capitalism. But neither space is free from guidelines on how to express diversity, and both can perpetuate social divisions.

It is not enough, under such conditions, to conform to domain cultural codes and express cultural and racial differences within them as a means of attaining equality, even though this is often the option most available to people in daily life. Progressive critics of multiculturalism argue that public cultural recognition must explicitly be tied to political change and must offer a counternarrative to conventional discourse on group differences in order to affect resource redistribution (Hing 1997; Young 1998). Popular multiculturalism within each domain, itself the result of years of struggle, is meant to simply give a larger piece of the pie to minorities without challenging the racist and class-based ingredients within capitalism (Davis 1996). In addition, treatment of Asian Americans varies not based on their own achievements but on international relations that often have little connection to their lives (Espiritu 1997).

Overall, then, actors were in a challenging predicament of navigating ethnic and racial differences in arenas that allow only selective displays. The domain codes offer deeper insights into how they experienced racializations and into their agency to respond. In reality it is very hard to directly challenge systemic inequality embedded within local cultures and social structures. Informants put in significant effort and took risks as they claimed the status of workers, moral families, and cultural citizens. Rather than try to assimilate and abandon their community, they sought acceptance for it in Dallas, which lacks the history of Asian American activism seen on the West Coast. In the process they may have furthered their role as a "diverse" population that suits the needs of the political economy and cultural discourse on the nation. Still, they took a needed step that others can build from.

KOREAN AMERICANS AND INDIAN AMERICANS: SIMILARITIES AND DIFFERENCES

This analysis of second-generation Indian and Korean Americans allows insights into what unites and divides Asian America. The two groups differ in their countries' histories with the United States, in the first generation's occupational categories, in their physical appearance, in religion and traditions, and in language and English abilities (Min 2003). Religion served as one of the most significant divides within Asian America and even within South Asian America. As conservative Christians, Korean Americans can have little sympathy for Hindus when they are criticized by Southern Baptists. For instance, when I asked Pastor Chung what he made of the Southern Baptists' condemnation of Hindus, he objected to the tactics and tone of the Baptists but not their overall disapproval of Hindus as a misguided faith. Indian Americans have other divisions from Asian Americans as well. At the college level they rarely join pan-ethnic associations, instead forming their own groups that emphasize cultural and transnational interests. Nor are they accepted as Asian Americans, for they often have their membership in the group questioned. Since 9/11, Indian Americans, along with other South Asian, Muslim, and Arab Americans, have been racialized in ways that cause them to have even less in common with other groups. Yet because of their religious, linguistic, cultural, and geographic differences, Indian Americans rarely identified with other South Asian Americans. Such factors even separated Indian Americans from one another, because they have a more heterogeneous homeland than do Korean Americans. Indian Americans also demonstrated stronger transnational ties than did Korean Americans, possibly because of their slightly greater economic and social resources, and correspondingly were more open to traditional practices, such as arranged marriages.

Korean Americans have more similarities with other East Asian Americans, in particular Chinese Americans. These informants noted more pan-ethnic friendships and a sense of pan-ethnic solidarity based on racist labels. They recognized the term "Oriental" as including them. Some even referred to themselves and other East Asian Americans as Orientals. Korean American participants also spoke of cultural ties to other East Asian Americans beyond "Asian" values, such as parenting styles that lacked expressions of affection, especially from fathers, unlike Indian Americans. Still, Korean Americans had significant differences from other groups. Most notably, the church served as a central meeting space for them and affirmed religious and social boundaries from others, even some co-ethnics. Many informants grew up attending Korean-based churches and were active in mostly Korean Christian fellowships at college, and they remained within EMs rather than joining either an Asian American Protestant church in Dallas or a mainstream one. Their families' experiences as small-business owners contributed to their shared interests, which led to such choices. As befits Korean Americans' national profile, most participants grew up helping in their parents' stores. Although few considered the 1992 Los Angeles riots significant to their lives, many still recognized the event as particular to their ethnicity. Cultural, religious, and social ties affirmed salient group boundaries separating them from other Asian Americans.

Despite these boundaries between Korean Americans and Indian Americans, a number of commonalities arise, as emphasized in this study. Similarities between the ethnic groups are important to document, for they give a deeper meaning to the politically constructed term Asian America. Examining only one ethnic group is the norm in Asian American studies, despite the field's attempt to unite a set of diverse ethnicities. The overlap in types of identities and experiences among informants results not in pan-ethnic alliances, but more in pan-ethnic "possibilities." Both groups stressed relatively standard "Asian" values from the first generation of respecting elders and family, achieving scholastically, somewhat conservative gender and social norms, language maintenance, religious participation, and so on (as discussed in chapter 3). Actors also experienced an equal amount of acculturation. Although it may have been easier for Indian Americans to hold onto traditions reinforced through their temples compared to the EMs, which resembled mainstream services, relatively few Indian Americans attended temples regularly. Second-generation Korean Americans also took part in cultural programs sponsored by immigrant associations. The groups maintained their ethnic heritage to a similar degree and cared deeply about doing so, as seen in chapters 3, 6, and 7. Women took on a disproportionate share of the challenges. Groups also expressed comparable racial identities, as seen in chapter 4, although pan-ethnicity was more prevalent among Korean Americans.

Part of the reason for the similarities between Korean and Indian Americans in their views toward ethnicity and race, as well as in their enactments of these identities, is their class status, their immigrant trajectory, and their geographic location. Parents of the participants have attained middle- and upper-middle-class status, with Indian immigrants often having higher incomes and more secure careers than owning a small business typically offers. Still, the second generation of both groups recounted the immigrant narrative of parents arriving with little means, of having less money than their peers while young, and of gradually attaining mobility over time by means of hard work. Even Indian Americans, whose parents entered professional careers relatively quickly upon migrating, often would mention how they knew what it was like to struggle financially while young and distanced themselves from a sense of economic privilege. Given their class status, both groups made sense of their ethnic ties in similar ways, as supportive of their mobility and as giving comfort. Their identical attitudes toward race as second-generation immigrants relative to Whites and Blacks also fit their economic location and other factors, as explained in chapter 4. One of those other factors is their location in Dallas. It has attracted a more focused section of the second generation in terms of occupational preferences and exposure to organized political activism, compared to the major hubs of Asian America. As illustrative of this demographic, both groups had organizations focused on the second generation's professional and social networking goals.

Ironically, these various experiences created similarities for both groups but also contributed to a concentration on ethnic boundaries at the expense of pan-ethnic solidarity. Individuals interpreted their encounters with racism, interest in family ties, political goals, desire for cultural citizenship, and so on through an ethnic lens, even if they recognized at some level that all Asian Americans had similar encounters. Given their shared outlooks and interests, even though they have little interaction with each other, there are a number of possible pan-ethnic links between the groups that could further an Asian American identity and lead to supportive institutions in Dallas.

IMMIGRATION INTO DALLAS

It is important to study the context of immigrants' reception (Portes and Rumbaut 2001). When I mentioned to people that I was researching Asian Americans in Dallas, I consistently received looks of surprise and disbelief, even from some scholars in Asian American studies, along with such comments as,

"Are there Asian Americans in Texas?" and "That must be much worse than in the North." Our commonplace impression of Asian America is that the population lives on the coasts, mostly in select cities considered international centers. The academic literature inadvertently fuels this image. Studies on Asian Americans in the South are few. Texas deserves consideration because it is an increasingly popular destination for immigrants (Kemper 2005). Moreover, it serves as a window on the growing racial and cultural diversity throughout the country. The Korean American and Indian American communities have established an infrastructure in the city, with religious and cultural institutions that target the first, 1.5, and second generation. Numerous organizations welcome newcomers, including churches, temples, cultural associations (based on dance, language, or other interests), women's groups, professional associations, pan-ethnic organizations, and more (Brettell 2005b). The current organizations try to offer a traditional version of their homeland's history and culture and are just numerous enough to give residents a means to affirm their ethnic boundaries rather than feeling adrift. The patterns of Asian American community formations are occurring here, but without the same degree of residential concentration for these groups, and with more capital.

Although general patterns remain consistent with other Asian immigrant experiences elsewhere, the location of Dallas impacts the community formations. Because Asian Americans in Dallas represent a smaller population in a conservative state, it is not surprising that the organizations present a nonconfrontational image of themselves—one that fits into the region. For instance, Asian Americans appear as business friendly, owing in part to the Asian American Small Business Association and other pan-ethnic associations, which suits the history and culture of Dallas as business oriented (Hazel 1997). Because of their membership's involvement in high-tech companies, IANA sponsored more finance programs than political programs relative to Indian American professionals in Washington, D.C., for instance. (Dhingra 2003b). Each ethnic group also took public pride in its culture and religiosity, which gained them currency in Dallas's religious environment. In particular, the Korean American EMs were conservative Christian denominations that matched the dominant style within the state. Hindus consciously portrayed themselves as comparable to Christians. In addition to religious practices, Korean American and Indian American leaders presented their racial status in ways that suited their impression of racial dynamics within Dallas as Black and White, with Latinos occupying a separate status albeit closer to Blacks, as discussed in chapters 2 and 4.

In everyday conversations informants had to be selective in what they shared of their ancestry with others in order to again appear "different" in an acceptable way. They were pleasantly surprised by the inquisitiveness of their co-workers, which they credited to being in the South, but did not take this as an invitation to be unguarded when communicating their background. Many commented on how much they stood out in Dallas, relative to more cosmopolitan cities, when they went out to eat, to museums, to sporting events, to bars, and so on. This distressed recent arrivals somewhat at first, but they gradually got used to it. They constructed a racial map of their surroundings, with areas of greater and lesser prejudice. They were relieved that the stereotypes of the area proved mostly false. They took part in the local culture and became used to being a perpetual outsider. Susan said:

> I went to a Garth Brooks concert with White friends, all blond hair, blue eyes, and who sticks out—me. And of course Garth Brooks being country, I was the only minority in there. It's different, you stick out.

They dealt with everyday discomforts without forming pan-ethnic solidarities, which lack a history and infrastructure in the city.

What the long-term impact will be of Asian Americans on the city is hard to tell at this point. Asian Americans are not as publicly recognized in local politics or civic discourse on race as are African Americans and Latinos. Asian Americans will only grow in political strength in Dallas, but it is not clear whether that will be within a pan-ethnic manner and if so, whether such alliances will be divided along class lines. Economic interests have guided most pan-ethnic formations in the city, most notably the small business groups. By the same token, occupational divisions within the community limit broad alliances. For instance, Korean American and Indian Americans, in particular of the second generation, might not have much solidarity with Vietnamese American refugees. Such alliances are especially unlikely if the communities continue to define themselves in terms of occupation and acculturation in order to advance within a dominant racial frame, as Asian Americans have done at other historical times (Loewen 1971). The ability to maintain their image as a model minority is itself in question as more Asian Americans arrive who have less human capital and access to social capital, which also creates uncertainty about how the Asian American community will grow politically.

Asian American populations contribute not only to the social and political diversity of the city but also to its cultural diversity. Through their festivals (which take place in high school gymnasiums, banquet halls, and outdoor spaces), temples and ethnic churches, dance troupes, and so on, they help create a multicultural Dallas, one that extends far beyond the city's stereotypical image of a cattle and oil town. This in turn makes the city more comfortable for future immigrants and encourages greater diversity in mainstream institutions, such as the media, the arts, and elsewhere. Cultural displays join with attempts by Asian American civic groups to further their members' acculturation, such as by acquiring English as a second language programs, health care, and other pressing needs. Matters of racial injustice may indirectly become downplayed in this process, which can have the effect of contributing to a broader shift in racial discourse toward government needing to ensure "equal opportunities" and away from addressing historic inequalities. Nonetheless, cultural respect is an increasingly important dimension of groups' social rights. Attaining equal opportunities and cultural representation requires significant effort by individuals. As new Asian American organizations arise with the arrival of new migrants and the growth of the current groups, this burgeoning community can change over time. It can pick up on the achievements of the current residents in attending to group preferences.

Overall, Asian Americans managed their multicultural lives in ways that would hopefully create respect for them from others. Their status as the margins in the mainstream informs the challenges and opportunities they faced, at both the personal and political levels, in dealing with conflicting sets of expectations. More attention should be paid to minorities' agency and constraints as they address their immediate needs within local cultures. Such research would add to our dominant frameworks on immigration, race, and identity, in order to understand the implications for social equality of how people make sense of and move through daily life.

Appendix

Appendix: Questions

The lists of possible questions to ask that follow served as templates, not scripts, for the interviews.

Demographic Questions:

Name:

Address:

Telephone #:

E-mail address:

Age:

Sex:

Marital status:

Sexual orientation:

Education:

Occupation:

Income:

Parents' occupation: Father: Mother:

Length of residence in D/FW:

Your legal immigration status:

Have there been any major events in your life within the past few years that have changed how you live your life or see things, such as a death in the family, moving, a new job, etc.?

Background Questions:

1. Where were you born?
2. When did you move to the United States (if applicable)?
3. Where did you grow up?
4. Where did you attend college?

5. Where did you attend graduate school (if applicable)? In what subject?

6. Please describe the community in which you grew up: mostly White, mostly African American, mostly Latino, or mostly Asian American (which ethnicity), or was it quite diverse? If diverse, then made up of which ethnicities?

7. Did you participate in ethnic organizations while growing up, such as church/temple, cultural performances, etc.?

8. Did you associate mostly with friends from school or from your ethnic community when you were in school?

9. Did you associate with Koreans/Indians at college? Why?

10. Is your current neighborhood: mostly White, mostly African American, mostly Latino, or mostly Asian American (which ethnicity), or is it quite diverse?

Domain Questions

Work

1. Take me through an average workday, including what you do for breaks.

2. Why did you choose this job? What did your parents think of this?

3. What are your relationships with co-workers and boss like?

4. Describe the last few times you talked with your supervisor.
   Do you talk about ethnicity, race, or gender?
   Did your ethnicity affect your impressions of the interaction in any way?

5. Has ethnicity shaped your perceptions of your co-workers or of yourself at work? Example?

6. Do you think that discrimination is an issue at your workplace?

7. [If yes] What is the cause of it?
   Have you ever talked about it with others?
   Overall, do you worry about discrimination?
   What is the best way to combat racism?

8. [If not] Why not?
   Is discrimination a problem for any group?

9. What is the stereotype of Korean/Indian Americans at work? Can you give me an example? How is this image communicated to you?

10. Whom do you feel more similar to at work, Whites or African Americans? Why?

11. What accounts for the success of many Korean/Indian Americans compared to other minorities?

12. Have you ever played down or accentuated your ethnicity at work? Example?

13. [For women] Do you think you face problems as a woman, subtle or direct?

14. What do you think of affirmative action?

15. Do you think that your experiences would be different in another state or not in the South?

16. Overall, do you feel Indian/Korean, Indian/Korean American, Asian American, or American at work?

Home

1. How would you describe your neighborhood?

2. How do you dress when you come home from work?

3. Tell me about the layout and decorations of your home. When I walk in, what do I see?
   Why did you choose these items?
   Whose do you think your place is most similar to: your parents', your Indian/Korean friends', your White friends'?

4. What do you think the expectations are for you in how you live your home life, such as what you eat, how you decorate, etc.? Where did you learn those expectations from?

5. How often do you cook Korean/Indian food? How often do you go out to eat it?

6. How often do you talk to your family?
   Thinking about the last conversation you had, what did you talk about?
   How does ethnicity affect how you approach a conversation?

7. Why do you live/not live with your parents?

8. Are there expectations from your family or community on how you go about your home life? Do you feel you've lived up to those expectations?

9. [For women] How does being a woman shape the expectations of your home life?

10. [For women] What are the major differences in how men and women are raised in the Indian/Korean community? What are your thoughts on these differences?

11. Do you think your relationship with your family members is similar to your friends', co-workers', or members of the community's?

12. Overall, do you feel Indian/Korean, Indian/Korean American, Asian American, or American at home?

Leisure

1. How often do you see people in your ethnic community?
2. For Indian Americans: Are your co-ethnic friends of the same regional background as you, or just national, or racial, or religious background?
3. For Korean American Christians: Are your co-ethnic friends also Christian?
4. What percentage of your friends are co-ethnics? Other Asian Americans? Other minorities?
5. What did you do the last time you saw your friends? What do you typically do with your friends?
6. Do the activities ever feel different based on who you are with? Example?
7. Thinking about your two or three better friends, what leads you to feel close to them?
8. Thinking of the last time you talked to your friends, what did you talk about?
   Does ethnicity ever come up?
   Do you think you approach the conversation differently if you are talking to a co-ethnic versus a non-co-ethnic? Example?
   How do conversations differ on whether the friends are co-ethnics or not?
9. What television shows do you watch or what movies have you seen lately? Have you ever been reminded of your ethnicity while watching? What is an example?
10. Have you encountered discrimination in stores, restaurants, etc.?

Civil Society

1. Who are the community leaders, if there are any?
2. Do you follow the news in Korea/India?
3. Do you pay special attention to news that pertains to Asian Americans who aren't Korean/Indian?
4. Would you say that you are politically conservative or liberal?
5. What organizations do you belong to?
   What do you like about these organizations?

6. Tell me about the last time you were at [name of organization person attends].
   Who was there?
   What did you do?
   What did you wear?
7. How important were ethnic events in terms of socializing you?
8. What parts of your ethnicity are expressed in these organizations?
9. Overall, do you feel Indian/Korean, Indian/Korean American, Asian American, or American in these gatherings?
10. Is it important for immigrants to partake in mainstream organizations, or simply ethnic ones?
11. Do you think that there needs to be a common bond between ethnic groups in the United States, or do you think that each group can focus mostly on its own needs?

Generic Questions

1. What does your ethnic background mean to you?
   How has that changed over time?
2. What are the differences and similarities between Korean/Indian Americans and other Asian Americans?
3. Did you ever feel ashamed of your background?
   Why/why not?
   Example of what happened?
4. How did you get interested in your ethnicity?
5. Do you want to maintain a heritage? Why/why not? How can you do this?
6. Do you feel a tension between being American and being Korean/Indian?
7. (If yes) when does that tension come up?
   How did you deal with the tension?
8. Is it important for your kids to learn about race and ethnicity?
   Why?
   How would you teach your children?
9. Overall, do you feel Indian/Korean, Indian/Korean American, Asian American, or American?
10. Is there anything else about your ethnicity that you want to talk about?

Questions For Community Leaders

1. What is the goal of your organization?

2. How many people attend your organizational meetings/services on average?

3. How do people hear about your organization?

4. What kinds of programs does your organization have?

5. What needs does the community have that your organization cannot address?

6. Which organizations do you see as most similar to yours?

7. What do you think draws individuals to your organization as opposed to a non-ethnic version of the same type of organization?

8. What are the major needs of the Korean/Indian American community in Dallas?

9. How much of the ethnic background should your members maintain? What does your organization do to promote that?

10. Does your organization have any interactions with other races?

11. What do you think is the relevance of race and racism for your community?

12. What similarities and differences are there between the Asian American and African American communities?

13. Do you see your organization as a "minority organization?" Why/why not?

14. Does the fact that Korean/Indian Americans are a minority have any implications for your organization, such as what programs you offer, what kinds of topics people bring up, why people attend, etc.?

15. Some people say that having an organization for a particular ethnic group continues to keep the group as "different" and outside of the mainstream. What do you think about that?

16. What are the major issues the Korean/Indian American and Asian American communities face in Dallas compared to other cities?

17. How do you see your organization changing as the Korean/Indian community expands?

18. Is there anything else you would like to say?

Notes

Chapter 1

1. Given post-1965 Asian Americans' relatively high human capital, many in the second generation do not maintain the same degree of shame over their ethnic group after adolescence, as was found for previous waves of immigrants, and thus can feel attached to both ethnic and American identities (Child 1943). Like other minorities, second-generation Asian Americans experience the development of their ethnic and racial identities in stages, as discussed in chapter 3 (Cross 1995). Many, but by no means all, feel ashamed of their background in their mid-teenage years but grow out of it as they gain more respect for their background, influenced in part by their parents' economic success.

2. This perspective stems from the Chicago School of sociology and race relations. According to Robert Park and his associates, immigrants gradually adjusted to their host society and became less attached to their ethnic communities as they and their descendants grew more comfortable with the individualism of the United States and encountered less discrimination. So individuals could have more than one type of group attachment but over time would find their ethnic community too constraining and embarrassing (see also Nahirny and Fishman 2005 [1965]; Shibutani and Kwan 1965; Simmel 1964). Those who had deep sympathies with more than one lifestyle were "marginal men," enduring an internal conflict because of the contradictory norms associated with each (Goldberg 1941; Park 1928; Stonequist 1937). This was mostly an unenviable position. Autobiographical and scholarly accounts commonly frame having an American allegiance as contrasting with having an ethnic one, with individuals being forced to choose between them. For instance, Rodriguez (1982) talks about having to choose between Hispanic and American identities and prioritizing the latter.

3. Much of the historical research on the second generation focused on European American populations that were removed from the majority in terms of their social structures (Gans 1962; Kivisto 2005; Morawska 1996). These second-generation groups lived in concentrated areas, worked in similar occupations or formed workplace associations with one another, and had easy access to co-ethnics generally. Gans (1962)

finds that second-generation Italian Americans in the 1950s chose the second of Child's strategies, forming a subculture of close relationships and institutions and still maintaining the binary of ethnic versus American. My informants, in contrast, are much more embedded in the mainstream thanks to their high human capital. The ability to deal with multiple identities becomes more complicated as a result.

4. Scholarship and popular opinion have moved from pitying those with bicultural interests to envying them. The focus of such research is often on the psychological and social difficulties of abandoning one identity for another, with the implicit message that it is better to maintain both (Sue and Morishima 1982). Still, the general view is that the multicultural individual has two or more very distinct identities that are inherently separate from one another.

5. I agree with those who argue that ethnic institutions and transnationalism need not result in social distance from Americans (Kivisto 2001; Kurien 1998). Yet not all cultural distinctions are accepted by Whites, as explained in chapters 3 and 5–7.

6. The fact that groups accept some but not all elements of another's background corresponds with the cosmopolitan social type. Robert Park (2005 [1914]) and others (Alba 1999; Hollinger 1995) refer to cosmopolitan individuals as more open-minded to others than is assumed for the general population. Yet even here there are limits to what parts of another's culture are embraced, and stereotypes of immigrant groups remain. Cosmopolitans may wish to consider themselves more enlightened, but they may not actually differ much from other Whites (Yu 2001).

7. Portes and Rumbaut (2001) find, for instance, that as it spends more time in the United States and encounters discrimination, the second generation forms a reactive ethnicity and stresses an ethnic-national or pan-ethnic identity instead of an American or ethnic American one. This is in contrast to first-generation migrants, who often refer to their homeland when making sense of their racial status in their adopted country. Similarly, other authors suggest that Asian Americans of postimmigrant generations are more likely form bonds with other minorities than do immigrants (Lee 1996; Singh 1996; Tuan 1998). This is likely the case, but such statements alone may misrepresent the lack of cohesion between immigrant descendants and other minorities.

8. Texas, like many states in the South, supposedly lacks the sophistication and open-mindedness of politically "blue states." High-profile criminal cases do little to counter that image. For instance, James Byrd Jr., a Black man, was murdered by three White men, beaten and then chained and dragged for miles behind their truck. Texas also is no stranger to use of the death penalty, an institutionally racist punishment. Amnesty International wrote in 1998, "The state of Texas executes more people than any other jurisdiction in the Western world. . . . A study conducted for the *Dallas Times Herald* in the mid-1980s showed that the killer of a white was anything up to

10 times more likely to receive a death sentence than the killer of a black victim." See http://web.amnesty.org/library/Index/engAMR510101998 (accessed July 11, 2006).

As explained in chapter 4, Asian Americans conceptualized race relations primarily as Black and White, with little reference to Latinos despite their significant presence in Dallas and Texas generally, which makes this gap noteworthy. Many were not from the Southwest, but even those from Dallas had relatively few impressions of Latinos because this group did not occupy the same mainstream status as they did. The general impression of Latinos was similar to and separate from that of African Americans: like Blacks they were generally working-class or poor and had low levels of education, but they worked hard and cared about family. Latinos, then, fell in between Asian Americans and Blacks in informants' mental hierarchy of race relations and so did not play much of a role in their discussion of race.

9. Scholars have articulated how minorities often uphold the ideals of the nation through their efforts toward social justice (Okihiro 1994), but this is different from actually connecting to other Americans at the individual level.

10. According to Swidler (2001), spaces impact behavior because they carry cultural codes. Friedland and Alford (1991) use the term cultural logics to refer to how local environments shape behavior. A logic is "a set of material practices and symbolic constructions which constitute organization principles and which is available to organizations and individuals to elaborate" (248). In other words, individuals' interpretations of a setting depend on its logic. The domains of work, home, leisure, and civil society come with their own logics, comparable to the notion of schemas (DiMaggio 1997). For instance, contemporary Protestant churches have four different types of codes, namely "house of worship, family, community, and leadership [styles]," that shape how members resolve conflict and interact with one another (Becker 1999). One cannot understand a person's behavior as a churchgoer without knowing which one of the four schemas applies to his or her church. As we internalize a society's codes and classification system, we learn its culture (Durkheim 1915).

11. For instance, U.S.-born Chinese Americans maintain both American and Chinese cultural orientations, without attachment to one necessarily influencing their interest in the other (Hall and Okazaki 2002). People can even maintain competing traits within the same identity. For instance, being American means both valuing one's individuality and enjoying volunteering and group membership (Bellah et al. 1985).

12. Identities with greater salience are more likely to be enacted, and an identity may become so salient that actors consider it always to take precedence over others (McCall and Simmons 1978; Turner 1978). Salience, as defined in identity theory, depends on one's emotional and instrumental commitments to a set of relationships associated with an identity (Stryker 1992). What leads to the salience of an identity is the number and emotional significance of relationships that people have that are tied to that identity.

13. This social-psychological conception overlaps with the sociology of culture formulations. According to Swidler (2001), we pick and choose a cultural repertoire (i.e., a set of skills, habits, and symbols) based on which behaviors best deal with a problem at hand. Cultural repertoires can be read as similar to identities and their various attributes. As one's environment changes, so does the best-suited repertoire.

14. For instance, Anderson (1999b) finds that many Blacks in white-collar occupations consciously choose not to associate with other Blacks so that they will be seen as "embracing the corporate culture" (12).

15. Historical research on immigration has also dealt with the integrating of backgrounds, although this has received less attention than the assimilation trajectory. One way is through taking part in common American activities but doing so with co-ethnics (Kitano 1969; Shibutani and Kwan 1965; Tuan 1998). Others argue that second-generation migrants who supposedly rejected ethnicity in order to be American actually carried with them the ideals and broad values of their immigrant parents, which guided their behaviors. Gans (1962) notes cultural mixing during major rituals, such as an Italian Thanksgiving by the second generation that consisted of both the traditional turkey dinner and Italian foods, side by side. Moore (1981) argues that second-generation Jewish Americans in New York City brought together ethnoreligious and American lifestyles through building their own minicommunities within New York City neighborhoods, introducing Hebrew into public schools, creating workplace associations, and other formal means. These are all important indicators of how seemingly contrasting identities can coexist, and I look for similar patterns for my informants. But I also examine how groups let diverse cultural norms intersect in daily practices and life-course decisions. I consider how this may be one of the rules (not the only one) of how groups manage their commitments, as opposed to an exceptional practice to the rule.

16. Morawska (1996) offers a similar insight with some cases of her "ethnicization" model, which refers to transforming traditional practices of one's culture into an Americanized version, such as East European Jewish immigrants' hybrid cooking or synagogue rituals. For example, instead of keeping kosher kitchens or preferring kosher restaurants, second-generation Jewish Americans preferred foods with mainly American ingredients but with some ethnic flavors and aura as well. Similarly, synagogues changed to become more cultural centers, with classes on Jewish history and English-language services rather than only orthodox sermons, as the second generation came of age (see also Moore 1981). These processes refer to daily life, not simply to isolated rituals. I focus on similar activities while examining the ways in which these lived hybridity practices affirm or challenge both the social expectations within their ethnic communities and the spaces in which the practices take place. That is, I assess the implications of a lived hybridity for the second generation's adaptation and inter-

group relations instead of assuming an assimilationist paradigm. I also concentrate on the cultural locations in which these hybrid moments occur. In a similar manner, Bakhtin differentiates between intentional and organic hybridities (Werbner 2001, 2004). The former are politicized cultural products designed to challenge notions of identities. The latter consist of everyday conversation styles and language use in which a person's choice of words involves more than one linguistic tradition. I examine the connection of contrasting identities at the level of daily life, focusing on subjectivities and practices, both linguistic and physical. Given the emphasis on daily life, such as what people eat at work, how they decide whom to date, what topics to discuss at a restaurant, and so on, I refer to actors' practices as possibly comprising a lived hybridity.

17. I take from cultural studies and related literature the challenge to the static notion of identities, highlighting artists' hybrid cultural creations (Hall 1990). Recent work on "borderlands" suggests that immigrants live in the figurative space where two cultures meet and are pulled in contradictory directions (Anzaldúa 1987). As a result, migrants and their descendants often feel fragmented as they go back and forth between identities. To overcome this fragmentation, they create a cultural hybridity—that is, they engage in practices that bring together elements of their discrete lifestyles to form a new entity. For example, the mixing of the Indian and the Western sides of oneself is represented by listening to bhangra music, with its combination of Indian folk music and western musical styles of techno, electronic, and hip-hop (Maira 2002). Listeners would not encounter the marginal-man scenario because the hybrid formation supposedly encapsulates the contradictory parts of oneself. Similarly, gay Christians in Atlanta bring together their separate identities at a gay club on Sunday mornings where drag queens sing gospel songs (Gray and Thumma 1997). Films, music (Gilroy 1993), clothes (Bhachu 1995), and other symbols (Hebdige 1979) also are believed to represent such hybridity. This perspective highlights individuals' agency in picking elements of their background to act on, not simply adopting one prescribed identity over another based on the context. Yet, outside of these liminal spaces, the existing research suggests that individuals return to segregating their identities to different realms (Hall 1995).

18. For instance, Gitlin (2001) argues that one reason Hollywood movies are so popular throughout the world is their inherent multicultural content.

19. The few studies that focus on the local level find that individuals conform to the space's cultural frame, seen in their behaviors and cognitive boundaries (Nippert-Eng 1996; Swidler 2001). In other words, researchers uncover the code of a setting, such as a church, by reading people's practices as illustrative of it and finding differences in behaviors across spaces (Becker 1999). Current research in cultural sociology has not considered how individuals negotiate cultural codes, that is, how they enact identities that are normally relegated to a different domain and that are not the best fit for the

situation. The strategies that people use to affirm their membership in a particular category, such as "being Asian American" at work, shape their group boundaries and so receive ample attention in each domain.

20. This is not to suggest that I ignore more standard ways of assessing immigrant incorporation. Involvement in white-collar occupations rather than in the ethnic enclave signals greater integration, as does speaking primarily English rather than an ethnic language at home and participation in generic as opposed to ethnically or racially specific civic groups. I concentrate, though, on overlooked ways of assessing adaptation, with the goal of revising how we assess adaptation rather than of giving a definitive statement on future outcomes.

21. There are multiple ways of conceiving of assimilation and multiculturalism as compatible outcomes (Kivisto 2005). I do not claim that this perspective is by any means a definitive one, in particular because it is based on a case study. I offer this as a model to consider.

22. "Study of North Texas Immigrant Communities." http://www .dfwinternational.org/_content/media/immigrants/ StudyOfNorthTexasImmigrantCommunities.pdf, p. 6 (accessed July 11, 2006).

23. http://www.census.gov/popest/cities/tables/SUB-EST2005-01.xls (accessed September 3, 2006).

24. For instance, Feher (1998) shows how messianic Jews maintain a commitment to Judaism through the boundary work of their choice of vocabulary and through giving Jewish festivals a Christian meaning, so that they can feel connected to both religious categories.

25. I refer to Dallas and Texas more broadly as part of the South, but this is not to deny its relationship to the Southwest as well. Dallas is distinct from cities farther west in Texas, such as El Paso (and, some say, even Fort Worth). Although it is not wrong to categorize Dallas as part of the Southwest, I refer to it as part of the South with a concentration on Asian Americans' reflections on Black–White race relations. Studies of Asian immigration are missing in both the South and Southwest.

26. A handful of quotes from informants throughout the book have appeared in other publications, namely in Dhingra 2003a and 2003b.

Chapter 2

1. I am not arguing that Asian America is not heterogeneous; perhaps heterogeneity is even greater in Asian America than among other races, given the group's extreme class disparities, linguistic differences, generational divisions, degree of interracial marriage, and so on. But a concentration on differences overlooks the similarities that do exist, as seen in this study.

2. Nativist laws include both those that limit immigration to the United States and those that restrict the privileges of current immigrants, such as English-only language

provisions or the need for employers to verify workers' immigration status (Ancheta 1998). Both types of regulations distinguish "real" from "fake" Americans and define the nation along racial lines that often overlap with concerns over cultural and political threats (Chang 1999).

3. Among this small number of migrants were Gujaratis who settled in San Francisco and became the first Indian motel owners in the country.

4. Even though the Immigration Law of 1965 is heralded as a marker of U.S. tolerance for ethnic diversity because it eliminated strict quotas on Asian countries, lawmakers did not expect a rise in Asian immigrants. In fact, the passage of the bill depended on the assumption that the racial balance of the country would remain stable. The law's first set of preferences for immigrants were relatives of current U.S. citizens, which meant European immigrants. Asian Americans entered mostly through the third preference for those skilled in occupations needed in the United States.

5. http://www.census.gov/prod/2004pubs/censr-17.pdf (accessed July 18, 2006).

6. http://factfinder.census.gov/servlet/DTTable?_bm=5y&-context=dt&-reg=DEC_2000_SF4_U_PCT113:001|013|023&-ds_name=DEC_2000_SF4_U&-CONTEXT=dt&-mt_name=DEC_2000_SF4_U_PCT113&-tree_id=4001&-redoLog=true&-all_geo_types=N&-geo_id=50100oUS&-search_results=05000US48113&-format=&-_lang=en (accessed July 18, 2006).

7. "Census Estimates Make Big D Feel a Little Smaller," *Dallas Morning News*, June 24, 2004.

8. For instance, there was a roundtable on how to conduct research in the South at the annual meeting of the Association for Asian American Studies, Toronto, 2001. Its 2006 conference is to be in Atlanta.

9. www.tsha.utexas.edu/handbook/online/articles/view/DD/hdd1.html (accessed July 18, 2006).

10. For instance, *Fortune* magazine rated Dallas the "overall best city for business in North America" (Payne 2002, 113). A major reason cited was the size and proximity of the airport, which was the third busiest in the world at that time.

11. "The Big D in Demographics: Research Portrays Dallas Differently than Rest of Texas, Even Fort Worth," *Dallas Morning News*, May 6, 2000.

12. "Study of North Texas Immigrant Communities." http://www.dfwinternational.org/_content/media/immigrants/StudyOfNorthTexasImmigrantCommunities.pdf, p. 6 (accessed July 18, 2006).

13. "D-FW Jobs Luring Immigrants," *Dallas Morning News*, February 29, 2004.

14. "Study of North Texas Immigrant Communities." http://www.dfwinternational.org/_content/media/immigrants/StudyOfNorthTexasImmigrantCommunities.pdf, p. 13 (accessed July 18, 2006).

15. As a way of distinguishing first-generation interviewees from the second generation, who make up the main focus of the study, I refer to the former by last name rather than by first name.

16. I attended all four, but was unable to interview leaders of the Catholic church, so I have detailed information on only three.

17. "Study of North Texas Immigrant Communities." http://www
.dfwinternational.org/_content/media/immigrants/
StudyOfNorthTexasImmigrantCommunities.pdf, p. 6 (accessed July 18, 2006).

18. As an example of its attempts to bring in various styles of worship, it has fifteen gods rather than the typical one god. Each specialized group of Hindus finds one of the gods the most significant.

19. Again, note that the name of all organizations have been changed. A national Indian American political organization also started a Dallas branch after my fieldwork was completed, with the goal of similarly helping people become more civically integrated by promoting political participation and outreach to local institutions. This general strategy of engaging in civil society receives attention in chapter 7.

20. An Asian American political advocacy organization started up after I had finished the bulk of my fieldwork. It serves as an umbrella organization for various pan-ethnic associations in the city. Its goal is to encourage the political participation of Asian Americans, as do other associations in the city, including the Asian American Small Business Association. It serves primarily the first generation; no informants during the follow-up fieldwork mentioned it.

21. http://factfinder.census.gov/servlet/DTTable?_bm=y&-context=dt&-ds_
name=DEC_2000_SF1_U&-CONTEXT=dt&-mt_name=DEC_2000_SF1_U_P001&-
mt_name=DEC_2000_SF1_U_PCT007&-tree_id=4001&-redoLog=false&-all_
geo_types=N&-_caller=geoselect&-geo_id=04000US48&-geo_id=05000US48113&-
search_results=01000US&-format=&-_lang=en (accessed July 18, 2006).

22. "D-FW Jobs Luring Immigrants," *Dallas Morning News*, February 29, 2004.

23. "Study of North Texas Immigrant Communities." http://www
.dfwinternational.org/_content/media/immigrants/
StudyOfNorthTexasImmigrantCommunities.pdf, p. 93 (accessed July 18, 2006).

24. One public issue that the Vietnamese American community dealt with in January 2006 was a police chief of a suburb reportedly saying about an application by a Vietnamese American police recruit, "As long as I'm chief, we won't have any gooks working in Farmers Branch." The chief resigned following critiques from the comment. http://cbs11tv.com/topstories/local_story_005225535.html (accessed July 18, 2006).

25. http://factfinder.census.gov/servlet/DTTable?_bm=y&-context=dt&-
reg=DEC_2000_SF4_U_PCT089:001|012|013|023&-ds_name=DEC_2000_SF4_
U&-CONTEXT=dt&-mt_name=DEC_2000_SF4_U_PCT089&-tree_id=4001&-

redoLog=true&-all_geo_types=N&-geo_id=05000US48113&-format=&-_lang=en (accessed July 18, 2006). This data is from Census 2000 Summary File 4, Dallas County. It refers to median household incomes in 1999.

26. The data comes from Census 2000 Summary File 4—Sample data. http://www .census.gov (accessed July 23, 2006).

27. Data from the 2002 American Community Survey Summary Tables. http:// factfinder.census.gov/servlet/DTTable?_bm=y&-context=dt&-ds_name=ACS_2002 _EST_G00_&-CONTEXT=dt&-mt_name=ACS_2002_EST_G2000_PCT035D&- tree_id=402&-redoLog=true&-all_geo_types=N&-geo_id=05000US48113&- format=&-_lang=en (accessed July 18, 2006).

28. http://factfinder.census.gov/servlet/DTTable?_bm=y&-tree_id= 402&-context=dt&-selections=002|DEC_2000_SF4_U_PCT001&-state=dt&-all _geo_types=N&-reg=DEC_2000_SF4_U_PCT004:001|013|023&-mt_name=DEC _2000_SF4_U_PCT004&-redoLog=true&-_lang=en&-SubjectID=10908851&- geo_id=05000US48113&-CONTEXT=dt&-ci_type=R&-format=&-search _results=01000US&-TABLE_NAMEX=&-ds_name=DEC_2000_SF4_U&- charIterations=008 (accessed July 18, 2006).

29. http://factfinder.census.gov/servlet/DTTable?_bm=y&-tree_id=402&- context=dt&-selections=002|DEC_2000_SF4_U_PCT001&-state=dt&-all _geo_types=N&-reg=DEC_2000_SF4_U_PCT035:001|013|023&-mt_name=DEC _2000_SF4_U_PCT035&-redoLog=true&-_lang=en&-SubjectID=10909265&- geo_id=05000US48113&-CONTEXT=dt&-ci_type=R&-format=&-search _results=01000US&-TABLE_NAMEX=&-ds_name=DEC_2000_SF4_U&- charIterations=008 (accessed July 18, 2006).

30. http://factfinder.census.gov/servlet/DTTable?_bm=y&-tree_id= 402&-context=dt&-selections=002|DEC_2000_SF4_U_PCT001&-state= dt&-all_geo_types=N&-reg=DEC_2000_SF4_U_PCT038:001|013|023;DEC_2000 _SF4_U_PCT086:001&-mt_name=DEC_2000_SF4_U_PCT038&-mt_name=DEC _2000_SF4_U_PCT086&-redoLog=true&-_lang=en&-SubjectID=10909265&- geo_id=05000US48113&-CONTEXT=dt&-ci_type=R&-format=&-search _results=01000US&-TABLE_NAMEX=&-ds_name=DEC_2000_SF4_U&- charIterations=008 (accessed July 18, 2006).

31. Similarly, Alba et al. (1999) found that Asian immigrants are residentially dispersed in urban and suburban areas throughout the country, even those of the first generation.

32. "Spreading Out, Staying Isolated," *Dallas Morning News*, April 4, 2001.

33. In fact, according to the African American tourist guide, put out by the African American Chamber of Commerce, there are more restaurants per capita in Dallas than in New York City. When I asked participants who were new to the area what they do in Dallas, almost all responded that they go out to eat.

34. http://www.bizjournals.com/austin/stories/2005/08/08/daily29.html (accessed September 3, 2006).

35. http://factfinder.census.gov/servlet/SAFFFacts?_event= ChangeGeoContext&geo_id=05000US48113&_geoContext=&_street=& _county=dallas&_cityTown=dallas&_state=04000US48&_zip=&_lang=en& _sse=on&ActiveGeoDiv=&_useEV=&pctxt=fph&pgsl=010 (accessed July 18, 2006).

36. According to a brochure published by the African American Chamber of Commerce.

37. "City Diversifying, Census Data Show Maps Chart Changes in Neighborhoods," *Dallas Morning News*, February 15, 1991.

38. http://factfinder.census.gov/servlet/SAFFFacts?_event= ChangeGeoContext&geo_id=05000US48113&_geoContext=&_street=& _county=dallas&_cityTown=dallas&_state=04000US48&_zip=&_lang=en& _sse=on&ActiveGeoDiv=&_useEV=&pctxt=fph&pgsl=010 (accessed July 18, 2006).

39. "Immigration Not Letting Up," *Dallas Morning News*, November 24, 2004. Because Texas is a border state with Mexico, it receives a large number of immigrants.

40. As an example, a discussion of domestic violence within Latino communities will consider how women can seek help without risking deportation. "Breaking from Abuse Without Being Deported," *Dallas Morning News*, March 15, 2005. A number of articles also deal with immigration policy at various governmental levels and its impact on both legal and illegal immigrants.

41. http://factfinder.census.gov/servlet/DTTable?_bm=y&-tree_id=402&- context=dt&-selections=002|DEC_2000_SF4_U_PCT001&-state=dt&-all_geo _types=N&-reg=DEC_2000_SF4_U_PCT130:001|013|023&-mt_name=DEC_2000 _SF4_U_PCT130&-redoLog=true&-currentselections=DEC_2000_SF4_U_PCT130 &-_lang=en&-SubjectID=10909265&-geo_id=05000US48113&-CONTEXT=dt&- ci_type=R&-format=&-ds_name=DEC_2000_SF4_U&-search_results=01000US&- TABLE_NAMEX=&-charIterations=008 (accessed July 18, 2006).

42. I did not rely on individuals to represent the social level but instead had in-depth interviews with organization leaders and conducted observations in community sites (Lieberson 1985).

Chapter 3

1. Because this study focuses primarily on the second generation, terms used to refer to those interviewed for the study, such as "informants," "participants," "actors," "interviewees," etc., refer to the second generation unless otherwise noted.

2. All of the immigrant leaders interviewed were men who led the major organizations of each community. That they were all men could bias the results of what constituted the social identity. However, the second generation of each group did not

suggest hearing different articulations of a social identity from mothers versus fathers, or from women versus men generally. This is not to say that second-generation women and men did not vary in the kinds of expectations they faced and the tensions that often ensued; they are discussed in this chapter and in chapters 5–7. As mentioned in chapter 2, the last names are used for interviewees of the first generation (except when first introduced) in order to differentiate them from the second generation. All names have been changed to protect confidentiality.

3. In a similar, although much more extreme, vein, the Taiwanese American Wen Ho Lee was a scientist at Los Alamos National Laboratories, working on national defense, which still did not clear him of assumptions of being a spy for the Chinese government.

4. "Southern Baptists, Expanding Effort, Target Hindus for Conversion," *Washington Post*, October 21, 1999.

5. "Southern Baptists Warned Chicago Religious Leaders Question Mission Plan," *Fort Worth Star-Telegram*, November 29, 1999. On the Sunday following the incident in Houston, the Metroplex Hindu temple hired two police officers to guard their doors (field notes, October 1999).

6. http://www.rediff.com/us/2003/mar/01us1.htm (accessed July 26, 2006).

7. http://www.indiausa-sc.org/co1.htm (accessed July 26, 2006).

8. Religious and non-religious-based intolerance and hate crimes against the South Asian American community are also nothing new. Even before 9/11, South Asian Americans endured the highest rate of hate crimes among Asian Americans. (See *Challenging the Invisibility of Hate: 1999 Audit of Violence Against Asian Pacific Americans,* compiled by the National Asian Pacific American Legal Consortium, the Asian Pacific American Legal Center, the Asian American Legal Defense and Education Fund, and the Asian Law Caucus.) Cf. the "dot busters" who terrorized Indian Americans in Jersey City, New Jersey, mentioned in chapter 2. After 9/11, the dangers facing South Asian Americans because of religious and racial prejudice have only intensified. A Sikh and a Pakistani American, in Arizona and Texas, respectively, were killed by individuals angry about the attacks soon following September 11, and an Egyptian American, coincidentally a Christian, was murdered in Los Angeles. Within two weeks of 9/11, hundreds of cases of aggravation and violence had been reported to the Council on American-Islamic Relations (http://web.amnesty.org/library/Index/engACT300272001?OpenDocument, accessed July 26, 2006). Many South Asian Americans, regardless of religion, worried about being classified as terrorists by both private individuals and government agencies, as evinced in the detainment and investigation of four Muslim American medical students in Georgia erroneously accused of plotting terrorism while driving to Florida, who in turn lost their internship positions as medical students (http://www.archives.cnn.com/2002/US/09/13/alligator.alley/index.html [accessed July 26, 2006]).

9. This is a strategy often endorsed by poorer migrants living in segregated urban areas with native minorities, who may experience downward mobility (Waters 1998; Zhou and Bankston 1998).

10. J. Kurlantzick, "Vote Getters," *New Republic Online*, posted May 26, 2004.

11. Asian Americans were criticized following the campaign finance scandal in 1996, in which politicians received illegal donations from Asian business interests. The Democratic National Committee responded by asking for the citizenship status of Asian American donors (Ancheta 1998). This image of the "Oriental" corrupting American politics made its way into popular media, such as the cover of the March 24 edition of *National Review* in 1997. For a critique of the image and the broader depiction of Asian Americans as "Orientals" in popular cultures, see Lee 1999.

12. Such an attitude fits with the overly personal advice given to Korean Americans after the 1992 Los Angeles riots. To ameliorate relations between them and African Americans, Koreans were told to smile more and learn different cultural norms (Abelmann and Lie 1995). This response reduces the source of the tensions to simple cultural misunderstandings and ignores the economic and geographic forces and the institutional racism that position Korean Americans as independent store owners in segregated black and Latino neighborhoods. Urban communities continue to be plagued by underinvestment, and therefore the need for middleman groups, often other minorities, continues. Prices in these stores will be higher because of their limited scale and other costs, and store owners will likely not live in that same neighborhood. The result is a lack of trust between store owner and clientele that fuels resentment.

13. The name of the organization, like the names of practically all the organizations and people in the study, is kept confidential in order to respect people's privacy. Few immigrants, including Korean and Indian Americans, join non-ethnic civic organizations. For instance, Hurh, Kim, and Kwange (1978) found that in Chicago, only 6 percent of Korean immigrants reported involvement in mainstream voluntary associations (78).

14. Interpersonal contact can limit prejudice between individuals but only under particular conditions, such as when the minority is in a position of authority over the White individual, or when members of the majority and minority must work together as equal partners to solve a problem (Allport 1958; Fiske and Taylor 1984). Reducing prejudice also requires the teachings of positive out-group attributes (Brewer and Brown 1998).

15. "Southern Baptists, Expanding Effort, Target Hindus for Conversion," *Washington Post*, October 21, 1999.

16. In addition to honoring the victims, leaders of various groups have used the discourse of having arrived in the United States "legally" rather than by surreptitiously crossing the border, as Latinos are popularly presumed to have done.

17. Espiritu (2003) argues that part of the reason Asian Americans have transformative experiences regarding their ethnic identities during college is the lack of information about their homeland and about their U.S. ethnic history in high school.

18. Although Asian Americans claim these attributes as peculiar to themselves, many European descendants consider such characteristics to define their groups as well (Waters 1990). In other words, these are relatively generic attributes rather than culturally specific.

19. Field notes, Thanksgiving 1999.

20. Field notes, September 1999.

21. Few Indian Americans went to the temple weekly, and about two-thirds went on special occasions, that is, between one and four times a year. Korean Americans attended services much more frequently. Regardless of whether they attended temple or not, people saw religion as central to what it meant to be Indian and had been to a temple on occasion. In popular imagination, India is a spiritual country where Westerners go to "find themselves" and discover religious guidance (Mehta 1991). The public image of India becomes part of how Indian Americans conceive of their own homeland, especially when they also have been exposed to temples in the United States that not only serve as religious bases, but also as cultural centers. Many temples host cultural performances that are only indirectly tied to religion, often in attached rooms dedicated to such events. How temples refer to the ethnic social identity, then, becomes significant in how the individuals understand it, even if they are not deeply involved in the temple.

22. Male authority in Korean American and Indian American religious institutions is normal, but this does not mean that women lack leadership positions. After moving to the United States, and especially if their paid work is valuable to the home, women often have more prominence in U.S. religious organizations than in their homeland (Warner 1993). The assistant pastor of God's Light EM was a woman.

23. Field notes, November 1999.

24. Although the other pastors did not refer to gender norms in the services I visited, one attendee at God's Light church said that the pastor had commented before on the need for traditional gender roles for Korean Americans, but suggested the division not be as imbalanced as among first-generation Koreans. All these acts place men more in charge of the public sphere and women of the private sphere, with the intention of reproducing the same codes of conduct that distinguished their ethnic groups from other races and helped lead to their mobility. Males were privileged in more subtle ways as well. At a ceremony of new parents dedicating their children to the church and to God at the Good Book, the fathers and mothers stood at the front of the church, facing the pastor (field notes, June 2002). Most of the fathers held their babies, and the pastor addressed the father when asking each set of parents if they were willing

to dedicate their baby to the church. Although the pastor addressed the husbands in particular, both the husbands and wives responded yes to the pastors' questions, not just the husbands. In the Swaminarayan temple men and women sat on opposite sides of the room, and people were not allowed to speak to anyone of the opposite gender while in the temple. The guru, who is male, faced the men as he spoke, not the women. Most of the women wore ethnic clothing, while about a third of the adult men did so. Indian meals are also served after these services, with men eating outside in the back of the temple and women often remaining inside. These cultural practices, endorsed by the religious institutions, prioritize domestic duties for women.

25. I even saw one boy, probably aged six, chastise a peer for wearing shorts to the temple, while all the other boys wore pants (field notes, September 1999). All women and girls wore traditional ethnic clothing.

26. Field notes, May 2002.

27. In 1990 in the Los Angeles region, just over one-third of native-born adult Indian Americans and just under a quarter of similar Korean Americans spoke a language besides English at home (Lopez 1996). Intermarriage statistics also support this view, with increased marriage rates between immigrant groups and Whites the longer groups have been in the country (Lee and Fernandez 1998; Wong 1989). The loss of ethnic cultural ties is especially likely in the United States because it has not institutionalized multiculturalism at the state level (Steinberg 1989; Taylor 1994). Transnational ties also may be weak because most in the second generation plan on settling in the United States and do not follow political or social trends in their homeland (Kasinitz et al. 2002).

28. Individuals have cognitive categories, or subjective boundaries (Lamont 1992), with which they make sense of their environment and their own place within it, including who is like them, whom they can trust, whom to avoid, etc. While Lamont focuses on macro cultural and social-structural factors in explaining the different categories found among upper-middle-class men in the United States and France, I concentrate on often micro-level variables, including types of interactions with Whites and involvement with the ethnic community, to explain participants' membership in different categories, because participants were not differentiated at the macro level given their similar class statuses, racial statuses, and geography.

29. This may constitute a disproportionate share of second-generation Asian Americans compared to the number in the other categories generally because of the sampling procedure, discussed in chapter 2.

30. A Hindu temple in Syracuse, New York, brought a young guru from India to serve in the temple and live near the facility (personal observation, fall 1998). The Swaminarayan temple, which Rupu attends, has guests from India as well as first-generation migrants speak to both adults and youth on personal values and religious tenants. Field notes, September 1999.

31. Immigration studies typically dichotomize immigrants into two types: sojourners and settlers. Sojourners intend to live in a new land for a limited time, accumulate resources, and then return home. They are visitors whose minds and hearts remain abroad. Settlers immigrate with the intent to stay, and while they may have nostalgia for their homeland, they dedicate their energy to integrating into the United States. Yet this dichotomy overlooks how groups mix elements of both immigrant types, a strategy that is becoming more common with increasing transnationalism, so that ties to one's homeland help groups adjust to the Unites States.

32. Psychological literature offers somewhat different versions of a stage progression model. Youth of color often—not always—identify with the majority, unaware of their ethnic and racial differences or ashamed of them. After experiencing a racist episode or sensing significant differences from the majority, the youth start to claim a traditional identity in order to affirm commitment to their previously neglected backgrounds and to "discover themselves," a normal adolescent process regardless of ethnic or racial status as youth try to find their place relative to the social groups around them (Erikson 1968). In the final stage individuals feel committed to both their ethnic and American identities and comfortable with their status as ethnic minorities. Like classical assimilation theory, these psychological models have been critiqued for positing a single pathway to developing identities and overemphasizing the marginal-man scenario (Kerckhoff and McCormick 1955). The revised versions of these models have broadened to account for other types of experiences, such as growing up continually attached to or relatively uninterested in their background. However, scholars still indicate the movement from opposing to embracing one's background as the most frequent trajectory (Child 1943; Kim 2001; Phinney 1990). The models, like assimilation theory, have also lost their normative tone and instead posit the final stage of identity development as a common outcome, desired or not.

33. Again, as Lamont (1992) found, individuals' cognitive categories shape whom they feel most similar to and empathize with.

34. According to Schudson's "How Culture Works" (1989), cultural elements "work" when they lead individuals to act, which he defines as resolution. Seen here, those elements that these participants promote themselves are often those that were learned from peers.

35. The practical application of post-ethnicity applies to European Americans more than to racial minorities, whose skin color continues to mark them as from elsewhere, which in turn leads to questions about their background; for them, communication of ethnicity cannot be completely voluntary.

Chapter 4

1. Racial identity refers to one's minority status as part of an ethnic-specific or pan-ethnic group. Indian American or Korean American, not just as Asian American,

can be a racial identity if it refers to one's status relative to another race as opposed to another ethnic group (e.g., relative to Whites as opposed to German Americans; see chapter 1).

2. Lien et al. (2003) found that encountering racism did not lead to a pan-ethnic identity among Asian Americans. However, it is unclear from the survey data whether this applied more to first-, 1.5-, or second-generation Asian Americans, and what kind of racism the respondents were referring to.

3. For example, both foreign- and native-born Asian Americans, male and female, showed an increase in marriages to other Asian Americans from 1980 to 1990 (Shinagawa and Pang 1996). More intermarriage takes place for native-borns. Asian immigrants rarely form pan-ethnic identities at the personal level, and few would expect otherwise, given recent immigrants' salient cultural, economic, geographic, and political divisions both here and in their homelands. Just when an Asian American pan-ethnic identity took root following the Asian American student movement of the 1960s, the influx of new Asian immigrants, many of whom had little connection to those Asian Americans already here, undermined it. This is not to say that immigrants have not pursued pan-ethnicity. Indian Americans lobbied to be classified as Asian Americans in the 1980 U.S. Census, a move that some other Asian Americans resisted, but that in turn allowed them to take advantage of government programs and protections targeted to Asian Americans (Espiritu 1992). At the micro level, however, pan-ethnic identities remain weak among the first generation.

4. Nazli Kibria (2002) also finds that a belief in a common racial, almost blood origin created a solidarity among second-generation Chinese and Korean Americans.

5. Many Asian Americans take pride in the model-minority image. See Ho (2003) and Wong, Lai, and Lin (1998).

6. See Steinberg (1989) for an account of the success of Jews relative to that of Irish immigrants and African Americans that stresses not their cultural attributes but their human capital, brought over from the homeland, and job opportunities within the United States.

7. This assumes that biological bases of differences in scholastic achievement have fallen into disrepute, which of course they have not totally (Herrnstein and Murray 1994).

8. Anderson (1999b) makes a similar categorical distinction among urban Blacks as "street" and "descent." He traces these cultural differences between groups to social-structural problems, including the lack of faith of inner-city residents in the police, the courts, and the schools.

9. The fact that one's self-perceptions do not overlap with one's actions is nothing new. However, this is often overlooked in accounts of immigrants' ethnic identities that rely on survey responses to a limited number of identity choices.

10. Theories of the self within symbolic interactionism argue that individuals develop identities by interpreting the labels assigned by others (Cooley 1902; Stryker 1992). According to symbolic interactionism, the self is a product of interactions with others—that is, one understands oneself primarily on the basis of one's perceptions of how others view one.

11. Although organizational links between Asian Americans and African Americans may be rare, historically and currently, there have been exchanges across national and racial boundaries. Prashad (2002) details these connections.

12. Most research on Indian Americans adopts a postcolonial and/or transnational perspective, with concentration on the political, religious, and gender dynamics within the diaspora (Prashad and Mathew 1999–2000). Indian Americans' degree of pan-ethnicity and attitudes toward racism are underexamined.

13. This image makes its way into popular media, such as in the cover of the March 24, 1997, issue of the *National Review*. For a critique of the image and the broader depiction of Asian Americans as "Orientals" in popular cultures, see Lee 1999.

14. Other ethnic groups also resist classification as members of a racial group as a means of self-definition and to avoid problematic terms. Latinos often choose "Other" on the U.S. Census form asking for racial background (Rodriguez 2000), and even West Indian immigrants may mark "Other" instead of "Black" and then write in their ethnicity so as to distance themselves from African Americans (Waters 1998).

15. According to Human Rights Watch, anti-Arab and anti-Muslim attacks in the United States are nothing new and tend to rise following publicized events that position Arabs and Muslims as threats to another nation's physical or economic safety, such as following the 1973 Arab-Israeli war and oil embargo, the hijacking of TWA Flight 847 by Shiite militants in 1985, the 1991 Persian Gulf War, and other events. Even when Arabs and Muslims are not involved, such as in the 1985 Oklahoma City bombing, they make convenient scapegoats and encounter threats and actual harm to their bodies and property. http://www.hrw.org/reports/2002/usahate/usa1102-03.htm#P221_29794 (accessed July 26, 2006). Even with the history of suspicion and hate crimes toward these groups, the number of such incidents rose precipitously following 9/11. According to Human Rights Watch, the federal government received reports of 481 anti-Muslim hate crimes in 2001—seventeen times the number it had received the year before. More than 2,000 cases of harassment were reported to Arab and Muslim organizations. http://www.hrw.org/press/2002/11/usahate.htm (accessed July 26, 2006).

16. Because of their physical differences from East Asian Americans, Indian Americans sometimes find themselves mistaken for Blacks or Latinos (George 1997). Yet participants reported this rarely happening to them, and they did not articulate a distinct relationship with these races as did other Asian Americans. Only one participant said he had been referred to as a Latino, and none had concerns about such

misidentifications. This is likely due to a combination of the different class levels of the participants compared to most Latinos and Blacks and to the racial segregation in Dallas. Participants frequently commented that they rarely saw Latinos and African Americans when they went out to restaurants, clubs, bars, and upscale clothing stores in Dallas, which lessened the possibility that others would identify them as such. If others mistook Indian Americans for Latinos or African Americans, they did not convey that to the participants.

17. This is not to argue that working-class and/or poor Asian Americans necessarily join other minorities in response to racism from Whites. Rather, interviewees' class status limits such alliances in specific ways. Social image and class alone do not account for why individuals do or do not join pan-ethnic groups; other factors include ideology, geography, population size, and group interests.

18. I had not heard of the event from interviewees anywhere else, neither at organizational meetings, nor from group leaders, nor in casual conversations at social gatherings.

19. Field notes, June 2000. This excludes the prevalence of Latinos working as busboys in Dallas restaurants and in other "backstage" positions.

20. Field notes, December 1999.

21. This is according to a representative (field notes, June 1999). Even the two second-generation Korean American informants who owned businesses had little motivation to be active in the organization.

22. Although not connected to their location in Dallas, participants' involvement in ethnic and religious organizations during college furthered interactions with co-ethnics rather than mostly with other Asian Americans. Even those Korean Americans who belonged to non-ethnic-specific religious associations, such as Brothers and Sisters in Christ [BASIC], stated that most members on their college campuses were Korean Americans.

23. The public image of Asian American groups changes depending on U.S.-international relations. For instance, during World War II, the Chinese were characterized as noble and courageous in their fight against the Japanese (Kitano and Daniels 1995). This image changed again during the cold war and with the rise of Mao Zedong, when some Chinese came to be suspected as communist agents. The current fears about terrorists could signify a positive image for non-Muslim (and non-Sikh) South Asian Americans on the backs of those who are being racially profiled.

24. For an analysis of the rise, popularity, and message of Hindu nationalist camps in the United States, see Mathew and Prashad (1999–2000).

25. Vincent Chin, a Chinese American, was murdered in 1981 by two unemployed White auto workers in Detroit who beat him with a baseball bat (Zia 2000). Earlier in the evening, one of the murderers had said to Chin, "It's because of you motherfuckers that we're out of work," referring to U.S. automobile corporations' growing competi-

tion with Japanese manufacturers. Collapsing Chinese and Japanese Americans into one group and treating them all as unwanted foreigners fuels a defensive pan-ethnic identity among Asian Americans. The two murderers, who confessed to the crime, were fined $3,000 and received probation; they served no jail time. Wen Ho Lee was a scientist at Los Alamos, New Mexico. He was indicted and imprisoned by federal prosecutors, who held him responsible for the loss of nuclear weapon secret designs to China. Robert Vrooman, former security chief at Los Alamos and an ex-CIA officer, claimed that Lee was wrongfully targeted in part because of his race. Lee was later found innocent of sharing nuclear secrets and released, but not before being placed in solitary confinement and shackled in prison.

Chapter 5

1. Most participants worked in large companies, which can encompass a variety of types of workplaces. Morrill (1995) finds a few major types of social structure and cultures within corporations. Although there was likely variation among informants in how hierarchies were established in informants' organizations and in rules for conflict management among employers, there was a similar sense of what a worker was, as defined by diversity management. I am less interested in the specific scripts of how to go about one's particular job or deal with a superior's weaknesses, and more interested in how workers were expected to present themselves in regard to ethnicity and race in the white-collar workplace. Some workplaces may offer more room to express one's background, but what "difference" means is defined by an organization's diversity management programs, which participants found to be relatively constant, as explained in this chapter.

2. Diversity management is separate from affirmative action and is intended to help retain minority employees already hired (Gardenswartz and Rowe 1993; Kirby and Richard 2000).

3. Field notes, June 2002.

4. For example, according to Holvino (2000), a workplace truly sensitive to the needs of Latinos allows for a prioritization of family over productivity at times, for family has traditionally been central to Latino identity; yet this rarely occurs.

5. Most co-workers were White unless otherwise noted, although few informants worked in otherwise exclusively White establishments. It bears repeating that the study's references to "Asian American" culture and "White American" culture reflect the views of the participants, not an attempt to essentialize and homogenize diverse groups of people.

6. Although expectations facing women inside the home and civil sphere are increasingly documented (Dasgupta 1998; Espiritu 2003; Song and Moon 1998; Maira 2002), how those expectations influence them in the work sphere needs more attention.

7. Religious differences did not present a significant problem, according to Indian American participants, in part because they did not bring them up. Some were vegetarian for religious reasons, which created little discomfort even though they felt conscious of this difference. After 9/11, Indian Americans stressed that they were not Muslim but instead Hindu or Jain when asked about their religion, and they encountered no explicit problems at work.

8. Brekhus (2003) similarly finds that some gay men prefer to segregate their sexuality, keeping it in their private lives, while others prefer to bring it into the workplace.

9. In fact, some scholars doubt that native-born Asian Americans will encounter a glass ceiling because of their acculturation (Min 2006a).

10. As social-psychological approaches to identity suggest, actors choose an identity based partly on what fits the expectations of others and so segregate their identities in distinct settings (Stryker 1992). African American women, for instance, maintain mostly African American friends at home but do not mention such friendships when at work, where they primarily associate with Whites (Bell 1990).

11. Workers are also turning to the Internet to express "marginal" identities. For instance, religiously devout individuals chat online with peers about spiritual topics while at work, often during their lunch breaks (Salopek 2000). They also express religiosity at work through the Internet ("Religion" 1999).

12. Vikram's lunch hour does not constitute a liminal space given its highly public nature and his participation in it by himself. Taken from Turner (1969), the term liminal space refers to almost metaphoric realms where people can negotiate ideas and identities as a collective, and then return to their normal lives (see Gray and Thumma 1997).

13. Jyoti had a staff of two other people and so could create her own "idioculture," which Fine (1996) defines as a small enough set of relationships that members can create their own specific norms. Those in larger organizations had less freedom to do so.

14. Field notes, June 2002.

15. Informants did not bring up class differences from their workplace culture because most had grown up in middle-class homes.

Chapter 6

1. In 2004 Paul Singh Ghuman wrote of the contradictions within second-generation Indian Americans: "They demanded 'more freedom': 'We want our lifestyles,' they said, 'but we don't want a bad reputation and we don't want to shame our mothers and fathers. It's just too much pressure; its hard because we can't be ourselves.'" http://www.youngminds.org.uk/magazine/72/ghuman.php (accessed July 27, 2006).

2. Whereas Morawska (1996) argues that second-generation Jewish Americans in both rural and urban locations tried to adopt more middle-class American goods for

their homes in the early 1900s, here we see a commitment by the second generation to keep their homes from seeming too American. The difference can be attributed to growing multiculturalism; to the respect accorded to Korean and Indian ethnic groups relative to Eastern European Jews at the turn of the twentieth century; and the high human capital and social integration of the informants, who did not need to prove their acculturation but instead needed to make sure not to appear too integrated, in violation of the home code.

3. Hardly any participants changed into ethnic clothes when returning home or performed other rituals, although this could have served as another means of marking an ethnic space at home. The reason is that few grew up wearing ethnic clothes around the home, and therefore doing so as adults was not part of the home schema.

4. The notion of identity talk fits with Lamont's (1992) discussion of boundary work, that is, the efforts one undergoes to affirm one's status within a cognitive category of similar people, distinct from others.

5. This process of reinterpretation as a means of dealing with discrepancies between one's desired lifestyle and the lifestyle one actually is living fits Arlie Hochschild's (1989) notion of "myths" used by women and men to reconcile the differences between how one wishes domestic chores were divided among husbands and wives and how they really are. Hochschild finds that some couples spoke of their housework as evenly divided despite evidence to the contrary, such as seeing the husband as in charge of the garage and the wife as in charge of the home as a fair distribution, even though the garage work took much less time.

6. Daughters have a more difficult time gaining permission to move away for college since parents often want to continue surveillance over their behavior, especially during a time of sexual and personal experimentation such as college (Dasgupta and Dasgupta 1998). No female informants said that they would not move away from their parents if the right job became available.

7. An emphasis on education and shared cultural upbringing could signify a middle-class dynamic more than necessarily an ethnic one. Lee (2004) finds that working-class Korean Americans did not have an affinity for other Asian Americans per se but for those of their own class background.

8. In a similar vein, Bhachu (1995) finds that Indian British female professionals maintained the traditional custom of dowry but updated it to fit their current upper-middle class lifestyles by choosing conspicuous-consumption items for themselves, such as designer clothes, jewelry, furniture, and other expensive goods. Bhachu refers to this as a hybrid cultural creation that blends their ethnic heritage with their upbringing in Britain and their current professional status. Similarly, interviewees try to satisfy traditional sets of expectations and social relations while attending to their preferences based on their upbringing as middle- and upper-middle-class Asian Americans.

9. At these meetings singles and a few married couples had a simple spaghetti dinner at the church and then sang songs and engaged in group activities. (Field notes, May and June 2002.) Those leading the service did not refer to dating or marriage. All the Korean Americans who were married had chosen other Christians, and over half had met their spouses through the Korean church.

10. Because of the image of Asian Americans as the model minority, individuals assumed that finding someone of their same "ethno class" would be easy and that such a person would be a good match for them in terms of both their "ancient" and their "current" tastes (Gordon 1964).

11. Although Indian American participants noted the importance of religion and language to their parents, they rarely mentioned caste. Because caste does not fit into the U.S. cultural or social-structural system, it lost relevance for many in the first and especially the second generation. Participants and their parents cared about a partner's class status and education level, as noted (see also Dhingra 2003b). A few respondents maintained the north Indian versus south Indian distinction in articulating marital preferences but did not go out of their way to avoid Indians from certain regions. For instance, Veera said that she wanted to marry a fellow Punjabi American but did not "know too much about [caste]. It doesn't mean anything to me. Never talk about it with friends. North and south are different. We'd like to stick to our own kind, but it's not a hard and fast rule."

12. This is becoming a more and more common practice. See http://www .nytimes.com/2005/08/23/national/23india.html?pagewanted=1&ei=5070&en= b65177e0c13fe524&ex=1125460800&emc=eta1 (accessed July 27, 2006).

13. Arranged marriages are changing within India as well, especially among those of the growing middle class. Parents are still involved, but youth have more control over the decision-making process. To facilitate marriages for the diaspora, web sites have started that provide personal ads from Indians throughout the world, e.g., http:// www.matrimonialsindia.com/ (accessed July 27, 2006). The same trend is occurring in Korea too. Koreans in Korea and the diaspora also can turn to the web to find partners. See, for example, http://www.koreancupid.com/ (accessed July 27, 2006).

14. Rituals take on an even greater importance in the diaspora because they ground migrants in a stable history during a time of change. Yet, rituals have less impact on preventing drug and alcohol use among the second or third generation than does limiting intergenerational and intercultural tensions between parents and youth (Bhattacharya 2002). Asian Americans who had high conflict with their immigrant parents reported more social problems than did others. Youth deeply involved in their parents' heritage tended to have limited intergenerational tensions, as did youth whose parents demonstrated a bicultural approach to parenting.

15. For instance, debates between Maxine Hong Kingston and Frank Chin regarding her book *The Woman Warrior* stem from this assumption, with Chin claiming

that Kingston was overly assimilated based on her critique of sexism within Chinese culture.

16. It should not be surprising that actors did not mention class. Few Americans think of their social location in terms of economic class.

17. K. Park (1999) finds that 1.5 generation Korean American men often return to Korea to find a wife because Korean American women, according to these men, often do not want to serve their husbands enough and prioritize money over strong family values. None of the second-generation male participants suggested this tactic.

Chapter 7

1. I am talking about these common activities rather than about hobbies such as playing guitar or painting because this is what actors referenced most as what they enjoyed doing with their leisure time.

2. In New York City, for example, there are frequent events that cater to one ethnic group, including art shows, public lectures and readings, nightclub themes, etc., not to mention pan-ethnic Asian American cultural productions (Khandelwal 2002).

3. According to Feagin and Sikes (1994), African Americans, once they are certain that discrimination has taken place, often address the wrongdoer and notify the person of their rights. This occurred with greater frequency in public establishments than in the streets. Most interviewees, however, avoided such confrontations, even when confident that they were unfairly treated.

4. This process bears resemblance to Morawska's (1996) discussion of "ethnicization," which refers to second-generation Jewish Americans taking traditional practices and making them more American. Here the opposite occurs—making an American practice more ethnic. The result is the same: integrating lifestyles through a lived hybridity. Actors' efforts to "ethnicize" mainstream hobbies also can be read as comparable to the process of ethnogenesis, whereby groups form boundaries that did not exist before (Roosens 1989; Tuan 1998; Yancey, Ericksen, and Juliani 1976). The emphasis here is on how the ethnogenesis allows for both differentiation from and integration with the mainstream. Actors, in effect, exhibited a subculture, as opposed to a counterculture, by fitting into the cultural norms of their age group but in a slightly unique way (Yinger 1982).

5. About a quarter of the men at the dance wore the traditional clothing of kurta pajamas, and practically all the women, regardless of age, wore saris or salvar kameezes. Field notes, October 1999. I also saw people of all ages and in similar attire at a variety show, held in the Dallas convention center, starring current Indian film stars who were touring the United States. The celebrities performed comedic skits and sang songs, all in Hindi. Their presence suggests the growing popularity of Hindi films for Indian Americans.

6. Field notes, October 1999.

7. For instance, at those EMs affiliated with a first-generation church, Thanksgiving and Easter services were often joined with the immigrant congregation.

8. Field notes, November 1999.

9. These observations were made throughout the fall and winter of 1999.

10. A couple of the EMs also have a Friday night singles ministry. The lay pastor running it at World Gathering explained, "We have a lot of people showing up to the singles ministry. We need to get them married and get them out of this group" [*laughs*]. Field notes, June 2002.

11. Although some Indian American cultural and secular organizations could be seen as bridges because they link different religious groups, these still appear to the general public as bonding a single ethnic group. The same applies to Korean American associations that link Christians and non-Christians.

12. Because this analysis concentrates on the second generation, it does not discuss the activities of organizations popular with the first generation with which informants had little, if any, contact. I draw from some observations, other primary sources, and secondary sources for commentary on the first generations' organizations.

13. This new organization (whose name, like that of the other organizations, is kept confidential) has sponsored discussions on race relations between African Americans and Korean Americans in Dallas, as well as on media depictions of Asian Americans. It fits a more progressive social-justice profile than do the other organizations. It started after my fieldwork was complete, so none of my informants could comment on its inner dynamics.

14. From the official magazine of Indian American Association [IAA]. August 2002, p. 9.

15. This also was sponsored by IAA. As another example, at IAA's fortieth-anniversary dinner celebration, it highlighted its goal of making Indian Americans more integrated. To that end it brought in local and federal politicians and officials, as it has done at its other major events (Brettell 2005b).

16. A national Indian American organization started a local charter after my fieldwork ended and furthered the goal discussed here to convince more Indian Americans to enter mainstream politics. An awards banquet for the Texas state chapter included the symbolism of honoring the flags and anthems of both India and the United States, with local politicians as guests and speeches on the need for Indian Americans to be more politically involved in their welcoming, adopted land (Brettell 2005a).

17. Field notes, June 1999.

18. Field notes, May 2002.

19. This is in addition to assistance that IAA gave to community members, including lessons on foster parenting, free medical checkups, psychological counseling, and more.

20. The Hindu temples also sponsored health fairs, held in their parking lots, that served both the temple attendees and local residents. Field notes, June 1999. During my fieldwork KAP did not engage in any volunteer work mentioned by Samantha.

21. Field notes, September 1999.

22. IANA, the EMs, and to a lesser degree KAP (because of its smaller size and lack of national organization) can be seen as part of a growing trend in one-stop civic organizations—a place to meet people, practice cultural or religious interests, and volunteer, with few if any commitments to sustain the organization (Wuthnow 1998).

23. Worth noting is that Maira (2002) finds that second-generation Indian American college students adopted hip-hop styles in order to indicate their Americanization. Here, informants adopt White middle-class styles for the most part. The difference in choices may not signal a difference in attitudes on race so much as a difference in what styles are more accessible and familiar to one's geography and/or place in the life course. Maira's subjects lived in New York City and were teenagers. These participants were older, lived in Dallas (often in its suburbs), and worked full-time.

Chapter 8

1. As another example, conservative Christians talk about the role of husbands and wives in a more conventional manner than do liberal Christians, given the dominant discourses within each group's religious institutions (Swidler 2001). Also, French urbanites understand the meaning of work differently than do their American counterparts because of national differences in culture and social structure (Lamont 1992).

2. This common culture can arise organically through interactions between members or through the intervention of the state to guarantee that marginal groups engage with the core culture on a level playing field (Parekh 2000).

3. Arguably, Robert Park did not consider multiculturalism antithetical to assimilation in his original articulation of the assimilation concept. According to Park, assimilation occurs when groups form a common commitment to national unity, which is measured by their ability to get along in public. They can have different beliefs and opinions in private but present similar ones to the public (Kivisto 2004). The private-public divide as a means of reconciling assimilation and multiculturalism remains constant through current theories, which I consider fruitful but incomplete.

4. This is a different perspective on specifying multiculturalism from that offered by Alexander (2001). He suggests that multiculturalism differs from assimilation and "hyphenation" (i.e., promoting hyphenated identities) because it calls for respect for marginal groups' cultural traits. Yet he does not elaborate on the practical tensions with which marginal groups must contend: trying to decipher between and then display their "good" cultural traits instead of their "bad" ones. Not all differences are accepted, even when cultures are respected. Marginal groups must go beyond simply declaring pride in their cultural backgrounds. They must demonstrate how their

backgrounds complement the mainstream as well as show their social and economic commitment to the mainstream.

5. Asian American women's complaint of a non-family-friendly environment that also punishes nonaggressive personalities fits White feminists' critiques of corporate culture (Moen 1992). Getting time off for family violates this ideal of placing the company first, which also affects women (and men) regardless of race.

Bibliography

Abelmann, N., and J. Lie. 1995. *Blue dreams: Korean Americans and the Los Angeles riots.* Cambridge, MA: Harvard University Press.

Abraham, M. 2000. *Speaking the unspeakable: Marital violence among South Asian immigrants in the United States.* New Brunswick, NJ: Rutgers University Press.

Adams, G., T. Gullotta, and R. Montemayor. 1992. *Adolescent identity formation.* Newbury Park, CA: Sage.

Adler, R. 2005. ¡Oye compadre! The chef needs a dishwasher: Yucatecan men in the Dallas restaurant economy. *Urban Anthropology* 34, no. 2–3: 217–246.

Agarwal, P. 1991. *Passage from India: Post 1965 Indian immigrants and their children.* Palos Verdes, CA: Yuvati.

Ahn, H. 1999. Juggling two worlds: Ethnic identity of Korean-American college students. Ph.D. diss., University of Pennsylvania.

Alba, R. 1990. *Ethnic identity: The transformation of white America.* New Haven, CT: Yale University Press.

———. 1999. Immigration and the American realities of assimilation and multiculturalism. *Sociological Forum* 14, no. 1: 3–25.

Alba, R., and V. Nee. 2003. *Remaking the American mainstream: Assimilation and contemporary immigration.* Cambridge, MA: Harvard University Press.

Alba, R., J. Logan, B. Stults, G. Marzan, and W. Zhang. 1999. Immigrant groups in suburbs: A reexamination of suburbanization and spatial assimilation. *American Sociological Review* 64, no. 3: 446–460.

Alexander, C., Jr., and M. Wiley. 1992. Situated activity and identity formation. In M. Rosenburg and R. Turner (eds.), *Social Psychology.* New Brunswick, NJ: Transaction.

Alexander, J. 2001. Theorizing the "modes of incorporation": Assimilation, hyphenation, and multiculturalism as varieties of civil participation. *Sociological Theory* 19, no. 3: 237–249.

Alexander, J., and P. Smith. 1993. The discourse of American civil society: A new proposal for cultural studies. *Theory and Society* 22, no. 2: 151–207.

Allport, G. W. 1958. *The nature of prejudice.* Garden City, NY: Doubleday.

Alumkal, A. 1999. Preserving patriarchy: Assimilation, gender norms, and second-generation Korean American evangelicals. *Qualitative Sociology* 22, no. 2: 127–140.

Ancheta, A. 1998. *Race, rights, and the Asian American experience.* New Brunswick, NJ: Rutgers University Press.

Anderson, E. 1999a. *Code of the street: Decency, violence, and the moral life of the inner city.* New York: W. W. Norton.

———. 1999b. The social situation of the black executive: Black and white identities in the corporate world. In M. Lamont (ed.), *The cultural territories of race.* Chicago: Russell Sage Foundation.

Anthias, F., and N. Yuval-Davis. 1989. Introduction to F. Anthias and N. Yuval-Davis (eds.), *Woman, nation, state.* New York: St. Martin's Press.

Anzaldúa, G. 1987. *Borderlands = La Frontera: The new mestiza.* San Francisco, CA: Spinsters/Aunt Lute.

Bankston, C. 2003. Immigrants in the new South: An introduction. *Sociological Spectrum* 23, no. 2: 123–128.

Barth, F. 1969. *Ethnic groups and boundaries.* Boston: Little, Brown.

Bean, F., and G. Stevens, 2003. *America's newcomers and the dynamics of diversity.* New York: Russell Sage Foundation.

Becker, P. E. 1999. *Congregations in conflict: Cultural models of local religious life.* New York: Cambridge University Press.

Bell, E. 1990. The bicultural life experience of career-oriented black women. *Journal of Organizational Behavior* 11, no. 6: 459–477.

Bellah, R., S. Tipton, R. Madsen, A. Swidler, and W. Sullivan. 1985. *Habits of the heart: Individualism and commitment in American life.* Berkeley: University of California Press.

Bhachu, P. 1995. New cultural forms and transnational South Asian women: Culture, class, and consumption among British Asian women in the diaspora. In P. van der Veer (ed.), *Nation and migration.* Philadelphia: University of Pennsylvania Press.

Bhakta, G. 2002. *Patels: A Gujarati community history in the United States.* Los Angeles: UCLA Asian American Studies Center Press.

Bhattacharjee, A. 1998. The habit of ex-nomination: Nation, women, and Indian immigrant Bourgeoisie. In S. Dasgupta (ed.), *A patchwork shawl: Chronicles of South Asian women in America.* New Brunswick, NJ: Rutgers University Press.

Bhattacharya, G. 2002. Intergenerational conflict, acculturation, and drug use among Asian Indian adolescents. In N. Benokraitis (ed.), *Contemporary ethnic families in the United States: Characteristics, variations, and dynamics.* Upper Saddle River, NJ: Prentice Hall.

Blair-Loy, M. 2003. *Competing devotions: Career and family among women executives.* Cambridge, MA: Harvard University Press.

Bobo, L., and R. Smith. 1998. From Jim Crow racism to laissez faire racism: The transformation of racial attitudes. In W. Katkin, N. Landsman, and A. Tyree (eds.), *Beyond pluralism: The conception of groups and group identities in America*. Chicago: University of Illinois Press.

Bonacich, E. 1973. A theory of middleman minorities. *American Sociological Review* 38, no. 5: 583–594.

———. 1976. Advanced capitalism and black/white race relations in the United States: A split labor market interpretation. *American Sociological Review* 41, no. 1: 34–51.

Bonilla-Silva, E. 2003. *Racism without racists: Color-blind racism and the persistence of racial inequality in the United States*. Lanham, MD: Rowman & Littlefield.

Bourdieu, P. 1984. *Distinction: A social critique of the judgement of taste*. Cambridge, Mass.: Harvard University Press.

Bourdieu, P., and L. Wacquant. 1992. *An invitation to reflexive sociology*. Chicago: University of Chicago Press.

Brady, M. D. 2004. *The Asian Texans*. College Station: Texas A & M University Press.

Brekhus, W. 2003. *Peacocks, chameleons, centaurs: Gay suburbia and the grammar of social identity*. Chicago: University of Chicago Press.

Brettell, C. 2005a. Voluntary organizations, social capital, and the social incorporation of Asian Indian immigrants in the Dallas–Fort Worth metroplex. *Anthropological Quarterly* 78, no. 4: 853–883.

———. 2005b. The spatial, social, and political incorporation of Asian Indian immigrants in Dallas, Texas. *Urban Anthropology* 34, no. 2–3: 247–280.

Brewer, M., and R. Brown. 1998. Intergroup relations. In D. Gilbert, S. Fiske, and G. Lindzey (eds.), *The handbook of social psychology*. New York: McGraw-Hill.

Buriel, R. 1993. Acculturation, respect for cultural differences, and biculturalism, among three generations of Mexican American and Euro American school children. *Journal of Genetic Psychology* 154, no. 4: 531–543.

Butterfield, S. A. 2005. "We're just Black": The racial and ethnic identities of second-generation West Indians in New York. In P. Kasinitz, J. Mollenkopf, and M. Waters (eds.), *Becoming New Yorkers: Ethnographies of the new second generation*. New York: Russell Sage Foundation.

Campbell, D., B. Masaki, and S. Torres. 2002. Domestic violence in African American, Asian American, and Latino communities. In N. Benokraitis (ed.), *Contemporary ethnic families in the United States: Characteristics, variations, and dynamics*. Upper Saddle River, NJ: Prentice Hall.

Caplow, T. 1982. Christmas gifts and kin networks. *American Sociological Review* 47, no. 3: 383–392.

Ceasar, J. 1998. Multiculturalism and American liberal democracy. In A. Melzer, J. Weinberger, and M. R. Zinman (eds.), *Multiculturalism and American democracy*. Lawrence: University Press of Kansas.

Certau, M. de. 1984. *The practice of everyday life*. Translation by Steven Rendall. Berkeley: University of California Press.

Cerulo, K. 2002. *Culture in mind: Toward a sociology of culture and cognition*. New York: Routledge.

———. 2001. Beyond strictness to distinctiveness: Generational transition in Korean Protestant churches. In H. Kwon, K. Kim, and S. Warner (eds.), *Korean Americans and their religions*. University Park: Pennsylvania State University Press.

Chai, K. 1998. Competing for the second generation: English-language ministry at a Korean Protestant church. In S. Warner and J. Wittner (eds.), *Gatherings in diaspora*. Philadelphia, PA: Temple University Press.

Chan, S. 1991. *Asian Americans: An interpretive history*. Boston: Twayne.

Chang, R. 1999. *Disoriented: Asian Americans, law, and the nation-state*. New York: New York University Press.

Chatterjee, P. 1989. Colonialism, nationalism, and colonialized women: The contest in India. *American Ethnologist* 16, no. 4: 622–633.

Cheng, C. 1996. "We choose not to compete": The "merit" discourse in the selection process, and Asian and Asian American men and their masculinity. In C. Cheng (ed.), *Masculinities in organizations*. Thousand Oaks, CA: Sage.

Cheng, C., and T. Thatchenkery. 1997. Introduction: Why is there a lack of workplace diversity research on Asian Americans? *Journal of Applied Behavioral Science* 33: 270–276.

Cheng, L., and P. Yang. 1996. Asians: The "model minority" deconstructed. In R. Waldinger and M. Bozorgmehr (eds.), *Ethnic Los Angeles*. New York: Russell Sage Foundation.

Child, I. 1943. *Italian or American? The second generation in conflict*. New Haven, CT: Yale University Press.

Chong, K. 1998. What it means to be Christian: The role of religion in construction of ethnic identity and boundary among second-generation Korean Americans. *Sociology of Religion* 59, no. 3: 259–286.

Chow, S. 2000. The significance of race in the private sphere: Asian Americans and spousal preferences. *Sociological Inquiry* 70, no. 1: 1–29.

Coleman, T. 1994. Managing diversity: Keeping it in focus; Tie diversity goals to business. *Public Management* 76: 10–16.

Collins-Lowry, S. 1997. *Black corporate executives: The making and breaking of a black middle class*. Philadelphia, PA: Temple University Press.

Coltrane, S., and E. Valdez. 1997. Reluctant Compliance: Work-family role allocation in dual-earner Chicano families. In M. Romero, P. Hondagneu-Sotelo, and V. Ortiz (eds.), *Challenging fronteras: Structuring Latina and Latino lives in the U.S.* New York: Routledge.

Cooley, C. 1902. *Human nature and the social order*. New York: Scribner.

Cornell, S. 1988. *The return of the native: American Indian political resurgence.* New York: Oxford University Press.

Cornell, S., and P. Hartmann. 1998. *Ethnicity and race.* Thousand Oaks, CA: Pine Forge Press.

Corsaro, W. 1992. Interpretive reproduction in children's peer cultures. *Social Psychology Quarterly* 55, no. 2: 160–177.

Cose, E. 1999. A dozen demons. In C. Ellison and W. Martin, *Race and ethnic relations in the United States.* Los Angeles: Roxbury.

Cox, T. 1991. The multicultural organization. *Academy of Management Executive* 5, no. 2: 34–47.

Cox, T., and S. Blake. 1991. Managing cultural diversity: Implications for organizational competitiveness. *Academy of Management Executive* 5, no. 3: 45–56.

Cross, W. 1995. The psychology of nigrescence: Revising the cross model. In J. Ponterotto, J. Casas, L. Suzuki, and C. Alexander (eds.), *Handbook of multicultural counseling.* Thousand Oaks, CA: Sage.

Danico, M. 2004. *1.5 generation: Becoming Korean American in Hawai'i.* Honolulu: University of Hawaii Press.

Danna-Lynch, K. 2004. How do they do it: The typologies and sociocognitive strategies of role switching. Presentation at the American Sociological Association annual meeting, San Francisco, CA, August.

Dasgupta, S. 1998. Introduction to *A patchwork shawl: Chronicles of South Asian women in America.* New Brunswick, NJ: Rutgers University Press.

Dasgupta, S., and S. Dasgupta. 1998. Sex, lies, and women's lives: An intergenerational dialogue. In S. Dasgupta (ed.), *A Patchwork Shawl: Chronicles of South Asian women in America.* New Brunswick, NJ: Rutgers University Press.

Davis, A. 1996. Gender, class and multiculturalism: Rethinking "race" politics. In A. Gordon and C. Newfield (eds.), *Mapping multiculturalism.* Minneapolis: University of Minnesota Press.

De Vos, G. 1991. Ethnic pluralism: Conflict and accommodation. In G. De Vos and L. Romanucci-Ross (eds.), *Ethnic identity: Cultural continuities and change.* Palo Alto, CA: Mayfield.

Dhingra, P. 2003a. Becoming American between black and white: Second generation Asian American professionals' racial identities. *Journal of Asian American Studies* 6, no. 2: 117–148.

———. 2003b. The second generation in "Big D": Korean American and Indian American Organizations in Dallas, TX. *Sociological Spectrum* 23, no. 2: 247–278.

———. 2004. "We're not a Korean American church anymore": Dilemmas in constructing a multi-racial church identity. *Social Compass* 51, no. 3: 367–379.

DiMaggio, P. 1997. Culture and cognition. *Annual Review of Sociology* 23, no. 1: 263–287.

Dimanche, F., and D. Samdahl. 1994. Leisure as symbolic consumption: A conceptualization and prospectus for future research. *Leisure Sciences* 16: 119–129.

Douglas, M. 1966. *Purity and danger*. London: Routledge.

———. 1986. *How institutions think*. Syracuse, NY: Syracuse University Press.

Durkheim, E. 1915. *Elementary forms of religious life*. New York: Free Press.

Ebaugh, H. R., and J. Chafetz. 2000. *Religion and the new immigrants: Continuities and adaptations in immigrant congregations*. Walnut Creek, CA: AltaMira Press.

Eder, D., and S. Parker. 1987. The cultural production and reproduction of gender: The effect of extracurricular activities on peer-group culture. In *Sociology of Education* 60, no. 3: 200–213.

Eliasoph, N. 1999. "Everyday racism" in a culture of political avoidance: Civil society, speech, and taboo. *Social Problems* 46, no. 4: 479–502.

Eliasoph, N., and P. Lichterman. 2003. Culture in interaction. *American Journal of Sociology* 108, no. 4: 735–794.

Epstein, C. F. 1992. Tinker-bells and pinups: The construction and reconstruction of gender boundaries at work. In M. Lamont and M. Fournier (eds.), *Cultivating differences: Symbolic boundaries and the making of inequality*. Chicago: University of Chicago Press.

Erikson, E. 1968. *Identity: Youth and crisis*. New York: W. W. Norton.

Espiritu, Y. L. 1992. *Asian American Panethnicity*. Philadelphia: Temple University Press.

———. 1997. *Asian American women and men : Labor, laws and love*. Thousand Oaks, CA: Sage.

———. 2003. *Home bound: Filipino American lives across cultures, communities, and countries*. Berkeley: University of California Press.

Farver, J., S. Narang, and B. Bhadha. 2002. East meets West: Ethnic identity, acculturation, and conflict in Asian Indian families. *Journal of Family Psychology* 16, no. 3: 338–350.

Feagin, J., and M. Sikes. 1994. *Living with racism: The black middle-class experience*. Boston: Beacon.

Federal Glass Ceiling Commission. 1995. Good for business: Making full use of the nation's human capital; The environmental scan, a fact finding report. Washington, DC: U.S. Department of Labor.

Feher, S. 1998. *Passing over Easter: Constructing the boundaries of messianic Judaism*. Walnut Creek, CA: AltaMira Press.

Fenton, J. 1988. *Transplanting religious traditions: Asian Indians in America*. New York: Praeger.

Fernandez, M. 1998. Asian Indian Americans in the Bay Area and the glass ceiling. *Sociological Perspectives* 41, no. 1: 119–149.

Field, S. 1994. Becoming Irish: Personal identity construction among first-generation Irish immigrants. *Symbolic Interaction* 17, no. 4: 431–452.

Fine, G. A. 1996. *Kitchens: The culture of restaurant work*. Berkeley: University of California Press.

Fischer, C. 1994. Changes in leisure activities, 1890–1940. *Journal of Social History* 27, no. 3: 453–476.

Fish, S. 1998. Boutique multiculturalism. In A. Melzer, J. Weinberger, and M. R. Zinman (eds.), *Multiculturalism and American Democracy*. Lawrence: University Press of Kansas.

Fiske, S., and S. Taylor. 1984. *Social cognition*. Reading, MA: Addison-Wesley.

Flores, J. 1997. "Que assimilated, brother, yo soy asimilao": The structuring of Puerto Rican identity in the U.S. In M. Romero, P. Hondagneu-Sotelo, and V. Ortiz (eds.), *Challenging fronteras: Structuring Latina and Latino lives in the U.S.* New York: Routledge.

Floyd, M., K. Shinew, F. McGuire, and F. Noe. 1994. Race, class, and leisure activity preferences: Marginality and ethnicity revisited. *Journal of Leisure Research* 26, no. 2: 158–173.

Foner, N. 2005. *In a new land: A comparative view of immigration*. New York: New York University Press.

Fong, C., and J. Yung. 1995–1996. In search of the right spouse: Interracial marriage among Chinese and Japanese Americans. *Amerasia Journal* 21, no. 3: 77–98.

Fong, L., and Gibbs, J. 1995. Facilitating services to multicultural communities in a dominant culture setting: An organizational perspective. *Administration in Social Work* 19, no. 2: 1–24.

Fong, T. 1998. *The contemporary Asian American experience*. Upper Saddle River, NJ: Prentice Hall.

Fouron, G., and N. Glick-Schiller. 2002. The generation of identity: Redefining the second generation within a transnational social field. In P. Levitt and M. Waters (eds.), *The changing face of home: The transnational lives of the second generation*. New York: Russell Sage Foundation.

Friedland, R., and R. Alford. 1991. Bringing society back in: Symbols, practices, and institutional contradictions. In W. Powell and P. DiMaggio (eds.), *The new institutionalism in organizational analysis*. Chicago: University of Chicago Press.

Friedman, R., and D. Krackhardt. 1997. Social capital and career mobility: A structural theory of lower returns to education for Asian employees. *Journal of Applied Behavioral Science* 33, no. 3: 316–334.

Fugita, S., and D. O'Brien. 1991. *Japanese American ethnicity: The persistence of community*. Seattle: University of Washington Press.

Gallos, J. 1997. On learning about diversity: A pedagogy of paradox. *Journal of Management Education* 21, no. 2: 152–154.

Gamm, G., and R. Putnam. 1999. The growth of voluntary associations in America, 1840–1940. *Journal of Interdisciplinary History* 29, no. 4: 511–557.

Gans, H. 1962. *Urban villagers*. New York: Free Press.

———. 1979. Symbolic ethnicity: The future of ethnic groups and cultures in America. *Ethnic and Racial Studies* 2, no. 1: 1–20.

———. 1992. Second-generation decline: Scenarios for the economic and ethnic futures of post-1965 American immigrants. *Ethnic and Racial Studies* 15, no. 2: 173–192.

Gardenswartz, L., and A. Rowe. 1993. *Managing diversity: A Complete desk reference and planning guide*. New York: Irwin.

George, R. 1997. From expatriate aristocrat to immigrant nobody: South Asian racial strategies in the southern Californian context. *Diaspora* 6, no. 1: 31–60.

Gherardi, S. 1994. The gender we think, the gender we do in our everyday organizational lives. *Human Relations* 47, no. 6: 591–610.

Ghosh-Pandy, S. 1998. Across many oceans: Asian Indians in the United States. In D. Cordell and J. Elder (eds.), *The new Dallas: Immigrants, ethnic entrepreneurship, and cultural diversity; A collection of student papers*. Dallas, TX: William P. Clements Center for Southwest Studies, Southern Methodist University.

Gibson, M. 1988. *Accommodation without assimilation: Sikh immigrants in an American high school*. Ithaca, NY: Cornell University Press.

Giddens, A. 1992. *Modernity and self-identity*. Cambridge: Polity Press.

Gilbert, J., and D. Ones. 1998. Role of information integration in career advancement. *Sex Roles: A Journal of Research* 39, no. 9–10: 685–687.

Gilroy, P. 1993. *Small acts: Thoughts on the politics of black cultures*. London: Serpent's Tail.

Gitelson, R., F. Bernat, and S. Aleman. 2002. A comparison of white and Mexican heritage older adults' leisure choices and constraints in two adjacent communities. *Leisure and Society* 25, no. 2: 471–494.

Gitlin, T. 2001. *Media unlimited: How the torrent of images and sounds overwhelms our lives*. New York: Metropolitan.

Glazer, N. 1997. *We are all multiculturalists now*. Cambridge, MA: Harvard University Press.

Glazer, N., and D. Moynihan. 1970. *Beyond the melting pot*. Cambridge, MA: MIT Press.

Gleason, P. 2001. Sea change in the civic culture of the 1960's. In G. Gerstle and J. Mollenkopf (eds.), *E pluribus unum? Contemporary and historical perspectives on immigrant political incorporation*. New York: Russell Sage Foundation.

Goffman, E. 1959. *The Presentation of Self in Everyday Life*. Garden City, NY: Doubleday.

———. 1963. *Stigma: Notes on the management of spoiled identity*. Englewood Cliffs, NJ: Prentice-Hall.

———. 1974. *Frame analysis: An essay on the organization of experience*. Cambridge, MA: Harvard University Press.

Goldberg, M. 1941. A qualification of the marginal man theory. *American Sociological Review* 6, no. 1: 52–58.

Golembiewski, R. 1995. *Managing diversity in organizations.* Tuscaloosa: University of Alabama Press.

Gordon, M. 1964. *Assimilation in American life.* New York: Oxford University Press.

Gram-Hanssen, K., and C. Bech-Danielsen. 2004. House, home and identity from a consumption perspective. *Housing, Theory and Society* 21: 17–26.

Gray, E., and S. Thumma. 1997. The gospel hour: Liminality, identity and religion in a gay bar. In P. Becker and N. Eiesland (eds.), *Contemporary American religion: An ethnographic reader.* Walnut Creek, CA: AltaMira Press.

Greeley, A. 1981. The persistence of diversity. *Antioch Review* 39, no. 2: 141–155.

Green, A. 1947. Re-examination of the marginal man concept. *Social Forces* 26, no. 2: 167–171.

Gross, J., D. McMurray, and T. Swedenburg. 1996. Arab noise and Ramadan nights: *Rai, rap,* and Franco-Maghrebi identities. In S. Lavie and T. Swedenburg (eds.), *Displacement, diaspora, and geographies of identity.* Durham, NC: Duke University Press.

Gutmann, A. 1994. Introduction to A. Gutmann (ed.), *Multiculturalism.* Princeton, NJ: Princeton University Press.

Hacker, A. 1995. *Two nations: Black and white, separate, hostile, unequal.* New York: Ballantine.

Hall, G., and S. Okazaki. 2002. *Asian American psychology: The science of lives in context.* Washington, DC: American Psychological Association.

Hall, K. 1995. "There's a time to act English and a time to act Indian": The politics of identity among British-Sikh teenagers. In S. Stephens (ed.), *Children and the politics of culture.* Princeton, NJ: Princeton University Press.

Hall, S. 1990. Cultural identity and diaspora. In J. Rutherford (ed.), *Identity: Community, culture, difference.* London: Lawrence and Wishart.

Hasnat, N. 1998. Being "Amreekan": Fried chicken vs. chicken tikka. In *A patchwork shawl: Chronicles of South Asian women in America.* New Brunswick, NJ: Rutgers University Press.

Hazel, M. 1997. *Dallas: A history of "Big D."* Austin: Texas State Historical Association.

Hebdige, D. 1979. *Subculture: The meaning of style.* London: Methuen.

Heiss, J. 1992. Social roles. In M. Rosenburg and R. Turner (eds.), *Social Psychology.* New Brunswick, NJ: Transaction.

Helweg, A., and U. Helweg. 1990. *An immigrant success story: East Indians in America.* Philadelphia: University of Pennsylvania Press.

Henthorn, W. E. 1971. *A history of Korea.* New York: Free Press.

Herrnstein, R., and C. Murray. 1994. *The bell curve: Intelligence and class structure in American life.* New York: Free Press.

Hing, B. 1997. *To Be an American: Cultural pluralism and the rhetoric of assimilation.* New York: New York University Press.

Ho, P. 2003. Performing the "Oriental": Professionals and the Asian model minority myth. *Journal of Asian American Studies* 6, no. 2: 149–175.

Hochschild, A. 1989. *The second shift*. New York: Avon.

———. 1997. *The time bind: When work becomes home and home becomes work*. New York: Metropolitan.

Hollinger, D. 1995. *Postethnic America: Beyond multiculturalism*. New York: Basic-Books.

Hollows, J. 2003. Leisure, labour and domestic masculinity in *The Naked Chef*. *International Journal of Cultural Studies* 6, no. 2: 229–248.

Holvino, E. 2000. Hispanics in the workplace: Assessing "best" and "worst" companies. *Diversity Factor* 8, no. 4: 12–16.

Howard, J. 2000. Social psychology of identities. *Annual Review of Sociology* 26, no. 1: 367–393.

Hunt, S., and K. Miller. 1997. The discourse of dress and appearance: Identity talk and rhetoric of review. *Symbolic Interaction* 20, no. 1: 69–82.

Hurh, W. 1998. *The Korean Americans*. Westport, CT: Greenwood Press.

Hurh, W., H. Kim, and C. Kwange. 1978. *Assimilation patterns of immigrants in the United States: A case study of Korean immigrants in the Chicago area*. Washington, DC: University Press of America.

Hurh, W., and K. Kim. 1984. *Korean immigrants in America: A structural analysis of ethnic confinement and adhesive adaptation*. Rutherford, NJ: Fairleigh Dickinson University Press.

———. 1999. The "success" image of Asian Americans. In C. Ellison and W. Martin, *Race and Ethnic Relations in the U.S.* Los Angeles: Roxbury.

Hurtado, A., P. Gurin, and T. Peng. 1997. Social identities: A framework for studying the adaptations of immigrants and ethnics; The adaptation of Mexicans in the United States. In D. Hamamoto and R. Torres (eds.), *New American destinies*. New York: Routledge.

Hylton, C. 2003. African-Caribbean group activities, individual and collective consciousness, and enforced "leisure." *Community, Work and Family* 6, no. 1: 103–113.

Ignatiev, N. 1995. *How the Irish became white*, New York: Routledge.

Jackson, S. E. 1992. A preview of the road to be traveled. In S. E. Jackson and Associates (eds.), *Diversity in the workplace: Human resources initiatives*. New York: Guilford Press.

Jeffres, L., K. Neuendorf, and D. Atkin. 2003. Media use and participation as a spectator in public leisure activities: Competition or symbiosis? *Leisure Studies* 22, no. 2: 169–184.

Jenkins, R. 1994. Rethinking ethnicity: Identity, categorization and power. *Ethnic and Racial Studies* 17, no. 2: 197–219.

Jeung, R. 2002. Asian American pan-ethnic formation and congregational culture. In P. Min and J. Kim (eds.), *Religions in Asian America*. New York: AltaMira Press.

Jo, M. 2002. Coping with gender role strains in Korean American families. In N. Benokraitis (ed.), *Contemporary ethnic families in the United States: Characteristics, variations, and dynamics.* Upper Saddle River: NJ: Prentice Hall.

Jung, M. 2006. *Coolies and cane: Race, labor, and sugar in the age of emancipation.* Baltimore, MD: Johns Hopkins University Press.

Kalmijn, M. 1991. Shifting boundaries: Trends in religious and educational homogamy. *American Sociological Review* 56, no. 6: 786–800.

Kamphoefner, W. 1996. German Americans: Paradoxes of a "model minority"? In S. Pedraza and R. Rumbaut (eds.), *Origins and destinies: Immigration, race, and ethnicity in America.* Belmont, CA: Wadsworth.

Kang, S. 2002. *Unveiling the socioculturally constructed multivoiced self: Themes of self construction and self integration in the narratives of second-generation Korean American young adults.* New York: University Press of America.

Kanter, R. 1977. *Men and women of the corporation.* New York: Basic.

Kasinitz, P., J. Mollenkopf, and M. Waters. 2004. Worlds of the second generation. In P. Kasinitz, J. Mollenkopf, and M. Waters (eds.), *Becoming New Yorkers: Ethnographies of the new second generation.* New York: Russell Sage Foundation.

Kasinitz, P., M. Waters, J. Mollenkopf, and M. Anil. 2002. Transnationalism and the children of immigrants in contemporary New York. In P. Levitt and M. Waters (eds.), *The changing face of home: The transnational lives of the second generation.* New York: Russell Sage Foundation.

Kelly, J. R. 1983. *Leisure identities and interactions.* London: Allen and Unwin.

Kemper, R. 2005. Dallas-Fort Worth: Toward new models of urbanization, community transformation, and immigration. *Urban Anthropology* 34, no. 2–3: 125–149.

Kerckhoff, A., and T. McCormick. 1955. Marginal status and marginal personality. *Social Forces* 34, no. 1: 48–55.

Khandelwal, M. 2002. *Becoming American, being Indian: An immigrant community in New York City.* Ithaca, NY: Cornell University Press.

Kibria, N. 1996. Not Asian, black or white? Reflections on South Asian American racial identity. *Amerasia Journal* 22, no. 2: 77–86.

———. 2002. *Becoming Asian American: Second generation Chinese and Korean American identities.* Baltimore, MD: Johns Hopkins University Press.

———. 2006. South Asian Americans. In P. G. Min (ed.), *Asian Americans: Contemporary trends and issues,* 2nd ed. Thousand Oaks, CA: Pine Forge Press.

Kim, C. 2001. Playing the racial trump card: Asian Americans in contemporary U.S. politics. *Amerasia Journal* 26, no. 3: 35–65.

Kim, D. 2004. Leaving the ethnic economy: The rapid integration of second-generation Korean Americans in New York. In P. Kasinitz, J. Mollenkopf, and M. Waters (eds.), *Becoming New Yorkers: Ethnographies of the new second generation.* New York: Russell Sage Foundation.

Kim, J. 2001. Asian American identity development theory. In C. Wijeyesinghe and B. Jackson (eds.), *New perspectives on racial identity development*. New York: New York University Press.

Kim, K., and S. Kim. 1998. Family and work roles of Korean immigrant wives and related experiences. In Y. Song and A. Moon (eds.), *Korean American women: From tradition to modern feminism*. Westport, CT: Praeger.

Kim, K., and W. Hurh. 1993. Beyond assimilation and pluralism. *Ethnic and Racial Studies* 16, no. 4: 696–713.

King, D. 2001. Making Americans: Immigration meets race. In G. Gerstle and J. Mollenkopf (eds.), *E pluribus unum? Contemporary and historical perspectives in immigrant political incorporation*. New York: Russell Sage Foundation.

Kirby, S., and O. Richard. 2000. Impact of marketing work-place diversity on employee job involvement and organizational commitment. *Journal of Social Psychology* 140, no. 3: 367–377.

Kitano, H. 1969. *Japanese Americans: The evolution of a subculture*. Englewood Cliffs, NJ: Prentice-Hall.

Kitano, H., and R. Daniels. 1995. *Asian Americans: Emerging minorities*. Englewood Cliffs, NJ: Prentice Hall.

Kivel, B., and D. Kleiber. 2000. Leisure in the identity formation of lesbian/gay youth: Personal, but not social. *Leisure Sciences* 22, no. 4: 215–232.

Kivisto, P. 2001. Theorizing transnational immigration: A critical review of current efforts. *Ethnic and Racial Studies* 24, no. 4: 549–577.

———. 2004. What is the canonical theory of assimilation? Robert E. Park and his predecessors. *Journal of the History of the Behavioral Sciences* 40, no. 2: 149–163.

———. 2005. The revival of assimilation in historical perspective. In P. Kivisto (ed.) *Incorporating diversity: Rethinking assimilation in a multicultural age*. Boulder, CO: Paradigm.

Kivisto, P., and G. Rundblad (eds.). 2000. *Multiculturalism in the United States: Current issues, contemporary voices*. Thousand Oaks, CA: Pine Forge Press.

Kondo, D. 1996. The narrative production of "home," community, and political identity in Asian American theater. In S. Lavie and T. Swedenburg (eds.), *Displacement, diaspora, and geographies of identity*. Durham, NC: Duke University Press.

Kozol, J. 1991. *Savage inequalities: Children in America's schools*. New York: Crown.

Knouse, S., and M. Dansby. 1999. Percentage of work-group diversity and work-group effectiveness. *Journal of Psychology* 133, no. 5: 486–494.

Kurien, P. 1998. Becoming American by Becoming Hindu: Indian Americans take their place at the multicultural table. In S. Warner and J. Wittner (eds.), *Gatherings in diaspora*. Philadelphia, PA: Temple University Press.

———. 2002. "We are better Hindus here": Religion and ethnicity among Indian Americans. In P. Min and J. Kim (eds.), *Religions in Asian America*. Walnut Creek, CA: AltaMira Press.

———. 2003. To be or not to be South Asian: Contemporary Indian American politics. *Journal of Asian American Studies* 6, no. 3: 261–288.

Kwong, P. 1995. Asian American studies needs class analysis. In G. Okihiro, M. Alzquizola, D. Rony, and S. Wong (eds.), *Privileging positions: The sites of Asian American studies*. Pullman: Washington State University Press.

Kymlicka, W. 1995. *Multicultural citizenship*. Oxford: Clarendon Press.

LaBelle, T., and C. Ward. 1996. *Ethnic studies and multiculturalism*. Albany: State University of New York Press.

Lamont, M. 1992. *Money, morals and manners*. Chicago: University of Chicago Press.

Lau, R. 1989. Individual and contextual influences on group identification. *Social Psychology Quarterly* 52, no. 3: 220–231.

Lave, J. 1988. *Cognition in practice: Mind, mathematics, and culture in everyday life*. Cambridge, MA: Cambridge University Press.

Lavie, S., and T. Swedenburg. 1996. Introduction: Displacement, diaspora, and geographies of identity. In S. Lavie and T. Swedenburg (eds.), *Displacement, diaspora, and geographies of identity*. Durham, NC: Duke University Press.

Lawler, E., and S. Thye. 1999. Bringing emotions into social exchange theory. *Annual Review of Sociology* 25, no. 1: 217–244.

Lee, J. 1998. Toward a queer Korean American diasporic history. In D. Eng and A. Hom (eds.), *Q&A: Queer in Asian America*. Philadelphia, PA: Temple University Press.

Lee, R. 1999. *Orientals: Asian Americans in popular culture*. Philadelphia, PA: Temple University Press.

Lee, S. 1996. *Unraveling the model minority stereotype: Listening to Asian American youth*. New York: Teachers College Press.

Lee, S. 2004. Marriage dilemmas: Partner choices and constraints for Korean Americans in New York City. In J. Lee and M. Zhou (eds.), *Asian American youth: Culture, identity, and ethnicity*. New York: Routledge.

Lee, S., and M. Fernandez. 1998. Trends in Asian American racial/ethnic intermarriage: A comparison of 1980 and 1990 census data. *Sociological Perspectives* 41, no. 2: 323–342.

Lee, T. 2000. Racial attitudes and the color line(s) at the close of the twentieth century. In P. Ong (ed.), *Transforming race relations: The state of Asian Pacific America*. Los Angeles: Leadership Education for Asian Pacifics.

Leonard, K. 1992. *Making ethnic choices*. Philadelphia, PA: Temple University Press.

———. 1997. *The South Asian Americans*. Westport, CT: Greenwood Press.

————. 1999. The management of desire: Sexuality and marriage for young South Asian women in America. In S. Gupta (ed.), *Emerging voices: South Asian American women redefine self, family, and community.* New Delhi: Sage.

Lessinger, J. 1995. *From the Ganges to the Hudson: Indian immigrants in New York City.* Boston, MA: Allyn & Bacon.

Levitt, P. 2002. The ties that change: Relations to the ancestral home over the life cycle. In P. Levitt and M. Waters (eds.), *The changing face of home: The transnational lives of the second generation.* New York: Russell Sage Foundation.

Lichterman, P. 1999. Talking identity in the public sphere: Broad visions and small spaces in sexual identity politics. *Theory and Society* 28, no. 1: 101–141.

Lieberson, S. 1985. *Making it count: The improvement of social research and theory.* Berkeley: University of California Press.

Lien, P., M. Conway, and J. Wong. 2003. The contours and sources of ethnic identity choices among Asian Americans. *Social Science Quarterly* 84, no. 2: 461–481.

Loewen, J. 1971. *The Mississippi Chinese: Between black and white.* Cambridge, MA: Harvard University Press.

Lopez, D. 1996. Language: Diversity and assimilation. In R. Waldinger and M. Bozorgmehr (eds.), *Ethnic Los Angeles.* New York: Russell Sage Foundation.

Lopez, D., and Y. Espiritu. 1990. Panethnicity in the United States: A theoretical framework. *Ethnic and Racial Studies* 13, no. 2: 198–224.

Louie, V. 2004. "Being practical" or "doing what I want": The role of parents in the academic choices of Chinese Americans. In P. Kasinitz, J. Mollenkopf, and M. Waters (eds.), *Becoming New Yorkers: Ethnographies of the new second generation.* New York: Russell Sage Foundation.

Lowe, L. 1996. *Immigrant acts: On Asian American cultural politics.* Durham, NC: Duke University Press.

Lyu, K. 1977. Korean nationalist activities in Hawaii and the continental United States, 1900–1919. *Amerasia* 1: 23–90.

Maira, S. 2000. Henna and hip hop: The politics of cultural production and the work of cultural studies. *Journal of Asian American Studies* 3, no. 3: 329–369.

————. 2002. *Desis in the house: Indian American youth culture in New York City.* Philadelphia, PA: Temple University Press.

Marable, M. 1995. *Beyond black and white: Transforming African American politics.* New York: Verso.

Martin, J. 1992. *Cultures in organizations: Three perspectives.* New York: Oxford University Press.

Massey, D., and N. Denton. 1993. *American apartheid: Segregation and the making of the underclass.* Cambridge, MA: Harvard University Press.

Mathew, B., and V. Prashad. 1999–2000. The protean forms of Yankee Hindutva. *Ethnic and Racial Studies* 23, no. 3: 516–534.

McCall, G., and J. Simmons. 1978. *Identities and interactions.* New York: Free Press.

McWilliams, W. C. 1998. Democratic multiculturalism. In A. Melzer, J. Weinberger, and M. Zinman (eds.), *Multiculturalism and American democracy.* Lawrence: University Press of Kansas.

Mediratta, K. 1999. How do you say your name? In P. Min and R. Kim (eds.), *Struggle for ethnic identity: Narratives by Asian American professionals.* Walnut Creek, CA: AltaMira Press.

Mehta, G. 1991. *Karma Cola: Marketing the mystic East.* New York: Fawcett Columbine.

Min, P. 1996. *Caught in the middle: Korean communities in New York and Los Angeles.* Berkeley: University of California Press.

———. 2003. Immigrants' religion and ethnicity: A comparison of Indian Hindus and Korean Protestants. Presentation at the American Sociological Association annual meeting, Atlanta, GA, August.

———. 2006a. Asian immigration: History and contemporary trends. In P. G. Min (ed.), *Asian Americans: Contemporary trends and issues.* Thousand Oaks, CA: Pine Forge Press.

———. 2006b. The Korean Americans. In P. G. Min (ed.), *Asian Americans: Contemporary trends and issues.* Thousand Oaks, CA: Pine Forge Press.

———. 2006c. Major issues related to Asian American experiences. In P. G. Min (ed.), *Asian Americans: Contemporary trends and issues.* Thousand Oaks, CA: Pine Forge Press.

Min, P., and R. Kim (eds.). 1999. *Struggle for ethnic identity: Narratives by Asian American professionals.* Walnut Creek, CA: AltaMira Press.

Misir, D. 1996. The murder of Navroze Mody: Race, violence, and the search for order. *Amerasia Journal* 22, no. 2: 55–76.

Moen, P. 1992. *Women's two roles: A contemporary dilemma.* New York: Auburn House.

Moon, A. 1998. Attitudes toward ethnic identity, marriage, and familial life among women of Korean descent in the United States, Japan, and Korea. In Y. Song and A. Moon (eds.), *Korean American women: From tradition to modern feminism.* Westport, CT: Praeger.

Moore, D. 1981. *At home in America: Second generation New York Jews.* New York: Columbia University Press.

Morawska, E. 1996. *Insecure prosperity: Small-town Jews in industrial America, 1890–1940.* Princeton, NJ: Princeton University Press.

Morrill, C. 1995. *The executive way: Conflict management in corporations.* Chicago: University of Chicago Press.

Mukhi, S. 1998. "Underneath my blouse beats my Indian heart": Sexuality, nationalism and Indian womanhood in the United States. In S. Dasgupta (ed.), *A patchwork shawl: Chronicles of South Asian women in America.* New Brunswick, NJ: Rutgers University Press.

Nagel, J. 1994. Constructing ethnicity: Creating and recreating ethnic identity and culture. *Social Problems* 41, no. 1: 152–176.

Nahirny, V., and J. Fishman. 2005 [1965]. American immigrant groups: Ethnic identification and the problem of generations. In P. Kivisto (ed.), *Incorporating Diversity: Rethinking assimilation in a multicultural age*. Boulder, CO: Paradigm.

Namkung, V. 2004. Reinventing the wheel: Import car racing in southern California. In M. Zhou and J. Lee (eds.), *Asian American youth: Culture, identity, and ethnicity*. New York: Routledge.

Nash, G. 1992. The great multicultural debate. *Contention: Debates in society, culture, and science* 1, no. 3: 1–28.

National Asian Pacific American Legal Consortium. 2001. *Backlash: When American turns on its own; 2001 audit of violence against Asian Pacific Americans*. Washington, DC: The Consortium.

Nee, V., and B. Nee. 1972. *Longtime Californ': A documentary study of an American Chinatown*. New York: Pantheon.

Newfield, C., and A. Gordon. 1996. Multiculturalism's unfinished business. In Gordon A. and C. Newfield (eds.), *Mapping multiculturalism*. Minneapolis: University of Minnesota Press.

Nippert-Eng, C. 1996. *Home and work: Negotiating boundaries through everyday life*. Chicago: University of Chicago Press.

Ogbu, J. 1994. Racial stratification and education in the United States: Why inequality persists. *Teachers College Record* 96, no. 2: 264–298.

Okamoto, D. 2003. Toward a theory of pan-ethnicity: Explaining Asian American collective action. *American Sociological Review* 68, no. 6: 811–842.

Okamura, J. 1981. Situational ethnicity. *Ethnic and Racial Studies* 4, no. 4: 452–465.

Okihiro, G. 1994. *Margins and mainstreams: Asians in American history and culture*. Seattle: University of Washington Press.

Omi, M., and H. Winant. 1994. *Racial formation in the United States*. New York: Routledge.

Ong, A. 1996. Cultural citizenship as subject-making: New immigrants negotiate racial and ethnic boundaries. *Current Anthropology* 37, no. 5: 737–762.

Ong, P. (ed.). 2000. *Transforming race relations: The state of Asian Pacific America*. Los Angeles: Leadership Education for Asian Pacifics.

Ong, P., E. Bonacich, and L. Cheng. 1994. *The new Asian immigration in Los Angeles and global restructuring*. Philadelphia: Temple University Press.

Outlaw, L. 1998. "Multiculturalism," citizenship, education, and American liberal democracy. In C. Willett (ed.), *Theorizing multiculturalism: A guide to the current debate*. Malden, MA: Blackwell.

Pang, G. 1998. Intraethnic, interracial, and interethnic marriages among Korean American women. In Y. Song and A. Moon (eds.), *Korean American women: From tradition to modern feminism*. Westport, CT: Praeger.

Parekh, B. 2000. *Rethinking multiculturalism: Cultural diversity and political theory.* Basingstoke: Macmillan.

Park, E. 1999. Friends or enemies: Generational politics in the Korean American community in Los Angeles. *Qualitative Sociology* 22, no. 2: 161–175.

———. 2002. Asian Pacific Americans and urban politics. In L. Võ and R. Bonus (eds.), *Contemporary Asian American communities.* Philadelphia, PA: Temple University Press.

Park, K. 1999. "I really do feel I'm 1.5!" The construction of self and community by young Korean Americans. *Amerasia Journal* 25, no. 1: 139–164.

———. 2000. Sudden and subtle challenge: Disparity in conceptions of marriage and gender in the Korean American community. In M. Manalansan (ed.), *Cultural compass: Ethnographic explorations of Asian America.* Philadelphia, PA: Temple University Press.

Park, L. 2005. *Consuming citizenship: Children of Asian immigrant entrepreneurs.* Stanford, CA: Stanford University Press.

Park, R. 1928. Human migration and the marginal man. *American Journal of Sociology* 33, no. 6: 881–893.

———. 2005 [1914]. Racial assimilation in secondary groups with particular reference to the Negro. In P. Kivisto (ed.), *Incorporating diversity: Rethinking assimilation in a multicultural age.* Boulder, CO: Paradigm.

Park, S. 2001. The intersection of religion, race, gender, and ethnicity in the identity formation of Korean American evangelical women. In H. Kwon, K. Kim, and R. S. Warner (eds.), *Korean Americans and their religions: Pilgrims and missionaries from a different shore.* University Park, PA: Penn State Press.

Pattillo-McCoy, M. 1999. *Black picket fences: Privilege and peril among the black middle class.* Chicago: University of Chicago Press.

Payne, D. 2000. *Big D: Triumphs and troubles of an American supercity in the 20th century.* Dallas, TX: Three Forks Press.

———. 2002. *Dynamic Dallas: An illustrated history.* Carlsbad, CA: Heritage Media.

Pessar, P. 1999. Engendering migration studies: The case of new immigrants in the United States. *American Behavioral Scientist* 42, no. 4: 577–600.

Phinney, J. 1990. Ethnic identity in adolescents and adults: Review of research. *Psychological Bulletin* 108, no. 3: 499–514.

———. 1996. Understanding ethnic diversity: The role of ethnic identity. *American Behavioral Scientist* 40, no. 2: 143–152.

Portes, A., and M. Zhou. 1993. The new second generation: Segmented assimilation and its variants. *Annals of the American Academy of Political and Social Science* 530: 74–96.

Portes, A., and R. Rumbaut. 2001. *Legacies: The story of the immigrant second generation.* Berkeley: University of California Press.

Prasad, P., and A. Mills. 1997. From showcase to shadow: Understanding the dilemmas of managing workplace diversity. In P. Prasad, A. Mills, M. Elmes, and A. Prasad (eds.), *Managing the organizational melting pot: Dilemmas of workplace diversity*. Thousand Oaks, CA: Sage.

Prashad, V. 2000. *The karma of brown folk*. Minneapolis: University of Minnesota Press.

———. 2002. *Everybody was kung fu fighting: Afro-Asian connections and the myth of cultural purity*. New York: Beacon Press.

Prashad, V., and B. Mathew (eds.). 1999–2000. Satyagraha in America: The political culture of South Asian Americans. *Amerasia Journal* 25, no. 3.

Preston, J. 1996. *Managing diversity: What it is and what it isn't*. St. Louis: Center for the Study of American Business, Washington University.

Prior, M., and R. Kemper. 2005. From Freedman's town to uptown: Community transformation and gentrification in Dallas, Texas. *Urban Anthropology* 34, no. 2–3: 177–216.

Purkayastha, B. 2005. *Negotiating ethnicity: Second-generation South Asian Americans traverse a transnational world*. New Brunswick, NJ: Rutgers University Press.

Putnam, R. 2000. *Bowling alone: The collapse and revival of American community*. New York: Simon & Schuster.

Pyke, K. 2000. "The normal American Family" as an interpretive structure of family life among grown children of Korean and Vietnamese immigrants. *Journal of Marriage and the Family* 62, no. 1: 240–256.

Qian, Z. 1997. Breaking the racial barriers: Variations in interracial marriage between 1980 and 1990. *Demography* 34, no. 2: 263–276.

Rajagopal, A. 1995. Better Hindu than black? Narratives of Asian Indian identity. Paper presented at the annual meetings of the Society for the Scientific Study of Religion and Religious Research Association, St. Louis, MO. Referenced in Kurien 2002.

Ravitch, D. 1990. Multiculturalism: E pluribus plures. *American Scholar* 59, no. 3: 337–354.

"Religion in the Workplace." *Business Week*, November 1, 1999, 151–158.

Resnick, L. 1991. Shared Cognition. In Resnick, L., J. Levine, and S. Teasley (eds.), *Perspectives on socially shared cognition*. Washington, DC: American Psychological Association.

Rodriguez, C. 2000. *Changing race: Latinos, the census, and the history of ethnicity in the U.S.* New York: New York University Press.

Rodriguez, R. 1982. *Hunger of memory: The education of Richard Rodriguez*. New York: Bantam.

Roediger, D. 1999. *The wages of whiteness: Race and the making of the American working class*. New York: Verso.

Romanucci-Ross, L. 1991. Matricies of an Italian identity. In G. De Vos and L. Romanucci-Ross (eds.), *Ethnic identity: Cultural continuities and change.* Palo Alto, CA: Mayfield.

Roosens, E. 1989. *Creating ethnicity: The process of ethnogenesis.* Newbury Park, CA: Sage.

Rudrappa, S. 2002. Disciplining desire in making the home: Engendering ethnicity in Indian immigrant families. In P. G. Min (ed.), *The Second Generation: Ethnic Identity Among Asian Americans.* Walnut Creek, CA: AltaMira Press.

———. 2004. *Ethnic routes to becoming American: Indian immigrants and the cultures of citizenship.* New Brunswick, NJ: Rutgers University Press.

Rumbaut, R. 1994. Origins and destinies: Immigration to the United States since World War II. *Sociological Forum* 9, no. 4: 583–622.

———. 1997. Paradoxes (and orthodoxies) of assimilation. *Sociological Perspectives* 40, no. 3: 483–511.

Saenz, R., and B. Aguirre. 1991. The dynamics of Mexican ethnic identity. *Ethnic Groups* 9, no. 1: 17–32.

Said, E. 1978. *Orientalism: Western conceptions of the Orient.* London: Penguin.

Sakamoto, A., and Y. Xie. 2006. The socioeconomic attainments of Asian Americans. In P. G. Min (ed.), *Asian Americans: Contemporary trends and issues,* 2nd ed. Thousand Oaks, CA: Sage.

Salins, P. 1997. *Assimilation, American style.* New York: BasicBooks.

Salopek, J. 2000. For God and company. *Training and Development* 54, no. 3: 77.

San Juan, E., Jr. 2002. *Racism and cultural studies: Critiques of multiculturalist ideology and the politics of difference.* Durham, NC: Duke University Press.

Saran, P. 1985. *The Asian Indian experience in the United States.* Cambridge, MA: Schenkman.

Schlesinger, A. 1992. *The disuniting of America: Reflections on a multicultural society.* New York: W. W. Norton.

Schudson, M. 1989. How culture works. *Theory and Society* 18, no. 2: 153–180.

Sewell, W. H., Jr. 1992. A theory of structure: Duality, agency, and transformation. *American Journal of Sociology* 98, no. 1: 1–29.

Shah, N. 1995. Sexuality, identity, and the uses of history. In D. Eng and A. Hom (eds.), *Q&A: Queer in Asian America.* Philadelphia, PA: Temple University Press.

Shamir, B. 1992. Some correlates of leisure identity salience: Three exploratory studies. *Journal of Leisure Research* 24, no. 4: 301–323.

Shankar, L., and R. Srikanth. 1998. *A part yet apart: South Asians in Asian America.* Philadelphia, PA: Temple University Press.

Sheth, M. 1995. Asian Indian Americans. In P. G. Min (ed.), *Asian Americans: Contemporary trends and issues.* Thousand Oaks, CA: Sage.

Shibutani, T., and K. Kwan. 1965. *Ethnic stratification: A comparative approach.* New York: Macmillan.

Shinagawa, L., and G. Pang. 1996. Asian American panethnicity and intermarriage. *Amerasia Journal* 22, no. 2: 127–152.

Shrake, E. 1998. Korean American mothers' parenting styles and adolescent behavior. In Y. Song and A. Moon (eds.), *Korean American women: From tradition to modern feminism.* Westport, CT: Praeger.

Simmel, G. 1964. *Conflict and the web of group affiliations.* New York: Free Press.

Singh, A. 1996. African Americans and the new immigrants. In D. Bahri and M. Vasudeva (eds.), *Between the lines: South Asians and postcoloniality.* Philadelphia, PA: Temple University Press.

Singh, J. 2002. The Gadar party: Political expression in an immigrant community. In J. Wu and M. Song (eds.), *Asian American Studies.* New Brunswick, NJ: Rutgers University Press.

Small, S. 1999. The contours of racialization: Structures, representations, and resistance in the United States. In R. Torres, L. Mirón, and J. Inda (eds.), *Race, identity, and citizenship.* Malden, MA: Blackwell.

Snow, D., and L. Anderson. 1987. Identity work among the homeless. *American Journal of Sociology* 92, no. 6: 1336–1371.

Sollors, W. 1998. The multiculturalism debate as cultural text. In W. Katkin, N. Landsman, and A. Tyree (eds.), *Beyond pluralism: The conception of group identities in America.* Urbana: University of Illinois Press.

Somerville, P. 1997. The social construction of home. *Journal of Architectural and Planning Research* 14, no. 3: 226–245.

Song, Y. 1996. *Battered women in Korean immigrant families: The silent scream.* New York: Garland.

Song, Y., and A. Moon (eds.). 1998. *Korean American women: From tradition to modern feminism.* London: Praeger.

Soni, V. 2000. A twenty-first-century reception for diversity in the public sector: A case study. *Public Administration Review* 60, no. 5: 395–408.

Spickard, P., and W. J. Burroughs. 2000. *We are a people: Narrative and multiplicity in constructing ethnic identity.* Philadelphia, PA: Temple University Press.

Stein, A. 1997. *Sex and sensibility: Stories of a lesbian generation.* Berkeley: University of California Press.

Steinberg, S. 1989. *The ethnic myth.* Boston: Beacon Press.

Stodolska, M. 2002. Ceasing participation in leisure activities after immigration: Eastern Europeans and their leisure behavior. *Leisure and Society* 25: 79–117.

Stonequist, E. 1937. *The marginal man.* New York: Charles Scribner's Sons.

Strauss, A. 1987. *Qualitative analysis for social scientists.* New York: Cambridge University Press.

Stryker, S. 1992. Symbolic interactionism: Themes and variations. In M. Rosenburg and R. Turner (eds.), *Social psychology: Sociological perspectives.* New Brunswick, NJ: Transaction.

Stryker, S., and A. Macke. 1978. Status inconsistency and role conflict. *Annual Review of Sociology* 4, no. 1: 57–90.

Subramanian, A. 2000. Indians in North Carolina: Race, class, and culture in the making of immigrant identity. *Comparative Studies of South Asia, Africa and the Middle East* 20, no. 1–2: 105–114.

Sue, S., and J. Morishima. 1982. *The mental health of Asian Americans.* San Francisco: Jossey-Bass.

Swidler, A. 1986. Culture in action: Symbols and strategies. *American Sociological Review* 51, no. 2: 273–286.

———. 2001. *Talk of love: How culture matters.* Chicago: University of Chicago Press.

Tajfel, H., and J. Turner. 1986. The social identity theory of intergroup behavior. In S. Worchel and W. Austin (eds.), *Psychology of intergroup relations.* Chicago: Nelson-Hall.

Takagi, D. 1992. *Retreat from race: Asian-American admissions and racial politics.* New Brunswick, NJ: Rutgers University Press.

Takahashi, J. 1997. *Nisei/Sansei: Shifting Japanese American identities and politics.* Philadelphia, PA: Temple University Press.

Takaki, R. 1989. *Strangers from a different shore: A history of Asian Americans.* New York: Penguin.

Tang, J. 1997. The model minority thesis revisited. *Journal of Applied Behavioral Science* 33, no. 3: 291–315.

Tannen, D. 1994. *Talking from 9 to 5: How women's and men's conversational styles affect who gets heard, who gets credit, and what gets done at work.* New York: W. Morrow.

Tatum, B. 2002. *"Why are all the black kids sitting together in the cafeteria?" And other conversations about race.* New York: BasicBooks.

Taylor, C. 1994. The politics of recognition. In A. Gutmann and C. Taylor (eds.), *Multiculturalism.* Princeton, NJ: Princeton University Press.

Thai, H. 1999. "Splitting things in half is so white!": Conceptions of family life and the formation of ethnic identity among second generation Vietnamese Americans. *Amerasia Journal* 25, no. 1: 53–88.

Thernstrom, S. 1973. *The other Bostonians; Poverty and progress in the American metropolis, 1880–1970.* Cambridge, MA: Harvard University Press.

Thomas, R. 1991. *Beyond race and gender: Unleashing the power of your total workforce by managing diversity.* New York: Amacom.

———. 1999. *Building a house for diversity.* New York: Amacom.

Tse, L. 1999. Finding a place to be: Ethnic identity exploration of Asian Americans. *Adolescence* 34, no. 133: 121–138.

Tuan, M. 1998. *Forever foreigners or honorary whites? The Asian ethnic experience today.* New Brunswick, NJ: Rutgers University Press.

Turner, R. 1978. The role and the person. *American Journal of Sociology* 84, no. 1: 1–23.

Turner, V. 1969. *The ritual process: Structure and anti-structure.* Chicago: Aldine.

Uba, L. 1994. *Asian Americans: Personality patterns, identity, and mental health.* New York: Guilford Press.

Um, S. J. 1996. *Korean immigrant women in the Dallas-area apparel industry: Looking for feminist threads in patriarchal cloth.* Lanham, MD: University Press of America.

Waldinger, R. 2003. Foreigners transformed: International migration and the remaking of a divided people. *Diaspora* 12, no. 2: 247–272.

Warner, R. S. 1993. Work in progress toward a new paradigm for the sociological study of religion in the United States. *American Journal of Sociology* 98, no. 5: 1044–1093.

Waters, M. 1990. *Ethnic options: Choosing ethnic identities in America.* Berkeley: University of California Press.

———. 1998. *Black identities.* Berkeley: University of California Press.

Werbner, P. 2001. The limits of cultural hybridity: On ritual monsters, poetic license and contested postcolonial purifications. *Journal of the Royal Anthropological Institute* 7, no. 1: 133–152.

———. 2004. Theorizing complex diasporas: Purity and hybridity in the South Asian public sphere in Britain. *Journal of Ethnic and Migration Studies* 30, no. 5: 895–911.

Williams, C. 1992. The glass escalator: Hidden advantages for men in the "female" professions. *Social Problems* 39, no. 3: 253–267.

Williams, R. 1988. *Religion and immigrants from India and Pakistan.* Cambridge: Cambridge University Press.

Wilson, J. 1980. Sociology of leisure. *Annual Review of Sociology* 6, no. 1: 21–40.

———. 2000. Volunteering. *Annual Review of Sociology* 26, no. 1: 215–240.

Wilson, W. 1987. *Truly disadvantaged: The inner city, the underclass and public policy.* Chicago: University of Chicago Press.

Wise, L., and M. Tschirhart. 2000. Examining empirical evidence on diversity effects: How useful is diversity research for public-sector managers? *Public Administration Review* 60, no. 5: 386–394.

Wolfe, A. 2000. Benign multiculturalism. In P. Kivisto and G. Rundblad (eds.), *Multiculturalism in the United States: Current issues, contemporary voices.* Thousand Oaks, CA: Pine Forge Press.

Wong, M. 1989. A look at intermarriage among the Chinese in the United States in 1980. *Sociological Perspectives* 32, no. 1: 87–107.

Wong, P., C. Lai, and T. Lin. 1998. Asian Americans as a model minority: Self-perceptions and perceptions by other racial groups. *Sociological Perspectives* 41, no. 1: 95–119.

Woo, D. 2000. *Glass ceilings and Asian Americans: The new face of workplace barriers.* Walnut Creek, CA: AltaMira Press.

Woodward, C. 1998. Meanings for multiculturalism. In A. Melzer, J. Weinberger, and M. Zinman (eds.), *Multiculturalism and American democracy.* Lawrence: University Press of Kansas.

Wu, D. 1997. *Asian Pacific Americans in the workplace.* Walnut Creek, CA: AltaMira Press.

Wuthnow, R. 1987. *Meaning and moral order: Explorations in cultural analysis.* Berkeley: University of California Press.

———. 1998. *Loose connections: Joining together in America's fragmented communities.* Cambridge, MA: Harvard University Press.

Yancey, G. 2003. *Who is white: Latinos, Asians and the new black/non-black divide.* Boulder, CO: Lynne Rienner.

Yancey, W. L., E. Ericksen, and R. Juliani. 1976. Emergent ethnicity: A review and reformulation. *American Sociological Review* 41, no. 3: 391–403.

Yinger, M. 1982. *Countercultures: The promise and the peril of a world turned upside down.* New York: Free Press.

Young, E. 2000. Asian issues in professional development: The "unwritten rules" of corporate America. Interchange Consultants Presentation, Cornell University, 3 October.

Young, I. 1998. Unruly categories: A critique of Nancy Fraser's dual systems theory. In C. Willett (ed.), *Theorizing multiculturalism: A guide to the current debate.* Malden, MA: Blackwell.

Yu, H. 2001. *Thinking Orientals: Migration, contact and exoticism in modern America.* Oxford: Oxford University Press.

Zavilla, P. 1997. Reflections on diversity among Chicanas. In M. Romero, P. Hondagneu-Sotelo, and V. Ortiz (eds.), *Challenging fronteras: Structuring Latina and Latino lives in the U.S.* New York: Routledge.

Zerubavel, E. 1993. *The fine line: Making distinctions in everyday life.* Chicago: University of Chicago Press.

Zhou, M. 1992. *Chinatown: The socioeconomic potential of an urban enclave.* Philadelphia, PA: Temple University Press.

Zhou, M., and C. Bankston. 1998. *Growing up American: How Vietnamese children adapt to life in the United States.* New York: Russell Sage Foundation.

Zhou, M., and J. Lee. 2004. Introduction: The making of culture, ethnicity, and identity among Asian American youth. In M. Zhou and J. Lee (eds.), *Asian American youth: Culture, identity, and ethnicity.* New York: Routledge.

Zia, H. 2000. *Asian American dreams: The emergence of an American people.* New York: Farrar, Straus & Giroux.

Index

Italic page numbers indicate material in tables or figures. Page numbers followed by "*n*" indicate notes.

adaptation: assessing, 9–11, 224, 264*n*20; and multiculturalism, 231–236; unintended implications for, 236–237
affirmative action, 93–94, 96, 121
African Americans: and affirmative action, 94, 96, 121; and Asian Americans, 88, 89; in Dallas, 37–38; dating, 176; educational attainment stereotype, 92, 93–94; explaining variation in relation to, 96–98; friendships, 278*n*10; and Korean Americans, 23, 39, 89, 101–102, 270*n*12; and model minority stereotype, 98; in racial hierarchy, 238–239; reaction to racism, 109, 281*n*3; social activism, 191; socioeconomic progress, 92–96; in white-collar occupations, 262*n*14; work ethic stereotype, 91–92
African Caribbeans, 191
air travel, after September 11 attacks, 100
alcohol, drinking, 194, 199–201
Alien Land Law (1920), 19
Alien Land Law Act (1913), 21
ancestry, survey questions about, 99, 152, 275*n*14
Arab Americans, 99, 116, 275*n*15
arranged marriage, 171–172, 280*n*13
Asian Americans: and African Americans, 88, 89; in California, 28; Dallas County population, *34*, 34–35; in Dallas politics, 33–34, 266*n*20; educational attainment stereotype, 92, 93–94; as "good immigrants," 55, 270*n*16; hate crimes against, 269*n*8; heterogeneity of, 16, 264*n*1; historical racialization, 18–19; and Latinos, 39, 260*n*8; political issues,

109–112, 120–121; role in economy, 16–17; socioeconomic progress, 92–96; student movement, 98, 106; Texas population, 28, *34*; work ethic stereotype, 91–92. *See also* Indian Americans; Korean Americans
Asian American Small Business Association (pseudonym), 34, 115, 153, 217, 276*n*21
Asian Small Business Association (pseudonym), 51
Asiatic Exclusion League, 18
assimilation: defined, 233–234; of European Americans, 239; and multiculturalism, 11, 232–234, 264*n*21, 283*nn*3–4; selective, 49, 187, 270*n*9
Association of Asian American Studies, 28, 265*n*8
athletes, 72–73
Avon, 125–126

balkanization, 190–191, 211, 235
Baptists, Southern, 48, 53–54, 244
bhangra music, 263*n*17
Blacks. *See* African Americans
boundary work, 14, 161, 279*n*4
Britain, 279*n*8
Brothers and Sisters in Christ (BASIC), 276*n*22
brown peril, 18, 99–101. *See also* yellow peril
Byrd, James, Jr., 260*n*8

California, 18, 19, 21, 23, 25, 28
caste, 280*n*11
Chan, Charlie (fictional character), 24, 45
charities, support for, 218–223

Chicago School of sociology and race relations, 259n2
children: economic attainments, 157; education, 279n6; family connection to ethnic
identity, 79; marital expectations, 60,
165–172; opting not to have, 3; raising,
69, 177–181
Chin, Vincent, 17, 276n25
Chinatowns, 114
Chinese Americans: and Korean Americans,
244, 274n4; public image, 276n23; Texas
and Dallas County populations, 29, 34,
35; U.S.-born, 261n11
Christians, 169–170, 261n10, 263n17, 283n1
Christmas parties, 127, 197
chuppels, 142
civil society domain, 204–223; dating
and networking with co-ethnics, 171,
209–210, 282n10; described, 190–191,
204–205; motivations for joining ethnic
organizations, 205–210; open-door
policy, 212–214; searching for safe
space, 206–209; support for dominant
institutions, 217–218; support for local
charities, 218–223; support of the state,
214–217
class status, 4–5. See also middle class
clothing: garba festival, 281n5; in home
domain, 160, 279n3; prescribing ethnic
social identity, 61, 272n25; in work
domain, 142, 149–150, 154–155
co-ethnics: community connection to ethnic
identity, 67–68, 69–70; dating and
networking with, 171, 209–210, 282n10;
family connection to ethnic identity,
78, 80; fitting in connection to ethnic
identity, 72–74, 75–76
college, financial support for, 219–221
communication skills, 137–138
community connection to ethnic identity,
66–70, 67
community involvement, local, 52–53
computer industry, 151, 154
consumerist attitude toward culture,
202–204
conversation styles, 199
cosmopolitan social type, 234, 260n6
Council on American-Islamic Relations,
269n8
cultural code, defined, 124
cultural displays, 56–57

cultural elements, framing, 53–55
cultural heritage, teaching to second generation, 58–62
cultural hybridity, 263n17
cultural logics, 261n10
cultural repertoires, 162, 262n13
cultural symbols, 60–62
culture: consumerist attitude toward,
202–204; racialization of, 103–105
curriculum revisions, public school, 233
curse words, sharing with co-workers,
146–147

Dallas: African Americans in, 37–38; Asian
American political activities, 33–34,
266n20; business in, 28–29, 265n10;
ethnic group population patterns, 36–37,
37; Hindu temples, 32, 266n18; Indian
Americans in, 31–33; influence on shared
interests, 112–116; integration into,
246–249; Korean Americans in, 30–31;
Latinos in, 38, 268nn39–40; population,
12, 27; racial diversity, 29; residential
segregation, 112–113; as study setting, 12,
27–28. See also Texas
Dallas County: demographics, 34–36, 34, 35;
income, 35, 35, 41; poverty rates, 35, 35
dating, 171, 172–176, 194, 209–210, 282n10
Davidson, Cheryl, 39
death penalty, 260n8
decorations, in home domain, 159–160,
278n2
democratic ideals, organizations' fulfillment
of, 211–212
Democratic National Committee, 270n11
demographics: Dallas County, 34, 34–36, 35;
Indian Americans, 24–26, 25, 26; Korean
Americans, 24–26, 25, 26; Texas, 34, 34
differences: celebrating, 56–58; censuring
expressions in work domain, 141–144;
expressing in work domain, 144–155
diligence, in model-minority stereotype,
1–2, 9
discrimination. See racism
diversity management, 125–129, 132, 277n2
divorce, 171, 177–178
Diwali, 75, 149, 154–155
domains: explaining conformity in, 237–238;
integration and stratification of,
238–244; performing identities in, 6–9
domestic chores, 279n5